THE SELECTED LETTERS OF
WALLACE STEGNER

THE SELECTED LETTERS OF

Wallace Stegner

Edited by Page Stegner

Shoemaker  Hoard

Library of Congress Cataloging-in-Publication Data
Stegner, Wallace Earle, 1909–1993.
[Correspondence. Selections]
The selected letters of Wallace Stegner / edited by Page Stegner.
p. cm.
Includes index.
ISBN-13: 978-1-59376-168-4
ISBN-10: 1-59376-168-6
1. Authors, American—20th century—Correspondence.
2. Historians—United States—Correspondence.
3. Conservationists—United States—Correspondence.
I. Stegner, Page. II. Title.
PS3537.T316Z48 2007
813'.52—dc22
[B]   2007011764

Book design by David Bullen
Printed in the United States of America

Shoemaker 〔S̲H̲〕 Hoard
www.shoemakerhoard.com

10 9 8 7 6 5 4 3 2 1

What does more to stay us and keep our backbones stiff
while the world reels than the sense that we are linked
with someone who listens and understands
and so in some way completes us?

WALLACE STEGNER

Contents

Introduction

My father was an early riser. By six o'clock every morning he would be rousting me from my nest of quilts and blankets to get up and get ready for school, a ritual that included downing a noxious potion introduced into our culinary repertoire by Robert Frost during one of his annual visits—raw egg, sugar, cinnamon, mixed up in a glass of milk—followed by a half hour of piano practice before a mile-long hike down our driveway to catch the school bus. While I sleepily mangled my fingering exercises, he would down a quick breakfast of toast and coffee in the bedroom with my mother, and be headed out the door to his study while I was beating to death the last of my Chopin preludes. What he did in that sanctuary was commence his own dexterity exercises by typing out letters in his two digit, hunt-and-peck style before getting down to the serious literary business of the day. He called it "warming up the fingers."

His letters were not notes dashed off in the rapid-fire, shorthand fashion of today's email. Virtually without exception they were thoughtful, articulate, and carefully crafted, with attention to minutia (spelling, punctuation, syntax); they employed simile, metaphor, poetic imagery, deliberation of voice, and, above all, attention to the melody of language. In short, they were literary compositions. He wasn't just "warming up his fingers," he was putting bellows to the fire of his imagination. What struck me most in reading and trying to choose from among hundreds and hundreds of these letters was how utterly attentive he was to the sound of written expression even in its most casual form. Like the company accountant in Conrad's *Heart of Darkness*, he would have been embarrassed to be found wandering about dressed in anything but an immaculate white suit, no matter how remote the exposure to posterity or the likely indifference of his audience.

My father's incomplete bibliography, compiled in 1990 by Nancy Colberg (see Biographers and Critics) lists 35 published books, including 15 novels, 5 works of history, 2 biographies, 57 short stories, 242 articles, and 164 first-appearance contributions and books edited (forewords, afterwords, introductions, essay chapters, and critical introductions). But he was not only a novelist, historian, biographer, short-story writer, and essayist. For four decades of his adult life he was also a full-time professor of American Literature and director of the Stanford Creative Writing Program, whose distinguished students would constitute a virtual Who's Who of contemporary American writers—Wendell Berry, Larry McMurtry, Edward Abbey, Tillie Olsen, Robert Stone, Tom McGuane, Evan Connell, Ken Kesey, Ed McClanahan, Scott Momaday, Ernest Gaines, Al Young, William Kittredge, Scott Turow, James Houston, Nancy Packer, Merrill Joan Gerber—to name only a few.

And, as this selection of his letters will indicate, he was a serious epistler with an extraordinary range of correspondents—not only writers of all kinds, novelists, poets, journalists, historians, biographers, but also politicians, conservationists, academics, literary critics, librarians, visual artists, editors, college presidents, seventh graders, ninth graders, graduate students, and, above all, fans. No admiring reader penning an appreciative letter ever went without a reply; Stegner would have found it unthinkable to ignore someone who had been touched by his work.

"Novelists," Stegner once wrote, "have few of the usual excuses for writing their autobiographies. They are not like politicians and generals. Though they may be just as intent upon leaving their mark on the world, they have no obligation to history and no lifetime of top-secret actions to reveal," and he went on to observe that while glimpses into the nature of personal experience can often be gleaned from a writer's work, they often use up their autobiographical capital in the creation of their fictions. Stegner had no interest in writing an autobiography. So these letters are as close as we will ever come (apart from the memoir portion of *Wolf Willow*, and his admitted roman à clef, *Crossing to Safety*) to many of his unedited thoughts and opinions, and to a factual narrative untransformed by the literary imagination, to life lived before being relived.

Like *The Letters of Bernard DeVoto*, which Stegner collected and edited in 1975, I have arranged these letters under topical headings so that reflections on writing fiction, or on a specific book, or conservation matters, or the Stanford Creative Writing Program can be easily referenced and read according to one's interest in a particular subject. Where there was a classification conflict, where a letter might cross several lines, I either chose the dominant theme or flipped a coin. Occasionally, in desperation, I succumbed to the ubiquitous default category of "miscellaneous," which I gathered under the title

"The Literary Life." It may be noted, by those who take note of such things, that these letters are arranged chronologically within their respective sections, with the exception of those reprinted in the chapter entitled "Reflections on the Works." It made more sense to me to keep correspondence regarding a specific book intact, irrespective of its date.

Page Stegner

THE SELECTED LETTERS OF

Wallace Stegner

Origins

S TEGNER WAS BORN in Lake Mills, Iowa on February 17, 1909, but spent only a few weeks in that small farming community before leaving for Grand Forks, North Dakota, where his father was the manager of a downtown hotel. That sojourn lasted a scant three years before George Stegner moved his family to Redmond, Washington where he temporarily abandoned them to seek his fortune in Canada, and it was there, in the raw frontier town of Eastend, Saskatchewan that the family was eventually reunited in 1914. At age five, Wallace was old enough to be profoundly imprinted by his surroundings, and although he would live in Eastend for only six years, the experience would inform his values and attitudes for the rest of his life.

The following account of those early years has been extracted and condensed without ellipses from the *Contemporary Authors Autobiographical Series*, volume 9:

I don't really know about [my parents'] years in North Dakota, where my brother, Cecil, was born in 1907. I don't know why my mother came back to her father's farm to have me, two years later, or why, after another year or two in Dakota and a couple in and around Seattle, my father disappeared from our lives. All I know is that Cece and I were put in a Seattle orphanage so that my mother could work, and that when she found out how miserable we were she took us out and retreated to the only safety she knew, Lake Mills. Home, Robert Frost has said, is where, when you have to go there, they have to take you in.

My memories of that time provide only random images. I remember too well that Seattle orphanage. I remember an autumn day in Lake Mills when I sat among colored oak leaves in the backyard and plastered the side of a shed with ground cherries, while I sang to myself a song my mother had taught me about Whistling Rufus, the One-Man Band. It was a song I sang for anyone who would listen, my first accomplishment. It brought exclamations of praise from my stepgrandmother and the neighbor women who drank coffee together in the kitchen. It made my mother proud. I was held to be a prodigy. And I could read a little, or thought I could. Jealous of Cece, who had started school, I badgered my mother to be allowed to go too.

The next thing my memory brings back is the waiting room in the railroad station at Weyburn, Saskatchewan, where I was impressed by the portraits of stern men in red coats who stared down from the walls. That, as nearly as I can tell, was June 1914, and we were on our way to rejoin the father I had not seen for a couple of years. . . . He was in the valley of the Frenchman River in Saskatchewan, through which something called the CPR was running something called a branch line. It would open up a whole new tract of country. We would be in on the ground floor, and would make a pile.

Eastend, Saskatchewan, was not yet a town, but only a construction camp on the railroad grade, when my mother, brother, and I arrived by stage from Gull Lake. For a while we lived in a derailed dining car next to Mrs. Torkelson's boardinghouse for construction workers. Later we rented a shack on Main Street. Still later—1916 as I remember it, but 1917 according to the Eastend Arts Council, which recently bought it as a literary landmark—my father built a four-gabled, two-story house in the west end of town, on a bend in the river.

We lived in Eastend from 1914 to 1920. We did not make a pile, though my father tried everything from poker—and he was a good poker player—to potatoes and wheat. In 1915 he homesteaded a quarter section and preempted another on the Montana line, fifty miles from town, and set out to feed the warring armies of Europe. Two good crops and three burnouts later, he turned to rum-running, first from Montana into Saskatchewan when Saskatchewan was dry, and then from Canada into the United States when the laws reversed themselves.

We gave up on Saskatchewan in 1920—abandoned the homestead, sold the house in town, delivered our horses to a river-bottom rancher who would keep them for half the increase, and moved out, as many other families were doing. Our destination was Great Falls, Montana, an awesome step upward and outward. At eleven, I had no memory of ever having seen a paved street, a lawn, a flush toilet, a house with a street number. My father had once seen an airplane close up, and he swore it was as solid as a democrat wagon, though even I knew that couldn't be true, else how could it get up in the air?

By the time we took off again the next summer, down through the Little Belt Mountains and the Smith River Valley and Yellowstone on our way to Salt Lake City, I was not desolated as I had been when we left Eastend. Already I had hardened myself for migratoriness.

But I was prepared for more rootlessness than I encountered. As it turned out, we lived in Salt Lake, with brief temporary interruptions, for the next seventeen years; and though my parents, because of my father's erratic and sometimes furtive businesses, never became part of the city but lived in it like mice in its walls, Cece and I found an unexpected home there.

I was fully a part of East High School and the city, contented with myself and my place in my world, when I graduated in 1925. Then came college—the University of Utah—a streetcar college then of barely three thousand students, but awesome to me, since my parents, who had never even attended high school, had no advice to give me. I was already out beyond them in that respect, and on my own.

Then, when I graduated from the university with no larger plans than to go on with my job and perhaps eventually work up to manager or part-owner, some of my professors put their paddles into me and stirred up my sediments. They said I had to go on to graduate school, at least for an M.A. I had won a little newspaper contest with a short story. I was literary. I should shoot higher than selling linoleum. It was not my own doing. Two roads diverged in a wood, and I, I took the one I was pushed into. I climbed on a bus in September 1930 and went off to Iowa City to take up the teaching assistantship they had arranged for me. I was barely twenty-one, having taken five years to finish college because I kept dropping out to work.

During my first two years in Iowa City my roommate at the old Quadrangle dormitory was Wilbur Schramm, one of the best friends of my life and a major influence on my life. Unlike me, he knew where he was going and had been preparing for his future (though he ended up somewhere else, not a literary figure but the father of communications research).

Wilbur found me an interesting barbarian, and without prejudice, and with real liking, tried to open my upstairs windows. But our friendship was interrupted when I went home in June to find that my two-year absence had cost me my girl,[1] and that my mother's cancer, operated on four years before, had recurred. My parents

---

1. Juanita Crawford.

were then living in Los Angeles. Rather than go back as far as Iowa, I transferred to Berkeley, where I roomed with an old friend from Salt Lake, Milton Cowan, an ex-Mormon missionary who was taking a Ph.D. in German and roared passages from the Niebelungenlied in his sleep.

That year in Berkeley at the very bottom of the Depression was a strange interlude, an underwater period. By the time it ended, my mother was clearly dying. The beginning of the summer we spent at our cabin on Fish Lake, which she loved; but when it became clear that she needed to be close to medical care, we moved to Salt Lake, still our little particle of a family, now three.[2] In November my mother died in a rented apartment, her husband gone off on one of his trips, nobody there but a nurse and me.

I was never lower in my life. Finally, in February, Milton Cowan and I drove back to Iowa City for the beginning of the second term, and in Iowa City I was reunited with Wilbur Schramm, now teaching there. He was true to his character. Within a couple of weeks he had found me a fill-in job at Augustana College, a Lutheran school in Rock Island, Illinois. Close to where my father was born. And he had introduced me to the girl that I would marry before the year was out. The job was artificial respiration; the introduction was a reentry into life.

The more recent letters in this section were written, for the most part, in response to questions about his Saskatchewan years put to Stegner by the historian Beth LaDow, author of *The Medicine Line: Life and Death on a North American Borderland*, and Sharon Butala, a best-selling Canadian author referred to by the *Toronto Star* as "one of [Canada's] visionaries," who herself lives in the province. Ms. Butala was a central figure in the move to restore the Eastend house built by Stegner's father in 1917, and to transform it into its current status as an Eastend Arts Council Residence for Writers. The letters to Sarah Barnard and Mary Page were written in 1933 and 1934 while Stegner was working on his Ph.D. at the University of Iowa and during his first teaching stint at Augustana College in Rock Island, Illinois.

◆ ◆ ◆

---

2. Cecil died of pneumonia in December 1930.

« *To: Sara Barnard* • *May 24, 1933* »

Dear Sally,[3]

I know it. I know what I am, and what I should have done, and what I neglected to do. Go on, call me down. All your callings down are but as sounding brass and tinkling cymbals. They don't bother me a bit, because I have a perfectly elegant excuse for not writing. To wit, I've been having altogether too much fun. Not that having fun keeps me from thinking about you and wishing you were here to go fishing and shishing, but it does keep me from writing. For another thing we haven't any ink and I just got a new ribbon for this antedeluvian (Sp?) contraption yesterday. Notice how fine and smeary she writes.

I said I'd been having fun. I insist on just that. Red[4] arrived the day after I did.[5] We went fishing with bad results but much Isaac Waltonish soulease. Last night I went over on the other shore and caught a fine mess on a fly, so now my soul-ease is pleasantly augmented by the consciousness that I can still catch fish if they'll bite. A couple days ago we went up on Seven Mile to fish the creek. It was several degrees below freezing when we hit the canyon at six o'clock. Snow and ice on the road, etc. We didn't catch any fish big enough to keep, but we had a fine time, and found out where Lost Lake is. (K.B., head ranger says Lost Lake is most beautiful spot in Utah. Report unverified as yet.) We had horses all spoken for to ride up there, but Doc dragged Red down to Fruita and Torrey, so that the trip was off. This morning we took about a ten mile hike up to Crater Lakes, on the East Rim, where we were pleasantly regaled with watching an eagle devour a mallard he had just caught. This evening two deer strolled through our back yard, and I took two or three pictures. The light was not too good, but I think they'll be fair at that. Aside from that, and running our brand new motor around, all I've done is house work and carpentering and had

---

3. Sara Barnard was one of Stegner's Salt Lake girlfriends during his undergraduate days at the University of Utah. The relationship ended when he met his wife-to-be, Mary Page.
4. Milton "Red" Cowan was one of Stegner's closest high school chums in Salt Lake City. He and Cowan spent a year rooming together at the University of California, Berkeley, before leaving in disgust over the antediluvian Ph.D. requirements. They enrolled in graduate programs at the University of Iowa—Stegner in English, Cowan in German—and remained close friends throughout their lives.
5. At the Stegner's cabin at Fish Lake in southern Utah.

a swell time doing it. Our boat has not arrived, for some strange reason known only to freight office employees, but we expect it up Monday or Tuesday. The motor works like a watch. If Red and Doc stay another day we are riding up to Lost Lake tomorrow morning. They say one can't find it without very explicit instructions or a guide, and that it is totally out of sight at fifty feet. There is also another place beloved of the ranger, which is known as Rock Springs. If I keep my health, and God and Love are willing, I am going to know this mountain like a book, or as Cowan knows Berkeley, within a week. So far my health is impeccable, and my beard sprouting lustily. Some tourists took Red and me for Reforestation workers this morning, which is a distinct compliment to our disreputable appearance.

Gad, I love to get dirty. Hain't washed my neck and ears since I arrived. Went swimming once and practically petrified in the wind. From now on I take my hard pleasures when the wind is down. I don't mind diving into ice water, but I hate a refrigerated blast blowing on me afterward. Goose pimples wit puffink wit pentink wit blowink wit rooshink hout from de wutta wit robbin down wigorously wit swinkink de homms wit stompink de feet wit roorink witsnizzink. Gift a left, de hudd plassures.

Mother[6] seems to feel as well here as in Salt Lake, so there is every indication that we shall stay. Better be calling Avine up and asking him when he is leaving. The porch is all screened, but we have had to wait for lumber to build the kitchen. It should be all done and the paraphernalia installed by next Saturday, so when you come up all will be ship-shape and tidy. There's nothing quite like tidiness unless it is good fun.

The lake is calm as a mill pond now. In a few more days just about the time you come up there will be a very large and incredible moon. Our boat will be here. The kitchen will be on. The floor will be scrubbed and the yard raked. I shall by that time have finished one of the fifteen books I brought down. The wren's eggs in the nest on the front porch, just exactly seven feet from me right now, when you hear the gong, will be hatched. The snow will be gone from the mountain back of us. My beard will be three quarters of an inch long, and will look very fine and scraggly and feel like excelsior with maggots in it. (Silk to you.) My nose will be purple—it's

---

6. Stegner's mother was suffering from breast cancer, from which she would eventually die in November of 1933.

maroon now, and my back will be the color of old mahogany. My ears will still be dirty. And I'll be awful glad to see you, you little snisp.

Degenerately,

Wishfort

« *To: Sara Barnard* • *June 28, 1933* »

Dear Sara,

I am most notoriously abused. (Malvolio.)
In misery, in woeful misery
This letter had its painful origin;
When Stegner underneath a heap
Of roasting blankets lay
And could not raise his head
A still small voice was heard within:
"My God, that I were dead!"

All hors de combat in my woe
I lay upon my bed of pain
And wished that I could die;
From misery, from woeful misery
This letter had its origin
From misery to misery
Through all the compass of despair it ran
To tell of me, the world's unhappiest man.

What can one do for pains across the back
That lay one like a culprit on the rack?
Or swooning fits, malaria, house-maid's knee
Or falling sickness? Oh, what woe is me!
My head is ruyined—eye, ear, nose and throat;
Upon my frame my once well-tailored coat
Hangs like a circus tent upon a broom.
With feeble steps I limp across the room
Leaving my bed because it's full of pain
And then, too weak to stand, I totter back again.

This little poem
Appeals to some
And others it repels.
For these last people
I hope deep sleep'll
Lay 'em among the asphodels.
    Respectfully,
    Steinblatz

« *To: Sara Barnard* • *July 11, 1933* »

Dear Sary,

Youse is a heck of a good egg, he said. Thanks ever so much for being so nice to mother when she was in town. Thanks both from her and from me. You are indeed most helpful, kind, considerate, and oke.

The jernt is about fixed up now except for a dab of painting here and there and a few odd nicknacks of work. Went fishing with Pa this morning at four thirty (two bells to you) and got me a mackinaw that weighed just an ounce and a half under five pounds. You should have seen us with our lines tangled, the motor dead, Pa's line off the reel, the boat going in circles and the sun stopping to see what the devil was going on. He had a bite just as we turned, but the fish broke water and got away. I was helping him get the line in, hand over hand, with the copper line tied temporarily around the oar, when all of a sudden the end of the oar went overboard and I grabbed the line and what do you think? There was a fish on. In the excitement Pa's line got tangled around his leg and he kicked the pole overboard so that it hung on the motor. Then the motor went dead, and there I was without a paddle, trying to reel in this horse, who was pumping like an oil well against the spinner. My such a fine fish. Gif a cheer gif a left gif a hop stap wit jomp wit waffing de hett wit roorink. Five pounds of good old he-fish. The thing wasn't but two feet long, but he was fat as a house. I've caught rainbow almost as long on a fly, but they didn't weigh half that much. That one with a good rainbow that Pa caught, and two brook I caught last night on the fly, should keep us in fish until you get down here, and then I'll catch another big one for you.

All of which reminds me that you promised the folks you'd be down if you could catch a ride. I don't think we'll be coming in before then for anything, but if you don't catch a ride down I'll smack you out from in between your ears. Or come on the train and I'll pick you up in Sigurd. You won't have to come on the train, though. There'll be plenty of people coming down on the 24th. If you feel like it you might call up Mrs. Jess Sharpe, somewhere about eighth or ninth east and thirteenth south, and ask them if they have room. They said they would be down about the 24th. Anyway, get down here. There's a lot of housework still left to be done. My only regret is that I scrubbed the floors and beat the rugs while the folks were away. If and when you come you might bring down a hunk of beeswax and a couple rolls of films, 116-A, eights. There's something to come down for, a chance to be helpful.

Our daily rainstorm is about to blow up, and I have to get this to Skougaard's before I get caught in it. Love and kisses and a barrel or two of thanks for everything. I really can appreciate something if it's appreciateable.

Ever thine,
Aristotle

« To: Sara Barnard • July 14, 1933 »

Dear Sary,

I'm behind again, but I have a good excuse this time. The mail hasn't gone down for two days. The films and the beeswax came today. Thanks ever so much. You're so danged helpful you hurt. I really didn't mean for you to send them out. I was just giving you something to do so you'd be sure to come yourself. In itself, beeswax isn't such a comforting article, but thanks anyway.

Did I tell you that we're expecting my aunt from Iowa in a few days? I expect Paw will meet her in Salt Lake while mother and I stay here. I wish I could come in, but I can't leave mother alone, and it's too damned hot in Salt Lake for her to go. We may perhaps go down to Zion and Bryce after my aunt comes. Neither of the folks have ever been there, and if mother feels well enough she'd like to go. One must show visitors the natural wonders, you know.

You should be thankful you didn't come down on the 24th. Everybody and his dog was here. And some very nosy dogs, I might add. One night when I was out fishin' Mother chased a couple out of our car in the back yard. That is she went out to see what was carrying on, and they ran like deer up along the pipe-line. You don't get the feeling of privacy when there are so danged many people about, don't you know. A bunch of Lambdas or Kappas were up for a couple days and tried to drag me off to the dance, but I resisted because that would have meant shaving. My whiskers are now between three and four weeks old, and prospering greatly.

Paw will bring the books in when he comes. Thanks awfully for those, too, and for not wanting them in a hurry. Paw will also recompense you for the fillums, etc. Please do not forget to add postage. Since finishing them I have been diligently poring over the holy writ. After great pains I have struggled through the Pentateuch, which God forgive me I didn't enjoy Mr. Moses at all.

Did it ever occur to you that you don't have to give up the idea of coming down just because you couldn't make it this time? Talk your Pa into taking a vacation, or something. I may come into Salt Lake for a few days in August, or I may come to live there during the winter. Mother practically insists that I go back to school, and I can't very well tell her why I can't.[7] If I could talk them into moving to Berkeley I'd go back. Anyway, I'll see you sometime in August, because even if I have to go to school I'll need to come to Salt Lake for my clothes. Or what I laughingly refer to as my clothes. If we move to Salt Lake I'll give you a heck of a fine chance to be helpful cataloguing my library. Or what I laughingly refer to as my library. I have a couple 17th century astronomy books that will curl your hair to catalogue.

The mail goes down pretty pronto, so I'd better get this in the box.

The folks send their best, with the wish (I incl) that you can come down again before we close up the shack for the winter.

Love and kisses (hairy),
Prometheus

« *To: Sara Barnard* • *August 2, 1933* »

Dear Sahara,
Well, why not a letter. I wrote the last one, even if it didn't go by mail. Special messenger service is none too good for my billets-doux.

Nothing is doing here except dishes. My aunt took most of the household

---

7. Hilda Stegner was dying of breast cancer and he did not want to be as far away from her as Berkeley.

duties off my hands, manger my teeth, so here I sit reading Shakespeare and the King James Bible. If I did this for several years I should be a well-read young scholar. I should be, notice. I shall probably become a bookfull blockhead.

I have practically convinced mother that I should not go back to Berkeley next semester. In fact, if the worst happens, as I am afraid it will, I may go back to Iowa to get my degree. I had to talk Iowa to mother because there had to be some excuse for avoiding Berkeley. At least I get a postponement, because Iowa doesn't begin until the middle of September.

There is nothing sure yet about our trip to Zion and Bryce. If mother gets feeling a bit better I suppose we'll run down for two or three days. I'm still hoping you can come down before the season is over. There is a moon now, with warm winds from the west that chase clouds all over the moon and make great dapples in the sage and across the benches. Practically no one is here now, and silence reigns. So does the rain—promptly at one every day. Fishing is putrid. Shishing has suffered from the exodus of the femmes. But there's plenty of good resting. Nine till nine I sleep, like clockwork.

No indication of coming in to Salt Lake for a couple of weeks. Until then, as I so plaintively asked before, why not a letter.

Till the sands of the desert grow cold,

Mojave

« *To: Sara Barnard* • *February 3, 1934* »

Dear old Celery head

Excuse me, Dear old Salad Fork,

I am about to read some Plato. I am about to discover those glorious realms of light denominated *The Republic*. In fact, I am about to spend a few hours with one of the greatest thinkers the world has ever known. As I said, I am about to read Plato. Yes, I am suffering. What's it to you? I no sooner get through reading *Innocents Abroad*, and having a wonderful time, than I have to tear back to Periclean Greece or someplace. I am indignant. Greece, especially those regions and periods of Greece with which I am unfamiliar, are the (or is the) most insufferable, most stomach-souring, most pestilential and disease-breeding bog-hole in the history of the human mind. I do not like the idea of reading Plato. (Omega, not omicron.) Betake theyself (or thyself. Damn this typewriter) to Mades, he said, and went away from there. Please do not think I compliment you by writing at such a time. You are merely better than Plato.

Now I shall tell as much as I can about MacRae et al. (alius, alia, aliud. I am reviewing my Latin again, for Heaven's sake.) Speaking of for Heaven's sake, I have written a pome. Hark:

> I ponder on the ways of fishes
> They always act so damned suspicious
> Do they consider men are vicious
> For Heaven's sake?

I wrote another, but it is obscene. I fear you will always have to be content with my more mediocre efforts. My muse cannot fly well in clear air. She needs the smell of stockyards before she gets going.

As I was saying. What was I saying. Oh yes, MacRae. When we hove into Iowa City I was very drunk. I meant to come in sober, but I weakened, and drank four or five beers in the last twenty-five miles. Previous to that we had been drunk with Ike in Ames. Well, I was drunk. We approached MacRae's room. It was locked, with a note on the door—"Get key at office. Be back at seven." We got key at office, sat down. Enter MacRae and Don Lewis. Cowan and I had on boots and breeches. Quoth MacRae: "Did you ride in, for Chrissake?" Then we got tight. MacRae has a girl who is secretary to the Dean. We went to her apartment, two by six if it is an inch. Lewis and wife, MacRae and girl, MacRae's roommate and girl, Cowan and I, were there. Girls were scarce. None could be gotten for Cowan and me. We used MacRae's. I don't remember much about the party except that at two o'clock MacRae was going around from person to person, very solemnly and affectionately, embracing them and telling them with a world of feeling: "Who I really love is you." Who is a dizzy ass is MacRae. Who got drunk was us. Who went out the next night and had a good old masculine bull session about Life, Death, Love, Prostitution, Society, Education, and all the other capital letter words was Cowan, MacRae, and me. Who thinks Cowan is the real stuff is MacRae. Who practically worships the MacRae manner is Cowan. Who likes them both is me. We have a mutual admiration society. Who is going to get drunk again Saturday night is us three musketeers. I have decided not to quit drinking. Already I have gained three pounds, and I have drunk an awful lot of tripe, read a number of books, and got an A on Foerster's reading exam. Who thinks I am a mighty scholar is Foerster. Who wants him to think just that is old Stegner. (I hope you like this style. It is the lastest thing out—MacRae special invention to add weight and pithiness to any conversation.

I cannot get a degree at the end of the summer, sad to say. I missed a German exam by a week, and another is not given until the end of the semester. What is impossible to get is a special exam. Said exam must be taken a year before the degree, or thereabouts. A semester plus summer term would suffice, but cannot be manipulated. So I am going to try to get all the exams out of the road except the final oral, and see how much I can get done toward a thesis. Probably not much. I have three nine-hour exams to take this semester. Who will need an occasional bath in alcohol is

Your devoted admirer,

[no signature]

« To: Sara Barnard • February 19, 1934 »

Dear Sally,

Thank you, thank you, my friend. I thrill at your proximity. No, the brownies were not stale, neither did I miss them. I just did not get my fair share. Who has really been the recipient of many birthday boxes is me, and who ate all of them was Cowan.[8] (Did I mention that MacRae sends thanks and thinks maybe you might be a Lily?) My kid cousin sent down a box of cookies, Mrs. Cowan sent Red and me each a fruit cake, and lo, all I got out of any of them was some of your brownies, which were the best, but I want my cake and I wanna eat it neither.

I went back to Iowa City last weekend to straighten out my registration and get some books and things, and last night the verdamnt train was two hours late, dumping me off at the station with a suitcase full of books and a typewriter at three A.M., and four below. I ache yet after that hike up the hill.

Let me tell you some more about our college,[9] he blatted. We have an enrollment of some six hundred, four hundred and fifty of whom are stenographers on CWA. When I want any typing or mimeographing done I beckon to any passing student, and four hundred and fifty times out of six

8. Stegner and Milton "Red" Cowan had grown up together in Salt Lake. They were undergraduates together at the University of Utah, spent a year together as graduate students in Berkeley, California, and completed their degrees at the University of Iowa in 1934.
9. Augustana College in Rock Island, Illinois. Stegner had a temporary teaching job there in 1934.

hundred he is my stenographer. I live with the seminary boys (quahhah); there are twin beds (come up some time), two rooms, one sleeping and one studying (not the rooms—me). From my lonely casement I can gaze across the rolling Mississippi with a couple more s's and a couple more i's to the Rock Island Arsenal in the middle. The town's on the bank. Between me and the arsenal is a large expanse of broad snow-covered nhyah (Old high Church Slavic term, meaning "Something terrible"). The town is smoky, dirty, ramshackle, disreputable, and mean. The college, with the exception of the two dorms and the library building, is ditto. In spite of that I think I like it. Most of my time is spent preparing lectures, for christsake, or in diverting my students with commentaries of Aristotle's ethics or Poetics or something equally inane. I dish out a lot of bromidical tripe and call it lectures, and the funny thing is, so do the students, and we get along fine. Maybe some day I'll get down and scratch out a good lecture, and ruin their faith in me. Today I was asked to write poetry for the literary journal, for the love of mike. Last week I was invited to a faculty poker party. I think the atmosphere will not be too thickly charged with the theses in spite of the theological seminary. The worst part of it is the smugness of these academic charlatans with their big fronts and their behinds just made for kicking. What I really love and admire is a college professor who is satisfied with himself and his work.

And you.

Wally

« To: Sara Barnard · March 29, 1934 »

Dear old fellow Stick-in-the-mud,

Everybody going to Chile and Los Angeles and places. And spring among our blood, and classes to teach and libraries to attend to. Oh fie! You and I are home bodies for certain. What is more, I am more than likely to be immured in the hot prison of Iowa for years and years. Letter from Neff Monday. No job, the old procrastinator. So I have been dickering with Foerster for a part-time job at Iowa, that will support me until I finish this never-to-be-sufficiently-damned and double-damned degree. So—no Salt Lake this fall, no moonlighting, no shishing, no fox-trotting, no Fish Lake, not even any pettifogging, and most of all no Sary. It is even doubtful if I can get back for a visit late in the summer, because who will be most broke is I, and believe you me, my pa's boy is not going back to the previous source of his support. That burden looks too heavy to be resumed after it is once got free of.

All kinds of changes in plans and plots. The Chicago trip looks distant—maybe not until June, or maybe not then. Got to save money, if I'm to live on a fellowship next year, without visible means of support. So your little sis is safe from the bold bad mans. I would like awfully to get in and see the gal and the town though. Maybe spring will make me reckless after a while. I have also changed my thesis, or practically done so. And Ah! Here is a chance to be helpful, Sahara. What I am maybe going to do for a thesis is an edition of selections from the literary portions of Dutton, from the *Tertiary History*, the *High Plateaus*, and some of his other works. Foerster seems to approve—perhaps because it will warrant another chapter to his book on nature in American Literature. The thing would be a selection, leaving out the technical geological parts, and with a critical and biographical essay sub, pre, or post-joined. I thought perhaps it would be possible to get the Caxton Printers to publish it, or maybe someone else. There are no copyrights to be considered, since almost all his work was published by the government, and is public property. So don't broadcast the subject. It would be too easy for someone to sneak in and do it before I get around to it. I'd like to have it all finished before I even submit it to Caxtons. But what I would like to know, and what you can be awful helpful about, is whether or not anybody around Salt Lake, particularly J. Cecil Alter, has done anything with Dutton, and if so, what. The libraries around here are not too well primed about western geologists, although I have found *The Tertiary History*[10] here at Augustana, besides some reports in the annual reports of the USGS. And if you run across any biographical data on Dutton I wish you'd send me the reference. I have found two short biographical sketches in the Am. Jour. Sc., Vol. 33, and the Seis. Soc. Am. Bulletin, Vol. 1, besides the account in Who's Who. I guess I'll write to Wallingford Connecticut, where he was born, and to Trenton, N.J. where he lived for some time, to see if I can dig anything out of the public libraries there. Who's Who says that Dutton published many articles in magazines and scientific journals, but I'll be able to dig those out at the Iowa library, I guess. So you know any guide to periodicals of the period from 1864, or there-about, until about 1890? I haven't even bothered to go back and see how early Poole and the Reader's Guide begin. As a matter of fact, I have only had

---

10. Clarence Dutton's *The Tertiary History of the Grand Canyon, 1882.*

this mighty inspiration a week. One thing I have done—have arranged with one of my many CWA student stenographers to type the whole of the *Tertiary History* off, which costs me just nothing except the paper and carbons. Pretty soft. If she gets that done before school is out I'll borrow a *High Plateaus*[11] somewhere and start her on that. Teaching school does have some advantages.

Please don't mention this Dutton thing to anyone. I'm afraid Pack or Alter or somebody would hop right to it if the idea ever struck them, and I'd have to change theses again.

Tusk tusk about your marginal notes. Feels good inside. The idea. Just at a moment when I was becoming mentally healthy and not even thinking about such things, haven't for weeks, as a matter of fact. Not even when it became spring all of a sudden. But I probably will, Oscar, I probably will. Right now I let the ineffably lustful subconscious and the automatic safety valves take care of all my activities in that line. I can't afford to be getting interested with you miles and miles and months and months away. Don't waste your youth waiting for me, Sally. I'm too decrepit, too variable, and too burdened with an unpleasant past to be worth much waiting. I love you a very great deal . . . you're the finest friend I ever had, but I think it dangerous to both of us to try to carry it beyond that. My crazy old body is not too well, and I think I know the cause. I'm putting off anything definite about it until after school is out—but unless some miracle or other happens, I am not the sort of person who would make a good husband. No matter what either of us may think or swear, pure mind without body never made a marriage. It is not very pleasant, that subject, but it is a good ironical joke, in a way, that my unhappy, unhealthy, haunted family should flower in something like me. The Last of the Stegners. What a distinction. It doesn't bother me much from my own point of view, because I've lived with it too long, but I hate it for your sake. It just is, and if I know you at all your chin will stay up. If you eat a thing like that down like a man, sooner or later you digest it, and it does you good—even gives you strength. Power to you, Sally dear.

You asked me a couple months ago if I were still honest. Was that what you meant? I still love you, I still admire and respect you, I am still dumbly grateful for everything you have been. But it will almost inevitably never be more than that. I wish to God it could. I'd like to kiss you when

---

11. Dutton's *High Plateaus of Utah*, 1880.

I tell you things like that. It sounds pretty blunt. But it is honest, and it's better than letting you be disappointed later. I do love you, Sally. You know it—don't you?

     Wally

« *To: Mary Page* • *March 31, 1934* »

Mary darling,

I can't say that I particularly approve of vacations unless one can go somewhere and do something with someone one likes. How's that for an English sentence. Where I should like to be is off in a tree house with you somewhere, musing sentimentally by a fire, with a cat (even a damned cat) purring by the hearth rug.[12] I am afraid you are romantic, my love. I am afraid you live in clouds, and in the future—an impossible future, and I am afraid you are one of these essentially skinless creatures whom every blowing cinder hurts. So am I, or was I. Then I developed a suit of armor, and then you came and undressed me again. I'm not sure that I mind, even on principle. I know that at present I love it, but I'm afraid when I think that both of us are going to get hurt. So I vacillate between, "Come on, Stegner, be sensible; get hold of yourself; you're only digging a pit for her and yourself by letting yourself love Mary," and "One crowded hour of joyful strife (maybe it's 'life') / Is worth an age without a name."

In fine, as Robinson and Cabell would say, I am completely polarized.

Had a letter from my father today,[13] and a package containing some shirts and ties. Think that over. The one man on earth that I hate as utterly as I love you sends me presents, writes letters that are almost pathetic in their loneliness. To me, whom he has never liked, and whom he knows has never liked him. I wish to God there wasn't so much of a moping, sick, gnawing Hamletism in me, so that I could hate him whole-heartedly

---

12. Stegner was introduced to Mary Page, the woman who would become his wife, by his roommate, Wilbur Schramm, shortly after returning to Iowa in 1934. He was teaching part-time at a Lutheran College, Augustana, and commuting back and forth between Rock Island, Illinois and Iowa City.

13. Many readers have thought they detected autobiographical elements from Stegner's early years in the conflict between Bruce and Bo Mason in *The Big Rock Candy Mountain*. Throughout his life, Stegner almost never spoke of his father, even to friends and family members, though he did offer a somewhat modulated appraisal in response to a direct question by Richard Etulain in *Conversations*. This 1934 letter to his wife-to-be is perhaps the most unrestrained outburst he ever made.

and be done with it. The hell of it is I have the unhappy faculty of seeing things from both sides at once. I can understand how he could crush my mother's life out, and never be conscious of the fact. I can even understand the woman he has picked up with. I suspect that he has married her, and is ashamed to tell me. Either way it is just as bad, and I hate him just the same with a fury that scares me. And he sends me gifts—clings like a drowning man to a straw to the one thing left of his wrecked and splintered and ship-wrecked life, even though it is the thing he liked least when he had the whole. And so utterly blind to the fact that he himself was the rocks he split on, himself the storm that ruined him, his greed and selfishness the reason that everything he seized turned to ashes in his hands. It's been a long time coming, but it is beautifully complete now. God be praised. The hell of it is that I am weak enough to feel sorry for him at times, he has so little bottom and character to understand and bear the catastrophe.

Can't imagine why I got on that sordid topic, unless it was to explain again why day-dreams are dangerous. I can never marry as long as that man is alive. As a matter of fact, I probably shouldn't then, because there is insanity in his family (I think he is slipping badly himself now, and has been for a year). But that is a more or less story-book reason for not marrying. One could practice your continence or something. The other one is real, however. I would never inflict even the shadow of that past on anyone. That is about the only thing I am completely sure of—that before I build any future I am going to be completely abgeschnitten from everything that ever happened to me previously.

And so here I am moaning and groping around through it, making you unhappy. Now I take it all back, or at least all the mopes. The prospect isn't entirely black. For one thing, I am practically sure that he won't live very long—none of his family does. I wouldn't feign any sorrow. It would be like a release from prison, and the best and kindest thing that can happen to him is death, if he only knew it.[14] And if he doesn't die within a few years I am as certain as that I am sitting here that he will be insane. I imagine this makes you feel like a ghoul, doesn't it. It does me too, but I can't pretend to any solicitude for him. If he fell in the gutter I should probably help him out, because there are still shreds of duty attached to his name, and because my mother would have helped him, and did, in the face of any and

---

14. George Stegner would take his own life, and the life of the woman with him, in a little over a year. It was hardly the "release from prison" anticipated by his son.

all insults and wrongs. It is for her sake I hate him, not mine. I sincerely thank whatever gods may be that I could never hate anyone this much for anything he could do to me personally.

Which is more than enough of that. Now I am going to forget the whole business until I get some other reminder like these damned shirts and ties. We decided to be contented with being in love, and letting the future take care of itself, didn't we? But I still think it is dangerous to day-dream more than a month ahead. Or maybe you weren't. Anyway it gives me a very solid and somehow criminal satisfaction that you do day-dream. I love it. Do it some more, but don't believe it until it happens, and then be pleasantly surprised. That is what is known as practical optimism. Only five more days and I can wrap you up and take you home for three days. And if you don't believe I am going to give you an evening wrap take another think. The diet I have down here is unbalanced. There aren't any kisses in it, and who needs your kisses more than he needs orange juice and vitamin B is

Yours truly,
Wally

« *To: Sara Barnard* • *May 1, 1934* »

Dear Sara,
Will you do something else helpful for me? Will you use these couple of dollars to put some kind of flowers on Mother's and Cece's[15] graves? Always before when I was away at school and the folks weren't in town I sent some money to Mrs. Hensdale, but I'm not sure they still have their little farm. Maybe you could call and see—could you—and let me know next time you write? Then I could drop them a note. I haven't even sent them a card since I left. You might tell Harriett that I sent you some money for flowers. It would give her faith in human nature a boost for another year. Then maybe you could put them out on Mother's day—would you?

Thanks awfully, Sally. I've only time for a note. Studying again. These examinations for your greater enlightenment, are as follows:

1) Exams over Masterpieces of World Literature. 9 hours. Written.

2) Exam over 5 hours projected registration on thesis. Oral, time indefinite.

3) Exam in German reading. One hour written, one hour oral.

---

15. Stegner's older brother who died of pneumonia in his early twenties.

And they all come on the 18th and 19th of May, so help me Gawd. About 13 hours of exams in 2 days. Woe. Woe. Woe.

Love in a rush,

Einer

« *To: Mary Page* • *May 21, 1934* »

Mary darling,

Do you mind if I have my date with you in the afternoon? I've been hibernating and getting work done, and I need the cool touch of your hand on my fevered brow. Who is industrious is me. I haven't been outside the room since yesterday afternoon, and I have finished what I had left to do in Hazlitt, read a volume of Uncle Remus stories (which are really grand), and read about three hundred pages of Mr. Howells' *Modern Instance*, besides an hour or two of German. If I could keep myself cooped up here for a week I'd have a semester's work done. That above is only since yesterday at four-thirty. Pretty danged industrious I calls it. Besides I went to bed at nine-thirty and got up at nine for a complete night's rest, albeit somewhat troubled by dreams of no spiritual nature. It takes time to conquer the unconscious. This afternoon I'll finish Howells and get a good long start on Lamb's Essays tonight. Tomorrow I can finish Lamb, do some more German, and begin a second volume of Carlyle or Hazlitt. Saturday night I go to the Theatre. Yes. *The Rivals*. I sit in lonely splendor in the eighth row all by meself without a lady friend. Wish you could come down, but it's probably snowing in Iowa City also, n'est-ce pas? We have six inches or so now, and still going strong. Let's talk about the weather.

In my sordid poverty I have been reduced to eating in the room. Crackers and cheese and pressed ham. Yes. I leave the ham on the window sill and it freezes and then I eat it like ice cream. At my present rate I can live from now till payday on a dollar and a half. I still have three dollars, so I may break down and eat out once, or have a shirt washed, or something. Who lives a monkish and sparing life is me. I have even made two packages of cigarettes last a week, and still have some over. (Editor's note: I roll them in between times, which is far cheaper.)

And so how about you? Dang it (please note restraint in color-words)—I had a chance to come in to Iowa City last night with some people who were going to see *Death Takes a Holiday*, but for one thing I didn't quite see how I would eat till payday if I did go, and besides, the invitation came from Ugly Mary, who I fear is getting a crush on teacher which it will not do to humor in any way. Damn the Undergraduate Mind.

The contemporary portraits will have to wait until tomorrow (I can hear you groan about that, Oh yes) because at present I have no subject but a pursy little priest with a bay window and not enough character to lend himself readily to my inimitable caricaturing. But tomorrow I go to see old Dr. Bartholomew, the former head of the department here, about some lectures he wants to give to the English majors, and I think he should be good material. For one thing, he has fine white mutton-chop whiskers like Oliver Wendell Holmes, and for another he lives in an old squat paunchy interesting looking house up on top of the hill. If he isn't interesting I'm sure his house will be.

Three cheers for Cowan (who would be fearfully hurt if he could see the way you spell his name) for taking you to the Budapest string quartet. I would gladly trade the Rivals for the Budapest string quartet, but no. Fate is adamant. So instead I have decided to write a learned article, modeled on Lowes' *Road to Xanadu*. It will be called *The Road to Skulleyville*, and will have to do with the sources of Popeye. In Uncle Remus last night I discovered that Brer Rabbit, when in the Dismal Swamp, is known also by the name of Brer Popeye, and I learned also that when he is reproached for anything his favorite defense is "I yam what I yam and that's all I yam." A clear case of literary borrowing. If it were not for the fact that it is high time somebody caricatured the scholarly method of research and rehabilitation of lost sources I should not bother myself with it, being of a naturally serious cast of mind, but as it is I have a good notion to do a little investigating. It would look elegant in print. *The Road to Skulleyville*. In the manner of the earlier John Livingston Lowes. By W. E. Stegner, Professor of English in Augustana College. I also have in mind a series of thumb-nail sketches based upon my researches for your letters, which would be written perhaps for College Humor or the American Mercury. Or I might do one on college buildings. Or on Dormitory Pests. Or on damned near anything. There is nothing like publication to bolster one's professional status. With a little encouragement I could become the Cotton Mather of Academicism.

It is about time I cleaned up this room and changed the bed and stuff. Come up sometime with your dust mop and we'll make a sweeping success of this place. And hasta I see you again, Fraulein, adios, and adieu and auf wiedersehen and keep your heart warm. Let me tell you about the dream I had last night. I dreamed that I had a piece of cold mince pie pressing against my heart, and I woke up and looked, and it was a piece of cold mince pie. So I took some soda and went back to sleep.

Hoping you are the same,

Your devoted

« *To: Mary Page* • *June 2, 1934* »

Mary dearest,

I finished Vardis Fisher's *Passions Spin the Plot* a few hours ago, and I don't think anything I ever read revealed so much or recalled so much of myself to myself. Damn, that is a grand piece of work. There just aren't any words for a book like that. And yet I can see how some people—perhaps you— might not get anything out of it but sordidness and swear words. He set out to write an honest book, because every other kind had been written. And he did. I thought *In Tragic Life* was good, but this is even better. If Fisher had been trying to write my life he could hardly have come closer to the self-torture and the pride and the vanity and the morbid eroticism that made my boyhood a miserable dark torment. And if he had had Juanita[16] for a model, he couldn't have drawn her portrait any more clearly than he has in Neloa Doole. And if he had been in my skin for four years he couldn't have dug out the restfulness and peace and freedom from the inner consciousness that happy times with her brought, or the hell that doubt created. She is complete even to the eyes, with the depths in them that meant something or nothing, the thing inside that showed through, and which was never readable. It was simply all life, all love, and all woman, all the dark mystery that lies behind and beyond consciousness, and is capable of being seen but never interpreted. It is the eyes, I think, that have made fools like Fisher and me love women like Neloa and Juanita so intensely and so utterly—because our half-mad adolescence is frightened away from actual women, and feeds on the Idea of woman, on the eternal mother, the life principle, the thing that stands for the opposite of unbeautiful death. And yet the thing we saw in those eyes was not in the woman at all. I have

---

16. Juanita Crawford, Stegner's first love, circa 1930–31. She is the prototype for Nola Gordon in his novel *Recapitulation*.

seen the same thing in the eyes of a cow . . . and I think it is in the eyes of all people and all animals, if we look closely enough. But in the eyes of this sort of woman, quiet, primitive, unable to read herself or what she stands for, it is a symbol that haunts me yet. Your eyes don't have it, except at rare moments, because there is intelligence in your eyes. This isn't an intelligent look. It is like quiet water, and you can look through it on and on until you get lost and bewildered in the shadows of it. I can read you in your eyes—I could never read Juanita, because the thing behind her eyes was not thought, was nothing that could be expressed. It was merely life, not even consciousness, but only life. And it was life I was trying to understand, and life I loved. The principle of fertility, of reproduction and continuity, not the woman, was what I wanted to know, and so my love for her was more agonizing than my love for you. I love you as a human being, as a mind, as a woman. I loved her as an abstraction and as a mystery. Looking back at her now, I know that she was not a fine woman; she was not intelligent; she was not a character whom one could love for herself. One loved her for the mystery that looked through her eyes, which she had nothing to do with. And the whole thing, probably, can be explained on the basis of pigmentation and lack of eye strain and lack of thought. Beautiful eyes rarely go with deep thought.

Please pardon me for talking about Juanita. I'm not reverting to old loves, or drawing comparisons between you and her, I'm only so damned moved by this book of Fisher's that all this comes back on me like a wave, and I remember and understand a great many things. I am amazed to reconstruct what I then was . . . amazed, and a little regretful. My skin is thicker now, and my brain is calmer, and I don't torture myself with thoughts, but it seems somehow as if I had lost something valuable at the same time, that I had lost the power to feel anything as brightly and terribly as I once could.

My brain has so far got control of my emotions that even my love for you, which is deep and wide and sure, does not put me on the rack as it once would have. The only torment I have now is that of being away from you. A few years ago I would have worried you into an early grave with my questionings and probings and attempts to analyze you and myself and our love to the deepest roots. It seems that I am content now to accept without too much questioning.

I was so blamed full of this book that I threw on a pair of pants and went walking in the rain for two hours. It was grand. In the lightning flashes I could see the long curved rain falling, and the clouds would light up so that I could see world beyond world, heaven beyond heaven, of piled cumuli with the light at their backs and the shadow on their faces, and just behind the nearest mass the hot stuttering drill of the lightning straight down to earth. The sky was completely covered with clouds, and the thunder rolled from horizon to horizon in long dying rumbles. It struck me that it was the first time I had had a sensation, a real sensation, in two or three years—not since the north wind blew at Fish Lake for three days a few summers ago, and I saw the sage fields bending under a high cold moon.

Darn it Mary, I wish you were here for me to talk to. I'm so full of something or other I feel as if I'm going to burst, and none of this transcendental drivel I've been writing says a thing. My conscience says that I should do my Latin—I have not touched it yet—but my love and my emotional state and the rest of what ails me say write to Mary and then go to bed and think, and let the Latin go to the devil. I really think that one evening like this per year is worth all the Latin in the British Museum. And I have discovered something else—I have not, as I thought, lost the faculty of reading for pleasure. If I read any more books like this soon I'll have to take aspirin to slow down my heart action.

Love me, darling, in spite of the fact that I'm screwy. If the time comes soon when we can be together for good, the first thing I am going to do is make you go walking with me in a thunderstorm, and the next thing, love you physically, mentally, and spiritually until you know how much I love your warmth, your actualness, your intelligence, your sunshiny affection. Thank God you are no abstraction, except at rare moments. I prefer to love a human being. But that book is nevertheless extremely fine. I have Lewis' copy, but if you want to read it let me know and I'll see if he'd mind my sending it up.

What are your objections to my coming up on July 4th and fixing Laura?[17] I'm quitting this board job on the first. Please advise.

All my love,
Wally

---

17. Laura was the name Stegner had given his car.

« *To: Mary Page* • *June 12, 1934* »

Mary dear,

For fifteen minutes I have been listening to Schramm[18] preaching marriage, and who cannot stand it any longer is guess who. All this talk of twin beds and study rooms and new drapes gets to me, pal, it gets to me. It gets to me worse even than Latin. I finally finished my Latin lesson last night at eleven, having been at it off and on since one that afternoon, and then to cap the whole affair with a weird and insidious capstone, I go to bed and find a mouse in my pillow. He didn't like me, I didn't like him, and we did our very best to get rid of each other for fifteen minutes, until I finally brained him with a shoe. That is a strange feeling, that rustling and tearing around among the feathers, after you have hit the snore slab very fagged for a long sleep. First little questing, probationary rustlings, then quick bursts of activity, then a determined and anxious effort to get out, and all the time you are lying there thinking what in the hell is wrong with me. Maybe I studied too long. Maybe it was those damnable daily meatballs at the hospital. Maybe I'm losing my mind. Maybe this is the first indication of a growing nitwittedness. Good heavens, what can it be. It grows. It whispers and rustles under your ear. You rise, turn on the light, see movements inside the pillow case. You see pictures of snakes coiled in your bolster—no, it can't be that. I haven't had a beer for five or six days. Then what is it. You lay an experimental finger on the movement. It leaps over and under the feathers. Ah. A mouse. But how to get him? If you crack him with a shoe you will ruin the pillow. If you shake him out he will escape, probably. And you do not wish him to escape. No indeed. Your fighting blood is up. No bird, beast, or reptile can inhabit your pillow and undermine your well-earned rest with impunity. You cogitate, keeping one eye on the twitching pillow slip. Ah. You will shake him into the wash bowl. No, he might get down the drain and clog the pipes and then the maid would be angry, and it is policy to keep the maid happy, or you find worse things than mice in your bed. You think some more. Finally you take the dilemma by the horns and with a shoe in one hand and the pillow in the other you shake gently, with distended eyes and a little green

---

18. Wilbur Schramm, Stegner's roommate at Iowa, and a colleague, years later, at Stanford. It was Schramm who got Stegner his first teaching job at Augustana College in Rock Island, Illinois, and introduced him to the woman who would become his wife, Mary Page.

reading lamp casting its pale illumination over your shoulder. Finally the intruder bursts from his nest, you beat violently on empty floor with the shoe, the mouse escapes under the bed. You follow wrathfully, intent on the kill. You corner him behind a suitcase, jerk it away, cripple him with a snap throw from the hip, and then beat out his pitiful little brains at your leisure, drop the remains into the waste basket, without military honors, and go back to bed tired but happy. It makes me tired to tell about it. This survival of the fittest, to the victor belongs the pillow-stuff is all right in theory, but it entails a lot of frenzied activity at times.

Same old assignment for Latin tomorrow, but I am sure I won't have to do all the translation, because we only finished half of what we had for today. Three cheers. Maybe I can read thirty or forty pages of Wieland for Clark. If things keep picking up this way I shall be able to read two or three books this summer, besides my Latin. Grand.

Please keep me minutely informed as to your immediate wishes, desires, and desiderations, because the more I think of this summer marriage business the more I think of it. Maybe I shall have to come to Dubuque and ask your father for your hand. What a job that will be.

Wilbur sends his love and expectations, damn his eyes.

Your,

Wally

« To: Mary Page • June 20, 1934 »

Dear old Mary,

Your letter this morning almost put me into Wertherian rhapsodies. What nice things you say, Grandma. Duplicate them and make them retroactive, and you have my sentiments exactly. A wire from Neff this morning. I have the Utah job, at $1700. Now what we going to do? Under the circumstances, the only thing I could do was apply at Utah, because if I stayed on here as a half-time assistant I wouldn't have a dime in June when I got my degree. I might even have had to borrow some money to finish. Now we can plan on things by next June, at least, and if you feel that you want to, we can get married before that. The only disadvantage of going to Salt Lake is that probably my father will be there, and I didn't ever want you to meet him. I think it would be very difficult for you to love me after you saw my father once. But that's up to you. Don't you like the way I leave everything up to you? It's the sign of a weak disposition. This morning also

I had the employment office call up and offer me a permanent board job in the Housekeeping Department of the Hospital. Despite the indisputable fact that I need training in housekeeping, I turned them down very cold. Still no word from the Irvines. I am beginning to think that perhaps they went right on through, and are planning to stop over on the way back. It is possible that Mr. Irvine[19] had to be in New York at a definite time, because he will be buying for the store, and that therefore he didn't want to run the chance of being delayed by pausing here. Anyway they hain't wrote, which is bad enough.

Now I have to go read *Deerslayer* and take some notes on Werther. I read that damned thing till twelve last night, and got up at six this morning and read some more, and finished it during the ten o'clock period. It is probably the worst thing ever written. Funke thinks it is swell. Zat is ze Baroque in literature. Who is definitely ill from the Baroque in literature is guess who. Love me some more as you did in your letter this morning. It gives me chills and fever. The vibrations from it coincided so perfectly with the shakings of my lean frame when I think of you that I practically shook apart when I read it.

Je t'aime,
Wally

« *To: Sara Barnard* • *June 23, 1934* »

Dear Sally,
I am afraid this letter is going to hurt you awfully, and very probably will make you hate me, or despise me, which is worse. You know what it is already—I have fallen in love, stupidly, goofily, insanely in love. I tried not to, honestly I did. I have been agonized for two months, trying to fight out of it, but it's no go, Sally. It's as if I'm being driven with whips. I have curs'd myself a thousand times when I've thought of you, and how sweet and grand you are, but I'm still driven back to where I started. The strange part is that I still love you, Sally, as much, and in the same way, as I always did. I admire you more than anyone I know—which sounds like a pitiful travesty, I know, but is true. The thought of your despising me turns me cold, but I can't help it, Sally, I can't help it. I've no more control over myself

---

19. Irvine owned the linoleum store in Salt Lake when Stegner worked as an undergraduate at the University of Utah.

than a child. The whole sickening background of my life comes back on me, and I simply have to try to make a desperate grab for whatever there is left in life for me. It may be much, it may be two or three years—the doctors don't know, and the only way to do is to wait,[20] they say. But I can't wait—and because I can't wait I have to stab my best friend. Oh, Sally, I'm sorry, so sorry, if this hurts you as much as I'm afraid it will. I wrote you once before, but your letter telling of your father's death made me tear the letter up. Please don't think I'm heartless, Sally. I suffered a great deal for you then, and cursed myself for a coward and a fool, but now I just have to be as honest with you as is still possible. No matter how you may despise me, you can't make me stop loving you and feeling deeply grateful to you, but it's no use pretending that I love you as a wife. I know my actions said otherwise, but you know by now that I am as weak as water, and that the thing I am is nowhere near the thing I'd like to be. And so, Sally, I am going to make a desperate plunge and be married as soon as summer school is out. Her name is Mary Page, and she's really an awfully fine girl, but I compare her with you in some ways and I loathe what my passions have gotten me into. What is worse for you, I am going to teach at Utah next year. I had to. Augustana kicked me out for being an atheist, which was more or less to be expected, and I had to take the only thing left. It would give me more pleasure than anything I know to have you and Mary become friends, but that is too much to expect, even from one as forgiving and gentle as you. Mary knows about you, and sympathizes with what I feel, and she'd like to know you. But that is too much to hope, and altogether too much to ask. I'm sorry, dear Sally, until it hurts down in the darkness of me, but what I'm doing is out of my control, forgive me if you can, but remember, however you feel, that I love and respect you, and always will.

Wally

« *To: Mary Page* • *July 11, 1934* »

Mary dear,

I'm awfully sorry about your cold. I've got one too. You feel sorry for me and I'll feel sorry for you, and we'll both feel better. Sorry also about the failure of shopping expeditions. As for the desert island, I invited you once

---

20. This was probably youthful melodrama, though Stegner would develop ulcers within a couple of years, and he had a mild heart condition in 1940 that disappeared over time.

to join my private nudist colony, and you refused peremptorily, and hurt my feelings. From now on you cannot go naked in my yard. Very glad about Ted, very glad about Red. I think she is a grand person, and he is not such a bad feller himself. I also have a theory that a love affair, ad finem, would be a fine thing for Ted, even if it never got to the point of marriage. If I were prescribing for her, I would tell her to go up with her boy friend to Minnesota and build her cabin all summer, and be as happy and lusty and lecherous and carefree as she pleased, and then come back to work a new woman, or something. Maybe I'm wrong. À chaque saint sa chandelle. But I'd hate awfully to see her shrink into being a timid and retiring maiden lady. People like you need different treatment, worse luck. You're in no danger of becoming an old maid. If I don't marry you some other poor sucker will (don't throw that).

Oh me. Went to chapel this morning, to the exercises meant to congratulate the president[21] on his seventieth birthday. I would not have gone if I had been able to attend the reception tonight, but I thought I should be in evidence somewhere, sometime. Chapel is a fine affair. I sat between the head of the Psychology department and the matron of the girls' dorm. We had a hymn book among the three of us, and both my companions stared very hard at me when I didn't join in on the doxologer. They both sang very loudly and very much off key to cover the fact that I was not among them. I couldn't. I had a cold, and there's nothing that aggravates a cold in me like old 422 in the Lutheran hymnal. Old Doc Bartholomew made the prayer. He is magnificent. His whiskers sweep down his cheeks in white billows, and then curl coyly away from his lapels. When he prays the words creep diffidently out from among the whiskers like rabbits out of a canebrake. One can almost see them float piously upward against those very white mutton-chops and that very pink face. He was going on with fervor when he came to the passage "In my father's house are many mansions," but he bleated so badly on the "ma-a-a-any ma-a-a-ansions" that he almost had to give up and sit down. But he stuck with it, and managed to get off a right smart prayer. I was suitably edified, especially by the bleating. I guess I am an infidel at heart. Old age, especially bleating and doddering old age, and most especially that sort of old age combined with cantankerous and spiteful religious bigotry, looks to me like something our poor suffering

---

21. Of Augustana College in Rock Island, Illinois, where Stegner taught for a year in 1934.

world could do without. Then the band played, and the male and female choruses, or chori, sang (and are not at all bad), and we listened to the president pour out his heart's blood for dear old Augie, and then we went to lunch. I can't get over the impression that these religious old coots around here are the most colossal hypocrites that I have ever known. Perhaps they're not, but how any sane, intelligent, and decently gutty man can talk like these people do is beyond the pagan comprehension of W.S. Stegner, Professor of English in Augustana College, with capitals. I cannot say yet whether I shall come back on Thursday or Friday. If I can get my check cashed immediately, I shall probably come Thursday; otherwise Friday. And who will be all bowed down with his emotion when he greets his great love is me.

All love,
Wally

« *To: Mary Page* • *July 15, 1934* »

Mary dearest,

Nope, I can't stand it any longer without a respite and a little Nepenthe. I have been going since ten bells, with only time out for a twenty-minute lunch. It is very hot here, and the flies tickle. If I put clothes on, the flies don't tickle, but it is hotter. If I take them off, it is still hot, and the flies tickle. To date I have killed forty-two flies with a rolled-up Popeye. Between killing flies, being tickled, and perspiring (sweating too) I have gotten half through the last of Cooper's novels, written a paper for Funke, and done some Latin. Woe. Now Cowan comes in and tells me I'm a masochist. Self laceration. Humbling of the flesh.

Every once in a while I would wake up from Cooper and discover that what I was thinking about was Mary, and how we would go for long boat rides at Fish Lake before settling down, and how we could organize a swell nudist colony all by ourselves in front of the fireplace, and how the wind would be rusting or rustling or something the aspens, and the birds would be heading south, and nobody much would be up at the lake, and we could get some horses from Elmer the dairy man and go riding up on top of the plateau by Rock Springs or Crater lakes, and how the deer would be coming down again now that the fishing season was about over, and how much fun it would be to chop wood again that you could use to fry me a boiled egg.

Oh my. We could climb up on top of the rim behind the cabin (two hours of climbing. Are you good and strong?) and look away down south, over Aquarius and Thousand Lake mountains, with the horizon rising in long swells and dropping off at the edges in sharp cliffs, and the sun slanting across red walls, and the aspens beginning to turn on the slopes. Oh my once more. I didn't realize until today how homesick I am, and I am just beginning to become aware of how much fun I'm going to have showing you God's country, and how sad I am going to be if you find it depressing or arid or too sage-brushish, or too lonesome, or too rough. And when we want a little minor exercise we can get horses and run up and down Frying Pan Flat, and scare up ducks from the marshes, or we can sit on the front steps and whittle, or watch the ants take in food for the winter. And at night we can wrap up in eight or ten sweaters and watch the moon come over the rim. If it isn't too cold we can take the boat and run up and down the moonpaths. In the mornings, when the wind hasn't come up and the sun is thin and warm we can drift along shore and watch the fish hanging motionless down among the seaweed. Hey, Mary—do you suppose you could make us two toweling bathrobes—with hoods, please—for exclusive Fish Lake use? But that's asking too much, when you've got plenty of other things to worry about.

Now I had better correct the rhapsodic impression. At Fish Lake there is no plumbing; the wasps frequently build their nests in the little house in the rear; the chimney sometimes smokes if the barometer is low; there is no hot water that you don't specifically heat yourself; it is very often extremely chilly at night; you may be bothered by the altitude for a day or so, and you may be bothered with the colic from drinking pure snow-water. Lots of people are.

Now what do you say? Shall we plan to get to Salt Lake by the 10th or so, and have a week at Fish Lake before settling down, or shall we plan to stay in Salt Lake once we arrive? If we don't go down at once I'm almost going to bind and gag you and take you down during the duck season when the leaves are the most beautiful sight you may hope to see between here and Harlem. What I would really like to do is go both times, and again at Christmas, with a party, for some skiing. You gather I rather like the place. But what makes it all of a sudden so overwhelmingly attractive is that there is our tree house all ready for occupancy, and when you can get the girl, the place, and the time all together, Heaven has not anything to show more fair. Mary, Mary, I love you until this miserable school is like an anvil on my chest. I wasn't particularly lonesome for the old lake until I began to daydream about being there with you, and all of a sudden I knew that if we couldn't have our perfect bodily, spiritual, mental, artistic union in front of the fireplace in that cabin, we might as well never expect to have it anywhere.

I need your body again, damn it, but I seem to need it a little in the spiritual manner, too. The spiritual need for the body. Sounds like a sophism or a paradox, or a parallelogram, or something. But I do—when I dream of your breasts I see your eyes above them, and your eyes are always full of something I want. I want my own eyes to look the way I dream yours. There's nothing you can add to eyes with that look in them. There's nothing they need, except me to look into them. Maybe I'm getting maudlin again.

Good hell, I sit here in my utter nakedness and the swea—(excuse me, perspiration) runs down my armpits in perfect streams. It's worse than the flies. I hate it. I won't have it. Time out while I get a wet towel.

Ah. Comfortable for a change. But as soon as I get comfortable good old Cooper catches my languid eye, and what do I do but half rise, pick up the volume, turn to page two-fifty, get out a pencil, and cut off the letter to my great love in curt haste. Thus.

All my love,
Wally

« To: George Stegner • May 17, 1939 »

Dear Dad,

I don't like at all to hear you talk the way you do in the last few letters. You have come out of tough times before, and you can do it again. But maybe it would be a good idea if you could get to Winnemucca or somewhere where you could get a job of some sort. I wonder if you haven't been shooting at the moon maybe, trying to make a pile of money all at once, where it would be safer and less discouraging to try for a living wage at something. I don't want to sound like Pollyanna, or as if I didn't believe you were hard up. I know you are, and I want to help you all I can. This check may give you another bracer until you can find something to do. But I should think it would be a hell of a good idea to try to find something, whatever you can, if it only pays you board and room, so you can shake off this despair that's got you down. I can manage ten dollars a month or so[22] maybe more if I happen to sell a piece for any money, and I think I could keep it coming if you could only find some place to stay where you can earn a bunk and three squares. I don't know how your health is—maybe real labor would be too much for you, but you could sell cars, or something that didn't entail too much hard work. Or if you know of something out at Winnemucca I'd take it. You can depend on a little from me every month, if you can make up the balance necessary for you to live. I've got a little article coming out about the middle of next month that I'll get twenty-five dollars for. I'll send that on as soon as it comes. After that the pickings may be a little smaller, but I ought to be able to manage ten every month.

Take a brace, Bo,[23] and shake it off. Mother would have stiffened her chin and gone along with you. Maybe we could both learn something from remembering how she could take it when it got rough.

Let me know if you go to Winnemucca, and give me your address because sometime during the summer I have to go east and I may be gone a month or so. I'll want to know where you are. And for God's sake try like anything to find something to do, even if it means swallowing some pride. Because when I stretch it as far as I can, or farther, I still can't send you enough to do more than help out a little. You ought to be able to get something from someone you know in Salt Lake. Try like hell, anyway, and keep your spirits up.[24] Try the WPA and the PWA and all the letter combinations—it's people in just such fixes as you're in that they started out to help. I should think they might find something, or tell you where something might be found.

I would have sent a check on the 8th of May when I got paid, if I had been sure that you were still in Salt Lake. But I was waiting to hear from you.

Get hold of your courage again, Pa. You've got to.

Wallace

---

22. Stegner was in his first real teaching job at the University of Wisconsin, but ten dollars was a significant sum to him in those days, one he could ill afford.

23. Bo was George Stegner's occasional nickname, and the name Wallace gave his avatar in The Big Rock Candy Mountain.

24. George Stegner, who had spent his life looking for the big strike, the pot of gold at the end of the rainbow, was old, broke, and desperate. Within a year he would take his own life, as well as the life of the woman he was hanging around with, in a fleabag hotel room in Salt Lake City. His son remarked, when Wilbur Schramm told him of his father's suicide at a lecture in Iowa City, "So now I know how my novel (The Big Rock Candy Mountain) ends."

« *To: Phil and Peg Gray* • *June 2, 1952* »

Dear Philpeg,

The enclosed may seem somewhat mysterious, since we could as well as not send it to Page in care of George Willey. But for fun and frolic and other causes we are traveling incognito, here in the town I grew up in, and knowing how postmistresses read all the postcards and hold all the envelopes to the light when there's a mysterious stranger in town, we thought it better to enclose this note to Page in one to you. Would you forward the masquerade by passing it on when you see him? It contains his driver's license and social security card, both of which he thought he lost while rowing a rented rowboat back through a gale in Glacier Park last week. We found it in the grub box when we shook the dust out of ourselves here.

Revisiting the childhood home,[25] especially incognito, has its interesting points. There is a moment when what—especially since it's never been revisited—has always seemed unreal, or like an especially vivid but unbelieved-in dream, has to be accepted as real, and that's an astonishing thing, almost as astonishing as the syntax of this sentence. This is earth, like other earth, even though that shadowy progenitor of mine walked it. Here is the river, smaller than I remembered it, but going around the same bends in the same directions and dimpling with the same raindrops and flopping with the same carp and suckers. Right across the street from where we have parked our trailer in a vacant lot is the Presbyterian Church where I recollect spending the bulk of my childhood. There it sits, unchanged, and I heard its bell twice today. Up the street is the old bank of Montreal, now the post office; the old hardware store, the old Chinese restaurant, now a tavern; the old railroad station and the old Pastime Theatre where I saw my first movie damn near forty years ago, this is all very strange, because I've written about this town until I think I imagined it. Now I have to imagine it over, because in thirty-five years it has grown a dense crop of trees all over itself, and the bare windswept flats I cut across are dotted with little old cottages and shacks hidden behind lilac and honeysuckle hedges and with cottonwoods sixty feet high all around them. The school where they carried out all the dead ones from the flu epidemic in 1918 is right through the hedge across the alley; I carry water from its

---

25. Eastend, Saskatchewan, where Stegner lived from 1914 to 1920. He was, at this point, doing research for a book that would eventually become *Wolf Willow*.

well every morning now. The cutbanks and the swimming hole and the footbridge are as specified, only smaller. The picnic ground, though now overgrown with man-planted trees, is much the same, and the sand feels the same underfoot and the chokecherry and wildrose smells the same, and when I went quietly through the willows on the old path and came down to the beaver dam rapids, two mallards took off from the quiet little watery place as if this were 1916 and I were a kid with large bare dirty feet and an air rifle.

The town newspaper is in the same building it used to be in. The editor, whose canoe I used to swipe to run riffles in in 1919, is a balding little Englishman who knows me now as Mr. Page and who gives me the run of his shop to look into the files. I can remember when this little man got aboard one of the first trains to go through this town, and went up to Swift Current to become a trooper in the Glengarry Horse. Somehow remembering that about him makes me feel older than he is, and I feel ashamed to be calling myself by a phony name, and long to throw myself on his mercy and say, Look, I was the guy that used to sink your canoe, and pull it out of your boathouse under water, and use it for an hour or two and put it back before you came back from the newspaper office at five to your tent camp down by the beaver dam. I am the kid who skinned the paint off your rowboat. I am the kid who on a dare jumped off your diving board at the high cutbank and bloody near killed himself, and thereafter looked upon you with awe because every afternoon you used to do swan dives off that thirty-foot board with great grace and ease.

Ah me. Probably just before we leave we shall remove the veil, but it's easier to get what I want as long as nobody here knows who we[26] are: the Norwegian woman into whose electricity we are plugged has already recommended that if I'm interested in the history of this town I should read *The Big Rock Candy Mountain.* I have shamelessly promised to do so.

We leave here next week. It will take us five days driving to make Greensboro, so our arrival will probably be not much before the evening of July 3. We shall let you know in advance, and we can always utilize the trailer for a while if someone else is using the cottage.

Yours from a half delighted and half aghast Limbo,
Wally

---

26. Stegner and his wife, Mary.

« *To: Ronald Rayman* • *October 12, 1975* »

Dear Mr. Rayman:

I'm afraid I can't testify to any enduring influence that Iowa has had on my character or my writing. Though I have a warm feeling for the state, and actually for the maligned Midwest at large, I'm hardly a native. I was born in it more or less by accident, when my mother was visiting her parents near Lake Mills, and I remained in it only a few weeks. That, plus a couple of academic years in graduate school, plus a few visits to my wife's home in Dubuque, is my total experience of Iowa. I'm probably a good deal more native to Saskatchewan and Utah and California than to the state I was born in. But I agree with your general thesis: geography does have an effect, perhaps the definitive effect, on the character of writers and the nature of their writing.

Sincerely,

Wallace Stegner

« *To: Mr. Steve Wilbers* • *February 26, 1976* »

Dear Mr. Wilbers:

Here in haste, before I get bogged down in something else and am lost without trace, is what I remember about the Iowa Writers' Workshop:

I went to Iowa in September 1930 as a very young, green graduate student in English. During my first semester there, Norman Foerster organized his School of Letters, which among other things permitted creative theses and encouraged creative and critical, as opposed to literary-historical, studies. I managed to get approved for an M.A. thesis in fiction, and attended the writing seminar conducted by Edwin Ford Piper, a poet. I was a member of that writing group for, I think, three semesters, and took my degree in 1932, with a thesis composed of three or four short stories. That thesis, *Bloodstain* etc., was not submitted under Wilbur Schramm, but under Piper. Wilbur Schramm was my roommate then, and had nothing to do with the writing workshop until after I left Iowa in 1932 to attend the University of California in Berkeley. I am not sure exactly when Wilbur took the writing workshop over, but I think he was already in charge of it when I returned to Iowa in February 1934 to continue work on my Ph.D. I did not continue in creative writing for the doctorate mainly because those were Depression times and I didn't think a creative Ph.D. was as good a teaching certificate as a degree in American Literature.

I was at Iowa only a few weeks in 1934 before taking a temporary job at Augustana College in Rock Island. I was back at Iowa during the summer of 1934, went to Utah to teach, and returned in the summer of 1935 to finish the degree. By that time I am sure Wilbur was in charge of the writing program. I came back only twice, I believe, each time to lecture. Once was in the summer (I think) of 1940, when Phil Stong, John T. Frederick, and perhaps others were also there speaking. The second time was later but I'm not sure how much later—Robert Frost, Red Warren, and Erik Knight were all there at that time. Later, as you know, Schramm became head of the Journalism School, still later went to Illinois as head of the Press and assistant to President George Stoddard, and still later came to Stanford, from which he retired a year or two ago to become head of the East-West Institute in Honolulu. All during the later part of his career he was working in communications research, not in creative writing.

Among the students who were working with Piper in those first two years were Paul Engle (he was still an undergraduate, and left in 1931 to take a Rhodes Scholarship); Donald MacRae, who was later head of the English Department at Reed College; Erling Larsen, the nephew of Henning Larsen of the Iowa English Department faculty; a girl named Louise Probst; and a gent named, God bless me, I can't think of his name. He wrote a book on the contemporary American novel which was essentially his class notes from a course taught one summer by Harry Hayden Clark of Wisconsin. There was nothing remarkable about the first creative writing classes. Piper was very permissive: we wrote and read aloud, the class discussed. Both poetry and fiction were being written in the class. *American Prefaces* was not yet in existence, though it came into being sometime fairly soon and published that Bloodstain story out of my thesis.

It should be said that Foerster, though a New Humanist and very sure of his philosophical ground, was also intellectually open: We spent most of our time disagreeing with his positions and liking him personally. He was strongly opposed to literary scholarship, especially of the Germanic/philological kind, and was not popular among the regular professors of English. All of us took his course in Literary Criticism, and all of us found it extremely stimulating. I suspect it was the most stimulating course I had in college or graduate school. Wilbur Schramm was for a number of years

Foerster's protégé—helped him revise his textbook in American Literature, later took over the writing program and expanded and enriched it. At some point there was a break between him and Foerster; or rather, there was a break between Foerster and the rest of the English Department in which Wilbur got caught. I don't know the details. Paul Engle ought to know, since he took over the writing workshops from Wilbur and carried them on.

That seems to empty the inkwell. You certainly ought to try to get some information from Wilbur Schramm, if you haven't already. I don't have his most recent Honolulu address, but a letter sent to the East-West Institute would reach him.

Sincerely,

Wallace Stegner

« *To: Ronald Rayman* • *September 7, 1977* »

Dear Ronald Rayman:

Many thanks for your encouraging note. I don't know what they said about me in *Current Biography*, since I haven't seen it, but I assume it dealt with the fact that I am a sort of belated frontier product. While that is true, I'm also fairly suspicious of frontier virtues—they seem to me anachronistic, they don't apply in the age of shortage into which we are moving, and the new frontier calls for virtues of quite another kind. Sure the frontier marks us—it makes us, I suppose, more amenable to change. It makes us alert, it forces us to adapt. And adapt we must, not by killing more grizzly bears but by learning to live with greater scarcity.

That, at least, is what I think in 1977. By 1980 I may have to adapt to something else.

Sincerely,

Wallace Stegner

« *To: Margaret Kecskemeti* • *May 29, 1986* »

Dear Margaret Kecskemeti:

It's taken me a month to get around to answering your good hearty belly-laughing Honyaker letter. It was like a wind off the curly grass—you brought me home. Roundup[27] is not so far from the Cypress Hills, or the

---

27. Roundup, Montana.

Montana plains so different from those in Saskatchewan, that there is any substantial cultural difference. Even the violin. The only violin I ever had was made out of a cigar box, but I know your cultural aspirations. In fact, I never met anyone, not anyone, who had grown up in shortgrass country with whom I didn't feel some sort of bond. I might not have liked them all, but I knew we belonged to the same tribe, we recognized the same things. One of the things I recognize most commonly is that same cultural hunger. Growing up in deprivation like that must be sort of like growing up in Siberia—the whole world, any part of it, looks exciting. And all of human accomplishment has to be realized, by hand, in a single lifetime. You don't say what you are doing now, but obviously you're reading books, which is more than can be said for 80% of the population.

I wish Roundup were a little closer. We ought to be paying visits back and forth. For lack of that pleasure, this note will have to serve. It is to say mainly how much your letter delighted me.[28]

Sincerely,

Wallace Stegner

« *To: Sharon Butala* • *June 19, 1988* »

Dear Mrs. Butala:

What you propose astonishes me. I have some trouble imagining our old house as an Historical Site, and I can't escape the perception that Eastend did a lot more for me than I ever did for it. All I ever did was remember it, fondly, probably inaccurately, and forever.

But no, of course I have no objection to what you propose. I am enormously touched and flattered. That was the only house my mother ever owned, and she owned it about three years. The rest of her life she lived in tents, rentals, and tenements. Having the house restored might anchor her poor ghost.

Whether or not I will be able to help you with the reconstruction, if it actually happens, I don't know. After all, I too lived in that house only about three years, and nearly seventy years ago. I'll append a sketch of the downstairs floorplan, so far as I remember it. It was a simple square house. My father both built and designed it, and it didn't have any architectural finesse. The furnishings, apart from the parlor heater, I don't remember

---

28. Stegner's responses to admirers were seldom perfunctory, as this one indicates.

much about. The woodwork, I remember, was just stained and varnished pine—Golden Oak, I think. Over the mantel, which had no fireplace under it, was Rosa Bonheur's picture of three white horses in a storm. There was an upright piano in the living room, and my mother's sewing machine was often operating there, too. During the flu epidemic, or just after we all got back from the schoolhouse hospital, my parents slept in the living room in order to feed the fire and keep the house warmer during the night. Upstairs there was no heat except what rose from below via the stairway, and on a winter morning you could just about freeze to the floor when you stepped out of bed. We never lingered to dress—we grabbed our clothes and fled down to the kitchen and hunkered back into the oven, sitting on the oven door to dress. That old kitchen range is all the kitchen furniture I remember except a wash stand that stood just inside the door. There were of course storm doors and storm windows all around in winter, and the house had tarpaper tacked all around the foundations and was banked with dirt nearly to the windowsills.

I am surprised that the records show my mother buying the lot, and in 1918. Unless I am badly mistaken, the house was built at least by 1917, and I never knew my mother to own much of anything. Perhaps she bought the lot with part of the little inheritance she had from an Iowa uncle—the same inheritance out of which she bought the piano. But why the records show 1918 I can't imagine, unless for some complicated reason my father sold it to her, or because he built the house before we had final ownership of the lot. Mysteries. The past is full of them, and nobody to answer the questions.

Somewhere, in an old album, I have a snapshot or two of the house in its early stages, with me, barefooted and strawhatted, standing like Huckleberry Finn on the porch rail. I also, I think, have a snapshot taken in about 1955, when the house was in good shape, surrounded by shrubbery and a white picket fence. I'll try to find those and send you copies, if you'd like. It may take a while.

And I'll look forward to receiving your novel with great interest. I hope you will let me know how your plans progress.

Sincerely yours,

Wallace Stegner

« *To: Sharon Butala* • *December 5, 1988* »

Dear Sharon Butala,

I must say I admire your energy and persistence. When you began this Stegner House agitation, I frankly didn't expect it would come to anything. But it seems it already has, and has the chance to come to something more. That result, I am sure, is due mainly to you.

Thank you for the samples of the notepaper you've been selling. I am amused and be-mused, and I want some for my own, for which I enclose a guess-work check. The drawing is full of nostalgia for me, for the window over the porch is the window of the room my brother Cecil and I shared, and looked out on whatever was going by in the road. I still remember the icy flow of air that came through the three ventilator holes in the frame of each storm window. The holes were no more than an inch and a half in diameter, and we were instructed to leave all six—three in each sash—open for the health-giving winter fresh air. But oh, my, how it hurt to get up out of bed in nightshirt and bare feet and shut those holes with their hinged covers. You could feel the cold air like a fire hose ten or fifteen feet away, and had to get back into bed for a few minutes to start the vital functions again before you got up the nerve to rush downstairs with your clothes in your arms and dress in the kitchen, with your behind in the open oven door and your teeth going like door knockers. The only heat in that whole house was the kitchen range and a parlor heater. Upstairs might just as well have been Labrador, especially in the morning before any warmth at all had risen from the just-started downstairs fires. I hope, for all your sakes, that <u>chauffage central</u> has come to Eastend.

Thank you very much for the copy of *Luna*. I am swamped with dead-lines until Christmas, but after that I will have time to get at it. I look forward to it, no matter what the critics may or may not have said. Who listens to critics is on the way to the bughouse.

I return your return-postage check, which is unnecessary, and enclose mine for whatever it will buy of notepaper and envelopes. And have a wonderful Christmas and a successful February 18. I'll be thinking of you.

Sincerely,
Wallace Stegner

« *To: Sharon Butala* • *February 8, 1989* »

Dear Sharon Butala:

It's beginning to look as if the most news-worthy thing I ever did was to survive, if I make it, to my eightieth birthday. It is not a distinction that I particularly cherish. As the man said, if I had known I was going to live so long, I would have taken better care of myself. On the other hand, facing the necessity of getting old, I am resolved to become as old as I can, and to stir around and look alive and alert so nobody will cart me off prematurely.

So I'd like you to do me a favor, and say hello to the people of Eastend for me, not forgetting to include yourself. What you are doing with the old house touches me. I wish I could get up to help you do it, not because I am being in a sense honored by the preservation of the house, but because the uses you hope to put it to are culturally admirable, and show the town to be as intellectually and culturally optimistic as I remember it. It surprises me to hear that our old house is one of the oldest houses in Saskatchewan—I really <u>did</u> participate in the Creation—and it pleases me to be associated with the continuing cultural and literary aspirations of all those good people. Please thank them all, from me, and pass on my best wishes for your collective success.

I enclose a little contribution (anonymous, please) to buy some shingles. I'll be thinking of you on the 18th.

Sincerely,
Wallace Stegner

« *To: Beth LaDow* • *March 15, 1990* »

Dear Ms. LaDow:

I have been out of the country for two weeks, and so am slow to respond to your February 26 letter. Apologies. Your interest in Saskatchewan and your association with Donald Worster both entitle you to a prompt answer.

You ask some sound and searching questions,[29] so sound and so searching that I would have great difficulty in answering them in a letter, or many letters, even if I knew the answers, which I often don't. Conversation,

---

29. Ms. LaDow's questions arose from her reading of Stegner's memoir and history, *Wolf Willow*.

especially if we had my wildly disorganized files at hand, would be better, and I'll be happy to converse, if we can find a time to get together. I'm here, up to my eyes in work, until probably the first of July, then I'll be in Vermont—distant from the files—until sometime in October. October and November I'm in and out, lecturing here and there. Maybe we could work out a meeting in June?

Meantime, here are a few quick stabs at answers to specific questions. I think your Chinook–Eastend–Maplecreek parallel is a good one, and should be revealing. I apologize for not getting into the farming frontier more deeply. For one thing, I left Saskatchewan in 1920, and have been back there only once, in 1953. I don't know the history of that homesteading frontier in any detail, and anyway, I excused myself because I was writing what amounted to a memoir, and that ended with our exodus. But what you call the "murky palette" of interpenetrating cultures is more apparent to a modern historian than it was to a boy living in the midst of it. For all I knew, that was the way the world was. The wild mix of people and cultures strike me in memory, but not at the time. My impression, and I have only memory to corroborate it, is that there were more Americans than any other kind of people there, but the Americans themselves were different kinds: Texas cowpunchers already on the fade when we arrived, who had moved north through the plains to Montana and then Canada; farmers, many of them Scandinavian by origin, who worked into the Northwest by a sort of migration route through the Dakotas and Montana; and various exotics like Jakie Klein, the butcher, who was American Jewish of some variety, and another storekeeper, Miller, of the same wandering-Jew species. The Syrians, whose name was Haddad, might have been American for a while—I don't know. The ministers were prevailingly Scottish Presbyterians without any American intervals. There were a certain number of English who we thought of as Cockneys, and a few professional people— barristers and doctors—who were mainly drunks and who disappeared fairly fast, by death or departure. There were some Métis families whom we didn't know well because they were Catholic and didn't seem to attend either school or Sunday School. There were a couple of Chinese. Out on the farm there were Duknobors—Ukrainians, I guess—whom we never saw in Eastend. But more people of American origin or at least some American experience than any other kind. I remember families—the Huffmans, the Bickertons, the Andersons, the Stegners, the Downs. The adults were transplanted Americans, the kids were essentially Canadian in feelings and certainly training. The English families that tried to import tennis were few and transitory, mainly the drunken professionals and real estate sharks. There was no way for any of us to know exactly who we were, and certainly neither the Boer war nor the Spanish American war left any ripples in that society. World War I did, of course, mainly because it was the one clash, or cause for clash, between American immigrants and British or Ontario immigrants: the consensus was that America was too yellow to get into it. That clash vanished in 1917 or whenever America entered the war. Gun-toting was not a cultural difference. We all toted guns, but the sidearm pattern had already gone out before we arrived. It was an issue only during the cattle period, which effectively ended in 1907. Cultural difference we recognized, and sometimes thought funny, and utilized as a reason for persecutions and prejudices of a certain raw kind, but between Americans and Canadians, as such, they hardly mattered. It was Jews, "Chinks," "half-breeds," and others outside the standard American–Canadian patterns who inspired it. Englishmen caught it some, because of their accents, their habit of taking tea instead of coffee (and their reputed inability to <u>make</u> a decent cup of coffee), and what was held, sometimes legitimately, to be their general incompetence in frontier or farming skills. Among the children, I don't remember any such feelings. We all—Jews, Canadians, Americans, English, Syrians—were a pretty equal democratic mix.

Whether my education was more European than Willa Cather's I can't say. I never memorized long passages of the *Aeneid*, but then I went to school in Eastend only through the 7th grade. I don't remember any subject that was really oriented to Western Canada. The history we got was mainly Montcalm and Wolfe, the poetry was mainly but not exclusively English or American (what else could it have been, in those years?). I do remember that the War of 1812, which had after all involved American incursions into Canada, was taught from a really anti-American point of view. As for the annealing tendency of religion in that town, that may have come about because the Presbyterian Church and the once-a-week movie theater were almost the only social and community meeting places, at least indoors. Outdoors, the town met at the river, swimming in summer and skating in winter.

This is getting windy and fruitless. We will have to talk. But if you do want to investigate the after-1920 development of cultural institutions in Eastend,[30] I suggest that you write to Sharon Butala, who is a good Saskatchewan novelist-cum-rancher, and who has recently stirred up the town to buy the old Stegner house as a sort of cultural monument, with the aim of using it as a hideout for Canadian writers in need of some peace and quiet. It is a quaint thought to me—and yet that old house of ours, built about 1917, turns out to be one of the oldest houses in Saskatchewan, and I'm flattered that the town thinks enough of literature, if not of me, to want it preserved. These cultural manifestations take a long time, and the town may die of inanition and soil exhaustion before they come to much of anything. A letter the other day told me that South Fork, a few miles east of Eastend, is a ghost town, like so many other prairie settlements. Eastend, I think, should last. It has a better situation, with the hills and the river, and it's on Canada's Highway 1.

As for what we did wrong, that seems to me easy. We plowed up Palliser's Triangle, one of the driest parts of the western plains, and destroyed the native grasses, imported weeds, mined the soil for wheat for a few years, created a dust bowl, and eventually abandoned what we should never have tried to settle. It is possible that an open-range cattle industry could have lasted longer, though that was very likely to lead to over-stocking and destruction of the range, and might have left the country just as bad off.

Finally, Turner. Turner works as far as the 98th meridian of west longitude. Beyond that, in the dry country, he doesn't work at all, and I have seen no evidence that even in 1895, when the Dakotas and the rest of the western plains were shriveling in drought, he recognized the difference that aridity would make in his frontier thesis. I hope you can settle that one.

If we can't meet, let me have some more questions and I'll try to give you at least off-the-cuff answers. If we can, we might look at some of the letters in my file from old playmates and other town residents, whose lives might give you an indication both of the backgrounds and the life patterns of the people who settled the Saskatchewan plains.

Sincerely,

[No signature]

---

30. Eastend, Saskatchewan, where Stegner lived until he was about twelve. In *Wolf Willow* he called the town Whitemud.

« *To: Beth LaDow* • *December 5, 1990* »

Dear Ms. LaDow:

I'm a month late with this, as you probably noticed. I'm sorry. Troppo da fare. And now that I get around to it, I'm not sure I can help you much with that schoolroom-hospital scene. I was delirious most of the time I was in there during the flu epidemic,[31] and my memory of the schoolroom itself is by now nearly seventy-five years old. I can't remember the name of that teacher, but I remember that she came from Kingston, Ontario and was thought to be snooty. I also remember once when I was late to class because I stopped for a drink at the water cooler by the door, she made me bend over it until recess, an excruciating matter of an hour and a half or so. She was considerably disliked, and perhaps that story of the bottle snuggled up to her in bed was the town's method of cutting her down to size. But there's no doubt that nearly everybody thought whiskey was a good idea to ward off the flu, and there were many, including most of the tobacco chewers, who insisted that a good chaw was the best preventative. There was also a superstition, which may not have been entirely superstition, that big husky men with deep chests were more likely to die of the flu/pneumonia than their frailer brethren. I think that may have been true. Too much chest capacity can't be a big help when your chest is full of pneumococci.

Now the schoolhouse. It was a square brick structure with four equal-sized rooms, two on each side of the central hall. Each room housed a couple of grades. I have forgotten what room I was in when we were all sick, but I think it was the 3–4 grade room. I haven't any idea what room Teacher was in. One room was referred to as the Death Ward because all the serious cases were taken in there and many did not come out alive. Beds were so short that I was in bed with my mother, and I'm sure made her illness twice as bad because I was delirious and had nosebleeds all over her and the bed. The principal medicines were soup and epsom salts. Men were in one ward, women and children in another. I can't remember, or never knew, who got the third room; the dying got the fourth. Because everybody was in it together, there was a good deal of yelling back and forth between wards, and jokes, and songs, and efforts to make everything

---

31. The 1918 influenza pandemic which Stegner writes about in *Wolf Willow* killed between twenty and forty million people worldwide. In America the number of deaths totaled approximately 675,000, or ten times the number of U.S. soldiers who died in World War I.

into a sort of picnic. The nurses were housewives who had somehow been missed by the bug; the doctor was naturally run to death, and besides that had no medical supplies or equipment. The school janitor came daily with a bobsled to haul the dead away to the cemetery.

But that teacher. I think her name was Miss Mangan, or something close. She would have held herself above all superstition, being a city girl condemned to the trans-Siberian provinces. But I heard that bottle story all over town, always told with delight, because Miss Mangan or whatever her name was had once sent home from school one of the Gilchrist kids, from the river bottom, with a note to her mother saying the child had pediculosis, and should not return to school until she was cured. The mother came tearing into town to see the doctor, thinking her child was sick; and when she found out that the girl was only lousy, she could hardly be restrained from tearing the snotty teacher's hair out.

None of that answers your principal questions, and it even removes the teacher from the stream of local superstition, which she would have looked down on. Yet she did take that bottle to bed, indicating that maybe she was influenced by the local lore, or perhaps only indicating that she was scared and needed some Dutch courage.

Further than this, deponent sayeth not. I'm sorry I missed that meeting in Reno. It would have been nice to see you again; and to see Patty,[32] Ivan Doig, and Don Worster. Let us say that I was in bed with a bottle.

Best,
Wallace Stegner

« *To: Sharon Butala* • *December 18, 1991* »

Dear Sharon Butala,
Many thanks for your letter and the pictures of the house. It doesn't look much like what it looked like during World War I, with its bare floors and Royal Oak parlor heater, but it looks a lot more comfortable. You have done something incredible, I think, and now you may begin to get some literary company in Eastend, and feel yourself expanding into a culture heroine. In *Wolf Willow* I sort of disparaged the dream of the rural Athens, but I think I under-estimated Eastend, and I didn't then know about you.

---

32. Patricia Limerick.

The other day I had a letter from George Haddad, who was/is a little younger than I but whom I remember well and whom I have seen once or twice at Ohio State, where he taught until his retirement. It was his brother Weddie and his sister Louise that I knew best, but there were a lot of Haddads, and George turned out to be the talented one. Maybe he will come and inhabit the house while he writes a symphony. Do you permit musicians into the fold, or only writers?

I have signed the two books, and added a little item to them. I wish my next book of essays was ready, but it won't be until March, after your February 29th dinner. If by any chance I get an advance copy I will shoot it on—it contains a couple of things that relate to Eastend. Meantime, I can only wish you a happy Christmas, with lots of snow, and immediately afterward a Chinook.

One thing: At the end of September I shared a platform during Stanford's centennial celebration with Prime Minister Mulroney, who apparently had specifically asked for me to be on the program. So I read a piece from *Wolf Willow* and talked about the Medicine Line as a model for all world boundaries. Just now I got a letter from Himself, expressing all sorts of friendly feelings. I don't know whom you apply to for the governmental money to help run your hostel, but I thought you might like to know that both Mulroney and what's-his-name, Joe?, the minister of state, seem to be very much aware of *Wolf Willow*, and friendly to its author. I have also talked with the Episcopal Primate of Canada, who tells me that in his youth he spent a year or so in Eastend and bears its memory tenderly in his heart. He's a fine man, but I forget his name, too. Isn't it nice to get old? Anyway, when you're applying, you might try to investigate what strings might be pulled at those several offices. A personal word from upstairs might not hurt our cause.

So have a happy Christmas and a prosperous New Year, and please keep in touch. My arriving on your doorstep seems less and less likely, because I just had a hip replacement and I am assaulted by several doctors, all after different germs or organs. But I will survive them, and if I can ever get back up there, I will.

Best,
Wallace Stegner

« *To: Sharon Butala* • *October 27, 1992* »

Dear Sharon Butala,

You are indefatigable, indestructible, and irresistible, and you deserve a monument more than I do. How about calling this the Sharon Butala House, and raising funds on your own behalf?

Your last letter sounded a little down and discouraged, this one is full of yelps of pleasure. I trust that Sean Virgo has arrived and is inhaling inspiration from the old house, and enjoying Eastend and the river. It's good news, too, that you get next year's Writer-in-Residence from the Saskatchewan Writers' Guild. It's also exhilarating to me, used to the jaded and jaundiced airs of this literary community, to hear how Saskatchewan (and especially Eastend) encourages and assists writers. I'm reminded of the years when I was teaching at Harvard, when my freshman class was filled either with boys from Andover, Exeter, St. Paul's, and Groton, or kids from Central, Iowa, scared to death and working their heads off to keep from sinking. In the first semester the prep school boys loafed and enjoyed themselves and found everything tedious, because they had had it all in prep school. Then at the end of the second semester the kids from Central, Iowa who had kept on running scared, won all the prizes. Old story; jackrabbit and tortoise. I must say I'm on the side of the tortoise, who is never as slow as he looks to the jackrabbits.

I'm sorry to say I don't remember Ira Schmitt, though I obviously should, and I'm even sorrier that I don't have range and township and all that dope on the old homestead. If you can find an old map with the now-extinct settlement of Hydro, Montana on it, just go straight north of that, along the section line, to the international border, and you can step across onto our scruffy old field. Our house was a half mile or more north of the line, on the bank of a shallow coulee. The remains of our "rezavoy," with a few willows, might still be there. I'd like to come sometime and help you hunt, but that's not likely. I'm getting to be a cheese that doesn't travel. If there was enough brandy, that might change things.

Here are the books, signed, for your February auction. I'm sending under separate cover a couple of copies of the *Collected Stories* for the same purpose, or for your personal use, whichever seems proper to you. Thank you again for all your effort, and congratulations on your success.

Yours,

Wallace Stegner

« *To: Sharon Butala* • *December 30, 1992* »

Dear Sharon,

I hope your vision of a little colony of fellow-spirits comes off, and that literary picnics in the sandhills or Chimney Coulee will become part of Canada's tradition, like the Philosophers' Camp that Emerson attended in the Adirondacks. Didn't Eastend set out to be a rural Athens, once? Why not a rural Concord?

But what I am writing about is to ask you if you'll be around this summer. Finally, it seems that we might get up to Eastend. I have to make an appearance at Middlebury College in Vermont on May 25, and after that we will go to our cottage in Greensboro for a month or so. But sometime around the end of June we should be coming back to California, and what we hope to do is to come by way of Eastend. I suppose we'll fly to Regina or Calgary, rent a car, and drive over. We could stay only for two or three days at the most. But I don't want to come at a time when you're not planning to be there, so if you'll be gone, please let me know, and I'll set up a new planning schedule. I would like to meet all of the people who have helped you in this miraculous operation of yours, and see if the sky is as I remember it. My most vivid memory of Saskatchewan actually comes from the Serengeti Plain in Tanzania, where I got out of the car and was struck absolutely dumb by a combined memory and vision: it was the same earth and the same sky I had grown up in, only it had some wildebeeste and zebras in it instead of horses and Herefords.

When your holiday chores are over, perhaps you can let me know if this proposal will work. Meantime, the very best to you in 1993. It looks good-news-bad-news from down here.

Yours,
Wally

Biographers
and Critics

◆

To Richard Etulain, March 24, 1980

To Forrest Robinson, October 16, 1981

To James Hepworth, May 5, 1982

To Richard Etulain, May 22, 1982

To Richard Etulain, July 15, 1982

To Nancy Colberg, September 26, 1982

To Nancy Colberg, August 12, 1983

To Nancy Colberg, November 29, 1983

To Nancy Colberg, December 31, 1983

To Nancy Colberg, May 24, 1985

To James Hepworth, June 5, 1985

To James Hepworth, July 2, 1985

To James Hepworth, July 31, 1985

To James Hepworth, August 15, 1985

To Jackson Benson, January 14, 1986

To James Hepworth, May 5, 1986

To Richard Etulain, May 20, 1986

To Nancy Colberg, September 20, 1986

To Nancy Colberg, November 19, 1986

To Nancy Colberg, January 11, 1987

To James Hepworth, January 19, 1987

To James Hepworth, January 30, 1987

To Nancy Colberg, July 27, 1987

To Jackson Benson, August 10, 1987

To Jackson Benson, August 21, 1987

To Nancy Colberg, November 8, 1987

To Nancy Colberg, November 30, 1987

To Jackson Benson, January 15, 1988

To Nancy Colberg, May 1, 1988

To James Hepworth, July 14, 1988

To James Hepworth, July 30, 1988

To Jackson Benson, September 9, 1988

To Jackson Benson, May 6, 1990

To Nancy Colberg, June 24, 1990

To Jackson Benson, October 17, 1990

To Jackson Benson, August 20, 1992

To Jackson Benson, September 12, 1992

To Jackson Benson, October 8, 1992

AGREAT DEAL has been written (and continues to be written) not only about Stegner's literary production, but about the man himself—"the dean of Western writers," as the *New York Times* put it, before proceeding in its article to get his name wrong. (Beyond the Hudson River, as the novelist Ivan Doig observed, he's known as Wallace, not William.) Although Stegner is unquestionably the major figure who pops to mind in any discussion of the American West as a literal or fictional living space, it wasn't a label he found particularly comforting because of its regionalist connotations. In his conversations with the historian Richard Etulain, himself a specialist on the literary West, he remarked, "I think we all feel the lack, somehow, in a lot of our literary criticism—and to some extent in the literature as well—of the breadth of view that can come from a regionalism which is expanding and going out toward the world instead of closing away from it. The establishment has a tendency to be more parochial really than the regions."[1]

Parochialism bothered him, as did the inclination on the part of his critics to read his work as thinly veiled autobiography. It is a topic that appears frequently in the following selection of letters to some of his closest and most sympathetic commentators. While the first book-length study of Stegner's work was Forrest and Margaret Robinson's *Wallace Stegner* (Boston: Twayne, 1977), the letters to Robinson are more appropriately included elsewhere. Richard Etulain and James R. Hepworth both published extensive conversations with Stegner, in Richard Etulain's *Conversations with Wallace Stegner on Western History and Literature* (Salt Lake City, UT: University of Utah Press, 1983), and James Hepworth's *Stealing Glances: Three Interviews with Wallace Stegner* (Albuquerque, NM: University of New Mexico Press, 1998). Nancy Colberg's *Wallace Stegner: A Descriptive Bibliography* (Lewiston, ID: Confluence Press, 1990), is the only book-length work of that type that has been done to date. Jackson Benson's *Wallace Stegner: His Life and Work* (New York: Viking Press, 1996), is the only major biography that has been written, though Philip Fradkin is undertaking a second study that will be published by Random House in January 2008.

◆ ◆ ◆

---

1. Wallace Stegner and Richard Etulain, *Conversations with Wallace Stegner on Western History and Literature* (Salt Lake City, UT: University of Utah Press, 1983), p. 124.

« *To: Richard Etulain* • *March 24, 1980* »

Dear Dick:

I've been trying for a week to find an hour to answer your letter of the 14th. Now here it is. Though distracted, I am essentially whole.

When I was in Salt Lake I talked with Trudy McMurrin two or three times about the Interviews book.[2] Whatever the Press committee thinks, there is no doubt about her enthusiasm for the project. I can understand your desire to have a contract before you commit yourself, though. All I could tell Trudy was that I was very willing to cooperate as I could.

I hesitate to amend or add to your list of possible conversations, because it seems to me that this is a book that should come from the reader's or critic's point of view. I come at the public from my own stance all the time; this book should be an appraisal from outside, don't you think? So I'd much prefer that you set the topics and the limits. I see nothing wrong with any that you suggest, except that I might want to evade airing my views about other writers, especially contemporaries. I am not like Mary McCarthy; I don't want to suggest the names of over-rated writers and by accident light upon my worst enemies. People I like, O.K. People I'm less than enthusiastic about, I'd better keep still about. Any writer has a hard enough time making it without being knocked by his colleagues. I would appreciate advance questions, as well as a chance to review the interviews when they are typed up. I find that I am often windy and unfocused when in front of a tape recorder. With a chance for review, I can make your book better, and given time, will be glad to.

My schedule right now calls for finishing the travel/geography/ history book I am doing with Page and Eliot Porter,[3] then doing a piece for American Heritage, then trying to scrape up an essay on Benny DeVoto for Golden Taylor's literary history. (Where does one write him, incidentally? Fort Collins?) In May we may go to France for just a couple of weeks. The summer we expect to spend here, or very largely here, while I brood about a (final) novel. I'll be glad to see you when you get loose from teaching. I can't offer you a bed, because we are without a guest room, but there's

2. Wallace Stegner and Richard Etulain, *Conversations with Wallace Stegner on Western History and Literature* (Salt Lake City, UT: University of Utah Press, 1983).
3. Eliot Porter, Wallace Stegner, Page Stegner, *American Places* (New York: E.P. Dutton, 1981).

everything else, including a new swimming pool beside whose dimpling waters we can talk. Just let me know as far in advance as possible so that I can arrange not to be in Santa Cruz or somewhere.

Incidentally, I just had a letter from a professor of history at U-Mass in Amherst, William Johnston, who asks why no one is organizing a conference to commemorate the 25th anniversary of Benny DeVoto's death. Is there anyone doing anything? Got any ideas?

As for the paperback situation. *Recapitulation* sold to a paperback house. *Spectator Bird*, despite being a Book Award following a Pulitzer, did not. I sold it myself to the Nebraska Press while we were up at Banff that time. There's a piece of literary curiosa for you.

Best,
Wally

« *To: Forrest Robinson* • *October 16, 1981* »

Dear Forrest,

What makes me grimace is not that you're messing around in my guts. It's that you think those guts you're messing around in are mine. I find no fault with the essay—it's actually very good if one grants its thesis—but I'm a little disturbed to have you reading several novels as if the protagonists were all W.S. Obviously there are pieces of W.S. in all of them; obviously you're right that *Recapitulation* is a trailer, a sort of revaluation, of *The Big Rock Candy Mountain*, and that both contain more autobiographical material than any of the other novels. "Family history, reasonably straight," is certainly there. But I think you have fallen for the common temptation to straighten out all the curves and even out all the grades and read the book as if it were indeed family history, and not a novel.

Selective evidence can give you a sort of computer reading of the author, if you want to work that way, from the reading of several novels. But what I think you do here is ignore some of the evidence that doesn't fit your thesis. Specifically, let me deal with the character of Bruce Mason in *Recapitulation*. You read him very accurately—he carries to the end of the book the marks his father put on him; he will never have the self-confidence he might have had if he had not suffered what he feels to have been all that childhood humiliation; he is indeed a walking Oedipus complex; he is indeed an unreliable witness about his father, and I indeed put into him a lot of submerged oedipal love for his mother, and emphasized it in such images as that shape-shifting image of Khamis. What I wanted to say in that novel is that a childhood such as his may never be fully recovered from, the father's dominance may be implacable through many years, the son may never develop fully, may always carry scars. O.K. What you forget is that I made that character. I didn't just copy him from a mirror, what you remember is autobiographical parallels; what you forget is art. What you forget is that I can do whatever I want with even my own image. I can exaggerate for plausibility or effect, I can push Bruce Mason in any direction I think his childhood may have started him in. In short, though I grant you that the parallels are sometimes close, I must insist that Bruce Mason is not W.S. He is what but for the grace of God, W.S. might be. Recall that Bruce Mason is blasted and loveless; W.S. is, thank God, not. Mason never married or had children. W.S. did. Mason returns to Salt Lake for the first and only time in more than forty years. W.S. has been back there, wallowing in old friends and even old girl friends, every year or so for the last fifty. Bruce Mason represents a possibility that may be shaped out of such a family history as mine. He doesn't represent the only possibility, or the reality. If you had read the first two drafts of that novel, you would know how many possibilities I juggled before I arrived at the chosen one.

Of course it's your privilege to publish what you please, short of libel or defamation, which this essay certainly is not. But I would suggest that you might temper the positiveness of your identification, and allow more for the shaping faculty of the novelist, before you put me in print as a warped, loveless, and probably impotent diplomat.

If Loretta Lorch calls, I'll certainly talk to her. But God knows I haven't time to become her guru or agent.

Reading this over, I see that it sounds a touch annoyed. I am not annoyed, only distressed that you have made the identification so precise. Mark Hunter in the *San Francisco Magazine* did the same thing. But what you both seize upon as the key to the books and to me is something I painstakingly made out of the scattered materials of my own life, out of imagination, out of logical probabilities, out of novelistic necessity, out of all sorts of things. I love to be taken as seriously as you take me, and I love to have my intentions read as accurately as you read the character of Bruce Mason. I simply want to protest, and keep protesting, "Is no true! Is novel!"

Yours,
Wally

« *To: James Hepworth* • *May 5, 1982* »

Dear Jim:

I'm afraid I'm not going to be very sanguine about a lecture-visit. For one thing, I hate lecturing. For another, I'm finally getting into this novel, and as it begins to move, I am not inclined to come out of my hole. For another, you don't say in your letter what time you have in mind. From internal evidence I deduce that it is March 1985 when your next conference will take place. My pessimistic mind tells me that I'll still be wrestling with this Midgard serpent of a book at that time. Finally, if I could come at all, and were to give a lecture, a creative writing session, and a reading, I'd have to soak you a fee that would empty your treasury, unless your treasury has a deeper bottom than you suggest. It takes me two weeks, these days, to prepare a lecture, quite apart from the interruption of the trip to deliver it, and it literally isn't worth it to me if I get less than $2000 for it, any other substantive labors to be in addition.

Considering all these points, which begin to cease looking like reasons and might almost add up to an excuse, I don't think you'd better count on me. But if, in spite of everything, you persist in wanting me, then you'd better tell me for sure whether I have the date right. That's basic to any final decision.

Best to you and your many labors.

Yours,

Wallace Stegner

« *To: Richard Etulain* • *May 22, 1982* »

Dear Dick,

Conversation No. 8 arrived on the eve of our departure for Italy. I have had time to go through it and make my corrections, and I think the best thing to do is to send it back to you so that you don't lose any time by my absence. You suggest my keeping it; maybe you'll want to send it back, along with Later Works, so I can double-check it when I return here on June 18.

Your summer sounds strenuous—Alaska and the Pacific Northwest. I imagine you hope to have the remaining conversations to me before you leave on June 15. I'll get at them as soon as we return, and should have them back to your secretary/office/editor within a few days after June 18. I see no reason, unless your northwestern commitments, why Trudy can't expect a manuscript in August.

Now Trudy's impulse to try sample conversations on the magazines, I certainly have no objections; but (privately between thee and me) I have found the Utah Press in the past willing to assume rights it does not have, or buy up universal world rights when what it really owns is first serial or one-shot prepublication. So let me ask you (I will read your reply after June 18) what you think: If Trudy sells any of those chapters to magazines, my understanding is that she's selling something that belongs, according to our contract, to you and me. I'm perfectly willing she should try the chapters; but I'm not willing that she should assume that the Press owns those rights, or should take any share of any possible fee. You can communicate this to her in your inimitable way. If she wants to peddle chapters for your benefit and mine, fine; if she isn't, then we should perhaps try the same caper ourselves. Is that the way you feel about it?

Anyway—here's the No. 8 conversation, complete with penciled emendations. As usual, I am dismayed by my own verbosity.

Have a splendid and productive summer.

Best,

Wally

« *To: Richard Etulain* • *July 15, 1982* »

Dear Dick:

I'm sorry to be slow with No. 10—other things crowded in. But here it is, along with No. 9, "The Later Works," which has been on my desk for quite a while because I kept expecting a re-type of "Early Works" so that I could X out overlaps. Overlaps are probably there, but maybe you can do that editorial job yourself when you have the whole text together.

You will find in No. 10 that I have cut a couple of passages, one on publishing because it wanders from your question, and one on western writers, Kesey especially, because I found myself sounding catty and ungenerous. So I cut it. You will find alternative typed pages to substitute, I hope without bumps and breaks, for the cut passages.

I hope your errand at your father's house is a hopeful, not a sad and hopeless one.

I'll go down the chapter titles and see if I can suggest anything, and let you know in a separate letter.

Best,
Wally

« *To: Nancy Colberg* • *September 26, 1982* »

Dear Nancy Colberg,

I'm sorry to hear that the Robinson book[4] is out of print. Maybe when I get home I can make a thorough search of the warren where I work, and find one of the copies I thought I had.

As to the manuscript page of *A Shooting Star*: Don't buy it, not for $278 and not for $269.50. It may be authentic, but I don't remember ever copying out a page in longhand and signing it, and there is rarely a time when I write in longhand except when I'm on the road. I wrote part of *A Shooting Star* while motoring down through the Dordogne, in France, and part of it in Aosta, in Italy; and I revised and retyped it while motoring back through France a year later, spending whole afternoons out in the weedy back yards of country inns, typing on a portable, on a portable table. It could be that some page of that erratic procedure might have survived somewhere, but when and why did I sign it? It is more likely, if the thing is authentic at all, that I did it for some promotion or for some fan or collector. But look at its teeth before you buy.

Sorry, I have no pictures up here in the woods. Maybe next time you come to California I can find something. We'll be at home, and receiving, after October 15.

Sincerely,
Wallace Stegner

« *To: Nancy Colberg* • *August 12, 1983*

Dear Nancy,

I did see Dunbar last week when he came over for a signature, and he says he and Diane are serious about the bibliography. But I have the strong

---

4. Forrest and Margaret Robinson, *Wallace Stegner*, Twayne's United States Author Series, 1977.

impression that he's a more active collector than scholar—and besides, he teaches at De Anza College. As for Diane, she peddles rare books and is also a dental technician. So they're at least as hard up for time as you are, and I would bet on you in a footrace.

I doubt that going to Utah, Twin Falls, Stanford, and points west will actually turn up much that you don't already know and that I don't have. I've got a closet full of old stuff—magazines with things by me and things about me, collections, books with introductions, etc. etc. Your discovery of *Fiction*, and of the Tanner Lectures, and the *Remembering* volume could have been taken care of here. They're in the closet, along with a lot of other things. So when you get your two or three days, come here first. I can't offer to put you up, because I don't know how Mary will be. She had a quadrant mastectomy two months ago, and a full bilateral one yesterday, and she's going to be laid up and languid for a while. But at least I can turn you a-loose in the closet and give you a tuna sandwich at midday and a drink at five. After that you can count your items and see where else you have to go. January ought to be all right, but check in advance.

Good luck,
Wally

« *To: Nancy Colberg* • *November 29, 1983*

Dear Nancy,

I'm delighted that you got some time off. Now I won't think of you, grim in some dim-lighted basement, poring over Library of Congress cards and keeping an eye out for the head librarian.

You have asked for April 11 to May 10. It is possible, in fact, a little more than possible, that we'll be away in May. But that needn't deter you. John Daniel, whom you met, and perhaps his wife, whom you didn't because she is still in school in Oregon, will be living in the cottage and looking after the place. He can keep the study open for you if we aren't here, and you can paw through those shelves to your heart's content. If we are here, of course, there will be even less of a problem.

Delphian Quarterly, you mention. My Goodness Godness Agnes. I had forgotten all about the *Delphian Quarterly*. When I was teaching at Harvard I used to write them potboiler articles for thirty dollars apiece. The Delphian Society is some sort of do-good-and-think-high women's group, and their magazine was edited by the wife of a Princeton professor, a friend of mine. I doubt that I have any Delphian Quarterlies around, but I can look. If no other leads turn anything up, you might inquire of the Princeton library, which may well have the whole series. But I hope you never find them.

We had a pleasant Thanksgiving in Santa Cruz, and hope (if Mary is up to traveling) to spend Christmas in Santa Fe. After that we'll be at home until (if) we leave for Israel and the Sinai Desert in late April or early May. I hope all gets straightened out with Sheri, and that she comes back from (where? Tours? Vienna? Oxford?) full of charity and forgiveness for her surly parents.

Best,

Wally

*The editor's name was Margaret Thorp and her husband was Willard Thorp (of the Princeton English Department). Both may now be dead, for all of that business was forty years or more ago.

« *To: Nancy Colberg* • *December 31, 1983* »

Dear Nancy,

Peace, perturbed spirit. I have dipped into the back corners of my files and discovered a whole folder of *Delphian Quarterly* articles—perhaps all of them. I find that I have things called "The Cooperatives and the Peace," "The Naturalization of an Idea," "Diagnosis and Prognosis," "Publishing in the Provinces," "The Tourist Revolution," "A Democracy Built on Quicksand," "The Colleges in Wartime," and "The Little Man with the Purchasing Power." Indeed, I have several clippings of two or three of these, so that you won't even have to copy them. Any one of them by itself would turn a vulture's stomach, and together they constitute the greatest emetic since the Book of Mormon. So save those until you come in April, and be confident that your shelves will not be bare.

And thank you extremely for the Pepperidge Farm soups. We got back from Santa Fe last night to find them waiting patiently on the kitchen counter. We are saving them for your April nourishment.

Santa Fe was very pleasant—cloudy and bleary overhead, but not cold in the way you were having it, and with all sorts of pleasant Christmas feng shui. We made a few Indian dances at San Juan and Tesuque and Taos, and the young went skiing a couple of days, and we saw some old friends and lived high on the herring.

Articles; I haven't seen the *American West* piece yet. And there's nothing else I can think of that's forthcoming except a review of the Steinbeck biography in tomorrow's *Los Angeles Times*, the introduction I did for Steinbeck's "Flight," to be published by the Yolla Bolly Press in Covelo, Calif., another introduction to a Sierra Club book called *The Wilder Shore*, by David Rains Wallace, and still another introduction, or re-introduction, to a new edition of a book called *This Is Dinosaur* that I edited twenty years ago for the Sierra Club when there were threats of dams on the Green and Yampa in Dinosaur National Monument. That will be published by the Rinehart Roberts Press in Boulder, Colo., but I don't know when, and I haven't yet written the introduction.

I hope that answers all your questions and lays to rest your anxieties. At least you can relax about those *Delphian* items.

Happy New Year, and a productive 1984. Keep us in your computer's memory.

Yours,
Wally

« *To: Nancy Colberg* • *May 24, 1985* »

Dear Nancy,
The Peregrine Smith reprint of Dutton's *Tertiary History of the Grand Canyon District* is faithful and beautiful and expensive. I can show you a copy when you come in July. As of now, it looks as if July 2 or 5 would be O.K., but keep in touch so that we don't miss connections. Drop the books off early if you want to, or bring them with you. I sign my name pretty fast.

I should tell you, sotto voce, that a couple of book collectors here have indicated an impulse to work on a Stegner bibliography. I don't know how serious they are—they seem to me more interested in acquiring than in the scholarly rigor required for a complete bibliography—but they may well be serious. Maybe you'll want to talk to them while you're here.

Nobody has my papers, but they will probably go to the University of Utah (don't broadcast this). Utah has been good to me, and consistently supportive, and it's where I came from, and its library could use a little strengthening. And any scholar who has to go to Salt Lake to study Stegner will get a bonus by being lured into good country.

No idea where you can find *Fire and Ice*, alas.

As for getting Ansel's signature, I think that can be arranged, though he's getting pretty old to be burst in upon. If you want to send the book to me, I can get his signature for you next time he's up here or I'm down there.

See you in July.

Wally

« To: *James Hepworth* • *June 5, 1985* »

Dear Jim,

I'm afraid you'll have to excuse me. For one thing, I'm flat on my back with back problems, and have been for a week, and may be for a week or two more. For another, I'm not inclined to spend my time refuting the scurrilities of the Walsh[5] woman—or giving her paranoias any further publicity.

I can't, of course, dictate what you will do about the Walsh article. My own decision, after the first angry impulse to sue, is to ignore it. So I'm not answering your questions, even if it were very convenient to do so in this flat-on-the-back position.

For your information—not for quotation—I used the Foote letters and reminiscences precisely as one uses any historical materials when adapting them to fiction. I used what I wanted, and changed when I wanted. I told Janet Micoleau[6] that was what I wanted to do and she agreed enthusiastically. I offered to let her see the manuscript before I sent it off, and she saw no reason to ask to. We agreed between ourselves that I should specifically not give footnote-like credit, because since it was a novel, and not about Mary Foote but about Susan Ward, Janet did not think she wanted Molly Foote identified. Hence the initials-only acknowledgement in the front matter of the book.

Later, when the book was published, Janet's sister[7] (who I didn't and don't know) was upset. She took the book to be about her grandmother,

---

5. Mary Ellen Williams Walsh, in an essay entitled "*Angle of Repose* and the Writings of Mary Hallock Foote: A Source Study," undertook what Jackson Benson called "a nasty piece of character assassination," promoting "the strange idea that *Angle of Repose* is essentially the work of Mary Hallock Foote." Ms. Walsh's contention is a little like arguing that a baleen whale is the product of krill.
6. One of Mary Hallock Foote's three granddaughters.
7. Evelyn Foote Gardiner.

and hence a slander. Walsh evidently talked to her at some time and got her notion that "the family" objected to my book. Janet, from whom McMurry and I got the Foote papers for the Stanford Library, was and is a good friend, and knew what I wanted to do.

And, of course, I did not accuse even Susan Ward of adultery, etc. It was my firm opinion that as a Victorian lady she was incapable of adultery, though not immune to temptation. Mary Foote I accused of nothing, nor did I show her _doing_ anything, though I adapted the [word obscured] of her character and her life for fictional purposes. If you, or La Walsh, or anyone else, think I didn't invent anything, I invite one and all to sit down with my book beside all the available papers and do a comparison.

But your interesting speculation about proper names—Ward, Lyman, etc.—are either borrowings from the Foote-Burling family trees, or out of the telephone book. My head doesn't work in those sly symbols. In fact, I suspect any ingenious critic can find comparable meanings in almost any novel you want to name.

You indicate that you intend to reprint the Walsh piece. That doesn't [word obscured] me. In fact, according to Dick Etulain, Walsh wrote it for some conference or other and couldn't get it published till Tony Arthur rescued her from oblivion by putting it in his collection of critical articles about me. Again, I can't tell you what to do, but I can tell you it won't please me to see this junk once again given new life.

I see that some of your questions don't concern Walsh, so I'll answer them.

9) No, MHF [Mary Hallock Foote] isn't any more reliable than any of us when we write about ourselves. She didn't know she was a snob, for instance.

10) She would have made a Ph.D. dissertation, not a trade biography. No recognition—nobody ever heard of her.

11) I helped George McMurry get them [MHF's papers] from Janet [Micoleau], to whom he introduced me.

12) I encouraged him but he was 66 years old, and gave up.

13) She [Janet Micoleau] was all for it, as above.

14) I was _very_ conscious of the shape this novel was taking, and I had great trouble making the Lyman story and the Susan story fit, and shed light on each other. Process was everything.

15) Of course Lyman is only partly reliable—reliable on his grand-mother, not himself.

That's about all the ink and strength I've got. Do what you want. But be very careful how you quote me. It's bad enough to be injured by the ill will of enemies; I'd hate to be injured by the good will of a friend.

Good luck,

Wallace Stegner

« *To: James Hepworth* • *July 2, 1985* »

Dear Jim:

Don't get me wrong. I wasn't asking you to ignore Walsh, or refute her, or anything else. I was only trying to keep from getting into the position of defending myself against her in a collection which dignified her slurs by taking them seriously enough to reprint them. On the theory that a lie goes a mile while the truth is tying its shoes, I would like to see her ignored, but that decision is yours to make, not mine.

So long as I'm not called upon to certify Walsh's slanders by patiently refuting them, I'm ready to answer any questions you want to ask.

You're irked by Stegner criticism. So am I, as it happens, by its absence, by its presence, and sometimes by its trend. A couple of people—Kerry Ahearn and a lady—was her name Hudson?—who did a piece on narrative voice in *Angle of Repose*—have said things that seemed to me sensible and perceptive. Bob Canzoneri I have to like because he flattered me more than I deserve. But otherwise there isn't much that comes close to what I've been trying to do.

You speak of realism. I begin with the real world, obviously. I hope I don't end there. It never seemed to me that Jack Barth and the structuralists were being anything but despairingly Alexandrine in insisting that the subject of fiction is the making of fiction. The subject of fiction is people in action, I think. What one makes of those people is something else, more subjective; and how one presents them is conditioned to a large extent by the tendencies of the times. At one extreme is the rather plodding reportage, omniscient and chronological, godlike judgment mounted upon objective realities and credible events, that fiction before about 1870 mainly showed. On the other is Nabokovian manipulation, sometimes (alas) for its own sake, which sometimes gets as incestuous as the bisexual bilharzias worm, incessantly engaged in mating with itself. I hope I am neither of those. I do believe that circumstances alter cases and that the viewer affects what is viewed, the reporter stains what he reports, the judge tilts what he judges. I try to become whoever is narrating my fictions, if there is a narrator, but I don't necessarily try to invent narrators who are totally unlike myself in education, background, and sentiments, any more than I try to invent places that I never saw. Nevertheless it would be an unwary critic who assumed that Lyman Ward or Joe Allston is Stegner, that those folks are just the Larry Speakeses of this fictional administration.

And as long as we're on that subject, let me admit that I don't respond to fictions in which the distortion of reality is extreme, whatever motives the writer had for his distortions. That means I don't worship Borges et al. They seem to me arbitrary. They seem to me too often not only to warp reality, but to warp it arbitrarily. Distortion has its function if it makes us see more clearly. Flannery O'Connor said she utilized the grotesque because when you are speaking to the deaf you have to shout. O.K. But I don't consider myself deaf, and I get to resenting her incessant shouting. The wrong lenses in the optometrist's frames can make the right ones, when they're finally dropped in, marvelously right. But what if the optometrist leaves the wrong ones in, and we go around with our astigmatism enhanced instead of corrected?

To that degree, maybe, I'm a realist. Reality is the aim of fiction. Aristotle said literature was the imitation of life. But any method that works is legitimate so long as it doesn't get bilharzified into thinking that the method is the aim.

As for symbols, I agree with you. Symbols rise out of reality like methane gas out of garbage. The moral here is that it's dangerous to think methane gas arises out of some parthenogenesis or spontaneous combustion. Never forget that the garbage comes first. Or to select a less odorous metaphor, don't assume that you can deal in shadows without having substantial things to cast them.

Finally, the West. You are right in thinking that I see it as a little America, a late (and by aridity modified and intensified) variant of the American experience. You are right in thinking that I resent the mythification of much western experience because, like the grotesque, like structuralism, like a lot of literary capers, it distorts, and misrepresents that experience. What is more, it simplifies as it distorts—simplifies experience, turns individuals into types, reduces ethical and moral responses to the consistency of the Reagan view—if it is a view. It's a peekhole, rather. It leads to the easiest and most dangerous sort of politics, and is the sworn enemy of intelligence.

I do think that if, in the characters of *Angle of Repose,* I am deconstructing myths and making individuals out of them, I may also be going back to the sorts of individuals from whom some of the myths derive, and to the experiences that, being shared by two or three generations and broad segments of a population, helped create some of the myths in the first place. For there is surely some validity in myth—reality has to match *somewhere* with wish fulfillment if the wish fulfillment is going to take hold of a whole people. My problem is that I just can't get interested in Louis L'Amour's mass production with interchangeable parts. It never tells me anything personal and it never tells me anything new. Nor does it tell me anything that is more than vaguely true, except about the map of the Louis L'Amour mind and the mind of the L'Amour audience.

Mainly this two-page garrulity is to reassure you that I don't feel threatened by your good will, or by your interest. Quite the contrary. Ask me another. As for the back, it has healed, and I am working on the woodpile again.

Best,
Wally Stegner

« To: James Hepworth · July 31, 1985 »

Dear Jim,
Here is a rainy afternoon when I can't walk or work on the woodpile, and so I am pinned to the wall by your questions. Maybe the rain will let up before I finish with them, in which case this will get delayed till the next precipitation.

1) Narrators. Strictly speaking, a narrator is a persona, created by the author, through whose mouth or mind a story is told. Omniscient novels and third-person novels have no narrators; they have authors, whose presence is apparent or otherwise. On the other hand, *Angle of Repose* has a narrator; *Lord Jim* has several; *Lolita* has one, a very unreliable one; *The Spectator Bird* has one. The narrator is another voice than the author's, and (as in *Lolita* and to some extent in *Angle of Repose*) may be untrustworthy, so that his story has to be read the way a desk sergeant would read a suspect's account of a murder.

2) "Books write their authors." You're being too cryptic for me.

3) "Try to become" the narrator: I say "try" because in spite of the

greatest care, any author is sometimes guilty of slipping into his created narrator's place, and talking in the author's voice instead of the narrator's. At worst, we create narrators in our own image so that we can speak comfortably in our own voice while pretending to speak from the narrator's. At best, we achieve maximum "negative capability," and pull ourselves completely out. When Hotspur speaks (he is not of course a narrator, but he is a participant) it is not Shakespeare we hear; we hear Harry Percy. When Lyman Ward speaks, you ought to hear authentic Lyman Ward, but sometimes you hear Stegner.

4) Borges et al. I don't mean to knock Borges, whom many people admire extravagantly. But his work is intellectual, not emotional; he operates by equations and theorems; he is a structuralist in the sense that he makes creative use of the act of creation, as do all of his imitators and devotees (e.g. Jack Barth). Me, I am more interested in people and their personal relations, emotions, and hang-ups, and I grew up thinking it was an error for an author to show his hands and feet above or below his little puppet show. When I say I don't respond to Borges, I mean simply that his elegant equations and mystifications don't interest me. He represents a maximum of manipulation where my impulse is to utilize a minimum.

5) My ideal reader is somebody who likes my stuff and is moved by it. I am more interested in moving him than in impressing or instructing him.

6) The objective realm. I know no alternative to acting as if it exists. If it turns out not to, I will probably never know.

7) Are my real concerns the unknowable? Maybe. I am interested in people in corners, people faced by dilemmas without horns. I am suspicious of systems and systematizers because systems achieve order at the expense of the large view and general probability. But when you suggest that my fiction "pushes at the limits of all thinking," I'm mainly embarrassed. I am no such pundit.

8) Am I part myth-maker? Somebody else will have to decide that. I am aware of no such intention. But I do, if this matters, try to make any story or character throw a shadow, sometimes a shadow longer than it/himself. But that isn't myth, it's only meaning.

9) I don't understand your question about deconstructing myths.

10) Neither do I understand your remarks about writers viewing

everything in terms of writing, making choices based on writing, friends based on reading tastes, etc. You see myth in this. It doesn't fit any definition of myth that I know. If, on the other hand, you say that every writer of any stature writes from a basis of belief (perhaps negative belief) then I'm with you. Some sort of code or feeling undergirds every story, and readers will usually catch it and accept it. If they don't accept it, the story fails. But is this vague unanimity or concurrence myth? I'd call it simply an expression of a society or culture, an expression of the social cohesion of human groups.

11) "Final belief." Certainly you can't make me out a religious man. I am what the religious somewhat stiffly call a "humanist," I guess. My (very cautious) faith is in a rough consensus, within any given non-disrupted social group, about what constitutes acceptable and unacceptable conduct. And conduct is what really matters to me: I'm a moral writer, if not a religious one. I don't mean behavior, I mean conduct. Some of what I'd accept as human decency surely comes from the Judeo-Christian tradition. Some of it comes from the Greeks. Some of it comes from Confucius, some from Native American animism. So be careful how you put me in the Judeo-Christian wagon. I suppose I represent that stage in the decline of a faith that Unitarianism came to; a code of conduct without any Godhead in it.

12) No, I have not thought of writing an autobiography. Nothing ever happened to me but long hours on my rump in front of a typewriter.

You do well to envy me Vermont. It's a fine place. Now if I could only move that literary rock.

Take care,
Wallace Stegner

« To: James Hepworth · August 15, 1985 »

Dear Jim,

In great haste, while about to pack for two weeks away, I'll try to answer your last ones.

Yes, I was looking, consciously or unconsciously, for ways to fuse the contemporary and the past. I had the Molly Foote story, and wasn't satisfied that it was enough, I didn't want to write a novel of the settlement, or of pioneering, or a triangle in prospector's boots—didn't want the <u>thinness</u>

of a straight historical story. So I deliberately invented a frame from which the story could be told, and a narrator to sit in it. When I had got through writing the first chapter (Lyman's son's visit) I sat helpless for nearly a year, trying other openings, not sure I could make the opening I had written tie to the 19th century stuff it was supposed to uncover. Eventually I found that I could, and I kept my original opening. The hardest job in that book was making the past and present fuse and merge and come apart again like strings that make a braid. I wanted each to shed light on the other. You know my feelings about the West's literary past—that most of the real past, which does melt into the present, has been lost under the mythic cowboy stuff, which neither was nor is. I'm a realist, as I have told you before. I think the best way to illuminate human life is to hold up real lives like candles. And I do believe in a continuum. I know there's history in the West, because by now I have lived some of it—about half of it, I'd guess.

You ask why Molly Foote, not Mary Austin or somebody? It never occurred to me to look around among the women writers and select one. I had one, Molly Foote, and I had her private papers and letters as well. It didn't matter to me whether she was a good writer or a bad one; she was an interesting case, as Henry James might have said. I had her papers, which gave me all sorts of intimate glimpses into how it was to be a cultivated lady in the crude West. Into other things as well that I would never have been able to imagine. I guess you should always bear in mind that I work most naturally from the particular to the general, not the other way around. So I didn't, as you suggest, start with a general notion of linking past and present, and then "narrow my subject to the particular life, the life of an artist." I had the life, and wrote it up as fact and imagination suggested it had to go, and let any general ideas about past and present, East and West, art and making a living, career and marriage, evolve from it naturally. In writing up Molly Foote's life, I am sure I shaped it, often unconsciously, with my own general conclusions about life in the West, past and present. But that all happened down in the basement, not up in the attic. That was close to your notion that the story writes the author; though I guess I see it in other terms. If one is a sausage machine, anything in the way of raw material that goes into one is going to come out sausage, ground to a certain fineness and encased in gut or plastic or whatever one's apparatus uses.

As for the God in those papers, don't forget that I knew what was in the papers before I ever invented Lyman. So it won't do to get exercised about the knowable and the unknowable. This is fiction we are dealing with, and fiction is a creation, to a greater or lesser degree. Or I hope it is.

Undenominationally,

Wallace Stegner

« *To: Jackson Benson* • *January 14, 1986* »

Dear Mr. Benson:

Of course I remember you—not by my review of your book but by the book itself,[8] whose thoroughness and objectivity I admired.

About the biography that you propose, I am of two minds. If a biography were to be written, I would be happy to have it done by someone so competent, experienced, and judicious as yourself. And no writer can afford to be totally indifferent to public notice. I suppose I have been too much that way, if anything, because I have a distaste for Tendenzlitteratur and Tendenz writers and writers who can't tell themselves from their own press agents. On the other hand, I am a private person, and my personal life seems to me the business of nobody but me and my family, and seeing it exploited or spread out—becoming the major character in a psychodrama—would give me nothing but a pain in the tail.

On still another hand, the books are public. If they aren't, why did I write them? And if they are public, then any part of me that went visibly into their writing is perhaps public too. The question is partly timing—before my death or after?—and partly the intention and style of the biographer. There is the further fact that I have led a very quiet life. I have no marital upheavals, spectacular alcoholism, sexual deviations, madcap adventures, or attempted suicides to report. You might find that even if I told you to go ahead, you would have little to write about. Actually, what I have meant, to myself and I hope to others, is an individual attempt to understand and come to terms with a dynamic, forming, and unstable society, that of the American West. The part of my life that is worth reporting is the part that bears on that extended study, as Dick Etulain well understood when he made up the questions for his *Conversations*[9] book.

---

8. Jackson Benson, *The True Adventures of John Steinbeck, Writer* (New York, The Viking Press, 1984).

9. Wallace Stegner and Richard Etulain, *Conversations with Wallace Stegner on Western Literature and History* (Salt Lake City, UT: University of Utah Press, 1983).

If all this doesn't dissuade you, I'm willing to talk, and it would be a pleasure to meet you in any case. With only short absences, I'll be here until June. If you feel like coming up for a talk, please call me and we'll work out a date.

Sincerely,

Wallace Stegner

« *To: James Hepworth* • *May 5, 1986* »

Dear Jim,

You can ask a lot of questions in one letter, and I probably won't get them all answered. But I'm going to be on the road for a while, and if I don't answer some of them I may never answer any.

Benson's biography: nothing settled, awaiting Etulain's return. If anything more comes of this, I'll sic Benson on you.

Your proposal to edit a book of Stegner on Writing. I think—you're mad—not dangerously, but mad nevertheless. The art of fiction that I practice is held by the reigning authorities to be the sort of fiction suitable for second-rate lady novelists. As for the interviews, they all ask the same questions, and not very bright questions at that. Etulain is the exception, but his interviews are already in print.

Your other proposal for a book of assigned essays. Again, I think you'll have real trouble getting any of the people you mention to write you a piece. Maybe Wayne Booth, if he isn't laboring on something big. But though Ernie Gaines and Evan Connell were once my students, I can't imagine that either one was in any way an admirer of my pellucid prose. Bill Styron is currently very depressed, and writing a piece on me would maybe be fatal to him. And John Fowles, though I know him a little, is almost the last person on earth I can imagine knowing my books, or being very interested if he did. What does he know about the country west of the hundredth meridian? What does he know about this forming sub-culture that I've been trying to illuminate or define in most of my books? And why does the world need a new collection of articles on Stegner when it already has Tony Arthur, including Walsh? Straighten up and lead a better life.

As for film options, these have come and gone like fog for many years. *Big Rock Candy Mountain* hit the fancy of Eva Marie Saint and her husband, a producer, and they tried for several years to sell it—Jeffry even scripted two or three pilot segments. PBS once had an option on *Angle of Repose*, also for a series. Nothing came of that. Parts of *Wolf Willow* have been made into film in Canada, but the big section, "Genesis," is still unmade. But sold. *Joe Hill* is currently under option in Hollywood, but I imagine that will wisp away too. *Beyond the Hundredth Meridian* has had nibbles, but never got to the option stage. The field is wide open. All you need is an angel with fifteen or twenty million dollars.

I hate to be discouraging to your youthful enthusiasms, but I am not very marketable. I applaud your taste, but you'll have a hell of a time selling me to those guys east of Iowa.

But coraggio.

Wally

« *To: Richard Etulain* • *May 20, 1986* »

Dear Dick,

I got back from Wisconsin last night, and have improved my morning by signing your box of books. One or two of them—that *Redbook* presentation copy of *Remembering Laughter*, for instance, and the copy of *Fire and Ice*, are pretty hard to find. The box will go out to you this afternoon. But it shouldn't go without my appreciation for all your efforts to publicize Stegner to the heathen. You wanna job?

Re: Jack Benson and the Oklahoma Press series. He came up and we had a talk. What he tentatively mentioned was the possibility that he could do this more limited book as a precursor to a full-dress biography—which sometime, maybe not while I'm alive, might make sense. What I tentatively mentioned was the fact that I didn't think a full-dress biography should be written for a series limited to western figures, if only because I'm already maybe over-labeled as a regionalist. What do you think? After you and Benson have talked, and he has made up his mind about what he'd like to do, we can know better how to respond.

As for the volume of letters, I can't think that you would, find much there. I have not had long literary discussions by mail with many people, and though I have written millions of letters, most of them are either personal-playful or merely businesslike. I'm sure whatever letters are preserved would be useful to Benson or any other biographer, but I'd have to be persuaded that there are enough with substantive worth to make a collection interesting to readers. Again, we can wait and see. If there ever is such a book, I'd be happy to see you do it, because I have no doubts about your competency, your carefulness, or your discretion.

I should say, too, that I like Benson's work and I like him. I would be lucky to get so able a biographer.

We're off for a short vacation in the South Pacific in early June, then we'll be driving to Vermont. From July 1 to October 20 our address will be Greensboro, Vermont 05841. The last week in October I'm giving the Cook Lectures at Michigan,[10] and then we're driving home perhaps via Santa Fe. If we come anywhere near Albuquerque I'll try to see if we can't get together.

I'm finally finishing that novel I was working on.[11] Whether I'll ever publish it is another matter. I might leave it for my biographer to defend.

Best,

Wally

« *To: Nancy Colberg* • *September 20, 1986* »

Dear Nancy,

Please send Dick Etulain two ounces of hemlock root with full instructions for use. I think that my writing an introduction to your bibliography is a terrible idea, something like calling me in post mortem to consult on the design of my tombstone.

So far as I can see, the purpose of an introduction to your bibliography of my works should be double: (1) to certify that in the opinion of sober scholars it is a worthy project, and (2) to certify, in the opinion of the same deacons of scholarship, that it is well and thoroughly done. I could testify to the latter, only a sober scholar could testify to the former. I don't know where you're going to find one who will so testify, but for starters you might try Jackson Benson, who has written a book or two on Hemingway and other competitors with Stegner for public notice, and has also written a big life of Steinbeck, and is now engaged in writing a biography of me.

---

10. Eventually published as *The American West as Living Space* (Ann Arbor: University of Michigan Press, 1987).
11. *Crossing to Safety* (New York: Random House, 1987).

He's in a bind—he'll have to testify, or else give up this Stegner biography and resolve to lead a better life. He can be reached at the Department of English, University of California Irvine.

Now be a good girl and do as you're told. "For him who list to hunt, I know where is an hynde / But as for me, alas, I may no more."

Best,

Wally

« *To: Nancy Colberg:* • *November 19, 1986* »

Dear Nancy and Don,

We have been home for two weeks, and I'm ashamed not to have written before this to thank you for that majestic sundial. Now we can count no hours but the sunny ones—as soon as I clear the desk a little more and get around to finding some sort of pedestal on which to mount it. It was very thoughtful of you to have it sent, and we do thank you.

When I called you from—where was it? North Platte? Maybe as far back as Ames—I knew what we were heading into, after four months away. I was absolutely right; it's been bedlam ever since we arrived, and we were right in not trying to stop off in Denver to see you, even though that would have been pleasant and instructive. As a matter of fact, we were in such a tizzy that we drove from Salt Lake to here in one flight—835 miles. I haven't driven that far in a day since I was 40.

Now it's beginning to ease off. I have to talk at San Jose State tomorrow night, and I still have some revising of the Michigan lectures to do, and the introduction to Ansel Adams' letters is coming up, and there is some busy-work about finding a title for the novel, and writing things to accompany the Italian publication of *Angle of Repose*, etc., etc., but those seem manageable now. I think I will retire in 1987 and see how it feels.

Mary stood the trip well—she will never convince me again that she has back problems, after that drive from Salt Lake. Or maybe it was that Chrysler, which is an unconscionably comfortable car. In any case, we're here, we're seeing light at the end of the tunnel, and we're very pleased with the sundial. How did we ever get along without one?

All the best,

Wally

« *To: Nancy Colberg* • *January 11, 1987* »

Dear Nancy,

I'm sorry indeed to hear about the difficulties with the bibliography. Of course you are not bound in the least to Nebraska, and I suspect other places, Utah and Peregrine Smith among them, would probably be interested. The only real negative is that now the new novel and the bibliography can't appear at approximately the same time, and wash each other's hands.

Our spring is up in the air. At the moment, we are thinking of Italy for a couple of weeks at the end of March, but that is still fluid. If we're here, we can put you up. If we're not, I suppose the house and the Daniels will be here, and you can camp. I'll let you know how our plans work out.

Nothing new on the publication horizon except an essay, "The Sense of Place," published as a fine-press, limited-edition (200 copies) pamphlet by the Silver Buckle Press, described as "a working typographical museum located in the Helen C. White Library at the University of Wisconsin–Madison." This will later be published as part of a larger study-publication by the Wisconsin Humanities Committee. At the moment I am finishing an extended review of James Welch's *Fools Crow* and Will Weaver's *Red Earth, White Earth* for the *Washington Star*'s magazine *The World and I*. (I discover belatedly that this is the Moony magazine.) The only thing assured in the immediate future is an introduction to the collected letters of Ansel Adams, which I haven't yet started on. *Angle of Repose* will be published sometime soon in Italian by Vallecchi of Florence, but I haven't yet seen a copy and don't even know the Italian title.

Health here is reasonably good, weather is cold and too dry. I hope your problems with Nebraska either smooth themselves out or that you find a better place to talk to. Our best to Don.

Wally

« *To: James Hepworth* • *January 19, 1987* »

Dear Jim,

I've been a good while getting back to the typescript of the Interview, because the copy-edited manuscript of my novel arrived, and there were a good many things to check before closing the forms. I hope you haven't been suffering for it.

As you will see I made a good many changes, reducing the first 20 pages to 13 and making, or trying to make, sense out of a lot of garbled gibberish. Since I am going to want to see the version of this that goes in to *Paris Review*, I suggest that you take a fairly free hand with the 30-odd pages that I have left unrepaired. If you mis-speak me, then I can straighten things out. But I really don't have time to go through the whole thing, writing it into intelligibility. When you get a typescript of the new conversations we had earlier this month, I ought to have more time to do a careful editing job on them without having to rewrite them. But it seems we are going to go to Italy around mid-March, so if time is a factor, better get the typescript to me by or before March 1.

I have had a letter from Gregory McNamee of the University of Arizona Press, asking about *The Uneasy Chair*. Did you put him up to that? Or is he muscling into your territory? In either case, I should tell you that I am very undecided about what to do with that book. I know that my agent is concerned that it not get lost in some small-press edition which would have the aid of neither assured longevity in the edition nor assured distribution facilities. It seems to me that the proper place for the book is with the others, in Bison Books; but so far Regier has been skittish about risking a book he feels has no great possibility of an audience. So I am inclined to wait and see what the new book, plus Nancy Colberg's bibliography, may do. I know you are eager for a book of mine; I hope you won't think me ungrateful if I spend a little time looking at my hand. Sooner or later there will be something, I expect. Maybe Hepworth's critical appraisal.

It was pleasant to have you here. I wish you the best of luck with the *Paris Review*.

Yours,

Wally

« *To: James Hepworth* • *January 30, 1987* »

Dear Jim,

I was just packaging up the edited tape transcription when your last letter came. First the transcriptions: they seem to me much more sensible and considerably more coherent than the first ones. Even so, I have scratched them up some; but I'm more contented with what they say. Go to—if you can't make a PR [*Paris Review*] interview out of all that stuff you have so painstakingly assembled, you've been witching over the wrong waterhole.

Now the matter of *The Uneasy Chair*. You are right that it has never seen a paperback edition. Nor a foreign edition. Benny was too colloquially American to interest Europeans, and he is limited, unjustly, by the common perception that he was a western wild man who thumped eastern noggins for fun. But he is also circumscribed somewhat by time—the times he wrote of are long gone. The environmental threats remain, bigger than ever, and those are what keep his memory alive in a few heads—those and his forthright attacks on the FBI and other police-state mechanisms. Regier, as you note, is afraid there's no market for the biography out there. Me, I don't know. But I'll tell you straight out what I think, even if it takes a while.

I think there may be more of a market than Regier thinks. Your guess of 2,500 copies may be optimistic, but it's not out of the ball park.

I think it would strain you too much to raise the capital to publish such an edition; and if it didn't happen to move, it could be a big burden on you.

I think I would rather not get the book back into print than to see it drop on you like copings in an earthquake; and I would rather not get it back in print if it's going to wither and die without notice or readers. I agree with you in general that people sell books, but the people who sell the most books are booksellers, and somebody has to sell them. Frankly, I don't know how good your distribution system is, how much attention that single salesman can pay to the titles of any single small isolated press. I don't think the University of Arizona Press could do it any better than you could, and certainly not with your enthusiasm and care. I suppose they could raise the initial funds more easily, and I suspect they could be surer of keeping the book in print and in stock for a few years. But Benny had no real contact with the Southwest; his contacts were all from Utah north, and a lot of his natural readership as well.

I think that before you pawn your g-string to try to put into print this book that you are kind enough to like, I should talk to Jack Shoemaker and to Turnbull, both of whom in the past have indicated that they would be interested in any book of mine that came loose. Would that satisfy your lust to see *The Uneasy Chair* in paperback? Would it hurt your feelings and make you feel that an opportunity had been snatched away from you? Would you accuse me of not thinking small?

The fact is, I am not afraid of thinking small, but right now there are pressures on me to think large. Strictly for your eye, and not for dissemination or incorporation in your non-fiction novel, I am interested in seeing my reputation climb out of the hole the NY Times et al digged for it. I appreciate your interest in helping it do just that. This last novel, Sam Vaughan thinks, may do it; and he will be playing the fifty-years-and-still-going-strong theme for all he is worth. Nancy Colberg's bibliography may help a little. The publication, to pretty good auspices, of an Italian edition of Angle of Repose won't hurt. Anything that looks cumulative and positive will help a little. But I tell you true, the re-issue of The Uneasy Chair or any other book by an obscure, however admirable little press in a lost town in Idaho is going to look to those people who make, break, and revise reputations, like an admission that I am not a world writer, or an American writer, but a regional western writer.

North Point has escaped that cage. There is a perfectly good chance that, like Regier, it will feel there's not enough market out there. If that's what they think, I'm not sure what I should do. But I probably would feel that The Uneasy Chair should simply be left, at least for the present, where it is. It came within a hair—one vote—of winning the Pulitzer Prize for biography, but it is a book about a pugnaciously western man, and in this present situation might better be forgotten than called to people's minds with the wrong vibes. Since Benny is remembered mainly as an environmental hero, it would not be a bad idea to reissue him in the Bay Area, which is more or less the capital of the environmental movement.

Now therefore, ponder all this and see what you think. I will do no more than inquire, discreetly, if Turnbull and Shoemaker might be interested, if. I don't want to snatch the book out of your hands. There may be other books, at other times, that can be steered your way! For now, just tell me what you think of all, or none, of the above.

I have passed on your flattering words to Mary P., who purred.

Best,
Wally

« To: Nancy Colberg • July 27, 1987 »

Dear Nancy,
You have every right to feel butchered and misused. When your advisers change the rules, after you have painstakingly followed their suggestions,

you have to ask where authority lies and what it says. I suspect that there is no right way—that the experts go by trial and error like everybody else. And it doesn't look good that they then tried to hide from you the fact that their suggestions were doing you in.

However, I don't think you should give up on it. You've put too much into it to quit it now. Let it cool. Let the press and the advisers settle down. Then, if there is some agreement on what the proper forms and method are, you can maybe pick it up and put it into a shape that—agreed on in advance—will satisfy Regier. It does seem that if Harlan suggested a lot of stuff that now he wants to un-suggest, it ought to be easier to take it out than it was to put it in. But I repeat, let it cool. Put it away where you can find it when you feel like finding it. And don't worry about my possible disappointment. I am disappointed only because your effort hit a snag. If you wait five years, I won't hustle you. I only want to see you get the benefit out of all your labor. As for lack of academic credentials doing you in—I dunno. I don't know libraries and librarians and bibliographers. Maybe they're that small, but I don't want to believe it.

As special information to my bibliographer, the pub date of *Crossing to Safety* is September 15. Sam Vaughan called a half hour ago to say that the *Kirkus* review was blah, but the *Publishers Weekly* was great. So I will see when I see them. Penguin has bought the floor of the paperback, and the Franklin Library is going ahead with its autographed first edition, which should appear a few days before the Random House edition. We are up here since Saturday evening, and will stay until the 29th. Then back to California for a couple of weeks, and then off again to Montana and Wyoming and (outside chance) Santa Fe, and to address the Intermountain Booksellers in Salt Lake on September 12. I had half hoped to see you and Don there, but that is probably not in the cards. Anyway, I'll have very little time, and that will be full of book signings at Sam Weller's and talk shows on Salt Lake TV stations. I hate this, but this one last time I will do it. And now I see that you need a copy of C. to S. Alas, I don't have one, not even a manuscript, and so far as I know, won't have one until well into next month.

Take heart, lady, and go to a lot of little league ball games and forget bibliography until the methods crystallize and the cold weather comes on. Our best to Don.

Yours,
Wally

« *To: Jackson Benson* • *August 10, 1987* »

Dear Jack:

I'll send this to La Mesa because I find I didn't bring your Sierra address with me, and I suppose you may by now be gone from the Loftis house. I trust the unfailing U.S. mails will get it to you sometime.

Since we last talked, in that hurried hour or so while we were packing to leave, I have been thinking some about biography in general and this biography in particular, and since for practically the first time in my adult life I haven't got any project on the typewriter, I have to do something with my mornings, don't I? So I've been thinking about biography. I have written a couple,[12] but both were biographies of careers—I realize that I was not interested at all in Powell's private life, and that Benny DeVoto's private life, minimal at best or worst, struck me as something that I, as both friend and biographer, didn't particularly want to publicize. So I didn't dwell on it, though I dwelt pretty heavily on his anxieties, phobias, frights, panics, and literary quarrels. I guess the most personal thing I wrote about him was his quarrel with Frost, which was devastating to him and uncomfortable for Marse Robert.

So now, thinking about our last conversation and the trend it seemed to be taking, I want to raise a question with you, for present thinking and later discussion. It seems to me that as we have talked, you have been running through one book at a time, trying to get a fix on the circumstances of its writing and how it derives from my own life. In the case of *The Big Rock Candy Mountain* you could hardly do otherwise. It's evident that that book is my *Sons and Lovers*, and pretty close to the bone of personal feelings, if not personal experience. In *Wolf Willow*, which is frankly autobiographical in many of its chapters, you are likewise justified in looking for the personal background. But some of the others don't lend themselves to that kind of elucidation (if indeed uncovering of autobiographical detail does elucidate a novel) nearly so well, and I thought I caught you going down a misleading road when we last talked. Specifically, I thought you were trying to assign real-life originals to characters in the novels. I have read a

---

12. *Beyond the Hundredth Meridian: John Wesley Powell and the Second Opening of the West* (Boston: Houghton Mifflin Company, 1954), and *The Uneasy Chair: A Biography of Bernard DeVoto* (Garden City, NY: Doubleday, 1974).

lot of biographies that do just that—it's tempting. But it's also, more often than not, misleading and perhaps harmful. It sweeps back onto the factory floor all the sawdust and iron filings and board-ends that were produced in the act of creation. It replaces the creation with the chaos it was made of. I can't think that is either very useful or entirely fair to the people who might be named as "originals." There is such a thing as a roman à clef, meant to be deciphered. None of my books is that kind. And, as I suggested at some point in our talk, my memory is a hell of a fallible instrument, more artist than recorder, and it takes its hints from experience and then does all sorts of mayhem to them. So that when Red Cowan[13] tells you that the "original" of Holly in *Recapitulation* was Helen Foster, and the original of Nola was Juanita Crawford, he was maybe 18% right, and the rest of the time he was jumping to a conclusion. Even when you assume that Bo Mason was my father and Elsa Mason my mother, you're on very boggy ground, like a floating island in the Okefenokee Swamp.

In all of those cases I took hints from reality. In all of them I so manipulated the reality that none of the people except maybe my mother would recognize the character on the page. And though it might be intriguing to the kind of reader who thinks that way to assume that *Recapitulation* is the record of my broken heart, smashed by a faithless babe, it would be dangerously inaccurate, and unjust both to those "originals" and to me, to link the novel character and any real life person by name. My heart was not broken. My vanity was hurt when I came back from graduate school and found myself Dear John-ed. After my vanity got well I found all that kind of amusing. I didn't stay celibate the rest of my life for loss of that dream girl. There are very few episodes in *Recapitulation* that come from reality (including all the romantic scenes and the Mormon wedding), except the circumstances of how I happened to get sent off by pure accident to graduate school. The people in the novel are there because the novel demanded them, not because I so vividly remembered them that I had to put them in; and they have the characters they do, not because that's the way any original was, but because I needed for purely literary purposes a Dark Lady, a Fidus Achates, and an Aegisthus (to mix a few allusions). The Bo Mason and Elsa Mason characters remain what they were in *The Big Rock Candy Mountain* because once I had decided to make this a trailer

---

13. Milton Cowan, Stegner's old friend from Salt Lake days. See note, p. 9.

to that book, they were fixed, with an unchangeable character and an unchangeable past.

What *Recapitulation* boils down to, ultimately, is the domination that a harsh and dominating father can exert even after his death upon a son. What is revealed in this novel is the incurable damage done to Bruce Mason, not by Nola but by his father. Nola is an episode, an instance of his traumatized nature. His refusal to marry is likewise from his father, not Nola. Notice whom he is communing with at the end of the book. In one draft I kept Nola alive and had her show up at that auntie's funeral. No way would it work. It was the father, not the girl, that had to be dealt with.

So at the end of this long rumination what I want to say to you is that any biography that goes very deeply into me is going to find not girls but parents, and that the characters in my books are characters of convenience, sometimes adapted from real persons but never portraits, and rarely recognizable from the old photographs in an album. If your research has been leading you in that direction, and you have been tempted, I urge you to get out your compass and set it 13 degrees east of the true north of reality, and proceed from there.

What you can say about *Recapitulation* is that it tries to be a true record of how it was to grow up in the 1920s, in a place like Salt Lake City, a little remote provincial capital—how family life and courtship and play and ambition felt to a boy in those years and those circumstances. The feelings I will admit to. Portraiture, or even caricature, I will not. And as I said, I even doubt the pertinence of these attempted "recognitions," because all they do is stir up the dust that, once the novel was done, had settled. Fiction is an imitation of life. I think I can imitate it pretty good. Sometimes I don't know myself what I borrowed and what I made up, but when I try to check, I generally find that other people don't remember things the same way I do. I think I know why. I fixed them so they would work better in the fantasy constantly going on in my head.

Thus sung, or could, or would have sung, your biographical subject, in tolerable verse and words of dry caution. I will sing this for you in person when we next talk. What you write about me after I am gone to my reward is your own business, though I would roil my cloud if it got too far from demonstrable fact. But I wouldn't want people named as being sources of my characters, not while I'm alive to squawk. They are about as much my sources as the egg and the sperm. Who's to say, short of the theologians and the physiologists, when life begins?

Life here is very mild and amiable—beautiful weather, plenty of thrushes in the woods, a rave review of the new book in *Publishers Weekly*, old friends, picnics, walks, even a conservation struggle into which we can stick our noses. We're here until August 29. I hope your research among all those dusty letters, lame reviews, red-ink royalty statements, and other relics of my past has inspired you.

Best,

Wally

« *To: Jackson Benson* • *August 21, 1987* »

Dear Jack:

Peace, perturbed spirit, as Benny DeVoto used to say. I didn't mean to upset your scholarly equanimity, and I certainly did not mean to suggest that I don't trust both your judgment and your discretion.[14] I only meant to put up a warning sign: DANGER, FALLING ROCKS. If you drive carefully, there's no problem. The only problem would be jumping from historical facts to literary conclusions—something that I was afraid Red Cowan may have started you doing, and something that Red himself seems to have done.

Sure I have worked close to life, sometimes very close. That is a conviction as well as a habit. I'm Aristotelian enough to think that literature is the imitation of life, and if it's going to imitate life, it's going to imitate the only life I know. The fallacy of critics arises when they make that leap of faith—Bo Mason equals Wallace Stegner's father, Bruce Mason's emotional relationships equals W. S.'s.[15] As I make somebody remark in the new novel, quoting Henry Adams, chaos is the law of nature, order is the dream of man. And the dream of order makes a lot of changes in the reality that is being imitated. It may even reverse the direction of the emotional current. It never fails to exaggerate, select, suppress. What looks like confession

---

14. Benson had written a response to Stegner's letter of August 10, 1987 asking for a little trust. Stegner tended to be exceedingly punctilious in his concern over the distinction between illusion and fact in his work, and instinctively fended off interviewers when they began to inquire into his literal sources.

15. Bo Mason and Bruce Mason are characters in *The Big Rock Candy Mountain*. They may or may not sometimes resemble G.S. and W.S.

may actually be protective coloration. And so on. You know as well as I do what happens when you make a fiction. I suppose you're right that some of these relationships between historical or biographical fact and fictional representation are "interesting," and even important. But I have caught biographers making a lot too much of them, making their revelation an end in itself; whereas so far as I am concerned they are only an attempt to dissect the living organism and lay out its now-dead parts. So I thought it might not be out of line to tell you early how I feel about that. I feel that I may have added to the truth of something by what I have done to it fictionally. I would hate to have that truth, if any, falsified by being analyzed back to its unassembled parses. Because I am a maker, not a copier; and I ain't Bruce Mason, however much I may have consulted my own albums while I was making him.

Of course you have to have the goods, and of course I don't want to put roadblocks in your way. Obviously the best way for us to handle all this is to talk a lot. If you will pose your questions (guesses, inferences, extrapolations), I will tell you frankly whether I think you're right or wrong; and if you get close to something I don't want aired, I'll tell you that, too—though I can't imagine what it would be. As I guess I told you, my father's life and death do not embarrass me, but they may embarrass some people close to me. So we'll talk that all out, when the time comes. And if you need some excitement in your biography, maybe we can even find some things that never got put into stories or novels.

We'll be back briefly early in September, then gone from the 10th to the 27th. After that, let's get together. By then you'll be more of an expert on Stegner than Stegner is.

Two happy circumstances this week. *Crossing to Safety* gets lyrical review in *Publishers Weekly*, and Tom Watkins writes a piece about me, so flattering that I literally blush, in *Audubon* magazine. May every week produce some such flowers. And may your studies not be agitated by my warnings. Every cold that Stegner ever had in his life is likely to appear as pneumonia or emphysema in his fiction—if it appears at all. And I even borrow germs, on occasion.

Best,
Wally

« *To: Nancy Colberg* • *November 8, 1987* »

Dear Nancy,

It is good to hear from you again. I hope the depression is over and you may be able to look at the whole project without swooning or bursting into flame.

A few days ago I ran into Florian Shansky in a parking lot, and he said with concern that he hadn't heard from you for a long time, was anything wrong? I told him I thought you had been discouraged by contradictory and confusing reports from the referees Nebraska had appointed. I did not tell him I knew he was one of the referees. He seemed distressed. Has he written you?

Anyway, I don't think you should quit on this, and I am now not thinking of the fact that this is a Stegner bibliography. I am thinking of the fact that you've put about four years into it, and it ought to result in some good to you, personally and professionally. You say in your last letter that the bibliography sits exactly where it was—you haven't opened the package that Nebraska sent it in. What did they tell you then? Do it over? Revise the system? No thanks? If what they told you is unacceptable, then if I were you I would send it somewhere else. The University of Utah Press, to mention only one small alternative, once expressed great interest in this project, and given the conflict of opinion on the proper form of bibliographies, they might be agreeable to letting you do it the way you want to. You may have been listening to too many voices, and the voices themselves may not have been consistent. But another publisher might not have any of those voices, or any will to call on them. Utah may not be any place you want to take it; there are plenty of others, including North Point, that could be queried on the basis of exactly the manuscript you now have in that package.

So much for fatherly advice. How is everything else in your life? We're going to Truckee for Thanksgiving, with the grandchildren. A good many book parties and signings. Pleasant reviews, in the main. Four printings, and I would expect that the book will hold up fairly well through the Christmas season. Penguin has bought the paperback. Nobody has bought the movie, but then I never did expect anybody to.

Let me know how things go and what you decide to do. If you want, I'll write to Regier and ask him what he thought he was doing, with his referees and hesitations about bibliographical form. But I won't accost him unless you ask me to. He's after the reprint rights to *Angle of Repose*, and I have some leverage on him.

Best to Don. And love,

Wally

« *To: Nancy Colberg* • *November 30, 1987* »

Dear Nancy,

First, your main question. Yes, I see no reason why you shouldn't try the bibliography, as it stands, on some other publisher. The worst they can say is no. You have a specific thing to offer. You can even let them know in advance exactly what you had in mind—the Pittsburgh format—and tell em (politely) take it or leave it. There's nothing sacred about Nebraska. My guess is that, since they have so many of my titles in the Bison series, they will regret letting your bibliography get away, but maybe I over-estimate their sense.

Crossing to Safety. I have no final word on printings and numbers, and neither will break any records. There have been four printings, of 17,500, 2,500, 2,500, and 5,000 respectively—or had as of a month ago, when I last heard. About three weeks ago, I had a note saying that the total sales to date had been 25,319. These figures are pretty modest, as Random House measures success, and may have been kept down by their caution in print-ing and by their almost-steadfast refusal to advertise. The ad you saw in NYTBR was the only one, except for a smaller one in the *San Francisco Chronicle*. Maybe they know what they're doing, but they're not lathering their horses to get us into campground. On the other hand, they do have justification, since they tell me that sales have been brisk only on the West Coast and that 55% of re-orders come from the West Coast. We have been on the *Chronicle* best-seller list for twelve weeks, anywhere from #4 to #11, but not at all on the *NY Times* list. So don't expect triumphant parades.[16] I'll send you the more final figures after Christmas, or you could get them from Sam Vaughan at Random House, telling him what you need them for. Of the Franklin Library edition I have only one copy, and I'd prefer

---

16. The sales figures for *Crossing to Safety* by 2007 would astound its author. It continues, with *Angle of Repose*, to be his best-selling (and continuously selling) book.

not to trust it to the mails until after the Christmas rush. Now I see you want the exact publication date. It was supposed to be, and officially was, September 21, but actually there were books in the bookstores very early in September.

Recent writings; nothing except an introduction to the letters of Ansel Adams, New York Graphic Society, to come in 1988, and a little article on Ansel to come soon in the magazine *U.S. West*, published in your town by a well-known public utility. Of publications during 1987, I remember these:

"Amicitia," (excerpt from *Crossing to Safety*). *Sequoia*, Centennial Issue, Vol. 31, No. 1, Dec. 1986. pp. 16–25.

"The Indian Voice," Review of James Welch, *Fools Crow*, and William Weaver, *Red Earth, White Earth*. *The World and I*, Vol. 2, No. 3, March 1987. pp. 397–401.

"Vision of Light," *Art and Antiques*, April 1987, pp. 101–105.

"La Citta del Vivere," traduzione di E. Tosques e E. Pellegrini. Stilema. Inverno 1987. Vallecchi Editore, Firenze. (A translation of the story "City of the Living.")

Angolo di Riposo. Traduzione di Edward Tosques e Ernestina Pellegrini. Vallecchi Editore, Firenze, 1987.

Crossing to Safety. Random House, New York, 1987.

"The Spoiling of the American West," *Michigan Quarterly Review*, Vol. 26, No. 2, Spring 1987. (A version of this also in *Los Angeles Times*, Sunday, May 31, 1987.)

"The Function of Aridity," *Wilderness*, Fall 1987.

The American West as Living Space. University of Michigan Press, 1987.

"What Makes a Westerner?" *American Heritage*, Vol. 38, No. 8. Dec. 1987.

I am working on a couple of stupid articles that I promised months ago, but until I make sure I can write the damned things, I won't even mention their names. In case you are still looking at interviews and articles-about, there have been several of those in connection with *Crossing to Safety*; and T. H. Watkins did an extensive profile of me as an environmentalist called "Typewritten on Both Sides: The Conservation Career of Wallace Stegner," *Audubon*, Sept. 1987, pp. 88–103.

Further than that, deponent sayeth not. Have a wonderful holiday season, snowshoe for exercise, and tell me after the first of the year what you decide to do. If I get any figures on C. to S., I'll pass them on. Our best to Don.

Affectionately,
Wally

« *To: Jackson Benson* • *January 15, 1988* »

Dear Jack,
Your plight at the Hilton reminds me of a time an Iowa writer named Phil Strong and I had to speak at a conference in Iowa City. But it was a hot afternoon, and before our turn came up we went out to a pub and drank two or three fishbowls (a quart each) of Foxhead Ale, which had an alcoholic content of about ten percent. We got a little happy, and had to hurry to the auditorium without proper preparation. I got through my turn early and stepped down, but Phil had to sit on the platform between Norman Foerster and John T. Frederick, each of whom was fairly longwinded. Sitting in the audience by then, I got out to the bath-room three times before Strong's turn to speak came. By the time he stood up he was sweating in marble-sized drops, and he could barely stand up to talk. I never heard a lamer or shorter speech, or heard such explosive relief in the men's room after he escaped. I trust your ordeal was milder.

That copy editor must have come from E. P. Dutton, or attended the same training school. *American Places* had the same kind. She changed all the that's to which's and all the which's to that's, rewrote my sentences, corrected my diction and my dates (invariably into error), and generally made herself lovable. There must be some grudging, envious, deep-seated malignancy among copy editors that makes them want to put their feet on the necks of their betters. Resist!

The week of January 25–29 is O.K. with me. I'm not sure I'll have time to sort out and get to the library any very substantial files, but if I can't get them down there, maybe you can find something to work on up here. There's plenty here; the only problem is to find the right box or file. I'll do my best to get enough ready for you, and I'll save all the time I can that week. I have to talk at a high school on the morning of the 27th, and stay through lunch. Otherwise my calendar doesn't show any extended obligations. Why don't you give me a call on Sunday, or Monday morning if Sunday isn't convenient, and we'll set up some hours.

Best,
Wally

« *To: Nancy Colberg* • *May 1, 1988* »

Dear Nancy,

I'm glad you're reviving somewhat on the bibliography. That is simply too much work to be thrown away.

You ask about Jim Hepworth. I will tell you all I know. I met him first years ago at the University of Arizona when I was making a speech dedicating their new library. He was about to start doing a Ph.D. thesis on me—he still is working on it, I guess, and maybe he will even get it done sometime. He is an enthusiast, a man of great energy, bright, full of ideas and projects. He takes on more and bigger projects than he is likely to be able to carry out, but he carries out more than you'd think he could, at that. He is, as a publisher, intuitive and imaginative and good; his problem is that he has no capital—he operates on a shoestring that is always in danger of breaking. He makes good-looking books and he promotes them shrewdly in the places where he has entrée. Whether he could help you at all with the form of your bibliography I don't know; I'm pretty sure he knows nothing about formal bibliography and cares less; that he would leave the form pretty much up to you. You would have to plan to proof-read very carefully, not because Jim is careless but because he is used to scanning content, not form—much of what he has published is poetry. Whether he could distribute a bibliography of this kind I don't know—you and Don can inquire and probe on that score. I know he could print it, and I know he would push it with enthusiasm, for he is a faithful admirer of Stegner, and he's ambitious to incorporate Stegner into the plans he has for himself and his press. He does know my work better, much better, than any other publisher you might find. And it could be that when you weigh him against some university press that might be interested—Utah let us say—you would decide he is the better bet. Check with him on his distribution system, what access he has to a sales force, and especially how he would expect to get the book into the libraries that will surely be its principal buyers.

That won't make your decision for you, but it may give you some idea.

Enthusiasm and commitment may be better than a well-known colophon. Personally I would be happy to see you go with Jim, but that's only because I know of his enthusiasm, and I like him. You'll have to make the decision on grounds more important to yourself.

Here, no news except aging skeletons and disintegrating physiologies. Mary has been having a series of ailments, the last of them an infected jaw after some root canal work. Ah, these golden years. You sound frantically busy, as usual. Don't overwork. Get in your trips. Stay in touch.

Best,
Wally

« *To: James Hepworth* • *July 14, 1988* »

Dear Jim,

The Stanford library has photocopied the letters to DeVoto in its archives, and they say the letters are in the mail to me. Since they have not yet arrived, I called the library just now; they will check and call back. One way or other, I will see that they're sent on to you, barring criminal revelations, before we leave here on Saturday morning.

Calling would not help you find my letters—they're wherever I sent them, and wherever the receivers threw them. I have never kept copies.

All I have here is a bunch of letters sent to me. So I cannot Xerox five million, or five thousand, or even five, for your edification.

I'm distressed that you seem to be at war with Tom Watkins, Dick Etulain, and other certified Stegner scholars. Charity, that's the word.

When you make errors, and you will, you will be grateful if the discoverer lets you know gently.

Which brings up the matter of your letter to Mary Lewis Bowen.

I confess I was not amused. I was distressed. Over a long lifetime, a lot of perfectly decent and well-meaning people have confused me with Wallace Stevens, or even with Wallace Sterling, the late President of Stanford. It is not an offense worthy of the stocks or the whipping post; most probably it is an inadvertent slip of the pen. And though I know your letter was prompted by generous indignation that not everybody in the world knows my name and principal works, and grants me Nobel status in the pantheon, I think your letter was a little hard on an office flunkey. Leave me to Heaven, as Hamlet said of his mother. God's justice is a little slow, but it's sure. By the year 2088 I will be in the textbooks a minor forerunner of the Western literary outburst. No reason to burst blood vessels trying to update the event.

From here on until October 12 we'll be in Greensboro, Vermont. Now back to that bicycle therapy and deep knee bends.

Yours,

Wally

« *To: James Hepworth* • *July 30, 1988* »

Dear Jim,

This is to clear the air before I descend into the caverns and grind out six month's work in six weeks. I wasn't seriously upset by your letter to Mary Lewis Bowen, but I get a little embarrassed when misguided people like you try to sell me to the world as the answer to all maidens' prayers. Maybe I don't like that reiteration of the fact that some people don't know my name. Anyway, let's forget it.

Of course, use the letters—publish them that is—in your dissertation. And Edith is of course Edith Mirrielees, who was very fond of Benny and sometimes acted as his comforter.

I'm glad you're not at war with Tom Watkins, who is a very good guy and who shares your delusion that I am a fine writer. I wish you'd now extend the peace pipe to Dick Etulain, who is also a good guy, did not kill Nancy's bibliography with Nebraska, and did not encourage Mary Ellen Williams Walsh (does she need four names before she'll believe she exists?) to publish that scurrilous and irresponsible piece about me. That was all the doing of the fellow at Cal State Northridge, whose name I have Freudianly forgotten. If I am going to develop a claque, how can I be at peace with my greatness if my supporters are all shooting each other like splinter-groups of Lebanese and Palestinians?

Your conference in the Wallowas put you in the company of some good people—Al Josephy, Jim Welch, Bill Kittredge are all friends of mine and deserving of great attention for what they know and can do. But I'm sorry to hear about your grandfather. Being a grandfather myself, I try to reconcile myself to my coming crucifixion, death, burial, resurrection, and deification, but I curse the sun every morning that makes me get up and dress. Putting on my goddam socks is getting to be something I can barely do, reaching down there blindly with a coat hanger to get them started.

As you will one day discover for yourself. May the discovery be delayed.

Onward and upward,
Wally

« *To: Jackson Benson* • *September 9, 1988* »

Dear Jack,

Your summer sounds active and idyllic. Whenever I have a summer like that I wonder why I don't make it permanent. Of course Mary will talk to you when you come, whenever that is. It wouldn't be very successful if you tried to come before November 1, though. We won't be back from Colorado until Oct. 21 or 22, and there'll be a week of cleaning out and gathering up and throwing away for both of us, and me personally, I will have two deadlines to meet and a couple of bookstores to talk in right around the first week of November. Mary, who is better organized than I am, should be ready earlier, given her health.

There are more papers if you're still game—files on books and stories done during the last twelve years or so, and personal files that I'll have to look through to eliminate all love letters and incriminating evidence and damaging information on my friends and colleagues. (I might remove a couple of letters.) No biographer should know everything, or how do we spell sanctuary? Incidentally, did you see Joyce Carol Oates' review of some tell-it-all biographer in the next-to-last *Times Book Review*? I am not Ms. Oates' greatest admirer, but she had it straight this time. And while I'm on that subject, I wrote a 10,000 word autobiography this summer for some sort of reference book to be published by the Gale Research Company. This you can look at, uncensored, when we get together. There is also a pretty autobiographical introduction to six stories that will be published as a hand-set, laid-paper, $300 job by the Yolla Bolly Press. Of course you will have to buy the book to see that. Biography is expensive.

Now back to work on a lecture on the future of the West. I am not quite sure whether I will be repeating the obvious or unscrewing the inscrutable.

The days draw in, the color begins (not very good this year), the nights get down close to or below freezing. When I have fears that I may cease to be before my pen can glean my teeming brain I wonder how I ever got into this rat-race. If I had lived a good normal respectable life I would have been loafing for the last fifteen years, with no more concern than the adequacy of my woodpile. But here I am writing lectures and preparing seminars for the University of Colorado, and writing a lit'ry speech for the New York Public Library, and writing another talk for the Dartmouth Bookstore and some Berkeley bookstore and the Stanford Bookstore, and the morning is gorgeous and my good wife would like to drive up to Lake Willoughby. Compromise: I will take her at eleven AM.

No bear tracks here. But last fall Page and Lynn saw one go down the path sixty feet from our south windows, so I can hold my own in tales of surmounted danger. And I've got a bear track preserved in plaster of paris on our coffee table.

Best,

Wally

« *To: Jackson Benson* • *May 6, 1990* »

Dear Jack,

Thanks for the clipping about Carvel Collins.[17] I hadn't seen any notice of his death, and I'm glad to know, though it's sad. Poor Carvel. He should be an object lesson to you. Ever since I first knew him, when we were both instructors at Harvard, he was gathering data for that Faulkner book—going down to Jackson every vacation, filling 5x5 cards, photographing thousands of pages of stuff, using every opportunity and excuse to keep from finishing his book. Finishing it? Starting it. I knew another one like that. "Dock" Marston, who was gathering data for the book on the Colorado River, its history, exploration, flow, topography, geology, wildlife, and tourist future, for more than twenty years. He died without ever writing anything but a few short pieces, and left a vast Berkeley basement full of filing cases of his gleanings. Now I don't want you to hurry, because this book is not supposed to be written until after I have been scattered over a Vermont hill. But I don't want my heirs to have to wait as long as Faulkner's, or students of the Colorado, while geologic time works itself out. Hey?

You didn't assault me in San Diego. It was refreshing to see a familiar face. Crowds of strangers like that scare me. Your petite assistant, however, would not have scared me at all, no matter what she said. I leer pretty good. And it was very nice finally to meet your wife.

---

17. Collins was a colleague of Stegner's at Harvard during the late 1930s and early 1940s.

We just drove down this morning from North Star, where our grandson was married yesterday. I am full of Mexican food (cinco de mayo, after all) and good will and grandfatherly benevolence, but suffering a little from a shrunken bank balance, which is worse than a distended bladder or an atrophied thyroid.

Now to write a speech for May 25, a speech for June 19, a foreword, and an article, and then by God I am going to Vermont where falls not rain nor hail nor any snow, nor ever phone rings loudly.

I hope you have a good, productive, but decorously unhurried summer. You have my Greensboro address, I'm sure. The telephone number, unless I have forgotten, is . . . I have forgotten. Write me a postcard, here before July 1, if you have to.

Best,
Wally

« *To: Nancy Colberg* • *June 24, 1990* »

Dear Nancy,

Just a line in great haste before some people descend on us for a drink, to say how sorry we are that you're having to look forward, dimly I suppose since you're looking at all, to a cataract operation. You're too young for that. Stop that proofreading.

As I guess you've already done. The word I have from Hepworth is upbeat, though as always a little behind schedule. Some day when he gets his pieces all in place he will go through a project like this like the grace of God through a Church of Christ Sunday School. He deserves better financial support, and maybe some time will find it. I look forward to seeing your joint effort sometime before we come back from Vermont, which will be around the middle of October.

I suppose Jim has told you that the *Paris Review* has finally decided to print the interview they bought from him several years ago. I have just worn out my old eyes updating the damned thing—I think the initial interview was a good ten years ago. Patched a little, it runs all right.

The Utah trip that you both threatened to come to and then chickened out at the price tag, as I would have too, was actually very pleasant, though strenuous. I had a hip go blooey on me about a month ago, and by the time we got to Salt Lake the Indocin and other pills they gave me for the hip had gnawed my stomach away and given me a good hot ulcer. So I came back in a basket, more or less, and have been sipping milk and taking de-acidifiers ever since. I will live. One thing we saw in Salt Lake was the first 15 minutes of Steve Fisher's film, which seemed to us quite good, with only a couple of misrepresentations. Those can be fixed, since all he had to show was a preliminary tape. Maybe it will make the screen just about the time your bibliography does.

We leave for Vermont on July 11. Take care of yourself this summer, and treat your eyes well. Fortunately, friends who have gone through that tell me that it is nothing like as unpleasant as it used to be, and that it is almost always miraculously successful. You will take one look at me on my cane and say, "My God, did I work seven years for that?"

Whether you regret it or not, I'm grateful.

    Yours,

    Wally

« *To: Jackson Benson* • *October 17, 1990*

Dear Jack,

In memory of the late lamented earthquake, I will dedicate this note to you.

So far as we could discover in Greensboro, nobody found you repulsive, everybody enjoyed talking to you, and everybody was eager to read what they told you when you finally write it. I think if you and your wife come back, you will even be welcomed. We will subscribe to that general welcome. I'm only sorry we couldn't be there when you were; we might have been able to illuminate a few corners.

The reason we weren't very close to getting there when you did was that my hip began to disintegrate, and to cure the hip they fed me anti-inflammatory drugs, which ate my stomach out. I found myself one morning on the kitchen floor with my pajamas full of black blood. Mary called the doctor, the doctor called 911, the yard filled up with fire engines and ambulances, and I rode in state from here to Emergency, and in a gurney, after while, from Emergency to Intensive Care. Very dramatic, considering I didn't even know I was sick. These days, they don't give you many transfusions—AIDS, I guess, as well as hepatitis—so having lost two and a half quarts of blood, I was given back two pints, and I spent the summer manufacturing the balance and getting my blood count up from 8 to 14. It should be 16, and will be, I trust, but the old bone marrow is not a speed demon. At least I'm past the period of severe anemia, when I fell asleep an hour after breakfast, and two or three times in the afternoon, and slept like a corpse for nine hours at night. It was not, as you can imagine, a productive summer, except in hemoglobin.

I hope you and Dick Etulain[18] have buried the hatchet. I like Bob Utley,[19] but I doubt that everybody should write like him. So far as I'm concerned, you're on your own.

Now to nibble and gnaw my way through the vast pile of paper—books, broadsides, appeals, magazines, annual reports, etc.—that accumulated while we were away. Pray for me, as I will for you.

Yours,
Wally

« To: Jackson Benson • August 20, 1992 »

Dear Jack,

I don't know whether you're still up on the mountain or back down in the desert, but I'll try the home address on the theory that if you aren't there, the mail service is up to forwarding.

I've got two questions, or rather, one favor and one question. First, the PEN West office in Los Angeles, Sherrill W. Britton, Executive Director, has written and then called, wanting to give me some kind of award—a Freedom-to-Write Award, it says——for turning down the President's National Medal.[20] This event will happen on October 4, and I have two reasons why I can't be there. The first is that I'm in every-other-day traction for a bum back, and may be for the next six weeks, and I don't want to risk a relapse by traveling anywhere. The second is that, even if the

---

18. Richard Etulain, emeritus Professor of History at the University of New Mexico, and author of many works on the American West, including *Conversations with Wallace Stegner on Western History and Literature*.

19. Robert Utley, Western historian and author of numerous works on the American Indian, including *The Lance and the Shield* (New York, Henry Holt & Co., 1993).

20. In a letter dated May 17, 1992, Stegner responded to Ms. Susan Houston at the National Endowment for the Arts declining the National Medal for the Arts for which he had been selected by President George Herbert Walker Bush. He did so to protest the firing of the NEA director, John Frohnmayer, and the institution of a "decency oath" imposed upon the NEA by its congressional and administration enemies.

See following letter to Benson dated September 12, 1992, and letter to Susan Houston, p. 289.

back gets all healed and I can travel, I'll have to go to Bozeman, Montana, where they are installing a chair in Western American Studies named for me, and where in all dutiful conscience I ought to be for the opening. In either case, I have told Sherrill Britton that I can't be in L.A. on October 4. She then asked if there was someone in the Los Angeles region who could appear and accept this award for me. God help me, you're the only friend I have in L.A., and I gave her your name and told her to try you, that you might be able to. If you can't, it's no great problem. If I can do without the national medal, I can do without the Refuses-National-Medal awards. But it's nice of them to want to do this, and if there would be anything in it for you (free drinks?), and if your heart feels especially swollen with goodwill, you can tell Sherrill B. when she calls or writes.

The question is simpler. How are you doing with the Oklahoma Press book? The reason I ask is that two people, one of them competent and the other a good deal better than that, have asked me in the last three months about doing some kind of book about me. I told them I had given the green light to you, and that I couldn't very well help your competitors with access to papers, etc. The better of the two is very hot to go to work, and keeps calling me. It would be handy to know where you stand, and what kind of time table you're working on. If you're a long way from the end, it might be that a sort of critical book, not a biography, could be allowed this gent. Actually I couldn't prevent him, but if I don't cooperate I can make it difficult for him. He is not talking about a biography, in any case. But I don't think you would want even a critical book coming out before or in conjunction with yours. Or maybe you wouldn't care. Just let me know if you can tolerate traffic or if you'd like a clear right of way.

I hope your summer was productive and pleasant. Ours, between the back and the Vermont season-without-a-summer, was pretty lousy till we got back here. It improves now.

Best,
Wally

« To: Jackson Benson • September 12, 1992 »

Dear Jack,

Here's a little spiel that you might want to read to the PEN meeting. I'm very grateful to you for taking this on. At the moment, I am not moving around much between sessions with the rack-and-thumbscrew folks at the therapy center. I guess the back improves—sometimes I think so, sometimes I wonder. But it won't stand much standing or sitting, nothing much of the same position for any length of time, and I'm not willing to risk surgery just for the gratification of hearing my noble stand applauded.

Carry on. Noble purposes must some day come to noble ends. And thanks again.

Best,

Wally

To the members of PEN Center West:

I deeply appreciate your action in giving me your Freedom-to-Write award. At the same time, I am sorry to receive it, for you give it to me because I refused the National Medal of the National Endowment for the Arts, and that was something I was not happy to have to do.

My quarrel was not with the National Endowment itself. I have respected the people I have known in that organization, and respected the job they have done. Twice before, when offered an NEA award, I have accepted gratefully. My problem this time was with the domination exerted over the NEA by its reactionary congressional and administration enemies. After Mr. Bush permitted and abetted the interference by political philistines, I could not imagine accepting any medal from his hand.

I believe that government should support the arts. I also believe that its function stops with support—it has no business trying to direct or censor them. Art must be left to the artists. If they sometimes make mistakes, or press too hard, or test too strenuously the boundaries of the accepted, that is part of the commitment and the excitement: creation by definition deals with what has not yet been made. The creation of any art is three quarters error. As Lewis Thomas said, it was only by making mistakes that mankind blundered toward brains.

I refused the NEA medal because the political and self-righteous right would not leave the NEA alone to do its job, and I thought the point could be made more persuasively by someone like me, who had never suffered rejection and could not be charged with sour grapes, than by someone disgruntled by refusal of a grant. I just wish I had not felt I had to do it. I hope nobody has to do it again. I hope the NEA can be allowed to help us make our necessary mistakes and create the things we dream of making. PEN Center West is one of the groups that may help bring that situation about. I am happy to be one of you, and grateful for your moral support.

Sincerely,

Wallace Stegner

« *To: Jackson Benson* • *October 8, 1992* »

Dear Jack,

Alas, poor Yorick. I saddled you with a pain-in-the-neck favor, I'm afraid,[21] and I'm very grateful that you could do it, and did it, and that apparently you don't now hate my guts for asking it. I think of you and Los Angeles and all that mess of 15 million folks down there as all in one pot, and I forgot that you had to buck the traffic to get there. Thanks, thanks.

Thanks, too, for the award package and the program. I'm pleased to see that both Random and Viking got out front and center. Actually I wish we had been able to come to the ceremony, which reads as if it should have been interesting. But it's just as well that I didn't, or couldn't. Instead, we went up to Bozeman, Montana, where Montana State was dedicating an endowed chair in Western Studies in my name. Fine weather, nice people, good preparations, everything set. So I collapse on the stage after fifteen minutes and they lug me off feet first to the emergency hospital, slap me into a monitor, tape an IV into my wrist, feel my pulse, lift my eyelids and peek at my eyeballs, and generally act as if I were about to croak. I felt that way myself, but really all I had was an acute attack of intestinal flu, complete with nausea and a blood pressure of about 500/200 that immediately went into something about 100/50. We were supposed to go up to a mountain inn that night. Instead, we slept in the bed of the university president, freezing out the golden lab that usually sleeps there, and the next day drove with friends to their ranch at Fishtail, over on the West Rosebud, where we convalesced. Before we got home, Mary had the bug too, and we're both rubber-legged yet. It would have been un desastro de la guerra if I'd been in L.A. and done a George Bush in the lap of the emcee.

You ask about the award. It's a very attractive quartz clock—desk clock I guess, which is what I'll use it for, anyway—with a brass plate on it saying

---

21. On Stegner's behalf, Benson accepted the PEN Center West Freedom-to-Write Award.

PEN U.S. West, and Freedom-to-Write Award, and my name. If they'd been on their toes they'd have added Courtesy Jackson Benson, by hand. I will show it to you proudly next time you come up.

So thank you once again. I owe you some favors, some postage, some undistributed goodwill, and I will find some means of retaliation. God grant us all our heart's desire on November 5.

Best,
Wally

Reflections on the Works

To Norman Foerster, October 15, 1957	(*Remembering Laughter*)
To Walter Harding, July 14, 1940	(*On a Darkling Plain*)
To Susan Parkinson, May 6, 1956	(*The Big Rock Candy Mountain*)
To Forrest Robinson, November 19, 1972	(*The Preacher and the Slave*)
To Carl Brandt, October 17, 1953	(*Wolf Willow*)
To Harold P. Jones, December 26, 1953	(*Wolf Willow*)
To Mrs. Grant Carlton, January 7, 1957	(*Wolf Willow*)
To Malcolm Cowley, June 6, 1960	(*A Shooting Star*)
To An Unidentified Query	(*Angle of Repose*)
To Mrs. Tyler Micoleau, March 3, 1970	(*Angle of Repose*)
To Blake Green, September 16, 1976	(*Angle of Repose*)
To Jackson Benson, June 26, 1982	(*Crossing to Safety*)
To Carl Brandt, May 4, 1985	(*Crossing to Safety*)
To Carl Brandt, July 7, 1985	(*Crossing to Safety*)
To Carl Brandt, May 4, 1986	(*Crossing to Safety*)
To Carl Brandt, June 16, 1986	(*Crossing to Safety*)
To Carl Brandt, July 25, 1986	(*Crossing to Safety*)
To Carl Brandt, November 29, 1986	(*Crossing to Safety*)
To Charles Schlessinger, February 11, 1988	(*Crossing to Safety*)
To Carl Brandt, April 5, 1988	(*Crossing to Safety*)
To Carl Brandt, May 10, 1985	(short stories)
To Carl Brandt, January 2, 1989	(short stories)
To Carl Brandt, February 10, 1989	(short stories)
To Sam Vaughan, June 15, 1989	(short stories)
To Carl Brandt, April 10, 1990	(short stories)
To Carl Brandt, May 30, 1985	(essays)
To Carl Brandt, January 24, 1991	(essays)
To Carl Brandt, February 10, 1991	(essays)
To Carl Brandt, July 16, 1991	(essays)
To Avis DeVoto, February 21, 1968	(*The Uneasy Chair*)
To Avis DeVoto, March 5, 1968	(*The Uneasy Chair*)
To Avis DeVoto, May 10, 1968	(*The Uneasy Chair*)
To Avis DeVoto, March 15, 1971	(*The Uneasy Chair*)
To Avis DeVoto, August 18, 1971	(*The Uneasy Chair*)
To Avis DeVoto, February 9, 1974	(*The Uneasy Chair*)
To Avis DeVoto, February 26, 1974	(*The Uneasy Chair*)
To Avis DeVoto, March 26, 1974	(*The Uneasy Chair*)
To Avis DeVoto, January 20, 1977	(*The Uneasy Chair*)

Works by Wallace Stegner

Fiction
Remembering Laughter (1937)
The Potters House (1938)
On a Darkling Plain (1940)
Fire and Ice (1941)
The Big Rock Candy Mountain (1943)
Second Growth (1947)
The Women on the Wall (1950)
The Preacher and the Slave (1950)
The City of the Living (1956)
A Shooting Star (1961)
All the Little Live Things (1967)
Angle of Repose (1971)
The Spectator Bird (1976)
Recapitulation (1979)
Crossing to Safety (1987)
Collected Stories (1990)

Nonfiction
Clarence Edward Dutton: An Appraisal (1935)
Mormon Country (1942)
One Nation (1945)
Beyond the Hundredth Meridian (1954)
Wolf Willow (1962)
The Gathering of Zion (1965)
The Sound of Mountain Water (1969)
Discovery: The Search for Arabian Oil (1971)
The Uneasy Chair (1974)
The Letters of Bernard DeVoto (1975)
American Places (with Page Stegner, 1981)
One Way to Spell Man (1982)
The American West as Living Space (1987)
Where the Bluebird Sings to the Lemonade Springs (1992)
Marking the Sparrow's Fall (1998)
On Creative Writing (2004)

• • •

« *To: Norman Foerster*[1] • *October 15, 1957* »

Dear Mr. Foerster:

It was very very kind of you to write, at length, about the book.[2] I was naturally flattered at the kind things you had to say, since I know of no one whose praise I would rather deserve. And I have been thinking about your comments on the ethical backbone of the book—or the lack of it. When I first began to write it, my sole and paramount aim was to create a situation which was hopelessly tangled, in which three lives got themselves so snarled that only a major miracle could un-snarl them, but a situation in which no one of the three was really wholly to blame. Even before Vardis Fisher's tetralogy, I felt that those lines of Meredith's were about the wisest in English poetry. Generally speaking, no villain need be, and no villain is. What is false within is enough to ruin almost any life. But here I see the point of your criticism: In making no one really to blame, I perhaps laid a little too much stress on what was false within Margaret, and not enough on what was false in Alec and Elspeth. I must confess that the sins of the natural man are a little more agreeable to me than the sins of the theologians. But I did not really mean to imply that the two lovers were pure Arcadians and couldn't be charged with their own acts. No one in this book is really to blame for the situation, but all are partially to blame and I meant to say so. It seems that I didn't. Yet neither am I quite ready to say that human weakness should be held to as strict accounting as human viciousness, if there is such a thing as the latter. There is plenty of room for tolerance and pity, even though they have to exist side by side with disapproval.

All this is proving is that I don't know what I think. But of one thing I have become convinced since I first came to Iowa. There is much to be said for what you humanists call "vital control," though no man, even Goethe, who seems to me the best humanist of you all, has control of himself at all times. That is where the pity comes in, and the botching of men's lives. That is the sort of situation I meant to present in the book, but that book isn't by any means as sound as it might be. It's cluttered up with echoes

---

1. Foerster was Stegner's Ph.D. director at the University of Iowa.
2. Stegner's first novel, *Remembering Laughter*, which won the Little, Brown novelette prize in 1937.

and conventionalities (probably the puritan-baiting is one of these), and it doesn't say exactly what my position is.

In my application for a Guggenheim the other day, I outlined a long novel which I hope will make that position a little more clear. The principal thesis of the work-in-progress is similar but I hope the edges will come a little cleaner. In this book, which I shall naturally write whether I get the Guggenheim or not, a man goes through a process of more than thirty years of degeneration, until he winds up completely vicious, completely selfish, and half mad. The villain might by some be called an unfavorable and washed-up frontier environment. I rather think the villain is again something false within, and that what is false is a complete inability at inner control. I used to take great joy in defining the humanist as "the man with the whoa." In the case of this character a good strong whoa would probably have kept him out of the gutter and made his life not only more productive but infinitely more happy. I am still naturalist enough to see the effects of a bad environment, but I imagine that I have become humanist enough, or sensible enough, to see that discipline is more than a mere word beloved of grade-school teachers.

The outline which I made for the Guggenheim people had to be done in a rush, and I'm afraid it is a bit garbled. But when that book is written I wish you would read it and tell me what you think. If it still lacks an ethical backbone, then I'm hopelessly lost to the cause of virtue, because I've been writing that novel in my head for a dozen years, and it will have more of my own faiths in it than any book I may write after it.

Sincerely,
Wallace Stegner

« *To: Walter Harding* • *July 14, 1940* »

Dear Mr. Harding:
If you were hoping for indications of direct borrowing from Thoreau in *On a Darkling Plain* I'm afraid my answer is going to be a little disappointing.[3]

---

3. Walter Harding was a professor at the University of North Carolina, interested in Thoreau's influence on fiction. He wrote Stegner a letter in July 1940 asking if "there might be an influence of Thoreau's philosophy upon the book [*On A Darkling Plain*] and if Thoreau might "have been in your mind as you were writing it."

The story is, naturally, a composite of a good many things. I don't know that it's worth anybody's while to sort them out, but here they are, roughly: a basis of real experience (I lived in Saskatchewan for six years, knew a person approximately like Vickers, went through the flu epidemic, and so on); a good salting of Arnold's schoolteacher pessimism which impressed me with its truth without convincing me of its usefulness or applicability in ordinary life; a walking trip in Vermont on which I had the double experience of reading MacLeish (in particular his favorite image of the world wheeling from light into dark: "You, Andrew Marvell") and experiencing something of the same feeling myself. That double-exposure recalled memories of how the light came and went during my childhood on the Saskatchewan prairie, and the weight of a pack on my back recalled Vickers, who used to walk forty miles and back for supplies, and the whole congeries of sensory impressions and memories brought up the general idea of solitude on the bare back of a continent. It is a difficult thing to say where a book begins, but I think that is where this one began, even though I had used the returned veteran and the flu epidemic before. I had written my first novel about the flu epidemic, and burned it; then I had written a short story about Vickers, killing him of flu, and destroyed that; then I had taken the last part of that story, added things to it, and made it into a story simply of Vickers' death and burial. That didn't sell. So when I came finally to the writing of the novel I incorporated the burial piece into it, and it was published in that form in *Redbook*; in the final version I transposed the burial scene and gave it to Ina, and generously allowed Vickers to live. The result is that the final version of the book contains practically nothing of the things I had previously written in an attempt to get around the material.

This tells you nothing of possible Thoreau influence, but I am trying to think back upon the writing of the book to see if I can see any myself. I can't see any direct impetus from Thoreau, since I hadn't been reading him at the time and so far as I can remember didn't think of him until, with the manuscript piling up, I recognized the essential problem as the Thoreauvian dilemma. Naturally I have read Thoreau, and inevitably he has impressed me very greatly. Probably my admiration for him had something to do with the attraction of the gathering theme of *Darkling Plain*. His disgust with certain sides of human society is easy to agree with in 1940, and easy and perhaps mistaken imitations of his primitivism are tempting. I have a feeling that in this novel I have been labeling myself a pessimistic meliorist, and I have an uncomfortable conviction that Thoreau wouldn't go all the way with my solution of the problem. But all that is after the fact; before I wrote the book I wasn't consciously aware that I was invading Walden.

Perhaps it is best to put it this way: Even though I did not consciously walk in Thoreau's footsteps in the novel, I immediately recognized what I had done when it began to take shape. And that may be significant for your general topic of Thoreau's influence on fiction. He is certainly a fountainhead in American thought and American writing of that incorrigible independence, that isolated human atom fighting for its toehold in eternity, that we look back on now with nostalgia. The problem changes when the atoms get too thick, but the impulses are still there.

So bracket me, if you choose. I am certainly influenced by Thoreau; I hunt up the most remote backwoods farm in Vermont to spend my summers on; I write things that have the inescapable stamp of his influence on them. Call it a pervasive rather than a specific influence, and I am ready to agree that *Darkling Plain* stems from Walden. It's a poor thing, but mine own, and I rather like the idea of its having distinguished ancestors.

Sincerely,
Wallace Stegner

« *To: Miss Susan Parkinson* • *May 6, 1956* »

Dear Susan:[4]
The question that you have been debating in your class is one of a kind that better heads than any of ours have failed to settle. I suspect that both sides are partly right—in fact, I know they are. You and your classmates are right in assuming that I was writing about things I had known and seen when I was a boy in Canada; your teacher and your textbook were right in that I dressed up the facts somewhat. It would take a long time to separate the fiction from the non-fiction in a story like this, but here are some hints:

The story, as you may know, was written in the first place as a chapter of the novel *The Big Rock Candy Mountain*. That means that the boy (who is I, clearly enough) was put into a family not mine. His relations with his

---

4. Susan Parkinson was a schoolgirl in Waynesburg, Pennsylvania who wrote Stegner on behalf of her class with questions regarding his short story, "Two Rivers." Characteristically, he wrote a thoughtful, non-condescending reply.

mother and father were conditioned by things I invented for the purposes of the novel, and both before this episode and after it the fictional elements thicken a good deal. But just through here, nevertheless, there is a good deal of almost straight autobiography, somewhat scrambled. The incident of the snake happened to my father, brother, and me on a drive to Chinook, Montana; the car that would not start (which just precedes "Two Rivers" and is told in a chapter-story called "Goin' to Town"), was the thing that missed me a Fourth of July celebration when I was nine or so. The look of the country, the mountains breaking the horizon to the south, the dog, even the memories of earlier childhood in Washington, are all as they were. But I regret to tell you, in case you laid any bets on this with your teacher, that the trip to the mountains never did come off. We talked plenty about it, but we never made it. So I took myself there thirty years later by imagination. The mountains I was describing, and the canyon we went up, pretend to be the Bearpaws. Actually they are Mill Creek Canyon in the Wasatch, back of Salt Lake City.

So you can divide the bets, or call them off. I quite honestly don't quite know where fiction ends and non-fiction begins, in my own stories or anyone else's.

Sincerely,

Wallace Stegner

« *To: Forrest Robinson* • *November 19, 1972* »

Dear Forrest:

I see your predicament. It's neither unusual nor, for my selfish purposes, particularly serious. I'll either make the suggestion to someone else, or let Bill Hogan pursue his own obscure way, which will probably be that of least resistance. But if I happen to see him, and the question does come up, I'm glad to know you'll do the review if asked. We'll have to leave it there for now.

I haven't seen the *Joe Hill* film. From what I have heard, it is a sentimentalizing and myth-making exercise, in the best tradition. Martyrs are queer phenomena. Under some circumstances I suppose Bruce Franklin could be built into one. Or George Wallace. Remember Horst Wessel?[5] A

---

5. Horst Wessel joined the Nazi party in 1926 and was killed by political enemies in 1930. Elevated to the status of martyr, his song became the official Nazi anthem.

Blackshirt goon killed in a street brawl. So out of him, like honey out of the dead lion Samson strangled, comes forth the Horst Wessel Lied, to which thousands marched and died.

When I was writing *Joe Hill*, first writing it, I was attracted by that there of the songs people died to. I thought Joe Hill probably was a victim and a martyr. The more I dug into the history, which was thin, and the more people I found who had authentically known Joe Hill (they were seven), the more I came to believe he was a thug with revolutionary sympathies. So I steered the book between the two possibilities and let the reader make up his own mind, which was probably bad strategy. The sources I used mainly were the several histories of the IWW; the letters and reminiscences of Ralph Chaplain, who conducted Joe Hill's funeral in Chicago and was in large part responsible for bulling up the legend; the recollections of the seven who had personally known Joe Hill, especially Harry McClintock, "Haywire Mac," an old saloon and early radio busker who first sang "Pie in the Sky" on Burnside Street in Portland when Joe Hillstrom brought it into the Wobbly hall on the back of a laundry ticket; the records of Joe's trial, since vanished except for the second half, which I put with other materials in the Hoover Library; the Salt Lake newspapers of the trial period; the memories of the family Joe Hill was said to have robbed in their grocery store, who were acquaintances of mine in Salt Lake; the Swedish vice consul in Salt Lake, an old tennis opponent of mine; the sheriff who commanded the firing squad; and the warden of the Utah State Penitentiary, who walked me through an execution routine from death row to the backstopped chair in the back alley of the prison.

As for biography, or autobiography: *The Big Rock Candy Mountain* and *Wolf Willow*, especially the latter, are the closest to autobiography, and they of course cover only a limited period. *All the Little Live Things* uses my house up here, but little else. I wrote a piece on growing up in Salt Lake City, once—it's in *The Sound of Mountain Water*—"At Home in the Fields of the Lord." That's about it. There is neither much biography nor much criticism available. Sinclair Lewis wrote a little piece on me in *Esquire* once. There have been various appraisals in western regional magazines—Ray West in *The Rocky Mountain Review*, a couple of pieces in the *South Dakota Review*. Howard Mumford Jones wrote a fairly extended essay for my German publishers, but I think it was never printed in English. There have been pieces in *Der Spiegel*. Charles Snow has written some highly pleasant reviews. But for biography you'd better depend on the tapes, and we can do those when you want—late spring is fine with me.

Best,

Wally

And yes, I'd be interested to see your review of *Hawks and Harriers*.[6]

« *To: Carl Brandt* • *October 17, 1953* »

RE: SASKATCHEWAN

My reasons for planning to spend part of this summer in Saskatchewan are partly personal, partly professional. I grew up on the Frenchman River, one of the headwaters of the Milk, which is in turn part of the Missouri system, in the years when this country was first being opened. It was still virgin buffalo grass in 1914, and the town of Eastend did not exist. My family helped found it; our first house was a derailed dining car on the half-built spur of the CPR that came down from Swift Current. The river was full of beaver and muskrat; my first honest dollars were earned trapping muskrat, a few beaver, mink, and ermine along the Frenchman and in the sloughs on the north bench, and my first memory of that town is of coming into it on a stage coach on the lap of a cowpuncher named Buck Murphy, who a few months later was shot off the seat of a democrat wagon and killed by a trigger-happy Mounty. This was, in other words, practically the last real frontier; the town started from scratch, as a thousand American and Canadian towns have started, and developed its institutions and its local history, personalities, lore, from nothing. I want to go back and spend a month or so seeing what forty years of the town's life have come to, and incidentally examining (for personal rather than primarily literary reasons) what the education it gave me amounts to now, in 1953. I want to see how a boyhood like that in a town like that fits a man for the twentieth century; I also want to see how a town on the bald-assed frontier, which was hit by the automotive revolution in its second year and whose patterns have had to change constantly to match a changing world, develops. When I was a boy there, in about 1916, there was a path along the irrigation ditch between our house and the center of town, and at a certain weir and footbridge the path branched three ways: one fork to the schoolhouse, one to the Presbyterian Church, one to the office of

6. Page Stegner, *Hawks and Harriers* (New York:, The Dial Press, 1972).

the Eastend Enterprise. Those were the town's institutions in 1916. Later we got a town-hall-movie-house that in winter was sometimes flooded to double as a skating rink and curling course. The livery stable that briefly rose declined into a garage. The train then came down once a day from Ravenscrag; now the transcontinental highway runs through the town, and undoubtedly has created miracles of change and a fringe of auto courts and trailer camps. The town footbridge, which my father put in every spring and took out every fall before the freeze-up, may or may not still be the center of community swimming; the bath houses where all the town used to dress and undress, and where secret sins sometimes went on, and where in the winter my family hung quarters and halves of frozen beef, may or may not still be there. The river itself may now be drained by irrigation canals and be no more than a trickle in the riverbed. The white clay cliffs may by now be the base of a pottery industry.

And so on. The changes wrought in half a lifetime in a frontier town seem to be interesting in themselves, because they put in a capsule much of the western, or even the American, experience. The country itself is not usually held to be glamorous, but it was once great Indian country, full of Assiniboines and Crees. Sitting Bull fled to the valley of the Frenchman after the Little Big Horn, Chief Joseph of the Nez Perce was on his way there when the dragoons cornered him in the Bearpaws. The coulee rims along the river in my boyhood were dotted with stone signal chimneys, and the Cree used to come through now and then and stay long enough to dry guts from the butcher-shop across the roofs of their brush shanties. When we lived there, the country was actually not much changed from what it was when Lewis and Clark poked through the upper Missouri country in 1806 and 1807. That country was alive with game then. In my time it still was, though the grizzlies were pretty much gone and the antelope were thinning out. As far as small animals go, I suspect it still is densely populated: coyotes, weasels, muskrat and mink and lynx and wildcat in the willow breaks along the rivers, badgers out on the prairies, millions of ducks and geese in the sloughs in the migrating seasons. In other words, I suspect that some of the romance still remains in that part of the high plains, though the same kind of country down in Dakota and Montana is supposed to be dull and uninteresting. It is my somewhat guarded belief that there never was a more interesting country; that its weather is more dramatic than any weather anywhere, and its sky makes up for the monotony of its plains. The plains themselves are as extensive, and quite as impressive, as the ocean, and almost as much life seethes through and across and under them. There is also a history of human (white American) failure to break these plains to the plow, a history in which I participated. I imagine, though I do not know, that hundreds of homesteads, including our own, which was directly on the Saskatchewan–Montana border, are abandoned. The buffalo grass won't have come back; maybe noxious weeds have replaced it—tumbleweed, for instance, which we used to call Russian thistle, and which we watched take over all the roadsides and the fields in a few years between 1916 and 1919.

As for angles, I suppose there are several: Nostalgic Native's Return to changed (or unchanged) Boyhood; more serious textual and photographic examination of how the institutions of village democracy have developed from buffalo grass to the present; socio-economic look at the country itself and its importance if any in the future economy of Canada and the continent; and included in this, perhaps, a grass-roots look at the CCF Party with its modified democratic socialism, and the roots of that semi-socialism in the hard conditions of the arid plains. I shall be looking at all of these aspects of the old home town when I go up, and I can make an article, with pictures, out of any of them.

Wally

« *To: Mr. Harold P. Jones* • *December 26, 1953* »

Dear Corky Jones:

I meant long ago to write and let you know how much I appreciated your letter this summer. I'm afraid I made some people mad by pulling that fool incognito act. My reasons were pretty vague, actually. I suppose some of them were on account of my father's probable reputation in the town, and some of them were very personal; I remembered Eastend so vividly from my childhood, and thought of it, in spite of all the things that I might have remembered unhappily, as such a kid's paradise, that I wanted to come back and look it over without anybody's memories except my own to interfere. But once I got into that incognito I was stuck in it, and I suppose Mrs. Ovre and Mr. Bean were both legitimately annoyed at being lied to. At least they never wrote, and Mr. Bean has never sent the subscription of the enterprise that I asked for. Well—having made a silly mistake, I guess I'm stuck with it.

My intention of writing a kind of village portrait is still with me, though.

It would involve no personalities, but would be, as I told you, concerned primarily with how village institutions—government, schools, recreation, cultural activities, social and religious activities, grow up when a town is built from absolute scratch. I want to put that sort of village portrait alongside one of a New England village whose institutions have been established—in somewhat different patterns—for a couple of hundred years, and then I want to put both of those against a village, say in Denmark which has been stable and steady since maybe the twelfth century. I would have picked an English village except that I think Scandinavia, especially Denmark, has developed more capacity for what you might call "rural culture" than any other part of the world. Denmark rode out the war, in spite of German occupation, with less disruption than any other country in Europe, and that must mean it has something solid. I want to see if we can learn anything from it that can be applied to our own rural life.

That's why I hope I can draw on you for some information, especially since Mr. Bean seems to be sore at me. For instance, was there ever, and is there now, a public library of any kind in Eastend? If so, who got it up, who supported it, how much influence did it have on the town's reading and outlook? You remember we spoke of the fact that you and the man who built the observatory were apparently the only two people in town with persistent cultural interests—and both of you imported them from some more cultivated place. How long would you say it might take for a town like Eastend to develop people with cultural tastes and offer them enough opportunity to practice them so that they wouldn't move on?

It's obvious that no sort of opportunity—economic, social, cultural, or anything else—holds Eastend's young people now. The town exports manpower. Its cultural activities, outside the schools, are the activities of immigrants like you from a more developed society. How long might it take for Eastend to develop some culture of its own that would stick? Is there anything like adult education going on in the town? Any debating societies, reading clubs, photographic or painting groups, ladies' literary clubs? How many people take an interest in your paleontological studies? How many, if any, really worked with the man who built the observatory? What about music in the town? As I remember it thirty-five years ago, music was one activity that was fairly actively supported: there were music teachers for the young, and the town and church and school all sponsored entertainments that included music, and the Chautauqua that came through a time or two was strongly supported. Anything now? Radio?

Anybody buy and play classical records? What response when George Haddad comes through and plays?

These are obviously shotgun questions. But I'd be more than grateful if you could find time to jot down things that you think I might like to know about the town. I have your reminiscences of the early history, before the town proper, and I'd like to know more, but the principal stuff I need is about a real town beginning to shape its institutional life. Probably I'll begin with Lewis and Clark, when they passed the mouth of the Milk River in 1806 or whenever it was, and for the first time ever, white men looked up into the country drained by the Frenchman. But I'll have to pass over that, and the fur brigades, and the cattle ranching times, fairly fast, all as a kind of first chapter. My story properly begins with a few people like you and J.C. Strong and the Cross brothers and others who bridged the gap between ranch and town and pinned it down where it is now.

This has been a long letter. I'll hope that sometime when you haven't much to do you will write me as long a one—or three or four or ten—in return. Mrs. Stegner sends her best with mine, to you and Mrs. Jones.

Sincerely,

Wallace Stegner

« To: Mrs. Grant Carlton • January 7, 1957 »

Dear Cora:

Excuse my addressing you as Cora: that's what I remember you as. You are right that we used to know each other in Eastend. I'm sorry I can't send you the greetings of the rest of my family, but they have all been dead for many years. Cecil died in 1931, my mother in 1933, my father in 1940. I'm glad to know that your family is well; please give them my greetings. It is always pleasant to hear from someone of the Eastend community. Neville Huffman, who you probably remember, is working in San Francisco for Standard Oil, but I have not managed to look him up yet. I intend to in the next few weeks.

Meantime, I wonder if I could ask a favor of you? In the process of writing a book about the last plains frontier, I have been digging a little into the history of the Cypress Hills and of some of the towns around them. I'd like to get as much dope as possible on the people who first came in as homesteaders—where they came from, how much money or property they had when they came, what led them to Saskatchewan, whether they had relatives or friends there or just lighted by accident, how well they did there, how many children they had, how much education the children got, what they do now, where they have moved to (if they have moved), and so on. Do you suppose you could summarize the Brummitts in something like those terms? I won't, of course, be using any of this with names on it—I want mainly to see if I can arrive at any general conclusions on what the effect of that frontier community was on the people who came there. And they came, as you know, from all over. You, I believe, came from England, didn't you?

I have got a good deal of data from Corky Jones, Bill Anderson, and some of the people I used to know as children. But I'm always wanting more, and if you can give me information not only on your family but on other people, particularly the children of about our age, it would be very useful to me. There isn't any hurry, actually, because I can't get back to this book before summer, probably; teaching takes all my time until then.

I enclose a photocopy of the article you say you heard a radio commentator speak about. It isn't much; actually it will be the introduction of the book I'm working on. But maybe it will stir up a gem of nostalgia in you. I find that everybody from Eastend is full of homesickness for the place. And that is a strange thing, isn't it? I remember it better than any place I ever lived.

Best wishes,
Yours,
Wallace Stegner

« To: Malcolm Cowley • June 6, 1960 »

Dear Malcolm,

I meant before this to write and thank you for that good and encouraging letter about Sabrina[7]—I needed the encouragement about then too—but I got your letter just after we came back to Rome from Maratea, where we'd gone to try to cure Mary's bronchitis and get my nose back into joint, and as soon as we got back we had to start getting ready to leave the Academy, and then we had to go to Florence for two or three days (by way of Spoleto,

---

7. The original title of A Shooting Star, published by Viking in 1961, was Sabrina. It was a Literary Guild selection, and enjoyed greater success than any of Stegner's previous work. Nevertheless, he was never very fond of it, and never wanted it reprinted.

Assisi, and Pergugia), and then we were on the road up through Veneto, and shaking down for this cruise back toward Le Havre and San Francisco, but not till it started to rain an hour ago have I had much chance for anything. But I'm just sitting down to put the afternoon and evening in on *Sabrina*, and I'll warm up my typing finger on you.

Don't worry about my killing her off—you were absolutely right about her not being a tragic heroine. I tried it that way and it doesn't work. So I am now trying it another way, and by the time we hit Le Havre late this month I ought to have only some retyping to do. I'll send the MS in from Los Altos in late July or August, and maybe come east around September 1 to talk it over with Marshall[8] et al. It will be better for your comments, I hope and trust. I'm particularly grateful for yours because they reassured me that I wasn't entirely off in what I'd done. I think the book was there in the draft you read, but with some wire edges and unsanded corners. Sabrina is less bitchy now than she was then, but she has to stay somewhat bitchy, or at least be capable of doing bitchy things when she's mad, or she isn't what I want her to be. The diary stuff is shorter, the father I did kill off so he doesn't make the red herring that Marshall smelled (the fact is, I was going to bring him in, and then x-ed him out, and that's why he looks like something that's going to happen). I have somewhat altered Burke, and the relationship between him and Sabrina, and I will have to cobble the ending so it neither seems rushed nor goes into a long anticlimactic decrescendo. The ending is the real problem, but I think I have it.

That's enough of that book: I'm sick sick sick of it by now. Cortina is a better subject. Until it started to rain, it was full of wildflowers, sun, meadows, water, peaks, snow, and general good feeling. We got in a picnic up on the Falzarego Pass before it clouded over. Tomorrow, granted weather, we'll go on over the Gross Glockner and on to Mayrhofen, near Innsbruck, where we'll settle down in some pensione for three days while I work eight or ten hours on the book each day and then walk it off in meadows sweet with hay. Then on to Innsbruck, then Grenoble, then Aix–Arles–Avignon, then Carcassonne, then the Lascaux Caves, then subito to Le Havre to put the car aboard ship, then subito to Paris to fly home over the Pole. If I hurry I can get back in time to watch the Olympic trials in the Stanford stadium, which will probably be better than staying in Rome for the Olympics proper.

---

8. Marshall Best, editor-in-chief at The Viking Press.

As you know, Peter Beagle is one of our next year's fellows. I have been reading his book, which is terrific. If I could only have hung onto Phil Roth we'd have had a red hot infield combination. Anyway you and Muriel will be there, come fall, and that gives us our battery. Me, I'm out in left field.

All the best,

Wally

« *To: An Unidentified Query Concerning the Writing of* Angle of Repose »

Years ago I helped acquire for the Stanford University library the papers of a genteel local color writer and illustrator who had married a mining engineer and lived her life in camps throughout the West, exiled from the art, music, conversation, and cultivated friends she had left behind. Reading her quaintly 19th century letters, I thought her interesting, but certainly not the subject of a novel. She lay around in my mind, an unfertilized egg.

Then at some point it struck me that she had been born in the 1840s and had lived into the 1930s. Her single life spanned the whole curve from the frontier to World War II, and her family spanned the rest of it, clear to the Counter Culture and the New Left. For years I have wondered why no western writer had been able to make a continuity between the past and the present, why so many are sunk in the mythic twilight of horse opera, why the various Wests seem to have produced no culture or literature comparable to those of New England, the South, and the Midwest, why no westerner had managed to do for his territory what Faulkner did for Yoknapatawpha County. Well, here was my chance to give it a try.

That sperm burrowed into the egg. What hatched, after three years, was *Angle of Repose*, a novel about time, about cultural transplantation and change, about the relations of a man with his ancestors and descendants. Through the eyes of my Victorian lady's crippled grandson, it appraises the conflict of openness and change with the Victorian pattern of ingrained responsibility and convention; and in the entangled emotional life of the narrator it finds a parallel for the emotional lesions in the lives of the grandparents. It finds the past in the present, the present in the past; and in the activities of a young and modern secretary-assistant it discovers that the most rebellious aberrations of our times follow paths that our great-grandfathers' feet beat dusty.

Angle of Repose got very complex on me before it was done. It gave me trouble: I had too many papers, recorded reality tied my hands. But a blessed thing happened. In the course of trying to make fiction of a historical personage I discovered, or half created, a living woman in Victorian dress. I forced her into situations untrue to her life history but not, I think, untrue to the human probabilities that do not depend on time or custom. In the end I had to elect to be true to the woman rather than to the historical personage. And I had to discover that time seen through quadrifocal glasses—past, present, future, and one other that I will not define—presents an astonishingly single image.

« *To: Mrs. Tyler Micoleau* • *March 3, 1970* »

Dear Janet:

Probably you thought I was dead, paralyzed, struck dumb, or otherwise incapacitated. I am none of those. I am only slow as a sinful conscience. The novel is now somewhere past page 500, with still the whole last section to go. I estimate that if I dive into my burrow and pull the hole in after me I can finish it by May, or the end thereof. Some parts of it I like a good deal. But as I warned you, the process of making a novel from real people has led me to bend them where I had to, and you may not recognize your ancestors when I get through with them. On the other hand, I have availed myself of your invitation to use the letters and reminiscences as I pleased, and so there are passages from both in my novel, stolen outright. Not long passages: a paragraph at a time at most. But even this selective theft raises some questions, especially since I had a call last week from Rodman Paul, a remote relative of yours I think, with that name. He is the man who got Mr. Hague to put the Hague papers in the Huntington. He tells me now that Mr. Hague has put up the money to see your grandmother's Reminiscences published by the Huntington Library, with an introduction by Rod Paul. I presume you know all about this.

Me, I think it is a splendid idea, and a publication long past due. But I am troubled about one thing. You suggested that I not use real names in any of my book, since what I am writing is not history or biography, but fiction. I agreed with that. But if the Reminiscences are now to be published, it won't take much literary detective work to discover what family I am basing my story on. It wouldn't have been difficult anyway for anyone at all familiar with Mary Foote's work. But the question arises: must I now unravel all those little threads I have so painstakingly raveled together, the real with the fictional, and replace all truth with fiction? Or does it matter to you that an occasional reader or scholar can detect the Footes behind my fictions?

I have agreed to look over Rod Paul's introduction; I have also invited him to come up and look through the letters, which he could not see the other day because I was not at home and the library was closed. I have told him about my novel and about Rosamund Gilder's probably-not-to-be-realized book of letters between her mother and your grandmother. But sometime before Paul gets the Reminiscences ready for publication, which won't be soon, I'd like your word on what I should do about my threads of actual fact. I can't shift the course of their lives—my characters go through Almaden, Leadville, Mexico, Boise, and Grass Valley just as the real ones did. But I could modify the actual language, and all the names, in a pinch. Will you let me know?

Sometime this spring I'd like to send you a draft of the novel. Would you read it? It'll take you a week. And it won't of course be final. Neither will it be true to all the details of the Footes' lives. For reasons of drama, if nothing else, I'm having to foreshorten, and I'm having to throw in a domestic tragedy of an entirely fictional nature. But I think I'm not too far from their real characters.

Best,
Wally

« To: *Blake Green*, San Francisco Chronicle · *September 16, 1976* »

Dear Ms. Green:
By now you will have heard from Janet Micoleau, as I have, and will know that by disregarding our mutual request and exploiting the misunderstanding between us, you have offended her as well as me.

In your letter you say, "While I do appreciate your feelings, I hope that you will understand that to do a story linking the opera,[9] the book, the author, and the subject would have been impossible without mentioning

---

9. Under the directorship of Kurt Adler, the San Francisco Opera transformed *Angle of Repose* into an opera, the music composed by Andrew Imbrie, the libretto by Oakly Hall.

the differences of opinion."[10] There is not much in that sentence that I believe. Do you appreciate my feelings? Certainly you disregard them. If you had both appreciated and regarded them you would not have (1) written the article as you did, or (2) been surprised that I was upset by it. What you mean is that you do not regard my feelings (or those of the Micoleaus) as sufficient reason for not suggesting publicly that either I am a plagiarist[11] or the Micoleaus and other members of the Foote family are rather ridiculously fussy. Neither, as it happens, is in the slightest true, but you can never rub out either impression—especially not by the usual newspaper method of printing in 2 point type on page 19 a retraction of what you have said in headlines on page 1. Do I have to tell you that the freedom of the press implies responsibilities of the press? That appreciating people's feelings in purely personal matters is not enough, unless you also respect them? That restraint, where no public issues are involved, is as important as accuracy? It looks as if I do.

You did not have to write your story focusing on that disagreement about my book. You could very easily have indicated Mary Foote's importance as a partial source of Susan Ward. You could have indicated that the novel never pretends to be biographical—it only uses facts from Mary Foote's biography as the basis for a fiction, and it alters facts whenever the fiction demands it. You could have indicated the parallels between Mary Foote's actual life and the career of Susan Ward; you could likewise have pointed out the ways in which the fiction altered and distorted all sorts of historical matters to the uses of the novel. Instead, you played the game of suggesting that Susan Ward is indeed Mary Foote, which she is not, and of exploiting the distress of some of the family, who never did quite

---

10. In spite of Stegner's well-documented attempts (see the previous letter to Janet Micoleau) to explain the difference between history, biography, and fiction, his warning that "you may not recognize your ancestors when I get through with them," his assertion that he was taking passages from Mary Hallock Foote's letters outright, and his repeated plea that the grandchildren read the manuscript before he sent it out for publication, the family's reaction to the published work varied from dismay to bitterness. "I thought he would write something like Irving Stone's biographical novels," Evelyn Foote Gardiner remarked in an interview. Mercifully, he did not. Regrettably, the ancestors did not avail themselves of the opportunity to express their opinion before the novel was published, as Stegner had requested.

11. This assertion appeared in a particularly asinine bit of academic twaddle by an Idaho State professor named Mary Williams Walsh, who put forth the bizarre notion that *Angle of Repose* was essentially the work of Mary Hallock Foote.

understand how a novelist might want to use the papers, and expected something like a biography. Actually you didn't have to mention any disagreement; you didn't have to mention the Micoleaus—in fact, they asked you not to. You mentioned them, and aired their disagreement with me, only to sensationalize what you perhaps thought a dull story.

Well, enough. That will indicate why I was bothered by your piece. As for the notes that you took and have not yet used, you would oblige me by touching a match to them.

Sincerely,
Wallace Stegner

« *To: Jackson Benson* • *June 26, 1889/1989* »

Dear Jack,
I just about set you back a century in dating this letter, and where would that leave you? Way behind. Like me.

You mention the few things you still have to go through. If by any chance you should want to go through them during the summer, while we're away, I suggest that you call my granddaughter, Rachael (in the evening or on a weekend so she's sure to be at home), and make a date to come down. A weekend would probably be the best time, so that she can close up when you're through. But there's no reason for you to stall yourself simply because we're not here. Make yourself at home in the dustbin where I work.

I had forgotten that I told you anything about the beginnings of *Crossing to Safety* but yes, it did begin as a California story. My original first chapter, at least, began here in this house, looking out into whatever wildlife was moving around, and on a morning when a telephone call came announcing the death of Sid. Charity had been dead ten years or so. Sid had remarried, and my gropings dealt with his (very much altered) relations with his second wife, and recollections of the old one. I never got far with it before I realized that the people I was writing about were so New England, rather than Californian, that they wouldn't ever be anything but remembered exotics in this setting. The only thing that's left of my original tentative tries is a little scene about a mouse drowning in the swimming pool, meant to be symbolic and a metaphor for survival—and in the final draft even it was moved to New Mexico. There was no "shape or form" to the original idea. I only knew that I wanted to write about that couple, and I was trying to find the handle, starting close to home. Very shortly I moved the story way back in time, before Charity died and before Sid ever thought of dying, and thereby saved myself the few dramatic crumbs the story contained. And as a matter of fact, the answer to your question, Couldn't they have been New Englanders transplanted to California? is No. In reality, they were; they lived for years in Claremont. In the story they couldn't be, they just felt out of place. Finally, I guess I realized that I had already written a lot about California, in *A Shooting Star, All the Little Live Things, A Field Guide to the Western Birds*, and *A Spectator Bird*, and I must have wanted to set this story where indeed most of it happened, in Vermont. I pay attention to these vague urgings—sooner or later they generally turn out to be right, no matter what I thought in the first place. I suppose I do subscribe to the notion that places (which include social habits, memory, attics, relatives, graveyards, and much else) have a lot to do with the formation of character—that at least in well established regions there is a sort of regional character. Maybe I felt that in California there is no such established pattern, and that characters who, though odd in some ways, would look appropriate in New England would only look bizarre in California.

We're beginning to pack and ship boxes. On the 6th, we're off. Have a fine productive relaxed summer in the Sierra. We'll look forward to seeing you in the fall. And do come down and use the files if you feel like it, just call Rachael first to let her know you're coming.

Best,
Wally

« *To: Carl Brandt* • *May 4, 1985* »

Dear Carl:

Many thanks for the word on the paperback situation. I'm sorry I had forgotten your November communique on *Mountain Water*. But I'm glad to know the current situation on all those titles.

Last week I gave your name, I hope not in vain, to a French writer who blew through here and more or less peremptorily demanded that a Stanford friend of mine tell him the name of a good agent so he could get published in the U.S. I have now forgotten the guy's name, but he did hand over a Dictionary of Authors sheet showing that he has published a good many things in France. He is also on the board of Reuters, which is where my Stanford friend came in.

Maybe you will win him undying fame, vast riches, and the Nobel Prize.

As for my book, I moved the constipated thing a full chapter last week, and I even kid myself that I can now see the way. This summer will see the end either of it or of me.

Coraggio,

Wally

« *To: Carl Brandt* • *July 7, 1985* »

Dear Carl:

Many thanks for all the thankless hours you've spent tracking down those copyrights. This will learn me to keep better records. And anyway, back here I don't have any records, and so the whole thing will have to sit till I can get back to California and do my end of the search. That won't stall anything, since the Yolla Bolly Press is gathering its powers and its capital, and will not be acting swiftly. Even if they were ready to act, this collection of stories should follow the novel by a dignified interval, don't you think?

The novel.[12] It does seem as if it might be one. It is pretty well combed out, up to page 235, and I give it the benefit of my presence every morning for four hours or so, and though I don't see the final four or five chapters with absolute clarity, I see them more clearly than I once did. I have even written one of them since we got here, and in four minutes will begin on another. The galleys from *Reader's Digest* interrupted me yesterday, and the Wimbledon finals completed my defection. Sundays, though, I am strong.

I am still shooting for a completed manuscript by fall. September may be a shade optimistic, since I have to go back to California for a couple of weeks in August. But October still looks possible.

Which reminds me that though Doubleday has been good to me, and I love Ken and Sally and Sam,[13] Doubleday has changed some since the last time I published a novel. We ought to consider what our options and opportunities are, since I played out my option and am a totally free agent with this book. Confidentially, I can't imagine switching, especially since

---

12. *Crossing to Safety.*
13. Ken McCormick, Sally Arteseros, Sam Vaughan.

Ken has already lined this one up for a Franklin[14] series of signed editions. But I would like, when the time comes, the best offer that Doubleday knows how to make, and to that end they should be aware that I am not a sure thing, signed, sealed, and delivered.

With that kind of start I am sure to deliver a manuscript that neither Doubleday nor anybody else will publish.

Pray for us.

Wally

« *To: Carl Brandt* • *May 4, 1986* »

Dear Carl:

You deserve an accounting, or at least an explanation of my long silence. Here it is, or part of it is:

1) Mary has not been well, and that has kept me from getting much done. She is now better.

2) I am presently engaged in writing the last chapter of the book,[15] having made sure that everything up to here is O.K. and will stick. Mary told me six weeks ago that the book was done, but upon examination I find that her usually reliable judgment was flawed. It isn't done, but it's close, and will be done by mid-May.

3) I have to check it out with members of the family[16] I will be recognized as writing about, before I send it to you or offer it to any publisher. There is nothing libelous, or anything like that; but I don't want even hurt feelings. So when it's done I'm sending it off for two or three people to read. Then I will get in touch with you.

4) I have to go to Wisconsin for an honorary degree on May 16. Be back here May 19 or 20. Then, if Mary is well enough, I am taking her on a little pleasure trip, like Bora Bora. On June 24 we will be leaving for Vermont, driving. We will arrive about July 1, and will

---

14. Franklin Library.

15. *Crossing to Safety*.

16. The novel is loosely based on the life-long friendship between the Stegners and Philip and Margaret "Peg" Gray. Begun at the University of Wisconsin in 1937, their close relationship continued for the next 44 years, largely during the summers in Greensboro, Vermont, where they both maintained summer homes. Stegner felt that if any part of the novel was hurtful or embarrassed any of the Gray's six children he would not publish it.

stay in Vermont till late October, when I have to give three profound lectures at the University of Michigan.[17]

5) It may be July 1 before I communicate with you about the book. By then I can tell you whether we're submitting it or, like old Ernie,[18] putting it in the safe for a while. Hold your breath.

Yours,
Wally

« To: Carl Brandt • June 16, 1986 »

Dear Carl:

I am sending you today a copy of the novel,[19] not because I want you to submit it yet, but because we are getting ready to start driving east, and I think it might save us some time if you have had a chance to look it over before we arrive in Vermont. As I told you, I want several people to read this before I submit it to anybody, and if there is any objection I will put it in the safe, like Hemingway. Only I hope it comes out looking better than *The Garden of Eden*.

There is little chance that there will be any objection. One member of the family has already read it, with enthusiasm both literary and familial. The others will be reading it in the next two or three weeks. When they have, and if they have no objections, we must start thinking about where we want to submit it. From all I hear and read, Doubleday is a shambles, and though Doubleday has been good to me, that goodness is attributable to Ken McCormick, Sam Vaughan, and Sally Arteseros, none of whom will be guiding Doubleday's policies or future. I have not told any of them that I will probably be leaving, and would prefer to handle that job myself when it comes up. I will value your suggestions and your wisdom about publishers. Because of the McCormick connection and my old friendship with Alfred Knopf, I lean toward Knopf; barring Knopf, then Farrar Strauss and Giroux or whatever they are now. Among editors, I like and know Billy Abrahams, but Billy would lead us directly to Holt, and Jack MacRae and I

---

17. The William W. Cook lectures, delivered at the law school at the University of Michigan in October 1986, were published as *The American West as Living Space* in 1987. Jackson Benson has called them Stegner's "final and most eloquent words on what the West was, is, and should be . . ."

18. Ernest Hemingway.

19. *Crossing to Safety*.

are not too simpatico. So Knopf or Farrar would be my initial impulses.[20] What are yours? Tell me when you've read the book.

You should know, too, that this novel has already been committed to a signed First Editions series of Franklin Library—this through Ken, of course—and I have taken their shilling as an advance. So whatever trade arrangement we make, the Franklin deal must be considered.

And naturally I want this book to make me rich and famous. Money, though not the major consideration, is a consideration. Whoever publishes this book has got to agree to push it, and that means, I suppose, has got to back his deal with a solid advance. Myself, I think it's a good book. Finally.

I'll be in touch after we reach Vermont. The address there is simply Greensboro, Vt. 05841. We'll be there till late October. But if this book begins to cook, we might come down to New York for a couple of days.

Cheers,

Wally

« *To: Carl Brandt* • *July 25, 1986* »

Dear Carl:

I find that I can't send the second copy of the manuscript for a day or two, but here are the corrected pages for the first copy. Can you just insert them where the page numbers indicate, and throw the original pages away? Within a few days I'll send you the other copy, to facilitate your labors. Or I suppose you have a copying machine, if the pressure gets heavy.

Yesterday I had a letter from Ken,[21] eager to read the novel,[22] which he has heard is finished. This distresses me no end, because I am very fond of him and I hate to seem to reject his partnership. But everything I have heard or read about Doubleday lately makes me very uneasy about putting this (undoubtedly last) book at the mercy of an executive office as crazy as that one appears to be. Besides which I strongly resent what Doubleday did to both Sam and Ken—thanks to whom my own relations with Doubleday have always been most amicable. And Sally. Damnation, I will have to write

---

20. The novel was published by Random House.
21. Ken McKormick at Doubleday.
22. *Crossing to Safety.*

a couple of difficult letters or make a couple of difficult telephone calls. But I still can't think that it would be safe or sensible to submit the book to Doubleday. Since that decision is mine, I'm where the buck stops. I will write or call both Ken and Sally today.

So let's see if Houghton Mifflin, Farrar Straus, and Knopf are interested, and how interested.

Best,

Wally

« *To: Carl Brandt* • *November 29, 1986* »

Dear Carl:

Still no revelations on the goddamn title.[23] My head feels like a theater marquee. No alternative but to keep trying.

I'm having another copy of the manuscript made, and will send it on in a day or two. I doubt the magazine possibilities, because unlike some of my books, this is one that doesn't excerpt well. I should tell you that I gave a piece of the Italian chapter to the Stanford literary magazine, *Sequoia*, for their anniversary number this winter. Since this is only for campus distribution, I don't suppose it would interfere with anything else, but I thought you should know.

Also, here's a note from Viking which I don't fully understand. I do understand about copyright renewal, and have always relied on your office to take care of it automatically. Maybe that was Carol personally, and if so, better let me know if the office needs reminders, or if somebody there has a list of at least major things. But what I don't understand about Viking's note is that they speak of renewing copyright not on the entire book *Wolf Willow*, (in which I think they no longer have any rights, though maybe they do), but of two pieces from it that are frequently reprinted. Is this their business or ours? In case it's theirs, I have signed where they ask me to. If that is what I should do, will you send it on over to Viking? And if it's not, will you throw their letter away and do what is proper?

Ah, now I see: *Wolf Willow* wasn't published as a book until 1962; these pieces were published in magazines earlier—"Town Dump" in the *Atlantic*

---

23. Stegner wanted to call the novel *(Crossing to Safety) Amicitia* (friendship), but Random House thought nobody would know what the word meant.

October 1959, "Genesis" in a little local magazine called *Contact*, sometime in 1959. But why is Viking taking the step of renewing?

Yours,

Wally

P.S.—Is Random House's first installment of the advance going to get here before Christmas? I hope so, for the sake of my loved ones.

« *To: Carl Brandt* • *April 5, 1988* »

Dear Carl,

I know not, me, what relevance the Commonwealth Clause has these days in foreign book contracts. I suspect, none at all. And it doesn't look as if we're jeopardizing any English profits by taking the Australian offer,[24] so if you see no impediments, let's do it. I confess I don't quite understand the English. They made a bust out of *Angle of Repose* and ignored *Recapitulation*, *The Spectator Bird*, and now *Crossing to Safety*. Hell with them. Let them go to their graves ignorant of my superlative beauties.

While we're on that subject, have you any answers to the question of why nobody has asked me for permission to put any book on a cassette? If print is on its way out, I ought to start insuring my immortality in some other medium. Years ago, the CBC put *Wolf Willow* onto tape and read it over the cold Canadian air for weeks or months, to what they reported as cheers. That's the only thing on tape, except for a few spot readings. If you see any light on that horizon, let me know, will you?[25]

Penguin seems to be taking the paperback seriously.[26] I'm going down to the AMA convention in Anaheim the end of May, and to Toronto and some East Coast (read Vermont) bookstores in October, and to a San Francisco lectern, also in October. Nobody ever asked me to do things like that for a paperback, until now. We must see that these nice people get their money back.[27]

No stirrings of a new novel. Too much clinic. Mary's been ill with one thing and another since January, the latest being an infected jaw from root canal work, and when I took her to Death Valley for a little break in March

---

24. An edition of *Crossing to Safety*.
25. *Wolf Willow* was eventually done as a book on tape by Northward Press, read by Page Stegner after his father's death.
26. Of *Crossing to Safety*.
27. Much of Stegner's work is now available in Penguin editions.

I lifted an ice chest the wrong way and put me back in a sling, until just about yesterday. Ah, these Golden Years, the orthopedist said to me as he authorized the off-taking of the corset.

Hoping you are the same,

Wally

« *To: Charles Schlessinger* • *February 11, 1988* »

Dear Charles Schlessinger:

I'm pleased that somebody finally came in for a foreign-language edition,[28] though I wouldn't have anticipated Brazil. So here are the signed contracts, pronto.

What's the matter with the European area God knows. I used to have some readers there—Sweden, Germany, Spain, France. Then it stopped. Either I got worse, or reading tastes changed. The Italian edition of *Angle of Repose* that a friend set up for me was a fizzle, so far as I know, though that friend has just come to teach a term in the Stanford Law School, and I will find out this weekend at dinner what he knows. But there was never a Danish edition of *The Spectator Bird*, for instance, though it was about Denmark and won the National Book Award. The English edition of *Angle of Repose* was the only foreign edition until this Italian one, and it was born dead, though *Angle of Repose* was a Pulitzer Prize winner. I guess I need to knife my wife, or be caught buggering a statue of Reagan in the park.

Anyway, I'm pleased with the Brazilians, and I hope their example is followed. Many thanks to you.

Yours,

Wallace Stegner

« *To: Carl Brandt* • *May 10, 1985* »

Dear Carl:

I think I wrote you some months ago that Jim Robertson of the Yolla Bolly Press in Covelo, California was trying to work out a way of publishing all my short stories (*The Women on the Wall*, *The City of the Living*, and maybe a half dozen uncollected ones) as a single fine-press book which he would design and print in a limited collectors' edition. Thereafter, he would want

---

28. *Crossing to Safety.*

to sell the assembled package to a trade publisher, or perhaps as a trade-and-paperback combination. Doubleday has said it is interested in the trade publication, Nebraska is probably the natural choice for paperback. But the whole deal was hung up by Houghton Mifflin, which refused to release the rights to *The City of the Living*.

But now I have a gracious letter from Wendy Withington, their manager of trade contracts, reverting, releasing, remising, and forever discharging to me the rights in that volume of stories. The decks are thus cleared. You will probably be hearing from Robertson; though he isn't the fastest man on four wheels, he is a good designer and publisher, and has done some exquisite things. He also designs a good many books for Houghton Mifflin, the Sierra Club, etc., and knows his way around the business.

One question arises out of Ms. Withington's letter. She says that Houghton Mifflin has not renewed, and can find no evidence of renewal of, the copyright on five stories: "The Traveler" (*Harper's*, Feb. 1951), "Pop Goes the Alley Cat" (*Harper's*, Feb. 1952), "The Volunteer" (*Mademoiselle*, Oct. 1956), "Impasse" (*Woman's Day*, Jan. 10, 1953), and "Field Guide to the Western Birds," which originally appeared in Ballantine's *New Short Novels 2*, 1956.[29] Can somebody in the office check the status of these? Carol used to renew copyrights automatically, and I suspect that these are all O.K. If they aren't, we ought to do something about those that aren't too late, I suppose.

All this sounds so déjà vu that I'm sure I must have written you about it before, when it was only a suggestion of Jim Robertson's. But you have lots of space in your files.

> Best,
> Wally

« *To: Carl Brandt* • *January 2, 1989*

Dear Carl:

Dan Frank[30] keeps indicating that he wants to know about any Stegner title that becomes available for his paperback series. He is waiting for *The*

---

29. Ballantine did not renew the copyright on its collection and this story reverted to the public domain.
30. Then an editor with Viking Penguin.

Spectator Bird to come loose at Nebraska in February, as you undoubtedly know. But it occurs to me that one of the short story volumes, *The City of the Living*, has been sitting there available ever since last year, when the Yolla Bolly Press was thinking about a Collected Short Stories. I guess I own the rights to both *The Women on the Wall*, which is still in paperback at Nebraska, and *The City of the Living*. There are also four or five uncollected stories.

Now the question. So far as I know, Sam[31] is not interested in a short story volume. He has known for two years they were there, and has never expressed interest. Viking Penguin, on the other hand, from Frank on down, has been enthusiastic and efficient, a bunch of boosters. Do you think there's any reason not to offer either *The City of the Living* or a Collected Stories to Frank? for a paperback? Would that be in any way a violation of my contract with Random House? Would it offend Sam? Or would it relieve him? Should the stories be offered to both Random and Viking simultaneously, so that they can be simultaneously trampled in the dust? Or shouldn't we test Dan Frank's claim, which I think he means, that he's interested in any Stegner title, and wants all of them he can get? I have little doubt that Viking Penguin, if it could be sold the stories, would do better with them than Random would.

Sam keeps inquiring about new books, perhaps an autobiography. I'll send him those scraps that I wrote last summer, but I have only minimal enthusiasm for the autobiography project, and I can't see another novel on the horizon. I'd kind of like to clean up after myself, and one act of cleaning would be to get the stories together in some sort of respectable and semi-permanent series. The fact that Nebraska has never bit on that bait is not entirely discouraging to me—they've never been as enthusiastic or as industrious as Viking, and they don't have as many weapons.

Anyway, let me know what you think. Yolla Bolly will have its little fine-press edition of six stories out in a month or two.

And a happy new year to you.

Wally

---

31. Sam Vaughan at Random House.

« To: Carl Brandt • February 10, 1989 »

Dear Carl:

I have definitely decided that On a Darkling Plain would be unprofitable for Dan and embarrassing for me.[32] Save it for the Collected Works, when even the failures are reprinted.

The short stories I put in the Book Post for you the other day. They should arrive in a week or so. I have been thinking, and Mary and I have been talking, about what we should ask you to do with those. I (we) do have the feeling that Viking's enthusiasm for Stegner is considerably greater than that of Random House, where we have never met or had a communication from anyone except Sam,[33] and whose promotion of Crossing did seem to us skillful but minimal. We can't see much sense in postponing a Viking paperback of the stories—one which would be pushed and promoted with enthusiasm—to a reluctant or half-hearted hardbacked Random edition, which would have little effect except to bleed off fifty percent of the Viking royalties. I say this diffidently, for I'm very fond of Sam; but I have the impression that Sam is not entirely master in his own house. Am I wrong?

If there is ever an autobiography, or a new book of any kind, Sam is it, of course. But this short-story number is really a reprint of a couple of reprints, with only three new stories in the whole package.

I guess what I am asking is that you look at the manuscript, and tell me what you think. (1) Is it worth publishing at all? (2) Should it go to Random or Viking? (3) Should we try to persuade Dan Frank to do a hardback simultaneous edition, mainly for library sale and reviews? I am in a mood to listen.

Best,
Wally

« To: Sam Vaughan • June 15, 1989 »

Dear Sam:

Thanks for your note. I'm glad to know that the short stories are being put on the assembly line, even though I have not yet had from

---

32. Stegner's third novel, published in 1940. Dan Frank at Viking Penguin was hoping to reprint it.
33. Sam Vaughan.

Carl the contracts and other minor details. They will probably be in today's mail.

And thanks for giving us the chance to participate in the cover design. The last one worked out very well, we thought. This one may be tougher, for there are so many foci in the book of short stories that it's hard to find the one central unifying unavoidable image that encapsulates the whole shebang. However, we will put what we laughingly call our minds to it.

Consulting some other books in my shelves—the collected stories of John Cheever, Eudora Welty, Willa Cather, the collected essays and letters of Cheever, Archie MacLeish, the collected poems of Frost, etc., I find that the general solution has been typographical rather than pictorial, though sometimes the typographical is supplemented with an inserted portrait or landscape, and in the case of Cheever, the whole typographical layout is enclosed within a big capital C. C is for Cheever. Maybe S is for Stegner. In any event, I don't have, and neither does Mary, an automatic painting or photograph to suggest. Maybe we will. Most of our favorite photographs are Ansel Adams, but the Italian publisher of *Angle of Repose* used "Moon and Halfdome" on the jacket of that edition, and it was wrong—"Moon and Halfdome" has nothing to do with small human heats and frustrations, which is what the whole novel was about.

In short, we will ponder and be in touch, and if it comes down in the end to a typographical jacket, I hope something mildly distinctive like Cheever Capital C can be utilized.

I have raised a question with Carl about how Nebraska's license to reprint *The Women on the Wall* is affected by these collected stories. When you have determined that, between you, I hope you will let me know.

Meantime, Summer has arrived, along with Jack Benson who is writing my biography and sharing my workroom. My oldest granddaughter is married off, my youngest one just reached her six-month birthday. And so from hour to hour we ripe and ripe, and so from hour to hour we rot and rot, and thereby hangs a tale.

Hoping you are the same,
Wally

« *To: Carl Brandt* • *April 10, 1990* »

Dear Carl:

Three cheers for our side, indeed. Though I maintain my well-earned caution, I have to be pleased at the reception of the stories, and I find the indignity of favorable notice singularly easy to bear. The funny thing about this is that those stories have been out there, none of them for less than thirty-five years, and some of them for more than fifty, without stirring up any great applause—and many of them, until Bernice[34] and I got tired of sending them there, turned down by the *New Yorker*. What has been ignored once can easily be ignored again, and so I will retain my aloof dignity, not to be ruffled until some real wonder appears.

But I'm glad Random House is upping its second printing and also, according to Sam, upping its advertising. Up to now I haven't seen any, but some is always better than none, and when I see some I will join the cheering.

Since Penguin has found a copy of *Joe Hill*, I would appreciate getting back the one I sent you. It seems to be the only one left around, and what if I should want to quote myself?

Yours,
Wally

« *To: Carl Brandt* • *May 30, 1985* »

Dear Carl:

You are right to be bothered by the smallness of it all,[35] but then there are only 1,500 people in Idaho who can sign their names. Cort Conley, the director of the Idaho Press, is a friend of mine, and I would just as soon let him go ahead as not, and so would Page, who was up here yesterday. But there are a couple of bugs. One is that since this is explicitly text, we don't suppose Eliot Porter would be entitled to a share; neither would we expect a share out of any photographs from the book that he used elsewhere. The second hitch is that Jack MacRae worked into the text, against our best

---

34. Bernice Baumgarten, Stegner's first literary agent, at Brandt and Brandt.
35. The University of Idaho Press wanted to reprint the text only of *American Places*, the book of essays the Stegners (Wallace and Page) did with the photographer Eliot Porter. The book was edited by Jack MacRae and published by E.P. Dutton in 1981.

judgment, some passages of Van Wyck Brooks. Can we arrange for those to be deleted? We have no right to reprint them again anyway, I suppose.

If those hitches don't derail the train, we'd just as soon let Idaho print its little edition. But we don't think there should be a five-year contract. If they want it for two or three, with the possibility of renegotiating at the end at that time, we think they should be allowed to. Whereupon Dutton stands to make $375 and you and Page's agent, harpies on the carcass of art, will gorge yourselves on $37.50 each. Each!

I went down this morning and copied off two copies of the manuscript thus far, to page 222.[36] Since I type with no margins, to save paper,[37] that is equivalent to three hundred ordinary pages. I have five chapters to go, and one of those is written but not revised. I do believe I'm going to finish this thing this summer.

Best,
Wally

« *To: Carl Brandt* • *January 24, 1991* »

Dear Carl:

Your embarrassment can't be greater than mine. Copies of *Beyond the Hundredth Meridian* seem to disappear from here. I don't even have the Nebraska paperback, though I think they must still have some, and I guess I will order a few this morning. Meantime, the only copy I can find is this—the original edition, but rebound in Carnegie Library Utility Grade brown. And considering that I have no other copy of the original, I would sort of like this back when Millman[38] has had a look at it. Meantime I will see if I can't get some paperbacks from Nebraska.

In between illnesses and having the house painted and having to write blurbs for the local environmental groups, I have been trying to put together a few essays[39] to go with those in *The American West as Living Space*,[40] some of them will probably repeat details, but those can be cleaned out. And some of them were written for specific wars or specific

---

36. *Crossing to Safety.*
37. Not only did Stegner type with no margins, he used a typewriter with elite type, and would not change the ribbon until the print was nearly illegible.
38. Michael Millman, editor at Viking Penguin.
39. The collection would become *Where the Bluebird Sings to the Lemonade Springs.*
40. Published by the University of Michigan Press in 1987.

purposes, and may have to be explained and given a setting. But when I get them together I will be sending them on, perhaps within the next week. With my new Christmas copier I may even send a copy for you personally, thus alleviating all sorts of snags and tangles.

Which is all life is at the moment. Pray for better days. You can even pray for the Critics Circle award for Tom[41] and me, but I suspect a bribe would work better than prayer.

Yours,

Wally

P.S. Just now in the mail comes a letter saying that I am one of four pieces of fiction nominated for the San Francisco Bay Area Book Reviewers Association award. Should this be examined into, the way we would examine into a simultaneous price jump by seven oil companies? Are the critics in collusion?

« *To: Carl Brandt* • *February 10, 1991* »

Dear Carl:

Here's a batch of fifteen essays,[42] including the three from the Michigan lectures. They seem to fall into three general categories—personal ones, ones concerned with the land and its character and its ills, and literary ones. That may turn out to be like wrapping three watermelons, but at least you can look them over. Many will probably have to be re-titled, and there may even need to be a little cartilaginous writing to fasten them together, but for now, this is as far as I've got. I would appreciate your input, as they say, especially if you are writer-friendly.

A copy of these goes to Sam[43] in the same mail with this. He wrote me the other day expressing the interest you had stirred in him and sounding happy that something might be coming up.

One problem: I don't know how the Michigan Press is going to like the idea of letting go of these lectures, which for a university press publication have moved reasonably well.[44] I don't know either if the University

---

41. Tom Watkins, author of *Righteous Pilgrim: The Life and Times of Harold L. Ickes, 1874–1952* (New York: Henry Holt, 1990).

42. The collection eventually entitled *Where the Bluebird Sings to the Lemonade Springs.*

43. Sam Vaughan, Stegner's editor at Random House.

44. Published by the University of Michigan Press in 1987 as *The American West as Living Space.*

of Nevada, which hired me to speak on Walt Clark[45] and then somehow assumed that they owned world rights in what I said, will happily give us a green light on the Clark essay. They published it in a volume of studies on Clark, which I am sure has not sold two hundred copies in ten years, but they have a certain provincial dog-in-the-manger attitude about their literary possessions. All that we can leave for now, though if the Michigan lectures can't be pried loose, then I think the whole volume is aborted, or at least postponed. Maybe you have some persuasive approach. I have not said anything to them about this project, preferring to wait until I have had some worldly advice from you and Sam.

One further off-the-subject detail: Has *Life* gone broke, or what? I sent them their little squib last December, and they published it several weeks ago. I could use that check, though of course if they're in financial difficulty I'll be glad to lend it to them interest free.

And further than this, deponent sayeth naught.

Best,

Wally

« *To: Carl Brandt* • *July 16, 1991* »

Dear Carl:

Here, as far as I can do it from here, is the dope on the first publication of the essays in the new book, which Sam[46] and I have decided to call *Where the Bluebird Sings to the Lemonade Springs*.

Several of these essays were written as introductions or contributions to books, and were never published in magazines. That probably makes things more difficult, though Sam indicates that Random House does not want to make a point of preserving its interest, but only wants to make reprinting of individual essays easier and less discouraging.

I have sent the list to Olga Tamowsky, at Sam's request, and I gather that Random House will go ahead and send out some form letters establishing the status of the individual essays. You may want to be in touch with them about this. Me, what I am mainly interested in is getting that contract signed and the money in the bank. I sent the edited MS to Olga this morning.

---

45. Walter van Tilburg Clark.
46. Sam Vaughan, Random House.

We're here till August 1. After that, back at the old California stand.
Best,
Wally

This is, as nearly as I can reconstruct it from here, a list of the essays to be included in *Where the Bluebird Sings to the Lemonade Springs*, together with publication data.

PERSONAL

"Finding the Place." Published in *Growing Up Western*, edited by Clarus Backes, Knopf, 1989. Backes is dead. His widow still lives, I think [in] Evergreen, CO 80439.

Crossing into Eden. *Ford Times*, 1989 or early 1990.

Letter, "Much Too Late." Published in *Family Portraits*, Doubleday, 1989?

HABITAT

"Thoughts in a Dry Land." Published first, about 1975, in *New West Magazine*, now extinct; republished in *Editor's Choice*, ed. Frances Ring, John Daniel, Santa Barbara, 1991?

"Living Dry," "Striking the Rock," and "Variations on a Theme by Crevecoeur," all published as *The American West as Living Space*, U. of Michigan Press, 1987?

"A Capsule History of Conservation." *Smithsonian Magazine*, 1990.

WITNESSES

"Coming of Age." *Los Angeles Times*, sometime to summer 1990. Check through the book editor, Miles.

"On Steinbeck' s 'Flight.'" A fine press edition of "Flight," Yolla Bolly Press, Covelo, CA. Jim Robertson.

"George R. Stewart." This was written as an introduction to a reprint of *Names on the Land*, and published by some obscure San Francisco house, probably now extinct, whose name I forget. I can send this information when I get home August 1.

"Walter Van Tilburg Clark." Originally a speech at U. of Nevada, later extracted from Nevada's clutches and published in *Atlantic*, later included on a U. of Nevada Press book of essays on Clark. A sticky and paranoid professor emeritus thinks he owns this, and will probably act like Fafnir guarding the gold hoard of the Nibelungs.

"Haunted by Waters." Written for a book of essays on Maclean, published by Jim Hepworth at Confluence Press, Lewiston, Idaho.

"The Sense of Place." Written for the Wisconsin Committee on Humanities, Patricia Anderson, and published to a fine-press chapbook and also to some sort of adult education course batch of materials.

"Letter to Wendell Berry." Written for a collection of essays on Berry, to be edited by somebody in Ohio and to be published (I think) by Hepworth at the Confluence Press.

"Law of Nature and Dream of Man." Unpublished, and so blessedly free.

« *To: Avis DeVoto* • *February 21, 1968* »

Dear Avis:

I have a question. Is anybody working on a biography of Benny? Have you authorized anyone to do so? Is there anyone besides Lee in the offing or in prospect? If not, are you still interested in having me do one? If you are, I am.

It would be, obviously, the work of several years, especially since I have a novel to deliver (and none of it yet written) before I could do more than occasional work on Benny's papers. But I find that I keep coming back to peck and chisel at Benny's monumental accomplishments. They intrigue me, and they come close enough to my own interests so that I can comprehend their drift even if much of what he did is beyond me. I would like very much to try it, and if I do try it I'll hope for your blessing and, in effect, your title of monopoly to the papers for a while. Can you let me know?

We got back here at the beginning of the year after a dispersed and not too profitable sabbatical, some of it in Vermont, some of it in Europe, some of it in the Middle East. Mary is in better health than for the past few years, and I seem to suffer no real wear and tear except a white thatch, a thickening waist, a reddening nose, and a distaste for the younger generation—all normal for my age and time. I'm about to start writing on the novel, having a light quarter ahead with a free summer beyond that, but since much of that time we'll be here, I'll hope (granting you approve) to poke around in the papers more thoroughly than I yet have. I know them in general, from having looked through them for various things, but they're now beautifully organized and arranged, and I know I will find much that I overlooked before. Late in the summer we'll probably go to Vermont, in which case we'll hope to see you, either at Breadloaf or at our place in Greensboro. We hear about you now and then, in flits and flashes. You sound busy. We hope you're contented as well. That would be the neatest trick of the year 1968.

Best,
Wally

« *To: Avis DeVoto* • *March 5, 1968* »

Dear Avis,

Bless you, then all's well. If you don't hear from me for a long time then you'll know that I am puttering away at the novel, and in my spare time reading DeVoto over, and maundering around among the papers. Nothing's going to happen very suddenly, but let us hope it will happen surely. I kind of had the feeling all along that I should tackle Benny, but I always had the feeling too that he was too big a coconut for this squirrel to handle. He probably is. But I don't see any other squirrels around.

We're a little frantic at the moment with an addition to the house (in anticipation of Armageddon, and not as bomb shelter but as guest room and bath, on the theory that even in Armageddon some friend might need a bed). And also Page is moving to the Santa Cruz campus of the University of California, and has bought a house, details of which are handled by guess who. We were down there last weekend looking the place over in anticipation of the arrival of the whole family on March 10. Naturally the whole house needs painting, etc. Guess who will be wielding one of the brushes. But it's pleasant to have them within an hour of us, and Page is so red hot among the books lately (he followed his Nabokov book with a novel, *The Edge*, and now has just turned in a Portable Nabokov and a text book o christ) that I need him around to stir my flagging ambition.

Which right now needs to confront the income tax situation. O christ again.

Best,
Wally

« *To: Avis DeVoto* • *May 10, 1968* »

Dear Avis,

Know anybody in Ogden or Salt Lake who could show me where Benny was born, lived, went to school, etc.? We have some Riser letters here, which I will look up before we go over there next week, but I thought you might know others. The reason for our trip this week is to get an honorary degree, laus deo, and help open the new library. I will have little time for interviews, but I thought I might set something up so that this summer, when we drive east, we can do some solid learning.

Where do I get the facts on Benny's boyhood? Can you tell me anything, or steer me to people who can? Bob Bailey, bless him, writes that he wants to write out everything he remembers Benny ever saying to him in thirty years, and send it to me. This is all the kinder, because he has an aortal aneurism, did you know? Naturally he had to be careful, but he sounds cheerful anyway, and very eager to help with this book.

Did I tell you the book will be Doubleday? I'm changing from Viking, which is a bunch of tight-wads and promise-breakers, and making enough of a package deal so that I can quit teaching almost entirely and live on the advances. Ken McCormick is enthusiastic about the Benny book, and Doubleday is so rich and willing that I anticipate nothing but roses and junior proms. Paul Brooks wrote about wanting Houghton Mifflin to do it, but the deal with Doubleday was already pretty well set. And anyway, how can you go back, once you've moved on. It's like marrying your ex-wife.

I'll write again and try to work out a time when we can talk this summer. If a car is all your problem, I can come over to Breadloaf and get you and bring you to Greensboro, where we will have nothing but thrushes to interrupt us. Or we can maybe see you in Cambridge.

I am just starting this new novel, and have had to submerge in it to get up some momentum, but I'm still hoping to do some work on Benny before we come east.

God bless,
Wally

« *To: Avis DeVoto* • *March 15, 1971* »

Dear Avis,

Bless you, if you were here you would not escape a good wet smack. I love it that you and Bess and Howard[47] all like the book. I love it especially because I just got an advance of the first review, the good old *Saturday Review*'s, and it forgot to say all those splendid things that one dreamed (can I deny the soft imputation) all the reviews would say. It used to be Granny Hicks[48] who harpooned me in that rag (could it be because I was a friend of Benny's? Or could it be that he simply didn't admire my writing? Not that, not that). Now it's this wishy-washy female who misses something she calls "gut reactions." Well. Write her a note, dear. Tell her she's in error. Tell her she has just passed Shakespeare in the street and kicked dirt on his white stockings. I wish to hell I owned a magazine, and the souls of fifteen competent reviewers into whose mouths I could put cunning words.

Well. I meant when I started to say thanks and then ask you something. What about a volume of Benny's letters, to be made incidentally while the biography is going forward? He wrote so damned many good letters it's a shame not to make a book of them. Any feelings on this? I haven't the slightest notion how Doubleday would feel if I proposed it, but I would bet money that either Houghton Mifflin or Lovell Thompson at Gambit would jump at the chance. Anyway, let me know. I've now read all of the DeVoto letters, outgoing, except some few in the Knopf file, and I know where a lot of beauties are, ready to be assembled. If you think it's a good idea, I'll keep a collection in mind as I proceed.

I've had to quit working on Benny to finish out the quarter, and to rewrite a film script of a part of *Wolf Willow* for the Canadian National Film Board. If I didn't have constantly before me the picture of Benny sweating out a hundred titles a year, I'd think I was working too hard. Another week, and I'm back on Benny. Take it easy in the slush time. Remember Don Marquis—

Through God-forsaken suburbs streaked with soot
And miserable with mud

47. Howard Mumford Jones.
48. Granville Hicks.

Past twisted trees that lack the sap to bud
Comes Spring . . .
　　Love,
　　Wally

《 *To: Avis DeVoto* • *August 18, 1971* 》

Dear Avis;
I've been pondering the calendar with your last letter in hand and it seems
to me you needn't fear a descent on your fold that will interrupt your round
of—it seems from here—giddy pleasures. The letters I have been picking out of the great mass don't all need your consultation, though I'll be
grateful if you'll read them through, make suggestions about editings, and
also make suggestions about areas that may be slighted. It will be selected
letters, with a vengeance, and the categories of selection we ought to talk
about. At this moment, I am going on the assumption that letters with
merely biographical interest can be left out—I'll handle those details, taken
from those letters, in the biography. What I'm picking now is letters that
express in memorable terms certain basic ideas and attitudes (freedom of
the mind, literary fallacy, a priori thinking, history, fiction, democracy, that
sort of thing); letters that deal centrally with his controversies (Brooks,
Wilson, FBI, Watch and Ward, McCarthy, Cousins, Lewis, et al); letters
revelatory of his personal demons; letters that throw new light on the
composition or intention of major books; letters expressive of his deepest friendships and his relations with people interesting in themselves
(Mencken, Zinsser, Elmer Davis, Frost, et al); letters that demonstrate
his extreme kindness and generosity to people, often nameless, who
want advice or help; letters that demonstrate his ruthless destructions
of fools and of people who attack him unduly, or out of ignorance; and
letters that set out to correct reviewers and others who have misconstrued
him.
　　Many of these will need some cutting; some will need some names
expunged; some will be subject to removal or replacement. This means
that I ought to go through the whole batch (not a small batch either) and
make penciled editorial suggestions, requests for identification, and so on,
before I bother you with them. I can do this, in my evenings, during the
next few weeks, and I can also assemble the remaining questions—some

of them getting intimate, I'm afraid, and you can shush me when they get too intimate, but there are some things a biographer ought to know.

Now therefore: In view of the jobs that remain to me, and the giddy round of pleasures you've got scheduled, how would it be if we plan to come to Cambridge for a day or two in late September? This would presumably be after you get back from North Haven and before you go to New London. I could bring the letters and leave them with you for the leisurely settling of the questions I've asked in the margins, and for the addition of any other question you want to raise. And I can set up my tape recorder and start you talking. Will that work? We can set the precise day later, but it looks now as if it's sure to be after the middle of September. Maybe you can drop me a card and say how this suits you, or propose alternatives. I'd suggest that you come up here, except that it looks as if you're already peripatetic, and except that we've got only a shack and a bed in the loft, and except that we're getting Page and his wife and family off to Caracas for a Peace Corps job in the next two weeks, and except that Mary is up and down with her emphysema and probably shouldn't take on any more than the family right now. That's a lot of excepts. It might almost be read as a collective injunction. So maybe we'll be accepting your brand new beds, if they're still vacant after mid-September; and in any event we'll probably be down. I want to try to see Galbraith and a couple of other people, too.

Thanks for the word on Kay.[49] Mary telephoned Ted just after the operation, and is calling again this morning. A quarter vision in one eye doesn't sound too damned inspiring to me. I am headed for the nearest glaucoma clinic as soon as I hit civilization—dust on my coattails, burrs in my cuffs, distraction in my aspect, hope in my voice, panic in my inner recesses. I don't want any of that.

Back to Benny. He wrote damned good letters, and they'll make a book full of cayenne and the voice of Tiresias, but some of them are very long for reproduction. So I am making little red ink brackets around what seem dead spots. As you will see in September.

Take care.

Wally

---

49. Kay Morrison.

« *To: Avis DeVoto* • *February 9, 1974* »

Dear Avis,

By now you have perhaps seen part of the initial response John Leonard, that least of editors, gave Malcolm Cowley's review the front page of the *Times Book Review* (that will be tomorrow). *Time* gave it lead space, the *Chicago Tribune* is front paging it, the *Sun-Times* (Paul Ferris) led with it, and the *San Francisco Chronicle* will lead with it next Sunday. Beyond that deponent sayeth not. I could write better reviews than some of these people, including Malcolm Cowley, who is a good friend of mine if not of Benny's; but I can't quarrel with the space they've given us. One thing I do regret—one or two of the reviewers, including Cowley, have seen fit to dredge up what they think Benny's belligerence and bad manners (surprisingly, *Time* was more temperate on that issue than some of the others, and at least granted the importance of what they called a curmudgeon). I feel partially responsible, and if this hurts you I do beg your forgiveness. In my intense desire to do Benny justice without becoming a sycophant about it, I may have over-emphasized the side that his enemies all saw. I haven't seen a review yet that grants him his full stature, though I have seen some letters, to me or to Doubleday, that do so.

The advance sale was not very extravagant, partly because, as Ken McCormick says, a lot of the salesman were children when Benny died, and never had experienced him. But he promises that with the generally first-class response to the book they will galvanize themselves and stir their stumps. On that we shall see.

I believe that either Ken or Sandy sent you up a Xerox of the text of the Letters volume, which is not scheduled until spring 1975. Would you, when this publication flurry has died down, go through those letters, identify anybody that you can and that I haven't, check the notes and headlines, and give me your wisdom on any changes you would make or corrections that are necessary? I will then incorporate your suggestions in the final copy, and Doubleday will go ahead getting it ready for the press during the late spring or summer.

Well, baby, this is my last thanks. You strewed my path with roses and lilies. I'd have been lost without your help.

Love,
Wally

« *To: Avis DeVoto* • *February 26, 1974* »

Dear Avis,

Don't be mad at Malcolm Cowley. He thought he gave us a nice favorable review—trouble was he couldn't help becoming autobioloquacious, as if he were writing another chapter of *Second Flowering* (a chapter he didn't put in the book). And he couldn't have got us better space—which I'm sure he did by simply writing at double length and putting the bet up to Leonard. And as you say, Anderson in *New Republic* and Russell Lynes in *Harper's* and Billy Abrahams in the *SF Chronicle* are all dandy. Weeks' review in *Atlantic* was a little snotty, perhaps because he has a competing book in the market, complete, as you say, with all those Weeksly sex experiences), and perhaps because he can't understand metaphors, and thought I was knocking Hans Zinsser. Has the *Globe* done a review yet? I can't find out whether the *Los Angeles Times* has or not—that's influential, out this way. But Bill Hogan of the *Chronicle* gave us a column the other day, talking Pulitzer, and though I will bet considerable sums against his prophecy, I do not knock it as promotion.

I'd be interested to see what Louis Lyons had to say. I gave a talk to the Stanford version of the Niemans a couple of weeks ago and found them lively and eager, and even informed about Benny, though some of them were no more than six when he died.

So all that is O.K. Doubleday printed only 10,000 in the first printing, and (for your ears only) the advance sale was poor. But last week they printed a second run of 10,000, and that indicates that the book started to move at once, because of the reviews. I get nothing out of this, having spent it long ago while living as a Doubleday pensioner, but I cheer nevertheless. I'd like to see a third printing tomorrow, but about that we will have to wait and see.

I have received the Letters, and am amending them, but waiting for Ken McCormick's final suggestions. I will amplify the notes where I can, but there's a dreadful problem of size and expense, and I may not be able to do as much as you and I would both wish.

Bless you. Come out like a crocus.

Love,
Wally

« *To: Avis DeVoto* • *March 26, 1974* »

Dear Avis,

Sorry about that *Herald* review. Sometimes I dream of a Book Review Academy where people who aspire to the job of literary arbiter could learn not only their trade but certain professional ethics. I have been unhappy to see some reviewers revive that old volcanic-ogre image of Benny, just for their own goddam chance to seem lively, and to see them also seize upon history and exaggerate Benny's private troubles and his departure from Harvard, and neglect the enormous solid contributions that he made in his life, and that my book deals with at length. When I read one like that, even though it may be favorable and even laudatory, I wish I hadn't put that sort of ammunition in the hands of fools and stupids and people of ill will. The ability to discriminate among ideas and values is so goddam rare its price ought to be above rubies. And it ought to be the first requirement of candidates for the Book Review Academy.

Sorry too that your freighter cruise is postponed. But think of those perfumed seas in May. Ah wilderness.

Incidentally, watch for the April 6 *Saturday Review*, in which Norman Cousins does a quite handsome double editorial on *The Uneasy Chair*, praising the book, praising Benny, and eating a little personal crow about the Lewis incident. It seems to me a generous sort of gesture, considering the blisters some of Benny's letters must have raised. It appears also that Naomi Bliven in the *New Yorker* will like the book; whether her review is a lead review, or only one of two or more, I don't know yet. And as you know, Russell Lynes is coming out with a very friendly reminiscence-review in *Harper's*. By and large, I don't think we can holler too loud about the reviewers, even though for the sake of color they do sometimes exploit the ogre image. Most of them show a real respect for Benny.

In case you inquired, which you didn't, there was a stupid but not unfriendly review in the New Haven Some-thing-or-other, a good one by Leon Gussow in the *Chicago Daily News*, a silly posturing one in the *Chattanooga Times*, a splendid one by Marshall Terry in the *Dallas News*.

Paul Ferris's review in the *Chicago Sun-Times* seems to have been syndicated, since I note it in the *Salt Lake Tribune* and the *Baltimore*

News-American among other places. If you haven't seen all these, I'll Xerox them and send them on. Some of them, at least, will soothe your soul.

So have a good time, already, on those perfumed seas.

Love,
Wally

« *To: Avis DeVoto* • *January 20, 1977* »

Dear Avis,

I don't know whether to thank you or not for that *Times Book Review* of Larry's third volume.[50] It is entirely true that old Robert[51] was often mean and sometimes diabolical and very frequently devious and always always focused on himself, but he was also a kind of titan, and it distresses me to see him chewed up by filthy little jackals like this Bromwich, who hasn't the intelligence to see that he is talking about something that is sad, even tragic, and can only jump up and down in glee finding the great man's zipper undone. It's one more instance, added to a hundred very like it, where the TBR has gone out and found the absolute most incredibly incompetent and unqualified person to review a book that deserves a judicial and careful and scrupulous appraisal. Larry's book is hard on Frost, but it also tries to understand him, and it doesn't gloat, the way this pipsqueak does. I'm half tempted to write a letter asking who this guy casting stones is.

Sutton is, as you suggest, another 25-watt genius, only on the other side. I have answered one or two minor questions, laconically and without invitations to continuance. Frost's shadow promises to be as complicated as his substance was.

No, I wouldn't send any of that advance back to Doubleday. They named the amount; we didn't ask for it. And they can afford it a hell of a lot better than thee or me. I'm as sorry as you are that they didn't sell the book better—but they probably got most of the library sale, at least, so Benny is out of the cold. Which must be something. Stay warm. Maybe see you next summer, if our drought doesn't become a disaster.

Love,
Wally

---

50. Lawrence Thompson's biography of Robert Frost, *Robert Frost: The Later Years* (New York: Holt, Rinehart and Winston, 1976). Completed after Thompson's death by R. H. Winnick.
51. Robert Frost.

Special Friends
and Family

◆

To Philip and Margaret Gray, April 8, 1942
To Philip and Margaret Gray, January 10, 1943
To Philip and Margaret Gray, May 1, 1943
To Philip and Margaret Gray, December 30, 1943
To Philip and Margaret Gray, March 27, 1944
To Philip and Margaret Gray, April 23, 1944
To Philip and Margaret Gray, September 18, 1944
To Richard Scowcroft, November 1, 1944
To Richard Scowcroft, December 10, 1944
To Richard Scowcroft, September 9, 1945
To Richard Scowcroft, October 28, 1945
To Malcolm Cowley, June 3, 1956
To Malcolm Cowley, July 7, 1956
To Malcolm Cowley, November 1, 1956
To Malcolm Cowley, November 7, 1959
To Malcolm Cowley, January 8, 1960
To Ansel Adams, January 26, 1963
To Malcolm Cowley, June 18, 1967
To Malcolm Cowley, July 22, 1967
To Malcolm Cowley, March 8, 1968
To Malcolm Cowley, April 14, 1968
To Ansel Adams, November 6, 1968
To Ansel Adams, November 12, 1968
To Wendell Berry, November 13, 1970
To Wendell Berry, August 14, 1971
To Page Stegner, October 1, 1971
To Page Stegner, November 21, 1972
To Page Stegner, No Date, 1973
To Wendell Berry, April 10, 1973
To Ansel Adams, May 19, 1973
To Ansel Adams, September 14, 1973
To Ansel Adams, October 26, 1973

To Ansel Adams, December 3, 1973
To Ansel Adams, December 29, 1973
To Ansel Adams, November 14, 1974
To Wendell Berry, April 3, 1975
To Wallace Page Stegner, July 3, 1975
To Ansel Adams, September 4, 1975
To Wendell Berry, October 1, 1975
To Ansel Adams, August 20, 1976
To Wallace Page Stegner, February 21, 1977
To Wallace Page Stegner, March 1, 1977
To Wallace Page Stegner, March 3, 1977
To Wendell Berry, May 27, 1977
To Rachael Stegner, July 29, 1979
To Page Stegner, No Date, 1979
To Ansel Adams, October 15, 1982
To Rachael Stegner, January 14, 1985
To Ansel Adams, July 4, 1985
To Marion Stegner, January 2, 1986
To Marion Stegner, March 7, 1986
To John Daniel, July 23, 1987
To John Daniel, July 11, 1988
To John Daniel, September 5, 1988
To John Daniel, November 24, 1988
To John Daniel, November 28, 1988
To John Daniel, February 2, 1989
To John Daniel, March 8, 1989
To John Daniel, October 9, 1989
To John Daniel, November 16, 1989
To Page Stegner, July 5, 1990
To Lynn Stegner, September 25, 1991
To John Daniel, October 7, 1991
To Rachael Stegner, December 20, 1991
To John Daniel, March 29, 1992
To John Daniel, October 22, 1992
To John Daniel, December 18, 1992
To John Daniel, March 14, 1993

STEGNER HAD a great many close friends, a correspondence with whom has sometimes been preserved, sometimes not. In a number of cases (Robert Frost and Frank O'Connor come immediately to mind) nothing has turned up in library archives or special collections, nor have direct channels of communication proved successful. The entire correspondence between the Stegners' oldest and closest friends, Philip and Margaret (Peg) Gray (the prototypes for Sid and Charity Lang in the novel *Crossing to Safety*) were preserved by the respective families, only a fraction of which has been reproduced in this volume. Similarly, the many letters over the years between Malcolm Cowley, Ansel Adams, and Stegner's former student and co-director of the Stanford Creative Writing Program, Richard Scowcroft, have been severely culled and only those that seem most revealing of these long-term friendships have been reprinted. Both Wendell Berry and John Daniel were Stegner Fellows in the writing program at Stanford, and of the great many students Stegner cherished over the years, these two were perhaps the closest to him in temperament if not style. As for family,

On my father's side I never had a family—in fact, I was past thirty years old before I ever met anyone with my surname. My father came from the little farming town of Anawan, Illinois, near Rock Island. He had brothers and sisters, but I never knew how many they were, or what they did for a living, or even their names. I never knew the first name of my grandfather, or of my grandmother either, though she lived with us for a while in her senile old age and impressed upon us all the concept of family as burden. That was probably the way it had always seemed to my father, for he left home at fourteen or fifteen, and never returned, and never stopped moving. His schooling stopped with the eighth grade.

My mother's stopped even earlier, with the sixth. She was twelve years old when her tubercular mother died, leaving her to take care of her father's house and bring up her younger sister and two brothers. Born Hilda Emelia Paulson, she grew up on a farm near Lake Mills, Iowa, a Norwegian enclave where most children, including herself, didn't learn English until they started to school. I know more about her family than about my father's because I too was born on Chris Paulson's farm, on February 18, 1909, and because with my mother and brother I spent the winter of 1913–14 at the Paulson house in the town of Lake Mills, and because I visited there in the thirties when I was a graduate student at the University of Iowa, and because for many years I kept in touch with my aunt Mina and her children, the only relatives I ever really knew.

I owe Chris Paulson for several things, among them a long clock (he lived past ninety), a full head of hair that has lasted, and perhaps— this is guess-work—a literary gene. Two of his grandsons became writers: I for one, and for another my cousin Tom Heggen, Minna's son, the author of *Mister Roberts*, whose career was cut calamitously short at twenty-nine. I owe him also for my mother, who was a saint.

Stegner's own descendants can almost be counted on the fingers of one hand—his son, Stuart Page, born in Salt Lake on the 31st of January, 1937, and three grandchildren, Wallace Page, born in Palo Alto, California on March 29, 1962, Rachael Mackenzie, also born in Palo Alto, on February 19, 1965, and Mary Allison, born in Santa Cruz, California on December 2, 1988. He lived long enough to know only one of his three great grandchildren, Wallace Page's son, Sheridan, born in Truckee, California in 1991. Rachael's two children, Dillon and Emma Sheedy, were both born in Santa Cruz after his death in April of 1993. He had two daughters-in-law, Marion Mackenzie and Lynn Moultray.

◆ ◆ ◆

« *To: Phil and Peg Gray* • *April 8, 1942* »

Dear Philpeg,

Oh to be in the Highlands now that picnic's here. In New England it's decent weather, but what can you do with it? In desperation we have taken a little beach cottage on Cape Ann for the month of May, which will undoubtedly be freezing cold, and will spend weekends there in search of vitamin D. I would, Sir and Madam, that you could come and go clamming with us (you eat the clams; I could never tell clams from clearing my throat). Last week during Easter vacation, we did New York. In the daytimes we made a tour of New York cooperatives—housing, wholesales, cafeterias, groceries, Rochdale Institute—and in the evening we did night clubs. Found Burl Ives singing in a little dive in the village, very fine. And if you don't know the Burl Ives Okay album called the Wayfaring Stranger go hear it. It's one of the best of the ballad albums. Also did Stork, LaRoux, etc., came home on the midnight, declined rapidly for two days, and then began to lift our heads again.

Just before we went to New York—and I probably shouldn't say anything about this, except that if it happened to me I'd want to know—Emily Perry called and said that Arthur, who was in Greensboro skiing, had telephoned down to say that the whole village was talking about Mr. Gray and that "Polish refugee girl" who were in a concentration camp. God damn a dirty little ingrown dung-heeled village anyway. Emily wanted to know exact data so she could telephone it back to Arthur and have him spike the gossip. Presumably he did; just possibly he was able to convince them that Mr. Gray had not yet faced the firing squad and that Maria was happily married in Rockford. Perhaps the nasty little business got to you by some other route. I don't know what you can do about it in any case, and I may only be making you unhappy or mad to say anything. I dunno. It's what might be called a delicate problem of conduct. I hope I chose right.

Our own lives are complicated by ten thousand questions. Our equation had six variables and ten unknowns, and how we find X is a headache. I am just now being voted on for the (presumably automatic, though the war changes all that) raise to faculty status as a Briggs–Copeland thing. It would gratify my vanity a very great deal to be promoted just once in some college. On the other hand, if I ever want to finish this goddam novel I want a year off; on that same hand I have been reading freshman papers for twelve solid years, and I'm sick and tired of the things. On the first hand, it will probably be impossible to get leave, especially at this time and especially on the heels of a raise, because temporarily at least there seems to be a staff problem in English A. So we are faced with the probability, though we haven't faced it yet and haven't peeped to the powers, that to get a year off we'll have to quit. If I could believe that this whole war business would have a heart and pass little me right on by, I might see more years ahead for such things as writing novels, but I don't think fate put that cloak of invulnerability on me, and when they start getting up to the eight million mark in the army I'm going to have another nice choice, which you already have made, and honor to your guts, Sir, between draft and labor camp. Worry worry. If I had any guts of my own I'd quit and be done with it, but what if they promote me—me, who has been grabbing for those promotion plums for too many years. Woe. I'm weak, I'm tempted, and I know bloody well that the pleasant little compromise I'm going to suggest will sit with ill grace on the departmental stomach. And here's another point, or question: If we do quit, or get leave, we can't go west as we'd like, on account of tires and funds. We can't live on the farm and get Page in to school. Could we maybe make a dicker to rent your winter house in G'boro for the price of winter wood, utilities, and a modest fee? We might splice a year's living out of the wreckage that way.

All that is speculation, but so is everything we rise to every morning. The summer makes me weep, but it could be so much worse that I don't really cry much except at nights, thinking of all that lovely fresh air. And we will have a month of it. Incidentally, your last letter or the one before it said that Peg might come east to get the Greensboro houses in shape for renters. If it weren't for possibly inducing Peg to stay away from Greensboro entirely I would say let us do that. We're going up late in May for a month, and could easily, with instructions about what you want done, take care of it. A much nicer way would be to have Peg not trust us to do the job, but let us help. Then we could see her and do something to boot.

And Sir, you ask me how I feel about it. I feel sick. I am fairly convinced by now that: I am not a C.O.[1] I am only a C.O. to certain kinds of war. If they made this one I could believe in I'd fight in it. But I see few signs that they're going to, and fewer yet that us little people can make them. The only things Mary and I can see to do are to support the Socialist Party all we can and work like hell to build up consumers' cooperatives, the

---

1. Conscientious objector.

last because they not only offer some sort of check on war inflation but because cooperation is a movement which has a good start in a great many countries and if it could be made strong enough would do an awful lot in making the peace turn out better than the war. If we can win the war. I take back the "we." I don't feel that affiliated, at least not yet. Like everything else in my mind, my attitudes on it are so tentative they're not attitudes at all. I would be much more comfortable in either army or work camp, but I haven't yet got up nerve enough to jump either way. I probably won't until I'm forced to it at the point of a bayonet. Fabian, that's me. Business as usual. It always was bad.

Now to Mormonism. I've hidden behind that most of the year, pretending it was a job I had to do, so I couldn't be bothered with non-essentials. But the bloody thing[2] will be done in another month and then I'm going to be in a hole.

Mary sends love. Give us another shot in the arm soon.

Yours,
Wally

« To: *Philip Gray* • *January 10, 1943* »

Dear Phil,
Your form letter at the . . . inst. Recd. And contents noted. In reply will state that I can use six longwear shirts, plain white, size fifteen and a half neck, at your special bargain price of $1.19.

Lessee, where do we begin? What waters have rolled under the bridge since last it was we had a drop together? We had built the shack. Yes. (We haven't used it a hell of a lot. It's been too damned cold. The thermometer hasn't been above zero for three weeks, and generally it's anything from five to thirty-three below, so we do our skiing no farther away than the Hyland Lodge, so we can run like hell for home after an hour or so.) But now Mary's in the hospital after a little operation (another hangover, the third I believe now, of having given birth to one small fry), and while she is in Barre I have determined to do a number of things, namely: Write at least a hundred pages—or re-write, rather—on the novel; go skiing up at the shack at least once; lug in the three sled loads of wood that George Hill and I brought down last week from the sugar bush, flailing the horses

---

2. *Mormon Country* (New York: Duell, Sloan and Pearce, 1942).

through snow to their bellies over Baker Hill, and mushing along in front like bloody Labradorians breaking trail through the crust; catch up on all my correspondence; wax the floor in the main room, etc., etc. So far I can't seem to get away from the damned novel with the result that I've rewritten seventy-two pages in three days. But I did bring in a little wood, and tomorrow I will go skiing. Your farmers George and Lucy are nice people. We were up there to dinner last week, and the sucker tried to cold-cock me out of a bottle of Seagram's Seven Crown. Hoaxing the city fellers. Fortunately it was one of my good days. I absorbed his poison and took his bait of a beer on top of three highballs, and remained not only upright but decorous. He respects me now. He ought to, considering the way he loaded my highballs. It's exactly the same thing they do in the woods. You tear in to show the farmers you're not a sissy, and they just go along with you and let you kill yourself. The truth is finally coming out as I get to know this Hill guy better. He admitted that he'd never got out so many logs in one afternoon as the first afternoon the two of us worked, and he admitted that the day we worked on the dragsaw the whole damn bunch was trying to run my tongue out. They did, but the dragsaw man told me the other day the same story—he never sawed as much wood in one day in his life. Next time, b'God, I won't be running my battery so far down thinking I have to keep up. But I think you got a damn good farmer.

Cold weather, some inches back, reminds me that we were thinking the other day, after your letter, of the oil shortage and the stoking and whatnot, and reminded each other that there are at least two or three electric heaters in the establishment here. If you'd forgotten about those, which I assume cannot be bought any more for love or money, I shall be glad to box them neatly and send them on. We have not used them at all, and shall not, and certainly nobody will after we leave in about three weeks. And if there's any other equipment, flat irons, vacuum cleaners, electric plates, foot warmers, or anything that you can use this winter please let us know. We'd be tickled to death to lend them to you.

Which brings me really to the burden of my song. The eight months we've been up here availing ourselves of your hospitality have been, no fooling, the best consecutive eight months any of us ever spent. We've had an awful lot of fun, and done enough work to satisfy us, and lived ten times more pleasantly and well than we probably have any right to now, or than we ever will again. We do thank you, and if there were words to match our gratitude I would use them.

It is now the witching hour of ten bells, and I'm off to beddy bye with a footwarmer. Let sanguine natures sneer and scoff, and throw their windows wide. I freeze when I kick the footwarmer off, and absolutely petrify if I open the window to let in all the fifteen-below zero weather that's outside. Ah, bless you, bless you. And just in passing, why doesn't the goddamn English department and the dean make up its (possible) mind? One more year, one more year. They know damned well they won't let you go, but they think they owe something to Scholarship or something to sweat a book out of you. I would tell them je m'en fiche, me boy. No devil can stand to see anybody out of torment, that's all their trouble. Anyway we're glad you're not on the town, and we'll be looking for the book.

Wally

« To: Phil and Peg Gray • May 1, 1943 »

Dear Philpeg,

Sing hey the green holly, college is oudt. Only this year we're not rushing to read three hundred thousand words of themes in the last twenty-four hours so we can burst up to Greensboro. That's one result of having small fry in schools which have not followed the syncopated programs of the colleges. So we're piously and indolently lying around tying up loose ends and putting seeds in the ground and wondering if there isn't something we could write. The novel is all revised and cut and dickered for and sold and will be out in September, according to present plans, and I haven't had anywhere to go after breakfast for so long that I've got out of the habit. Maybe in the next couple of weeks I can begin pretending I'm a writer again. Which brings me to the middle of my song. What we wondered (here are those people again) is this: Are any Grays, Days, Cases, or other creatures going to infest the Gray mansion for the first two or three weeks of June? If not and if we could, we'd sholy admire to go up and finish up the jobs we left unfinished last winter. By debating the draft board a little (scuse me, ration board) I find that we can get twenty gallons of gas extra "to go up and look over our property and keep it from deteriorating." That will almost get us there and back, and since I am now dedicated to teaching Basic Army units whenever they arrive (sometime after June 15), and am deferred therefore for one year beginning July 1, and since there is a vacation entirely unlooked for between now and the time the army moves in, we got thinking nostalgically of Greensboro and peabody birds and wondering if that tennis court pole that I was gonna brace and never did ever fell down, and thinking about the pile of spruce and hemlock cordwood I left down in the woods because I was too lazy to haul them up and saw them, and other matters (who started this sentence) we concluded to write and ask were you giving the house to Days or Cases or others. Emily Perry has offered us her mother's house for June, but those unfinished jobs bother me, and I'd like to make sure that George Hill brings down the wood he still owes the Gray farm, and see if Louis burned out any bearings in the furnace, and one thing and another. We're going up anyway, probably the last week in May, but I find that I caretake better on the ground, so to speak, and living at the Stuarts or Athertons I might never get that pole braced. So would you drop us a note and let us know? And any jobs other than trimming out around the pine trees and scything the paths?

Having asked for more lend-lease, I can now sit down like Mr. Litvinov and pass diplomatic or even dipsomatic gossip. Claude writes that he is about through at Coral Gables and about to be transferred somewhere. Undoubtedly he has been by now, but we don't know where. Harvard is in effect taking over Radcliffe (maybe you saw the co-educational scareheads that had the alumni on their ears), so we get a raise July 1. Army teaching looks from here like a head-and-belly-ache. Speech, too. Not to mention the split infinitive. To say nothing about ending sentences with prepositions, up with which the army will not put. But cheer, there's always a bright side, which in this instance is the spectacle of all the old guard girding itself to take over the regular freshman English. Hyder Rollins and Magoun et al shouldering the white man's burden is a pleasant warmth around the funny bone.

We met the Causes from Madison a few weeks ago, and discussed you with mutual enthusiasm. Nize people. Also we have been to dinner with Kay-franchot-brown-howells and her latest husband, who also seems like a nize guy but has some rather peculiar friends, such as an eight-foot Englishman with a six-foot tux and furlong-and-a-half wrists and the habit of swallowing his adam's apple on every consonant and regurgitating it again on every vowel.

Now to make out my final grades and put my house in order. When are you out? When's Peg coming east as she promised, or has she been and gone and slighted us? How's the house, the water system, the furnaces, the garbage-destroyer (the one in the kitchen, not any of the kids), and the country dancing? How's the book? How's the draft status? How's the state of mind? And isn't it about time for one of your nine-page letters (semi-annual but worth the wait) even if I didn't barge in and ask for something?

Mary sends her best, with a yell from the bedroom that there's one possibility that I haven't covered—that you might yourself be coming to Greensboro, in which event we would toss our hats in the air and write Emily Perry post-haste for reservations down the rud.

By God, sir, it's a nice walk up past your farm to Barr Hill.

Yrs,
Wally

« *To: Phil and Peg Gray* • *December 30, 1943* »

Dear Philpeg,

Nomam, every time I think of the miserable news in your card I curse the decrepit minds of Wisconsin. We're terrible sorry, Phil. It's an object lesson in how narrow minds working within a rigid formula can operate. Those same people would have kept Kittredge out of an assistant professorship because he didn't have a doctorate. We appreciate also what problems must immediately arise. I don't know what the situation about jobs is, but I suspect that nothing except annual appointments as instructor to regale army units is floating around. If I hear of anything fitten I shall certainly wire. But maybe you don't feel like moving a household—and house—like yours around the world, and that doubles the problem. Roots take up a hell of a lot of packing space.

I am leaving an unenviable opening at Harvard about March 1, which will undoubtedly be filled by a teaching-fellow appointee, because what I've been doing is teaching-fellow stuff. But what I shall be doing after March 1 is going about the United States sticking my bill into various American prejudices (with pictures) for *Look* magazine.[3] It's just my luck that by the time I get to *Look* they have cut out their sex angle, and become a family magazine (something for everyone from Grandpa to Baby Snooks), so I don't get no fun. But I get to go a lot of places on *Look*'s money, and for a year (for which I got a leave) it might be fun even without the sex. Also I might arrange to come through the Middle West a time or two, and

---

3. This eventually became the book *One Nation*, which won the Houghton Mifflin Life-in-America Award in 1945.

then I could see you, and that would be fine, and if as we expect we'll be sending Page to a camp this summer maybe Mary will be with me and that will be finer still, because then we can both see you, and that, as I said, will be fine. For us.

Meantime, as a concession to Mary's operations, an unexpected windfall of time off in February, and the New England climate, we hope to fly to Mexico on February 1, to stay about a month before I start for *Look*. The Eastern Airlines seem to think they can get us there, and if they think so we're willing. Hey—how about a reunion in San Angel or Taxco or Uruapan or somewhere? No fooling, isn't Len getting lonesome and isn't Peg in dire need of a rest from hospitals, and aren't you in a mood to celebrate February among the flowers? We could all sit just quietly and smell them.

I should report also that we went up to Greensboro for a couple of days early this month, and found everything in order, Louis firing the furnace, George with his sugar house all built and his rig in, and a temporary chicken house installed. I guess he couldn't get seasoned lumber for a new one, and hadn't had time, because of the long and rainy haying season, to cut and skid any, so he just cobbled up a hencoop in the old barn. I didn't get to see him, because on the second day we all got flu, and thereafter saw nobody but Esther, who came out and played Gray lady one day. Between us and Freddie Pleasants, Sam Ladd had quite a grouch on about the damn summer people that didn't have sense enough to stay home in the winter, but otherwise we survived. Lovely snow, beautiful skiing, every kind of weather, but no healthy participants. With my little candid camera I shot fifteen or twenty frames of snow scenes, which I shall send on if and when I finish the roll and get it developed.

Please let us know what you turn up in the teaching business, and what you decide to do, and how you be, as Mr. Drown says, and what day we can expect you in Mexico, and so on.

And incidentally, the reason I can take the *Look* job is that I am assured by a battery of doctors that nobody with a history of gastric-ulcers would get past the first medical examiner. I never thought I'd see the day when I would look back on those two years and a half of milk and crackers with something approaching affection.

Hoping you are the same, and expecting immediate wires about Mexico, we remain, Sir and Madam and Madam Patterson,

Your affte. and lvng frnds,
Wallmoll

« *To: Phil Gray* • *March 27, 1944* »

Dear Phil,

I believe that the Modom has just completed a letter to Peg which undoubtedly details our interesting movements and prognosticates our immediate future. We beat around the bush about moving west in the fall, but pretty clearly we're coming as far as Iowa, at least, and we sho hope we can see you then. I'm enclosing a letter, at your suggestion, to Scudder Mekiel, asking him if he can give me some dope on Chicago's black belt. That job will come up, I imagine, the first couple of weeks in August. Then I have to run back to Breadloaf the last two weeks of August, while Mary stays in Dubuque, and after that—maybe—we start moving west. Los Angeles ought to be a better headquarters for Mexicans, Japanese, and whatnot than Cambridge. But we dunno. Maybe we wonno till we start. Anyway, would you forward this letter to Mekiel, who looks misspelled or mistyped but is the way he appeared in your letter?

How goes Madison? Is it still fraught? I haven't seen enough of Cambridge since we came back to tell how it is here. I've had to be in New York twice and New Haven once, and the rest of the time I seem to write letters asking people to give time to the cause of *Look*'s campaign against prejudice. I am not advertising too widely what I'm doing, for various reasons, one being that I've got an article in the *Atlantic* in a month or so that will have most of Boston howling for my head, I imagine. Not that I said anything very brusque. Only that I implied, with truth, that the Boston Irish and the Catholic Church were mainly responsible for the outbreaks of anti-Semitism here. I shall be fighting duels with Bill Cunningham within the month.

And meantime my draft board has me 1-A, and I ponder the agenbit of inwyt and wonder if my ulcers and sinuses and sacroiliacs are going to stand up under official scrutiny. If you do not see us in August you will know that I am giving my all, being too goddam inert to make a move one way or the other. It is a very curious thing how one gets involved in a country or a place. I never felt involved at all until we went to Mexico, and there I got at once so ashamed and so proud of being an American that my conscience and my various other emotional agencies all told me quite plainly that I was sold down the river for good, and could never be either an expatriate or a five-to-one boy because I would be gnawed at all the time by the responsibility of belonging to something. So I guess we'll never migrate to New Zealand, as we had half wanted to after the war.

And incidentally but finally, it occurs to me that among the more rabid prejudices in this country is the prejudice against groups like the Fellowship of Reconciliation—at least around here. I wondered if your Sauk Prairie farm might make a picture story which could show C.O.s[4] being human beings and doing a human job. I dunno. I haven't seen the farm and I haven't consulted with *Look*. But they're willing to have a chapter on the Japanese internment camps, and that looks hopeful. Let me know what you think, anyway. I'd sho love an excuse to spend a week in Wisconsin, and the only excuse I can think of is a picture-story.

Best,

Wally

« *To: Phil and Peg Gray* • *April 23, 1944* »

Dear Philpeg,

What cheer? We keep waiting for that letter your postcard promised, but no soap. In between mailmen we fiddle around among the mysteries of racial and religious discrimination, and read a great deal too much ponderous sociological jargon, and run down to New York occasionally, as we're doing day after tomorrow. Mary's going along, for a wonder and a change, and if we could get tickets we might even see a show, though it's about like getting into Buckingham Palace nowadays. A week or so ago we had some fun shooting a mess of very fine Russian-Jewish immigrants in Dorchester, getting our teeth stuck together with Passover raisin wine, and winding up with a very high opinion of immigrants if this family is a sample. I don't know why I think talking with rabbis and drinking raisin wine during the First-Night Seder is more fun than reading themes, but so help me I am pretty glad, I discover, to get away from those paper clips and rubber bands. On May 8th I'm going down to Chapel Hill to talk to some more sociologists, and then I meet J. Saunders Bedding of Hampton Institute and case out a job on the faces of Jim Crow, which might be more fun even than Jewish immigrants. I got a nice note back from Scudder Mekiel, incidentally, but he wrote from the New Weston Hotel in New York and never gave me his permanent address. Hence this little insert again. I hope you don't begin feeling like Pandarus.

---

4. Conscientious objectors.

Plans shake down a little, though not too definitely. Draft board has laid off for a while, and there's some chance I can get a six-month sentence into 2-A. If so, then I can pretty well finish up this *Look* business, at least, before they call D-day on me. And I think I'm going to shoot one job in Chicago and another in Dubuque, as I guess I told you before, so that if you're around I don't see any excuse for our not getting together. And I guess we've about decided to move west for good, no matter what comes up after this *Look* job. I wouldn't advertise that yet, since I'm still technically on leave, but I don't expect we'll come back to finish up our three years here. Instead we shall probably make the 2,000,003rd immigrant into California since the outbreak of war, and rent us an abalone diver's shack at Santa Rosa or somewhere. What of you? Are you westering, as you threatened? Leave a guy know. And what of the possible *Look* story on the FOR[5] fare? I was at least eighty percent serious about that, if you and Peg were. I'd promise to put it right next to the chapter on Jehovah's Witnesses. Or more likely, I'd substitute it for Jehovah's Witnesses, who seem to me a dreary subject to illustrate prejudices against C.O.s,[6] and one I couldn't stir up much objectivity about.

Spring comes slowly up this way. Last night for the first time a sort of springy feeling in the air as we walked from Milton station over to Arthur Perry's house, where were assembled some Greensboroites, and we had ourselves some beer and a sing and a very fine time without catching a single pneumonia. And Pops concerts begin, and the crocuses are out. But a New England spring is a fraud, really. You wait and wait, and tentatively go without a coat, and catch a cold, and recover, and it snows, and then it rains, and the sun shines a little, hopefully, and the much-postponed baseball season gets in a game or two, and then it blows up an east wind and freezes the statues in monument square, and then it rains, and then one day all of a sudden it's hot as hell, with a humidity of ninety-eight, and that was spring that you just suffered through.

Give us news, chums.

Yrs,

Wallmoll

---

5. Fellowship of Reconciliation, an interfaith movement encouraging nonviolent resistance to World War II.
6. Conscientious objectors.

« *To: Phil Gray* • *September 18, 1944* »

Dear Phil,

Well, damn it, the poems came back from *Atlantic*, with a letter saying that Dudley was enclosing a letter to you. He (and the other editors) apparently liked parts but not wholes, which seems to be a fairly common failing of critics. I'm sorry there wasn't more in this, but maybe Dudley's letter to you may be helpful. He's an honest and forthright guy with sense.

Our hegira was fairly hot and hectic, but much fun. Every time I come west I swear I'll never go back east. This time maybe the swearing gets somewhere. We hit a good many places—Mexican villages, half a dozen Pueblo towns, the Navajo reservation, Hopi reservation, Hualapai reservation, divers Acclamation Service, Soil Conservation Service, Indian Service, Tourist Service, and Forest Service offices and files, and gobs of marvelous country. Four or five nights we stayed out on the reservations, and once I even gave a speech through an interpreter to a bunch of Pueblos at Acoma. They were not impressed, though their bloody governor had asked for it. Maybe they scalped him after we left. Coming out, we even got in five hours at the south rim of the Grand Canyon, and we found a desert terrapin in the Mojave Desert that made the trip complete for Page. He is not a housebroke terrapin, I just discovered.

The house here,[7] apart from the Southern Pacific which runs through the back yard like a banshee every hour, is really fine. Hibiscus trees and palm trees and eucalyptus trees and pine trees and a thousand flowering shrubs, a nice sweep of lawn, a view of the Pacific seventy feet away through the pines, etc., etc. Despite the trains, we feel few pains. We're just settling our haunches, as I imagine you are also. How's the World Over Press, and how do you like your dictophone? Give us letters and dope, and for God's sake make it necessary for yourself to come to the West Coast for business reasons. For a change we've got space to put people up, and we think of no one we'd rather put up, temporarily or permanently.

In three days I have written thus far twenty-seven letters, and there are still thirteen on my list. You're relaxation, but a busman's holiday can't go on very long and I ain't up to being funny. Flash—we did see Stuart and Mildred in Grinnell on our first day out of Dubuque. Mildred very much

---

7. In Montecito, California, where the Stegners lived for one year before Wallace was offered a job at Stanford.

pregnant and expecting in two weeks, Stuart lying around taking it easy because he'd had a mild heart attack. Of all the goddam luck those two people have I would not want any of it. Still, they seemed cheerful and not particularly worried. We could stop only for a couple of hours. I suppose Mildred has been delivered by now. We are holding our thumbs for fear something may be wrong with this one.

Leave us hear, Sir. Mary has been wailing for a month at the thought of your leaving your fine house. She's shore house-conscious. I give her a new one every six months, but it don't do no good.

Best,
Wally

« *To: Richard Scowcroft* • *November 1, 1944* »

Dear Dick,
Seems to me a long time since I last saw you staggering home from anywhere. Once in a while Mary wakes up screaming and hollering that Scowcroft is after her, but otherwise we hardly ever hear of you. Or anybody in Cambridge, for that matter.[8] We have a hell of an intelligence service. If I write to Conant, Buck, Morrison, Munn, and the Corporation suggesting that you all be promoted to associate professors and have your salaries raised fifty percent, will you write us a letter?

At long last we seem to be breaking loose from our temporary moorings here, and tomorrow we're bound for Hollywood to go to the studios and see all the stars and maybe have a drink at the Brown Derby and see Voyle and your charming sister. Then Mary will come home to recuperate and I'll stay on to shoot Mexicans.[9] All the kids who are arranged for to show me and the photographer around are just fresh out of San Quentin, the races open in L.A. Monday, election night is Tuesday, etc. I look for a moderately vigorous few days. We don't know yet what we're going to do with Voyle und frau, or what night we're going to do it on, but we have no doubt we'll remember it afterward, or maybe not.

Rumors leak back to me, via Ipswich, Baton Rouge, and ultimately Palo

---

8. Stegner had left his teaching job at Harvard and was living near Santa Barbara, California, working on *One Nation* and gathering material that would eventually result in the novel *A Shooting Star*. Scowcroft had been a student of Stegner's at Utah, and had gone to Harvard to do graduate work.
9. With a camera. *One Nation* was originally written for *Look* magazine.

Alto, that we are living in a mansion with six baths.[10] Tain't so. Is only three, one of which is tired and won't work any more. House is a little tired all over, really. But we still like the palms and the eucalyptuses and the pines and the beach and the private golf course, on which today, b'God, shooting golf for the first time in eight years, I almost breaks eighty. Which reminds me of something else. I wonder if you could do me a great favor, Sir? It's a hell of a thing to ask, so bat me down. But when we came out here I had no idea I was such a hell of a fellow on a golf course, so I left my clubs moldering in that landlocked back hall which is crammed with our dusty boxes and bales, and I could use them here, considering that we were swimming last week and could have gone today if we hadn't been playing golf. (I work nights). Do you suppose that sometime when you're in the latitude of Warren House you could call up Lt. Com. Perrin Snyder, who now occupies our apartment and to whom I shall write a note so he won't be surprised if you call, and see if you could pick up the bag? I'm ghastly afraid there isn't a padlock on the thing: that calls for a brisk walk to the Bicycle Exchange, Bow Street, and the expenditure of thirty-five cents. Then maybe you can sit on the green pad on the Warren House [11] bench in Warren House 9 and hang out your tongue and gasp for Jinny to call the express company. They'll do the rest.

God. Now that I lay it out so neatly it sounds like a week's work. Don't sprain yourself, but if you happen to think of it when nothing else is stirring, I'd go your bail sometime. Assorted stamps scattered through this letter may almost cover the padlock. I'll send you another collection next time I write. Express can come collect.

How does the novel go? How does the navy or whoever it is now go? Who's who at Warren House? Who's who at the Old Howard? Is Ted's [12] book out (I live in seclusion deeper than the shades of hell or the Ides of March), and so what of the inscribed copy the sonofagun was going to send me, and what of Jinny and Car and Mary and others, and what of the status of our Harvard minorities, and watchman, what of the night?

In front of my window the moon climbeth the sky with how sad steps, and the sea moaneth. I pray for storms during our absence in Hollywood,

---

10. Stegner was living in the "gardener's cottage" on the old Hammond estate in Montecito, a property that included a private golf course, a small landing strip, and about a mile of beach.

11. Where the English Department is located.

12. Theodore Morrison.

for during storms the sea casteth up logs and ships' timbers and wooden legs and old chair backs and lobster pots with which I replenish the fire in our simple cot. Yea, and strange monsters out of the deep, octopuses and jellyfish and men whose heads do grow beneath their shoulders.

Hoping you are the same,
Wally

« *To: Richard Scowcroft* • *December 10, 1944* »

Dear Dick,

Sir, I am deeply indebted to you for sending on those golf clubs, even though I haven't had much of a chance to use them yet. But I am incensed with you, Morrison, Burnham, and all the other vermin who crawl on the body of the laboring world, for implying that I sit among the roses and smell the flowers, and don't know there's a war on. I know there's a war on, because I am the slayer and the slain, and I know too damned well the paths I keep. I've worn a rut in it with my backside. When I asked you to send the clubs I had a plan; I would work from eight-thirty to three-thirty, see? Then I would take my golf bag in hand and go shoot nine holes. Then I would return for a good highball by the fire with my good wife, who would have supper smoking on the hob, and after supper and an hour's companionship with wife and child I would return upstairs at eight and work till ten thirty or so. It's worked out, actually—all except the middle part. But I still keep those hours—eight-thirty to ten-thirty, and if you think I like working that hard for my paltry dollars you can, Suh, change your mind or accept my challenge.

But enough of vain recrimination and regret. I got into something that works my can off. So who's the sucker, I ask you? Only once in a while I yearn with a childlike, plaintive, heart-tugging yearning toward those sunny greens, those caves of ice. Weave a circle round me thrice, remove the blankets and the spread, for I have wet the heavenly bed and soiled the sheets of paradise. Who said that? (Somebody's following me.)

We had a nice time with Voyle, but saw Ruth only briefly because she was down with flu bugs or something. Voyle very properly took us down to the Earl Carrol Vanities where we ate tough steak and looked at some awful tough titty, and as for belly buttons, there were enough in sight to repair the damage to the trousers of the ten thousand service men present. Placed end to end they . . . Jeesus, away, foul specter.

Nice about your book. I'm as they say anxious to see it. And did you know we're probably fellow-authors? From what I can gather from the New York office, who are not communicative, the picture book is going to be done by HM.[13]

I enclose some more stamps. I like this stamp idea, because it has a nice old-maidy frugal kind of sound. And also I can charge stamps up to *Look*.

Merry Christmas, m'son. And if I don't get around to writing Xmas cards, distribute my greetings around, will you?

Yrs,

Wally

« *To: Richard Scowcroft* • *September 9, 1945* »

Dear Dick,

I know what you think. You think I read your damn book[14] and didn't like it and didn't have the nerve to write and tell you so. Or you think I never read it at all. But I did read it, see? I finished it day before yesterday in Carmel, after starting it three months ago in Santa Barbara, getting halfway through it last week in the Sierra, and matching chapters while Mary bought groceries in Fresno and Hollister. But I finished her. What is more, I liked her. I liked her to beat hell, see? It's the only book I've read all summer that wasn't prescribed for some goddam job, and maybe my taste has got conditioned by floods of local-color short stories, but it seemed to me a very percipient, sensitive, intelligent picture of people you know from the hide inward. Your Esther is a really good job, and your Burton likewise. But the thing that is somewhat surprising is how good the minor people are, the Johnsons and Templetons and all those good people. You really did it, Sir. Honestly, such people. There isn't any other picture of contemporary Mormonism, but if there was it would have to be good to show up in the light of yours.

On the whole, we thought the press was good, too, and we cheer when Lovell and the business boys kick in with a half page here and there on the advertising front. The *New Yorker* review we thought was simply stupid: maybe you could have written a book about the returned missionary, but that wasn't the book you wrote. You weren't really interested in the

---

13. Houghton Mifflin published *One Nation*, written for Look Magazine, in hardcover.
14. *Children of the Covenant.*

returned missionary as such, but in the young Mormon without a dragon to fight.

See, son, this is how it is with us: Long ago would I have finished the *Children* and written a blurb for the ads and all that, only working for Houghton Mifflin I couldn't, so I waited till I could read it in peace. And I am very glad I did, because I kept stubbing my toe over people I know, and I thought the people and the architecture and the writing were all first-rate. This job of looking over talent gives me a notion of how many ways a first-novelist can stub his toe, especially if he has a contract for his book before he's finished it. You didn't stub your toe at all, for which we have stood at attention, raised steins to shoulder level, enunciated three clear Heils, and put one away.

I'm sorry we didn't get to see you when you were out on the coast. Just when you were there, we were in process of fighting out from under masses of manuscript, and by the time we came to, it was too late even to telephone. Next time, come to the right town and make it easy for a guy.

We've just come back from ten days of camping out in the Sierra and down at Big Sur, and my loins are blistered from nuding on the deserted beach by Thurso's Landing, which isn't called Thurso's on the map; also my tail is blistered from riding a stiff-legged horse up into the Santa Lucia Mountains behind Big Sur, which are really something, when you pop out onto the ridge two thousand feet above that incredible coastline and look down on waves that have rolled in from Japan and redwoods that were growing there before the Shoguns, and headlands that have been wearing away ever since the coast range first poked its snout out of the sea. You better come over sometime.

Best to Jinny and everybody. Page and Mary blow kisses.

   Yrs,
   Wally

« *To: Richard Scowcroft* • *October 28, 1945* »

Dear Dick,
Those are kind words, I hope deserved. I'm glad you liked, gratified you respected, etc. If you read some of my recent mail you'd think I'd advocated the revival of polygamy,[15] that twin relic of barbarism, and you'd probably

---

15. The reference is probably to Stegner's book, *One Nation*.

shudder for my personal safety. I do. I have a theory I'll tell you some time about Georgia boys brought up by Mamies.

That deal with the blonde from Nahant interests me strangely. It's homeric, that's what it is. As a swift stallion from the hills spurns the ground with his hooves, striking fire from flint and quartz as he scours over the plains, arching his neck and letting the wind take his long flying mane, so Scowcroft scoured the Nahant countryside from shore to shore and back, turning his windswept head in anguish to spy his grim enemy, the blonde mare, etc., etc.

> There once was a blonde from Nahant
> Whose panties were silken and scant
> Her boy was diminutive
> And split his infinitive
> You finish the damn thing, I can't
> Or maybe a gal from Cape Ann
> Who desperately wanted a man

Or maybe I'd better leave this for them as can do it. Sunday night is letter night, and holy Christ the desk is full, so this will be the shortest letter you ever had from old runs-off-at-the-type-face. Weather persists, Stanford persists, the opera is a stinking art form, the U.S. Navy as witnessed yesterday is a powerful aggregation, as the freshmen say. And Page's music lessons are not an aid to either digestion or study.[16]

Stay away from blondes, either artificial or natural. But if you must pry, stick to natural ones. There's only one way to tell.

Hey—get a job out this way. But before you leave, say hello to them that deserve it.

Our best,
Wally

« To: Malcolm Cowley • June 3, 1956 »

Dear Malcolm,

I am slow in replying to your letter about Patchen[17] because we have been out of town for several days. Actually I don't know what to say. We were prepared to give him fifty dollars for a reading of his poems whenever he

---

16. Page enjoyed them equally.
17. The Beat poet, Kenneth Patchen.

called or came in to set a date. He never came in, and never set it—which I assume to mean either that he is in such distress he forgets important (even fifty is important if you're that down!) items, or that he isn't interested in money he has to earn. We are still ready to put him on in the Jones or Bender Room if he shows up, but up to now at least haven't had time to go hunting for him.

There is one possibility for a foundation, if you think more charity is what is called for. At least I am sure that the San Francisco Foundation would accept and disburse money for Patchen's relief, thus making it tax deductible, if you have some donor willing to provide it. This is the foundation which is handling the memorial fund raised in Joseph Henry Jackson's name, and it handles as well a dozen or two other charitable funds of the smaller kind. If the Rosenthal Foundation doesn't work out, write me again and I'll go to the City and snoop around to see if the S.F. Foundation may be available.

Great about Michigan—I hope it isn't half as pleasant as Stanford. As for Los Altos Democrats—Suh, we've got two to three hundred, all registered. Our best to you both—a brave if ragged cheer reaching from Los Altos Hills to Conn.

Yours,
Wally

« *To: Malcolm Cowley* • *July 7, 1956* »

Dear Malcolm:
The enclosed letter from John May of the San Francisco Foundation will carry its own unsatisfactory message.[18] Whether the suggestions May makes about New Haven and Hartford are worth anything I'll have to leave to you. Since I have been out at pasture, or on the shelf, I haven't had much contact with the local literary scene, and so I don't know the latest word on Patchen. I do know that he has never come back to renew the contact with Dick, though Dick is certainly not the kind to give anybody the freeze-out. So I guess we wait till he does. We'll put him on for a reading anytime he wants, but that's about the best we can do.

The summer, as you will have been advised, is already past the solstice,

18. Stegner had appealed, without success, to the San Francisco Foundation for financial aid for Kenneth Patchen.

and beginneth to wane, and like a solar myth, I wane with it. The book[19] (books are supposed to grow in your hands, I hear, and grow satisfactorily heavier week by week) seems to stand still, though with the proper instruments one might measure a snail-like movement. With God's help, on which I am afraid I can't rely, I may finish the damn thing before school starts again.

Have you seen the reviews for our next year's fellow, Jacobson? Maybe we'll put him in the saddle and let him rule the local tribe and communicate the arts of life and letters to the young.

Our best to you and your delightful Missus.

Yours,
Wally

« To: Malcolm Cowley • November 1, 1956 »

Dear Malcolm,

I don't know why it should have to be practically the anniversary of your arrival out here before I get around to writing a letter that is not concerned with Kenneth Patchen. And speaking of Patchen, God knows what the poor devil is doing. He wrote me asking for an appointment as poet-in-residence, and I wrote back renewing our offer of a paid reading or two, and that is the last I have heard.

The rains begin rather earlier than usual. Your former house is occupied by an Australian Writing Fellow, the group this year looks several cuts above that of last year's—I wish, for your sake, it had been the reverse. Of your crowd from last year, I still have Comito, Harss, and, once he gets his red tape organized, Lovell. The rest are new, and several of them red hot.

In another package, I am sending you a copy of my latest book of stories.[20] I hope you like them, but don't have them on your conscience as something you think you have to acknowledge or comment on.

One thing, however, I would like to ask, if it isn't a terrible burden. We are putting together now the next *Stanford Short Stories*, which will contain, among others, Lovell, Joanne Hardy, Comito, Harss, and Murphy. Could you find it in your heart to write us a few hundred words of foreword sometime in the next two or three months? I could send you a set of galleys,

---

19. *A Shooting Star.*
20. *The City of the Living.*

probably in January. Whatever you chose to say, either about the class, the stories as a whole, or any individual stories, would be fine and would gratify the kids very much, not to speak of us and the Stanford Press.

Dick is off duty, writing some stories of his own. I am on duty and doing nothing of the kind. I hope that you and Muriel thrive. Our love to you both.

Yours,
Wally

« *To: Malcolm Cowley* • *November 7, 1959* »

Dear Malcolm and Muriel,
We have the enormously invigorating news from Dick Scowcroft that both you and Frank O'Connor will be at Stanford for six months next year. This is worth coming home for. I gather that you will be there autumn and winter, so that we can start all over again together. Benissimo, benissimo. I'm particularly grateful to you for agreeing to six months! I never felt in the other two fits that we had time to do more than say hello and goodbye. This time we will plumb the deep-down-going-much-mud-upbringing depths, by god.

Mary is at a concert of the Vienna Chamber Chorus; I am at home with my fourth European cold. If you detect a note of bitterness here and there, va bene, you detect it. I have had this thing, I am entitled to be exempt. However, I have had the pleasure this afternoon of looking into Bill Wiegand's novel (the second Joe Jackson fellowship book) which McGraw Hill is just publishing. It looks good; I hope it does him proud.

I have followed your advice, and stuck very sternly to the novel,[21] except for a brief spell in England when I was writing the introduction for Mary's O. Henry book,[22] and for a time when we were traveling. I arrived two or three weeks ago at page 420, and stuck. I was stuck, and not very nice to live with for two weeks. The only thing that saved my reason was a commission to do a $25 article for *Collier's Encyclopedia*. When I came out of that I was not <u>well</u>, but was better. And this morning I think I finished the first chapter since the Great Breakdown, and even in my thick-headed and sore-throated and angry mood, I have hope of seeing daylight out that cave

---

21. *A Shooting Star.*
22. The annual O. Henry Short Story Collection, edited for 1959 by Mary Stegner.

door sometime soon. The hell of if was, I had had this girl self-consciously making her life into a soap opera, and suddenly I had to say why. Maybe I know, now.

Mary thrives. As I may have written you, our quarters are very pleasant and the food is fine, I can't blame anything on the working conditions. Lawrence Roberts and his wife, along with Elizabeth Bowen and some architects, blew through our town two or three weeks ago, and we had a drink and some talk with them. It seems we can stay at the Academy[23] about as long as we want into the summer, and so I have no fear of not finishing the book before we go home. But I hope to finish a draft of it in the next month, and then go to Vienna for Christmas. Ora pro nobis. Maybe Prague, too.

Our very best wishes for the merriest of Christmases and happiest of New Years—half of it in Palo Alto. Hurray.

Yours,
Wally

« To: Malcolm Cowley • January 8, 1960 »

Dear Malcolm,
I have been wanting to write you about the Leaves of Grass and the pleasure I took in both it and your introduction, but my own book[24] has had me where the wrestler in the Great Hall of the Palazzo Vecchio in Florence has his opponent, and I hadn't had time to read quite through old Whitman. Now I have, and I agree with you, it is incomparably more a single thing, a book, a testament, than what I once waded through as Leaves of Grass. I think you have done a service, and I thank you for my copy, you and Marshall.[25]

Life at the Academy[26] is lively but industrious, by and large. The admirable Assunta, of whom we grew swiftly fond, has been laid off because of illness, and is having to give up her apartment below the Villino for the portiere and his wife. This gives Assunta delusions of persecution, naturally, and she goes around the garden like a witch at the Battle of

23. The American Academy in Rome.
24. A Shooting Star.
25. Marshall Best, editor-in-chief at Viking Press.
26. The American Academy in Rome. In 1960 Stegner was appointed Writer in Residence following the tenure of Elizabeth Bowen.

Pharsalia muttering charms and curses and giving certain people the Eye. Marguerita says she really shouldn't work because of her heart, and that she's quite well taken care of with pensions and an apartment house, but she acts like the most abused woman since the Christian martyrs, and it makes us unhappy to see her so gloomy.

Our apartment is the one next to the Villa; the Tommy Churchs are in the next one, but leave tomorrow; then comes a composer named Finney to be our neighbor. Your villino is occupied by Rico LeBrun, a painter, but he's had a kind of breakdown and has not poked his nose out in the nearly six weeks we've been here. Dick Kimball, the new director, has already gone back to New York for board meetings. The two writers on the ranch are Edmund Keeley, from Princeton, and Harold Brodky. Saul Bellow is in town and lecturing this week. I have met no Roman writers except the crowd around Botteghe Oscure, mainly Irish poeticules, and Ignazio Silone. We sightsee only casually, though Mary went off for a week and took that trip to Salzburg and Vienna that illness kept us from taking at Christmas time. In two weeks we have to remove the car from Italy and bring it back in again, and for this we will go to Corsica. Know any writers in Corsica? Greece we are saving up for April or May, when the novel is presumably done.

Speaking of which novel, I have revised it up to page 413, and I have one solid chapter ahead that will go fast. Then there is a hundred pages of tough going, the last part of what I wrote in Florence, which is still in real first draft. If you see our esteemed editor, as you will, would you tell him that by the time I have to go to Corsica I should be part-way but not all the way through that last 100 pages? And that therefore he won't see the MS quite as soon as I had hoped? But that after our four or five days in Corsica I shall come straight back here and finish it in at least shape to be seen. That is, barring disasters, a manuscript in March. I do not dare comment on it: It is as it is.

Dick writes that all arrangements are made for you at Stanford. Half the pleasure of going home will be to find you two shortly there. Mary, who just crawled into a hot tub after an icy tour of the Vatican museum shouts her greetings to mingle with mine like incense from a pan-Hellenic altar.

Our best to you both,

Wally

« *To: Ansel Adams* • *January 26, 1963* »

Dear Ansel:

Clearly both the books you mention are GREAT BOOKS.[27] The fact that you like one better than the other is a commentary, not on the author, but on the reader. A fine but narrow taste, posterity will say of you. If you hadn't liked either one, I would have given up on you. And if you should press me, I might even admit that, assuming you had to like only one, you picked the right one.

The map error you noticed is one that I howled my head off about. I never saw proofs—the idiot who made the map moved all of Canada 500 miles west of where it ought to be. Second printing will correct. Meantime I patiently answer angry letters from Canada.

And thank you for your superb card. Mary has mounted it on her easel and stares at it often. I pass the easel less often than she does, but I certainly look as I go by. It's a beauty. Now that you're down among the cypresses, you may turn out to be a photographer of the sea and no longer of the mountains. Though that would be a pity.

See you Monday night, maybe, at the publications committee meeting.[28] Love to Virginia.

Yours,
Wally

« *To: Malcolm Cowley* • *June 18, 1967* »

Dear Muriel and Malcolm,

This is mainly to hope that your singular and collective ills have eased up, that Muriel is no longer stoking up on digitalis and nitroglycerin and that Malcolm is walking without a cane, upright, firm, the very picture of a country gentleman. We haven't heard from you in a good while, and we can see why even though we fear your silence, which may mean you're still hurting. Please, don't.

We're hoping to leave here in about seven or eight days, depending mainly on the temper of our renter (erstwhile), to whom we have given summary notice after I found my whole goddam hill planted with marijuana. I don't give a damn what he does in his private life; what I object to

---

27. One was *Wolf Willow*. The other is unknown.
28. Of the Sierra Club.

is his practicing agriculture with neither lease nor license. And since we're turning over the house to a Harvard pair on July 1, we suspect we'd better clear the premises first, lest they get involved in a lot of questioning by the boys in blue. The difficulty is that the renter feels no sense of sin, and is sullen at the shortness of our notice, which in the circumstances couldn't be more than about three weeks. So he may stage a sit-down, and then what do we do? Arrive with the bailiff and set his furniture in the street? Alas. I doubt that we have deserved this, as landlords, but we had better learn to deal with it. I could turn over some carefully preserved evidence to the sheriff, but though if it got that far I might be pleased to see the sucker in jail, I'd have to stay here all summer testifying against him. Aren't you glad you live in a climate too arid to grow pot?

A brief conversation with Marion and Page, in Greensboro, an hour ago told us little other than that the weather is beautiful and Pagie caught a lot of perch. Page is reading galleys on his novel,[29] and wondering whether they're going to publish him in the fall or in January. Me, I got doodling with a story a few weeks ago and the thing is now nearly fifty pages long—just the wrong length to be anything. Ah, the beautiful and blest nouvelle.

Since for complicated reasons we're driving east, and for still more complicated reasons by a far northern route, we won't be seeing you on the way. If you'll once let me pay your goddam room rent, I'll invite you both to Greensboro for a good rest, or we may well see you if we come down to New York during the summer or fall, as seems likely. In any case, take it easy. Both of you. And let us hear. We'll be in Greensboro around July 4.

Best,

Wally

P.S. Have you heard that Page is coming to Santa Cruz, beginning spring quarter next year? Goodbye, Columbus.[30] In a way he's sad, I think.

« *To: Malcolm Cowley* • *July 22, 1967* »

Dear Malcolm,

We were just getting the feeling that we were terribly out of touch with you and Muriel when your inscribed copy of the Faulkner book arrived, and that was a fine and stirring way to get back in touch. I sat down and

---

29. *The Edge* (New York: Dial Press, 1968).
30. Ohio State.

promptly read it through when I should have been preparing a speech for the University of Vermont next Tuesday, and I am much better off than if I had worked on the speech. It's a fine, solid, humane, undazzled, judicial, and admiring book, and it says a great deal about Cowley as well as about Faulkner. God send every neglected novelist such a friend. Does it ever give you the twitches to think that you may go down in history as Faulkner's St. Paul or Huxley? Or maybe Jean Baptiste, saying Prepare ye the way of the Lord? You did us all a service, sir. Back in Prohibition times it used to be customary among the better bootleggers to put a little glycerin in the bathtub gin—it precipitated out the foreign bodies and left things sparkling. That's what you did, if you don't mind the metaphorical company.

I guess I should bring you up to date on us. We got back to Philadelphia on July 1, having spent two weeks before that on the Dalmatian coast and the three months before that teaching at Semmering, 60 miles out of Vienna, where Dick Scowcroft is teaching right now. We cut our Dalmatian trip short because Mary, who had had a heart upset a while before, in Austria, got some more symptoms on the island of Hvar. In Philadelphia they told her she had a damaged heart muscle and that her cardiograph was out of whack. She has been pretty much resting, with only very minor walks and sociability, since we came up here on the 7th. Too early to tell how she's doing; they said she might get all over it in a month, or it might take six. So we are not in the jolliest frame of mind, and poor Mary is bored stiff to lie around and not get anywhere or see anyone. But we are acquiring some good books (witness yours) and some good music, and she will damn well have to submit herself, and in the constructive element immerse. I am a pretty feeble cook, mainly because all my instincts and temptations run to carpentry. But we manage; and I even get in a little carpentry on the work shack, and a little writing on the book, which is just heaving out of the mud where it had been stuck since last Christmas. Pray God it runs when I get it back on the road: I estimate I have about four good solid chapters to write, and with luck I will write them before we go back to Stanford in September. I guess I told you that because of Michael's death[31] I am postponing my sabbatical a quarter. We'll piece out the rest of the year after I depart in January. We did not, as we had hoped, see Harriet abroad, though we had some letters. She is back in Dublin, unless she has finally closed things

---

31. Michael O'Donovan (pen name, Frank O'Connor).

up there and come back to her family's place at Annapolis. You know that Trinity had a memorial service for Michael in early June—that was one thing Harriet went to Dublin for.

Page writes that you have been reading galleys of his Nabokov book.[32] I hope you found it worth an encouraging word. Me, I sit outside this whole development pinching myself black and blue and hoping that it doesn't all turn out flash in the pan, or too-kind friends, or something dreary like that. Nothing would please me more than to have Page turn out to have a talent. JESUS, I'd turn cartwheels. But I have learned, through many burned thumbs, not to reach too greedily. I shall wait, though not patiently.

Any chance you'll be touring north this summer? We are not much more civilized than we were, but we're some—I hung a screen door today after I finished your book. We'd love to see you—hopefully without that busted tailbone you were dragging around last time. And we now have a telephone—give us a call. Send us a postcard. Drop by. I'll be up there in the shack trying to resolve the problem of whether to yield to temptation and do a little carpentry, or whether to spend another while on the book in order to justify building the damn shack all.

Our love to your sainted Muriel. And may you both be in health. And many, many thanks for the book and the inscription.

Yours,
Wally

« *To: Malcolm Cowley* • *March 8, 1968* »

Dear Malcolm,

By now, how do you like Oaxaca? No yearning for the melon vines emerging from the snow in the Sherman garden? No faint itch for acacia yellow all over the Los Altos hills? Better come by on your way home. That would make a pleasant break for us, since all I've done since getting back is read fellowship applications, admissions applications, and student manuscripts. The quarter ends in a week, and I have only one class next quarter, and the fellowships will be settled by early April, and the admissions are almost done now. God willing, I can get back to the book in a few weeks.

News from here is meager. The Kronenbergers are Regents Professoring

---

32. *Nabokov's Congeries*, published by Viking Press in 1968 and reprinted as *The Viking Portable Nabokov*.

at Berkeley, so that we've seen them a couple of times. Tom Moser retires as department head in June, and the corridors are full of murmurs and caucuses, without a clear candidate to show for them. Or rather, Claude Simpson would be everybody's candidate but we're all sure he won't take it.

It makes not much difference to me. I've just about decided to retire early and spend my declining years writing books instead of reading bad manuscripts. And something that may disturb you: I'm leaving Viking. Where, I haven't yet decided. But just to be leaving. Reasons I will tell you at length when next we see you. I just don't feel particularly well used. Used maybe, but not well. I will miss the one incomparable thing that Viking gave me: your editorial advice. So far I have done nothing but write Marshall that I was leaving (he is on vacation and I have not heard from him in reply) and write Carol to ask her to look around for another stall.

Page and Marion arrive next week to take up their new job and new house at Santa Cruz. There's a hell of a lot of painting and cleaning up to do, but basically the house is a good one, with a good big yard and a fine view and lots of country around it, and only a half mile or so from the university. School bus picks up the children at the end of the lane, etc. etc. They should be well set after a couple of months of frenzy.

Write us. And come by. We've always got a bed, and a lecture to help pay the expenses. And a crust to gnaw on, though that may not last. Our very best to you both. Have a great year.

Yours,
Wally

« *To: Malcolm Cowley* • *April 14, 1968* »

Dear Malcolm,

I appreciate your letter and I understand your distress. I feel it myself. But I would not want you for one moment to feel that my decision to move has anything to do with you. As you know, your editorial advice on both *Wolf Willow* and *All the Little Live Things* was invaluable to me. I will not get its like again, in any editorial office I land in. And quite apart from that utilitarian matter, I will miss the friendship that the Viking office contained. Nevertheless, I was not getting at Viking what I left Houghton Mifflin hoping to get, and what I thought was assured me. And I haven't got a hell of a lot more time. So I will have to go hunting.

I'm coming east this afternoon, but in such a hurry, with such crowded and limited time, that I probably won't even have time to call you. I'll be in New York one bare day, with both publishing and movie problems to discuss, and then I have to be in Washington Tuesday morning at 9 for an award to Ansel Adams, and then I have three days of meetings, and then if the meetings end anywhere near their scheduled terminus, I'll fly up to Montreal for one more tight day, talking to the National Film Board, which is talking of making a movie out of parts of *Wolf Willow*. Then I will come home on a shutter and resume teaching, but not for long. I've applied for a year's leave without pay (assuming something comes out of these talks) and will spend it working on the new novel, intensively I hope, uninterruptedly I hope. It doesn't look as if we will be in New York again until August. Is that a time when a drink can be arranged with a Century member? We hope it's a time when the Cowleys can make their annual pilgrimage to Vermont, to walk on moss and swim in icewater. We've even got a bedroom for you now.

The news about the volume of poems is great. I have never forgotten the one you read in Greensboro, about your sister (?), the thrice-dead, and I like the new one. In fact, with your permission, which I assume, I am going to give a copy of it to Stewart Udall, who is always looking for eloquence to work into a conservation speech or essay. So if you get a letter asking permission to quote, blame me. He will go for that final prayer, I will lay money.

Page and Marion have settled down in Santa Cruz, up to their pistol pockets in clover so far as I can see. They have a good house, a good view, a good job, neighbor kids for their kids to play with, open land around for their dog to pee his corners on, and a state beach at the foot of the hill, a mile away. Moving has interrupted his writing some—moving and reviewing books—but he should be back in the groove before I am.

We are both rather better in health than you remember us. We hope Muriel is rested and fattened and invigorated by Mexico, and we pray for your abdominal rumblings, which from here do sound themselves like a distant mutter of prayer.

Yours,

Wally

« *To: Ansel Adams* • *November 6, 1968* »

Dear Ansel:

I tried to reach you by telephone and missed. So here is a note with several subjects.

1) Christmas is coming around again, the third since I tried to buy Mary an Ansel Adams photograph for her wall. We have had a mighty pleasure out of the Varian portfolio that we took in partial exchange for the $250 I paid you, but we would like a print too. Or another portfolio. Almost anything. I know you're terribly busy, but could you cast a look around the studio for loose objects that might satisfy the pesky Stegners? If it turns out to be a portfolio, I know that the one Mary loves next to the one she has is the one with many Yosemite prints in it.

2) Would you be interested, for *American West*, in writing a fairly brief appreciative, biographical, or critical essay to accompany a fairly lavish spread of Maynard Dixon pictures? I think you knew him since your portrait of him is much displayed. Did you like, admire, or respect him enough to write out your response to him and his art for our readers? We could pay you $250—about enough to supply you for a year with typewriter ribbons and maybe erasers. And we would love to have you in the magazine. If the Dixon idea doesn't appeal to you, maybe you'll have another, to use Adams pictures instead of Dixon's.

3) I hear lamentable things about the Sierra Club. Almost I hate to ask anybody what's happening, for fear I'll find out. So don't consider yourself asked unless you feel the need of a listening and probably sympathetic ear.[33]

Our love to Virginia,

Wally

---

33. Ansel's reply refers to the famous dispute between the board of directors of the Sierra Club and David Brower, its executive director. "The Sierra Club is in a truly lamentable situation. I do not like to be a Jeremiah, but we are confronted with possible financial disaster. The obdurate, recalcitrant, myth-weaving, unilateral character of our Executive Director hath brought upon us the stark possibility of catastrophe. I hope and pray for some SIGN from above—some miracle . . . One choice bit: he [Brower] set up a London office and (in effect) a London corporation—without the knowledge or approval of the Board or Ex. Com. He then obligated the Club for around 180,000.00 for producing the Galapagos Books (without knowledge or approval) and without a formal contract."

« To: Ansel Adams • November 12, 1968 »

Dear Ansel:

Don't grovel. I've been a vague demander. But now that we've made contact—and I don't mean print—I hope we can get a real Adams to hang on our nail. We have been looking through all the books we own that contain Adamses, and this is what we would most like. We would like almost anything.

As you remember, our first enthusiasm was for trying to buy the great big "Sierra Nevada from Lone Pine" that you had hanging in the studio in the Valley. You said it was defective, and wouldn't sell it at any price. So I bought the same picture in about a 20 x 30 (whatever was $250 at that time) and Mike brought us down a standby-print so Mary could have her Christmas stocking. This was fine, except that the print was smaller than we wanted, and its values ran toward the darker ranges, whereas for this room, on this particular gray wall we thought the lighter range would be better. He brought the standby print back to you one day, and you were going to make another, of the larger size and lighter range of tones. Later still, desperate for an Adams, we took a Varian portfolio at some price ($125) leaving us still into you for some kind of print. Alas, the University of California and other intruders intervened. So with that preamble, let me say that we would still love a big print, 20 x 30 or bigger, and would be glad to pay any difference we might still owe. Our favorite is still "The Sierra from Lone Pine," but others would make us very happy—for example "Frozen Lake and Cliffs," or "Burnt Stump and New Grass." We don't want to force you into your cave, when you are already swamped with work, to make us a special print. What we hope is that you have on hand some larger print of some photograph we will fall upon with cries of joy. We have enough books here to check out specific pictures pretty well. If you'll let us know what you've got on hand, maybe we can drive down and pick it up between now and Christmas.

I don't even comment on the Sierra Club, though I feel enough, until I have talked with more people and heard the latest decisions of the Board. Maybe Savonarola had to be burned. And I make a separate letter out of the *American West* proposal, according to the best business practice. Our love to Virginia.

Yours,
Wally

« *To: Wendell Berry* • *November 13, 1970* »

Dear Wendell,

We've been back home only about ten days, and most of that time I've been shoveling out from under the accumulated pile of mail, including a good many books by former students here. It is getting so that I do very little other reading. But one such opportunity that I thoroughly enjoyed was *The Hidden Wound*. I read it with the deepest sort of respect, not only for its prose, which is as usual eloquent and even elegant, in the way an equation is said to be elegant, but for its qualities of wisdom and dignity—I guess the combination really is what Ed Abbey says it is; nobility. You take care, hear? You're a great man. Even when I think you're overstating your case, as I think you do when you imply that only black men know the American earth (you yourself are the best confutation of that implied thesis), you overstate it in a way that does you honor and the world good. You are so old-fashioned (which is a good thing to be) that you sound like Lincoln (who is a good man to sound like). I thought the *Long Legged House* essays were splendid, but this is more, this is a document. I am going to give some of these to people who need to read you. I'm only sorry to have got here too late to write a comment for Houghton Mifflin, or to get somebody to let me review this. If there is still any point in it, you have my eager permission to use anything from this letter, in or out of context, with or without ellipses. And I will tell you something: I never wrote that kind of blank check about any book or any writer before this moment. I think the book is absolutely great.

In my enthusiasm for *The Hidden Wound* I have not yet got to the latest book of poems. I have to admit it—I read prose with more comfort and probably with more discrimination than I read poetry. I will read your poems because they're yours, but I read *The Hidden Wound* because after trying two paragraphs I couldn't help myself. I suspect that when I read the poems I will find the same integrity I find in the prose, and many of the same convictions.

I thought I understood why you had made the decision to stay on the farm in Kentucky, I understand a little better now. If anyone tries to woo you away, as I did, send him to me and I will talk him out of it. You belong right where you are. That's good ruminating country.

Our best to Tanya and the children, and thanks—this is from Mary too, who was up half the night with you night before last—for a book that I am going to read, and quote, many times. So are a lot of other people.

Yours,
Wally

« *To: Wendell Berry* • *August 14, 1971* »

Dear Wendell,

Your letter made me passionately wish you were employed by Columbia University as a member of the Pulitzer Prize Committee, and by the Swedish Academy or whatever it is as a chooser of the Nobel Prize. But even though your note comes without gold seals and checks attached I'll take it. It pleases me exceedingly that you find the book good. Though I should tell you in warning that on the same day as your note I got a fan letter from Pearl Buck, and what does that make me? I'll tell you what it makes me. It makes me think more highly than I ever did of Pearl Buck's literary stature. As for yours, you know what I thought of that even before this.

Rumination, once our favorite country pastime, seems a little harder to maintain this summer. Motorboats on the lake, visitors one didn't ask to drop by, drudgery of reading through the documents for this bloody biography. But I finished all that yesterday and from here to October 1 is going to be purest meditation under my favorite bo tree, which is actually a basswood (tilia Americana). I have built two lean-tos, which is about par for the summer, and have only a woodshed to go before snow flies.

Very little word of anybody. Dick[34] has been at Yaddo, but I think has now gone back. Dolly[35] is in Sweden with her mother. Page goes to Caracas next Tuesday, and after he hunts up living quarters, Marion and the children will fly down to join him. Frantic last minute preparations. At any moment I expect to be called on to help put the sailboat away. So I had better be ready. Our best to you and Tanya.

Yours,
Wally

---

34. Richard Scowcroft, co-director of the Stanford Writing Program.
35. Dolly Kringle, secretary of the Stanford Writing Program.

« *To: Page Stegner* • *October 1, 1971* »

Dear Page,

That letter of transmittal the other day had no room for a reply to your remarks on *Angle of Repose*. I am embarrassed that you had your arm twisted into making them—I was not bothered, I knew you were frantically busy and distracted, and I knew we would talk about it sometime—and that if we didn't, it would be because there was nothing there to talk about. I find your faulty judgments about art and posterity and such easy to condone, and I agree with you about Susan Ward. If you didn't dislike her gentility you weren't reading me. On the other hand, and I hope this was clear too, without her gentility she didn't exist. She was, like all of us, the product of her qualities, and the good and the bad are so entangled in that gentility business that it's like Hawthorne's birthmark. Cut it out and you kill the patient. In the same way, Oliver's (and Lyman's) mule-headedness and unforgiving rigor is all tied up with their integrity, which is quite as real. I may have been trying to do something impossible in showing, through two long lives and several shorter ones, that in any social context individuals will be colored by their times, for good and ill, and that in the end one social context is about as good as another, so long as it is subscribed to fully, and as binding on the people born to it. I suppose I also wanted to throw in the notion that one time, despite its assumed freedom and emancipation from history and human cussedness, can be about as foolish as another. As for Julie, sure she ain't very convincing. I modeled her on one of our Fellows, who is now off to join a commune in Cambridge and live by ripping off grocery stores. But I wasn't very privy to the most intimate thoughts of that girl, and anyway she's 25 or 26, and behind the times. I guess I didn't worry too much about her being entirely with it; the argot and the attitudes change about every three years, and it's impossible to keep up to date. But I'm sorry she didn't turn out to be more of a person.

Also the ending. I feel like that guy who brought in his watch to be fixed and the man said we don't fix watches, we fix cats, and the customer said why the hell have you got a watch in the window, then? And the shop-keeper said what would you put in the window? How would you get out of that book? I tried writing the wife's reappearance in real terms, and it was both long and wrong—the introduction of a new character merely to end the novel didn't ring right. The dream bit was a kind of cheap way out but the only one I could think of. It was meant to be final, in that it suggested the inevitable: somebody, probably she, was going to come and get Lyman sooner or later, and his independence was going to get bent by vile neces- sity. But you're not alone in finding the ending wrong. Malcolm[36] objects to it too. Its tone I think I could defend; I think it hooks together past and present, it tilts the historian into a stance not too unlike the Shelly modern stance, sexuality and all. Or it was intended to.

Word this morning about some abduction of a Dominican Republic diplomat's wife and a search for her through Caracas. Keep your family inside that broken glass, hey? And let us hear—we're very fond of letters from all members of the family. Our departure date looks like about Oct. 12, and we'll take a couple of weeks at least on the road. I'll write you when we know exactly. Love to all.

Pop

« *To: Page Stegner* • *November 21, 1972* »

Dear Page,

There's a fair chance that this won't reach you before you all leave Caracas, so I'll send it to Quito, and maybe it will be waiting for you. It's mainly about your story,[37] which as Mom probably wrote you, we both found lively, persuasive, often greatly amusing, and worth a lot of discussion. I've just read it for the second time, to check out some questions that rose in my mind, and in talking it over with Mom I find that some of the same questions rose in hers. You will find it endlessly amusing, I know, to be told that though we're both absolutely certain there's a good story here— already here, most of it—it isn't yet quite clearly articulated. Part of our uncertainty about some points may arise from the fact that this is part of a longer story, and some of what seems almost irrelevant or misleading here may be a legitimate part of the whole. But all we have is these 89 pages, and here is what we both think: (Remember, as you read this, that I found Mom chuckling and giggling out loud while reading it in bed, and that I too read it with great respect. The surface, the detail, the backgrounds, the characters, are first rate. It's primarily the relation between the two

---

36. Malcolm Cowley.
37. This was the opening section of a novel, *Sportscar Menopause*, eventually published by Atlantic/Little, Brown in 1977. Page Stegner was in Venezuela working as a deputy director of the Peace Corps.

principals that puzzles us, and since that's central to the whole story, it's important enough to entrust to the Ecuadorian mails.)

1) There is a real doubt in both our minds that you need the child, whom anyway you introduce—as a name or an image, not really as a person—and then totally forget. At the end, when Eliot has his last errands to run, saying goodbye to his child never enters his head. I think you had forgotten he had one. In any case, I suspect you can quietly abort him, even if he is two years old. He only confuses the issues between husband and wife; he is in no sense part of the issues, except to give you a little diaper caper which, though it's funny, you can give up. Think about that, anyway.

2) I wonder if you've quite settled on what the central issue of this story is? From the beginning until well into the story, Eliot strikes us two rigid old squares as eminently justified in his attitudes toward the aberrations of the young and the way the university yields to them helplessly. And he has good strong attitudes, and expresses them forcibly. He likewise has good strong attitudes toward those same, or similar, aberrations as they surface in his wife, and he expresses those too. I thought the communication was pretty clear, both in the scene at home when we first meet her, and in the narrative and expository stuff that communicates their past together. I never saw him failing to talk to her, ignoring her, putting her down, diving into a magazine, and so when I was told (by her) that he was guilty of those things, I wasn't at all sure but what she was a most unreliable witness. Especially since she has already been identified with the permissive and half-baked fads that blow around the campus. Maybe he expects her to play a role that she's no longer willing to play, and maybe there is a real, hard conflict between his moralistic responses and her do-your-thing permissiveness. But that doesn't mean he's uncommunicative, as she says, or morally wishy-washy, as he thinks. So far as I'm concerned, he's a hell of a lot more sensible than she is, and though he's ironic with her, I don't see the justifications for her desperate and vengeful effort to get noticed and be a woman. I take that as one more aspect of her contamination by the fads of the counter culture. Up to near the end, I follow him in his effort to shuck the false and the wishy-washy, I applaud his flunking the 12 deadbeats, I agree he has good cause to leave his wife (but not to forget that he even has a child). When their final

confrontation comes, I'm prepared for her to make her defense according to her own new warped code, but I don't expect it to be persuasive, either to him or to me—though the wrench of separation might be, and should be, harsh and emotional. What troubles me is that I seem to be asked, right at the end, to accept her defense and therefore transfer the blame to Eliot. When he steps-slinks-wafts out the door I guess I am supposed to feel that his departure is only another sign, among many I am supposed by now to know, of his weakness and tendency to cop out and blame others for his own mistakes. And I don't.

Back in class, while Arington is reading, you seem to be preparing us for this switch by half-justifying Arington's idiocies by the atomic uncertainties of world peace and world economics and human ecology. But you don't sell me. We owe God a death, as we owe him a life, and the Arington justifications for the cop out are simply whines that your Eliot is too sensible to take seriously. I make note of those remarks about the older generation and its rigid narrow codes, and all that. O.K. But I think you've made Eliot much closer to that—and asked our sympathy with his position—than to the cotton-candy philosophizings of the Aringtons or even the Erins.

What this comes to is that you start me toward one sort of understanding of the story, and then switch me over when I'm not prepared to switch. I can see a story between these two precise people that reveals the clash between his moralism and her somewhat self-indulgent acceptance of the New Freedom. I can see that as a pleasant story of how the trapped animal escaped, or as a more pitiable story of two people who began by liking one another and were forced apart by a social revolution that one followed and one could not. I can even see it, though I don't think you'd write it this way, as a story of how a stuffy old-fashioned husband was shocked into recognizing the new free permissive code. But I can't see it as what it seems to me to be now—the story of a reasonable and intelligent man who wants to chuck the vulgar frivolity of his job and the growing promiscuity of his wife, and then is made to realize at the end that he is the cause of all his own troubles. If you want that last, then I think you have to show us the way he has of putting his wife down, making her feel foolish, treating her grumpily or shutting her out with his silence. Maybe you could start, not with the nude-in at the Provost's, but at the house while he drinks his morning coffee and puts his wife down for the day before going off to the college. Anything that will let us feel him as a subtly unreliable narrator.

Then we can agree with most of his responses while still reserving judgment about whether he's entitled to have those responses. It's not, as you know, done with brickbats. Just let a petal fall at the right place.

With that fundamental problem of what the story says taken care of, it goes as smooth as a swan on the Avon. You can't spell any better than you used to, and Jere Whiting is JERE, not JERI, and I wouldn't use an expression like "raised their ugly heads" (p. 9), but those are nitpicking objections. It's got great life and vigor; even your retrospection doesn't sag as is the case with most of us mortals. But in that connection—once he has spied the naked arses outside his window, he ruminates for about 3½ pages. It's quaint but hardly normal, because his ruminations touch not at all on naked arses, and it seems an odd time to lose himself in meditation. If we had seen him first at home, we might have a ready explanation for this odd behavior, and we might need just a little less of the retrospective and expository right there at the beginning of the tale. But that too is essentially unimportant, a suggestion only. I like the story and expect to see it in print. And if I have misread you as your Eliot misread Arington, you can set me straight, as that great mind set straight his tutor.

Now we're about to go to an evening Spanish class, just to see. Since Mom wrote you yesterday, there's nothing to report. See you in print.

Love,

Pop

« *To: Page Stegner* • *No Date, 1973* »

Dear Page,

I have a feeling I didn't give you much of a comment on your boar-hunting piece when you brought it up. Maybe the reason was that it obscurely bothered me, and I couldn't tell why. The tone is the good humorous tone of the first one,[38] the subject matter is the same absurd bunch of innocents living off the land in their zany fashion, and it ought to be as amusing and satisfying as the first one. But it didn't seem to me to be that funny, and I've been trying to figure out why. At the risk of putting sand in your peanut butter, here is what I think now:

I think it just misses. I think it leaves a reader not with belly laughs but

---

38. "Headin' for the First Roundup," *Atlantic Monthly*, October 1974.

with an obscurely uncomfortable feeling. And I think I can see about three possibilities why. Whether the places where it misses are susceptible to repair is a question for you to ponder. You may also want to ponder if I'm right in my diagnosis.

1) The people in the first piece were all engaging—Houston with his unstretchable budget that got stretched, Robinson in his tennis shoes, all of you in your cowboy costumes, and so on. The people in this one are not so engaging. They do nothing but sit around drinking too much and bragging too much, and when they do get into action they go out and <u>kill</u> things. In these times, a lot of readers are going to feel sorry for the pigs, and offended at those drunks who slew them.

2) (These considerations are all tied together, and probably are all the same thing.) The tone of the talk is not so much funny as—I use a word from Victorian times—coarse. Coarse to no particular purpose. Coarse as if the author thought coarseness was funny. I'm thinking of Eamon's kid particularly. Granted his language is the language of these times. I still feel like spitting when I see it in print, and so, I am afraid, will a lot of the elders who really were gassed by your first essay. When you add up the drunken idleness, the ostentatiously shitty language, and the fact that these guys go out and shoot innocent little pigs, you have probably lost the reader's sympathy for the funniness of the situation.

I <u>think</u> that's why I didn't respond to this one as much as to the other. And I at least wanted to give you my honest opinion, instead of the hey-ho kind of comment I made when I first read the piece. When you told us the story first, you told us about the girl who had to butcher the game for the great hunters. How did she get lost? She represents a potential moral judgment on their destructive manliness. Or maybe it's possible to get to that ear tag recognition without actually shooting any pigs at all. Could they try to capture a boar? Could they be out to hunt boars with spears, in the good old-fashioned risk-yourself way, and get collared by the swineherd? I dunno. But I think maybe something's wrong with their activities as they are now presented, and with them as characters too.

Now go out and mourn and shiver and get right with God.

Pop

« *To: Wendell Berry* • *April 10, 1973* »

Dear Wendell,

We came home from a month's visit with Page and Marion in Ecuador a while back, and among the books waiting for us was your *Country of Marriage*. It's a splendid country—Tanya ought to be putty in your hands for years. You've immortalized her, or rather your relation with her, and said something memorable about the poor old abused institution of marriage. We kept reading along, saying lovely, lovely. Sweet Kentucky River, run softly till I end my songe.

Then I got to your poem to Ken Kesey and Ken Babbs, and I said, in the idiom of my time, Shit, what can Wendell be thinking of, commemorating that garbage? He's too good to be raking around among that old two-holer privy. Then I thought, Maybe he's composting it. On that comfort I rest. But you stopped me reading, and I haven't got past that page. Prejudice, no doubt. But if it's really being composted, I forgive you.

Love to Tanya.

Best,

Wally

« *To: Ansel Adams* • *May 19, 1973* »

Dear Ansel:

I'm glad the Graphic Society book is on the tracks, and that they like me for the introduction. Me, I don't care about the Graphic Society that much, but I love the association with A.A. (What suggestive initials you have, Grandpa.) So I will await their communication.

Also Pat Cauldfield. I have seen some of her things in the *Audubon* magazine, and I'm very interested in seeing somebody really good take on the challenge of that big flat characterless land-and-sky, grass-and-clouds-and-wind of the northern plains. I want somebody to take some pictures that match the pictures in my mind, and I've never seen them yet. So I might be interested, if she wants to get in touch. Not for a while. We're going (to the northern plains, in fact—to Saskatchewan, to get an honorary degree) the middle of next week, and we'll stop in Toronto and Montreal and Vermont before we come back. But we'll be here from June 12 until we take off for Santa Fe and the reunion of the True Brotherhood in Christ. So she can either write me in Vermont (Greensboro, Vermont, 05841) between May 27 and June 11, or see me here after June 12.

As for you, repent, for the last days are at hand. How are the mighty fallen, and how I would enjoy their fall, if they didn't bring down so much of the library and living room with them. What were you doing on the night of January 17, 1973? Answer yes or no.

Love to Virginia.

See you,
Wally

« *To: Ansel Adams* • *September 14, 1973* »

Dear Virginia and Ansel,
Forgive the lateness of this note, I had to come home and dive into the g.d. galleys, from which I just emerged, bloody but unbowed. I'm about to go put them in the mail, with a sigh of supreme satisfaction. I'll also put in the mail three books that I found spare copies of—*Wolf Willow, The Big Rock Candy Mountain*, and *Second Growth*. Also the *Trader to the Navajos* that Mary borrowed and read with pleasure.

We're about at the stage of cleaning house and clearing desks before going to Toronto. One of my first acts will be to box up all those precious A. Adams picture books so that I can lighten the gloom of the Canadian winter by looking at some great images. I'll be in touch as I get closer to producing a text of some sort, which I hope to do by the end of November.

Meantime, this will inadequately express our thanks for a lovely and profitable day with you. It's always an experience to be with you two—the world is warmer where you are. We hope Ansel's indisposition is over and that every morning you are awakened by the blowing of passing whales.

Love,
Wally

P.S.—Could you tell us where we might order a copy of the new Portfolio, if by chance we stay that solvent for the next few months? I presume we would have to order from the New York gent who commissions or publishes the Portfolios. Could you put his name and address on a postcard? Many thanks.

« *To: Ansel Adams* • *October 26, 1973* »

Dear Ansel,

Today, having made all the immediately necessary notes for speeches, symposia, etc., I started to write an essay on A.A. The morning generated one page that will stand, and a couple more that I will steal from. If the university will leave me alone for a week or ten days I may get a rough draft of something, and at that point I will have to get in touch with Ackland, who said that he would like a text, or a version of a text, so that he could beard the Book of the Month Club about Thanksgiving. I hope to gratify him, though the locals may shanghai me into too many dinings-with-the-dons and with too many participations in panels on Whither Canadian Literature, and I may have to read day and night the latest outpourings of Canadian cultural patriotism. In any case, I wondered if you have yet made your selection of the photographs that you're going to want in this Graphic Society book. If you have, I'd love to have the list. I think I've got enough books of yours around here so that I can identify almost all the well-known images, and that will be enough for the occasional mention that I'd like to work into the text. But only if it's no great trouble to you.

Toronto so far is pleasant and not very demanding. The reason is that the university runs year courses, not semester or quarter courses, and it is very relaxed about getting started. But I have three appearances to make next week, and one tonight, and I suspect I will not feel quite so free and neglected after another ten days. The colleges of the University of Toronto are suitably Scotch and medieval. Women, according to their lights, do not exist, so poor Mary is spending her time practicing on the piano (a rented one, electric). She sold her violin some time ago, and now gets her musical solace in an unfamiliar medium. Fortunately, right across the street there is a Record Library, part of the Toronto Public Library system, in which she can sit and listen by the hour. A great public idea that California might well copy. The Toronto parks are numerous and pleasant, and we get our exercise running Susie[39] around in them. Musical things are hard to get tickets to, as in SF, but we have had some chamber music and tomorrow will hearken to the university's symphony. I have met Marshall MacLuhan and he is mine. Tonight I'll meet Northrup Frye, and he won't be mine by a long shot. The weather so far has been splendid Indian Summer, but I

---

39. Stegner's Airedale.

look out the window right now at some tired and sagging clouds. Blizzards for the weekend, probably.

Well, forward. When I get a draft for Ackland, may I ask you to look it over for boners? I don't want to embarrass you by asking you to judge it, so if you'd rather not, let me know. But I'd like to have its facts and general tenor right. I'll only send you the negative. What comes out in the final print is my own dark (room) secret. Our love to you and Virginia.

Yours,
Wally

« To: Ansel Adams • December 3, 1973 »

Dear Ansel,

This in haste, in the midst of the last-minute chores and packing, to ask your indulgence about my not finishing a see-able draft of the text yet, and to tell you that Mary and I have gone through all the books we have, checking out the photographs you have starred for the book. It will be some book. We are not going to quarrel with you about any photograph you like enough to star. All we can do is lament some mighty images that for one reason or another—I don't doubt good—you have left out. Probably you omitted some because they have been on greeting cards or in ads, or for some similar reason. I hope you didn't leave them out because you're tired of them—because we're not. So we do lament the absence of "Autumn, Yosemite"; "Sierra Nevada from Lone Pine"; "Rails and Jet Trails"; "Banner Peak and Thousand Island Lake"; "Pine Branches and Snow"; "Court House Mariposa"; "Grass and Burned Stump"; "Winter Forest"; "Slide Lake," and a lot more. But we applaud every one you left in. I hope the Graphic Society agrees to stretch its table of contents.

On which subject: I wrote Ackland saying I had 10–12 pages he could use for dummy text in his presentation to the Book of the Month Club, but have had no reply, and so I haven't sent it on to him. Nor to you. The reason is that I'm not satisfied even with that more finished section, and not at all with the rough draft of the remainder. I want to work on it with everything else shut off. It will be shut off Wednesday evening here. Thursday, we fly home. It will take us the weekend to get settled. A week from today I'll sit down to the Adams photographs and stay with them until there is a whole text I can send to you for comment, correction, and cussing. I fully expect to have it more or less right and done by New Year. Will that do, do you think? If it won't, I'll bloody well get it done sooner.

Toronto has been pleasant but somewhat odd—Torontonians are a cross between an Englishman and a red Angus calf. They get in their own road. They do not get high marks for imagination and alertness. But they're very law abiding and they run a clean town. We're glad to have been here, we'll be glad to get home.

Please—our love to you and Virginia, and expect a call from me over the weekend.

God bless,
Wally

« *To: Ansel Adams* • *December 29, 1973* »

Dear Ansel:

Many thanks for the second thoughts. I have sent the script in to Mrs. Childs, since she wanted something for a dummy presentation, but it is by no means locked up, and all of your suggestions can and will be incorporated. I have eradicated the word "shoot" from my vocabulary, root and branch, and sown the place where it grew with salt. I shall eradicate it from the manuscript also, but will wait until I have had Mrs. Childs' comments, if any. At that same time, I'll make the other changes you suggest, and any more that you may suggest in the near future.

We were in the City yesterday and took in the Paul Strand show at the De Young. He is good, plenty; but he's not in your class. Also he taught me something: one reason why I don't respond to your portraits as much as to your big magnificent natural scenes is that I don't respond to any photographic portraits much. That goes for Karsh, certainly, and now I find it goes for Strand, good as he is. I guess I want a more distorting medium for portraits. Most of us need to be distorted before we become interesting. Nature doesn't.

God bless, take care, read good books, practice charity. We'll all need it in 1974. I am about to start trying to put a new novel on the page beginning after New Year, and I am all quivers and quakes. It's like starting out to swim across Lake Superior in winter.

Buss your lovely blue-eyed bride for us. Some angel blood got into her veins, probably by sinister means.

Yours,
Wally

« To: Ansel Adams • November 14, 1974 »

Dear Ansel:

I don't know where you are by now—autographing books somewhere, I guess. But I'll send this to Carmel and hope you come home sometime.

After all this time I have finally seen The Book. For a while I wondered if I was ever going to, since New York Graphic didn't send me one, the ones I ordered didn't arrive (still haven't), and the bookstores I went to had sold out. Then Betty Childs wrote to reassure me, saying that one of the Super-Edition had been "saved" for me (whatever that means—it hasn't come, in any case)—and finally my neighbor below the hill, who had ordered one through the Yosemite shop, got his, and let me peek.

You don't need me to tell you—it's magnificent. Adrian's design and type, the printing, the quality of the reproductions, for once do almost complete justice to the photographs. There just aren't any weak spots unless maybe the text, but Adrian's typography so dignifies that that even it seems superior. The reviews I've seen have been peals of triumphal bells. Well, God bless, say I. You've had this coming for a long time. On top of the New York show, it ought to give you that suffusing glow of accomplishment that will let you sit back upon your tired can and say, or sigh, "Factus est," And maybe "In-factus sum."

Give us a call, a visit, or a notification when you get back, and I will break out the VSOP. Our love to Virginia—I hope she loves this whole triumphal march.

Cheers,

Wally

« To: Wendell Berry • April 3, 1975 »

Dear Wendell,

The other night I got a copy of "Not Man Apart," the little paper published by Friends of the Earth, with a note from Tom Turner clipped to it, saying Mr. Stegner, see p. 7. So I saw page 7, and there was a poem dedicated to me. I thought it was Tom Turner's. As a matter of fact I had read the first page, and said to Mary, Hey, this is no little old newspaper poet. This fellow Turner is good. So I turn the page and see who did it, and I am about equally divided between pleasure at your act of friendship, and self-satisfaction at being able to tell a real poet when I read him. It really was a most agreeable thing for you to do—I feel as if I'd got an honorary degree without having to wonder what to do with the hood—and it really is a lovely poem. It's a blood-warmth kind of poem. It grows off the page like bulbs coming out of the ground. I like the silences, the peaceful silences, between songs. I remember that you call yourself a ruminator. I think you are. If you clove the hoof as well, you would be taken strictly kosher, as maybe you are. Five stomachs are in any case a blessing for those that have them, considering what we are asked to put and keep on them. So I melted into your poem like a rain on plowed ground. I damned near took it along to read the last section, as an object lesson, to last night's meeting of the Los Altos Hills town council, which is busily helping the greed in developers' minds become the cancer of their dream. I didn't, but the spirit came on me anyway, and I prophesied. And at the end of the meeting, not because of anything I said but because the general temper is getting short, I had the satisfaction of hearing that council booed by its constituents. I can hardly wait for election day.

We're in a somewhat more than usually hectic phase, since we're going abroad later this month (the Rockefeller study center at Bellagio, on Lake Como, and later a cruise, on which I'll lecture, through the Baltic and up to North Cape). Now comes the outside possibility of a Book Award for the DeVoto, and Doubleday wants us to come to New York, which cuts our preparation time short by a week. I have no expectation of winning the thing, and I have no real lust to go to New York and drink too much while being an also-ran, and so we'd rather not push that fast, but we may not be able to get out of it. If you hear, in the silence of the night, a steady humming noise, that'll be my generator, and I'll be hating it. I'm getting too old to rush. Mary too.

Everybody well here—Dick and Anne, Nancy, Dolly.[40] Everybody full of fellowship manuscripts except me—I can take comfort in some things. Please give our best to Tanya, and remember what I warned you about once before: Take care, you're a great man.

Best,
Wally

---

40. Dick and Anne Scowcroft, Nancy Packer, Dolly Kringle—staff of the Stanford Creative Writing Program.

« To: Wallace Page Stegner • July 3, 1975 »

Dear Pagie,

I am a cement-head. Before you went back to camp, I wanted to tell you how much fun Grandma and I have when you are visiting us, and how we enjoy having you around, and reading with you, and playing games with you. But I forgot, so I tell you now, by mail.

I also wanted to ask you about one or two things I noticed yesterday. When we were all playing badminton, and for a while you kept taking the bird from David instead of letting him knock it back, I gave you one little suggestion—that you give him his turn. After that, you not only gave him his turn, but you gave him yours too—you handed the bird to him and let him start a new rally. That was generous. I approved of that. Later, when you got to spitting watermelon seeds onto Grandma and maybe other people, I was not so pleased with you. You needed a good swat with the fly swatter to make you remember your manners.

So I was going to have a talk with you about being a Good Camper while you're at Highfields Farm. A Good Camper has some rules he goes by. (1) He gets along with the other campers and stays out of fights. (2) He doesn't break up campfire singing, or any other camp activity, by snickering and talking to his pals. (3) He respects other people's things and expects them to respect his. (4) He remembers that he is a good scout, and not a slob—He has too much pride in who he is to be rude, loud, or a smart alec. (5) He does not have to show off. He gets attention by doing things right, not wrong.

That's what I was going to talk over with you, before you went down to camp again and tied a canoe to an alligator, like Cement-head Roger. You can be the best kid in camp if you try to live by the rules, and people will like you better than they like the noisy smart alecs.

Whenever you feel like knocking somebody, ask yourself how you would come off if he started to knock you. We've all got scabs. Be gentle with other people's, and maybe they won't pick yours.

That's a conversation. We'll go on from there when you come back. Meantime have a good time, obey the rules, remember your manners, and be a Good Camper.

Much love from Grandma and me. We're looking forward to your next weekend with us.

Love,
Grandpop

« *To: Ansel Adams* • *September 4, 1975* »

Dear Ansel:

A couple of weeks ago I had lunch with Don Ackland, who clued me in on your plans. Who do you think you are, everybody? What is it, a book a month? God rest you, and I mean rest. You sound too busy.

Don mentioned the possibility of my doing the text for a book a year or so hence, Adams on Yosemite. Deadlines being humane, I'd like nothing better. As I told Don, I have just signed up for another novel, and taken a big advance so I can't chicken out, and that has precedence simply because I'll be living on that advance for the next couple of years. But if, as I hope, I get a decent start on the novel by the end of this year, I'll be in good shape, because the deadline isn't till January 1978. I should live so long, already. In order to get the start, Mary and I are going up to Angora Lake for a week or ten days to do nothing but walk, read, and think. We solicit your intervention with the muses. I might even get a few inspirations about Adams and Yosemite.

Meantime, remember that daily nap. Meantime, emulate the sleepy autumn fly, not the incessant autumn cricket. Love to Virginia.

Yours,

Wally

« *To: Wendell Berry* • *October 1, 1975* »

Dear Wendell,

Again I owe you for a cluster of perceptions and observances. You go on like a lemon tree—ripe fruit, green fruit, and flowers all on the same bush at the same time. Not that any of these poems in *To What Listens* are green—they just have the promise of further ripenesses in them. I wish to hell I didn't feel so much like a March potato bin, musty and dark and with spots of rottenness, and the whole place haunted by long white sprouts. I am supposed to be starting a new novel, and though I know what must happen, and how, I can't for the life of me determine to whom. I seem to lack the invention to create me a passenger for my vehicle. In the end, I suppose, I'll fall back on myself, with a crash.

That was not supposed to be the subject of this letter. This was and is to thank you for the poems. I respond to them more than to any I can think of among the contemporary poets. You have more Frost in you than I had been aware of. Your poem to Gary Snyder is generous in granting him his way of seeing and his things to see, but insistent on difference. I'm less generous. I find Snyder interesting, and personally he always makes an intelligent sound when he is knocked upon, but I can't imagine seeing things his way. He thinks you can recreate the whole accomplishment of mankind by meditation. I think maybe there has to be some hard stubborn work, and it is as a worker in the natural world that I hear you making poems. I can't imagine Snyder composting his privy by meditation. He's crossed some boundary, he's like a windigo, he lives outside the safe limits of my tribal territory, we step around each other cautiously when we meet. Whereas I hail you as the farmer from over the hill, and might even con you into helping me get in the winter wood.

We enjoyed Tanya's visit, brief as it was. Next time instruct her to bring you along—she'd find you quite good company, we think. Which reminds me further that several times you have produced poems on marriage that Tanya ought to frame between the right and left ventricles. "Seventeen Years" is an example. One of those verities of which Gary Snyder would be incapable.

No news from here. We haven't seen anybody from Stanford except the Scowcrofts. We have managed to avoid Mr. Ford's walkdowns through the area, and to concern ourselves primarily with means of keeping the deer out of our tomatoes. No Vermont this year, for various reasons. In compensation I am making a three-cord woodpile.

All the best,
Wally

« *To: Ansel Adams* • *August 20, 1976* »

Dear Ansel and Virginia,
Welcome aboard the continent again—though it is obvious the strain of travel has deranged you, at least temporarily. Next time you want to have a dream about me, check the script with me first. It will not do for my public to get the impression that I commit experience just to be able to write it up, or that I scribble while Friends Freeze.

I'm not surprised that you find Europe unsatisfactory. I do too, except Italy. Mary keeps getting these dreams of living abroad and (whisper) I am silent, because I'd rather go to southern Utah or Santa Fe. Which we may do for a couple of weeks in September, to get away from the fall smog here.

From the Lands, with whom we spent a day in Peterborough, we have heard that the London exhibition was a triumph. As why shouldn't it have been? Now for God's sake settle down and enjoy Carmel and potter around among the million great images you've already got. Don't be greedy, Ansel; you can't leave it all behind you in impeccable black and white and shades of gray.

Which reminds me, we saw some high-resolution pictures from Mars the other day when some of the scientists involved were having a show, and you wouldn't believe them. Twenty-six shades of gray, from velvet black to creamy white, and detail so clear and clean you could see the crests on the dunes, and tell the direction of the prevailing wind. From 240 million miles away. That's the place you should travel to.

Read this at arm's length—I've got some sort of flu bug and am up-and-down. Be happy and healthy, both of you.

As ever,
Wally

« *To: Wallace Page Stegner* • *February 21, 1977* »

Dear Pagie,

You're doing all right. These paragraphs aren't perfect, as you can see by the corrections, but they have something to say, and when you set out to explain how something works, you do it clearly. Your paragraph on how the internal combustion engine works is the best one.[41]

Now I want you to do something. Sit down and read these all through, studying the mistakes especially. Write out the words you have misspelled or misused, and make sure you know how to spell or use them. Next, read through the paragraphs you have written but not yet sent me. Check the spelling of everything, and read the sentences aloud to yourself to listen for bugs in the carburetor. If you have a lot of errors, re-copy the paragraphs. In fact, it might be a good idea to do that with all of them, just for practice in making a manuscript look fit to read. No mixture of pen and pencil, please. Pen only. Each paragraph to start with an indentation. All proper

---

41. At the time of this letter, Stegner was working with his grandson, age 16, on improving his writing skills. In defense of the tutee (here, and in the two letters that follow), he suffered from severe dyslexia that was not diagnosed until he was twelve or thirteen.

nouns like Thursday to be capitalized. All apostrophes to be put in, and in the right place.

That's the way to make the surface of the paragraphs clean. The way to make them better in what they say is to loosen up, give yourself a chance to say something well. Take a chance. Even if you say something silly, at least it won't be monotonous or dull. If you read every sentence aloud, you may find that all of them have the same tune—they all rise and fall in the same pattern, they all begin with their subject and go on to their verb and end with their object. Mix them up. Try writing longer and more complicated sentences, with different rhythms.

The purpose of all this paragraph-writing, I hope you will agree, is to get you writing better and more correctly. Some improvement will come with practice, but some more will only come with the hard work of going through the things you've done, seeing where you've made mistakes, correcting the mistakes, and then avoiding those mistakes in the next batch. Go over them with your tutor if you want to, and if she will. (Incidentally, she is a tutor, not a tuder. Pronounce it right and you're more likely to spell it right.) It would be a good idea to keep all these paragraphs in a ring notebook so that you can have them to look back at when you begin to feel eloquent. Nobody can know where he's going, but it's fun to know where you've been.

See you Saturday.

Adios,

Grandpa

« *To: Wallace Page Stegner* • *March 1, 1977* »

Dear Page,

Not too much improvement, I'm sorry to say. You're using the right method when you write a draft, check with your "tuder," and then re-write it. But you're depending on the tutor to catch all the errors, instead of looking for errors yourself, and hunting ways to improve the phrasing, punctuation, organization, and whatever else. Result: Your second draft is just about as be-slubbered as your first. And that isn't the ideal.

You've got one more round to go, or maybe two. Let's see you really revise from now on. Don't just re-copy, errors and all. Re-think, re-phrase, try to make it sound better and look better.

Spelling is your worst bugaboo. And I'll tell you something: <u>There's no excuse for misspelling a single word</u>. You know why? Because you've got a dictionary and can look every word up. Don't just look up the words you're sure of: if you're sure of it, it's probably wrong. Also, pin a few things down;

UNTIL (only one l)

MAKING, SKATING, RAKING, SMILING (no <u>e</u> before the <u>ing</u>. This is very close to a foolproof rule)

Finally: When you're writing a story, there's a different sound to it than there is to the same story spoken. You don't want a lot of "Well, things went great," and "Well, people were pretty tired" cluttering up the page. When in doubt, leave out Well.

I'll check these over with you when we see you this weekend. By now you should have got the other batch that I mailed to you two or three days ago.

Coraggio.

« *To: Wallace Page Stegner* • *March 3, 1977* »

Dear Page,

If you will look carefully at my comment on the last page of your composi-tions, you will find that I was a little irritated when I read them.[42] You are finding things to write about, you <u>don't</u> have that verbal constipation that you had at first. But you're making exactly the same mistakes—the same kinds of mistakes—that you made from the beginning. That means you aren't paying enough attention as you write. You aren't reading your things over and checking them for errors. You're still spelling by ear, and your ear changes from line to line. If you had read your paper over, you would have discovered that you have spelled coyote or coyotes three different ways within six lines. First you tried <u>cayoties</u>, then <u>coyots</u>, and then <u>coyoty</u>. The word is <u>coyote</u>, which is pronounced <u>ki-yot</u>, without any y sound on the end, although plenty of people, imitating the Spanish pronunciation, do put that y sound there.

Another thing you didn't watch was the <u>n't</u> kind of compound words. Whenever you find yourself writing <u>ent</u> at the end of one of those negative compounds, back up: you're wrong. <u>n't</u> is short for <u>not</u>. The apostrophe

---

42. Hence the absence of the diminutive, Pagie, in favor of the more sternly formal, "Dear Page."

means that the o in not is left out. What results is a sound very like ent, but it isn't ent. It's n't. You're spelling by ear again. The only way to quit spelling—or misspelling—by ear is to put your eye to work.

So here's what I want you to do. I want you to take your next batch of paragraphs and read them over with a red pencil in your hand, marking all the errors you can find—spelling, awkward sentences, left-out words, all the things you're prone to. Then I want you to recopy the whole batch, in ink, correcting the old errors and not putting any more errors in. Then I want you to send me both the old and the new copies. O.K.? The purpose of all this is to get you writing better. You won't start writing better until you start taking pains. If you take pains now, sooner or later you will write better automatically, and won't have so many errors.

And while you're reading over this present batch and my comments thereon, ponder these truths:

TUTOR is not spelled TUDER or TUTER or TUDOR, but TUTOR. THEIR does not mean THEY ARE. It means OF THEM. When you want to say THEY ARE, you say either THEY ARE or THEY'RE. And when you want to say IN THAT PLACE, you say THERE.

So get busy chum. You're doing pretty well on the adelante, but not so well on the arriba. If I find that you haven't improved the mechanics of your writing by your birthday, I'll have to give you that guitar without any strings.

Arriba.

Grandpa

P.S.—This sounds rough, as I read it over. It's only meant to indicate that you can do better. The best paragraph you've written for me is the copy of your letter to the Sierra Club. There you wanted to do well, because you wanted the letter to get you something. Try that hard on all of them!

« To: Wendell Berry • May 27, 1977 »

Dear Wendell,

I've been sweetening my mouth before sleeping with alternate readings in your two new books, which as you are well aware are one book in two moods or movements. What you're saying is in drastic need of saying, and you do it, in the poetry, with felt eloquence, and in the tract, with passionate logic. You cut through a lot of confusion and guff and special pleading, and I think you're absolutely right that our spiritual malaise is at least partly the product of our broken communion and that our broken communion is in good part traceable to our contemptuous and industrial mistreatment of the earth. Naturally the county agents will dismiss you as a horse-drawn crank, but that could be the highest compliment. And in the great and terrible Last Days you may find some of us making a strategic withdrawal to the Kentucky River, where with a few small bags of seeds for a gene pool and an aging team of Belgians for energy we will try to reconstitute a world fit to survive. It could be that the American Dream, from Raleigh to Butz, is the worst disaster ever to strike the race and the planet. I thank you for these books and for earlier ones; you're saying it for a lot of us.

But I've got a question: What do the Amish do for poets?

Anyway, keep plowing. I'm writing a blurb for Jon Beckmann.

Best,

Wally

« *To: Rachael Stegner* • *July 29, 1979* »

Dear Rachael,

We enjoyed getting your card, even if it wasn't a letter. It sounds as if you did a good deal of sitting on the merchandise tables with your chin in your hands and perspiration on your chin.[43] How are you as a boots-and-shoes salesperson? Gummed up any orders yet? Charged people the wrong prices? Failed to smile at a customer? There's nothing like being a salesperson (well supervised) to teach the young to show their teeth. I learned that just a little later than you're learning it. When I was 16 I started working in a rug and linoleum store whose owner was a ferocious merchandiser (he paid me 25 cents an hour at first, later raised it to 40 after I had three years' experience). He used to snarl at me, "SMILE when you go up there to meet a customer!" I nearly wore out my face trying to please. Good practice. It keeps the face from getting wrinkled, too.

We had a good letter from your mother yesterday, along with one from Ellen Patterson and one from Beth Watson. Lots of news from Greensboro. It seems that Louis isn't doing very well. He's old and terribly tired. If you have an extra five minutes sitting on the table in Willey's loft, why not send him a postcard? Esther too. They'd love to be remembered.

---

43. Rachael had a summer job working in the clothing department of Willey's General Store in Greensboro, Vermont.

Please tell Page that I have put insurance on the car, so that at least I'm not liable for million-dollar suits if he gets a few innocent bystanders. But I'd still like you all to use the car only for essentials. And if you wonder what is essential, stop and think whether it's essential to you or essential to me, essential for business or essential for convenience and fun. You know me. I'm against fun. Also I'd like a few miles left in that old heap if Grandma and I finally make it to Greensboro again. It doesn't look likely this year. Grandma is still dragging to doctors, three or four of them. All doctors seem to know one thing only. If they know hearts, they don't know lungs. If they know lungs, they don't know lumps. But by going to about three a week, Grandma is managing to stay afloat. She's having some people in for a picnic this evening, and that's a good sign.

It's also a sign I have to go sweep the deck and patio. And as I go out, I will SMILE. Grandma, grinning horribly, is baking bread. She sends a bundle of love.

You too.

Love,

Grandpa

« *To: Page Stegner* • *No Date (1979)* »

Dear Page,

I've meant to write you all week, and have been prevented by too many damned chores. I read through your three chapters[44] a week ago, and as Mom told you over the phone, I think the Sedona one is first rate—though pretty hard on Sedona and likely to raise cries of anguish. I had only one question about it: you go out of your way to smear up your own image in the way that Lasch in *Culture of Narcissism* says is characteristic of our times. Most of the way I didn't object, because you're looking back, ironically, at your gummed-up adolescence. But there is just a touch, that yum-yum tone about bourbon and porkchops, that bothered me.

The botheration increased somewhat as I read on through the San Juan and Humboldt sections, and it arose from that same tendency to uglify your own authorial image. That's a good trick in fiction, especially when you're dealing with a somewhat messed-up modern man. I wonder about it

---

44. Part of Page Stegner's contributions to *American Places*, with Wallace Stegner and Eliot Porter (New York: E. P. Dutton, 1981).

here, partly because this book is going to have an audience of nature lovers and clean livers if it has any audience at all, and I think they're going to be bothered if they constantly find their guide yearning for five o'clock and squirming in anticipation of his love affair with sour mash, as on page 22. It does seem that the principal sources of information are bars and beer parlors, and as one reads through the three chapters consecutively, the impression is cumulative, rising to a climax as your hero staggers out of the Jambalaya to inhale some of Humboldt's gross national product. The tone, in these passages, is just a little raffish for the general subject and thesis, it seems to me; and any humor you gain by it is offset by the uneasy sense of disaffiliation you produce. I would seriously consider—and here I'm repeating what I said before—pruning those somewhat self-conscious capers and making the tone somewhat more judicious, with less mugging and hoofing. I'm not, I hope, suggesting that you modulate your tone to mine. What I think I'm saying is that you make some slight revisions to modulate the tone to the seriousness of the subject and the relatively earnest nature of the people likely to read you. I know there is always Abbey. But Abbey is outrageous, deliberately, and even when he's throwing beer cans out into the Montana landscape he is making a point about the landscape, not about himself. Anyway, ponder this. It would require only a little cutting and trimming. In all other matters the three pieces are very sound. The descriptions are clean and washed and accurate, and will gain you the adherents that the yum-yum-bourbon passages might lose you. The perceptions of modern feelings and certain sociological movements of the young are accurate, too, and all three of your places are real places. So I don't fear for these chapters. The thing in them that troubles me I could fix with a red pencil in about seven minutes.

You have probably already sent this section to MacRae, and perhaps to your agent. That's no problem. If you decide that I have a point, you can do the red penciling as fast as I could. Maybe, in fact, you'll get a clue from MacRae's response whether he notices what I notice, or whether it doesn't bother him.

Here, incidentally, are some 1099 forms for the kids. If they file tax returns, you'll need them, or they will. There should be a couple more of these in the next week or two.

Arriba.

Pop

« *To: Ansel Adams* • *October 15, 1982* »

Dear Ansel,

Here is a draft of what I might say to kick off the shindig on the 24th.[45] It seems to run about eight minutes, leaving us 52 to do our talking. If you have comments, suggestions, or objections I would appreciate having them. Or if you think we should simply start talking, without any such preliminary, I'll listen to that opinion too, though I think myself that something like this ought to be in there.

Here too are 8 proposed questions, designed as starter-uppers and un-pluggers. As you see, they are nearly all concerned with artistic rather than environmental questions. They take that line partly because most of your questions open up the environmental debate, and also because I have the feeling that a lot of people will be there to hear you talk, at least part of the time, about photography. I have added no environmental questions to yours, because I am sure that once we get started on that topic we will not be short of material. I'll comment on your questions in a minute. Meantime, here is what I gather from the committee running the show:

It will be moved to Memorial Auditorium, which seats 1,700, and will be videotaped, without Klieg lights, and not for live broadcast, but for educational use in classes etc. at Stanford. The original hall was over-subscribed by 260 names. So now there will be 800–1000 Friends of the Library and their guests, and when they are seated the doors will be opened to students with student-body cards, to the limit of those wanting entrance or the limit of the hall. We will be introduced as we sit at a table onstage. I will then (if you approve it) deliver your eulogy, as at the best of funerals. We will then sit down and be edifying. You might want to pick the question or questions, yours or mine, that you think will best open up the proceedings. My own guess—but it's only a guess, and easily retracted—is that the artistic questions and discussion might come first, and the environmental ones at the end, where they can expand to the end of the hour. After the talk there will be a brief gathering, without food or spirits, in the rotunda of the old

45. The Library Associates and Committee for Art at Stanford University sponsored a special program entitled "Ansel Adams and Wallace Stegner: A Conversation" on October 24, 1982.

library. I have asked that they have a place ready where you or Virginia or any of us can retire and put our feet up if we feel that way. About six we're due to go to dinner at the Wreden house in Atherton, so that the rotunda gathering, designed to let old friends and admirers shake your hand, will not last above three quarters of an hour.

Now for your questions: I have the feeling that the first two, however important they may be to you and me, will be less interesting to this general audience. At the same time, this general audience is precisely the kind of audience where we might strike a blow and convert somebody who has hitherto been indifferent. Can you rephrase those questions, moving them from the "techniques of propaganda" area where they now rest, and into the "public education, public crisis" area where we hope to touch people? Perhaps we can do this by starting with your question 4, with its concern about reaching the great indifferent unschooled mass of well-meaning people who don't know they're being destructive.

Your question (3): I see no reason why we shouldn't say right out loud that the Reagan administration is accountable for the attacks on environmental protection, and that the Watts and the Gorsuches are only instruments. It is the philosophy of exploitation, without regard for consequences, and the 19th century good-old-American-initiative myth that supports it, that we want to nail.

(5) Absolutely. All the resources—the web in which we live and by which we live, up to and including the desert pupfish. Against this, everything that dulls our perception or perverts our desires—advertising, TV, Las Vegas, the whole bit. You can ask me, or I will ask you, the value of wholeness, wildness, wisdom, husbandry, stewardship, for this generation and the future, and then we can join in a duet.

(6) I don't know that your political proposals are feasible, but they can sure be enunciated. Those people are our employees, or started out to be. They are what America has developed to replace the "authorities" who suppress people elsewhere, and the more they come to resemble the authorities the less I like them. The buying of elections with excesses of money is certainly something we might talk about, especially as it relates to threats to the environment and to the arts and education. It might well come up in conversation how much certain interests are putting out in anti-environmental war chests (the SP, Valley growers, etc. on Prop. 13, for instance) and how we have only the guerrilla forces of

volunteers to fight them with. You can be as eloquent as you please on the disgrace of a less-than-40% turnout at elections that will affect us now and will affect the country for generations. You can be eloquent on the subject of the quality of life we would like to see available to all (though there are plenty of slobs who will prefer Las Vegas and the Atari arcades).

I agree we can't make campaign speeches, but if we ask the right questions of each other we can be led (surprise) into speaking our minds on things that matter.

That's it for now. Let me hear how any or all of this strikes you. Love to Virginia.

Yours,

Wally

« *To: Rachael Stegner* • *January 14, 1985* »

Dear Rachael,

Grandma and I were glad to have your letter the other day, and know that you made it back to Rainsville safely. We were sorry not to see more of you at Christmas, though it was our own fault for going to Greensboro. We had a very pleasant time there as restored members of the Gray–Rainey family. Pam and Pat were up, both looking good and happy, and Penelope of course was there, and Clive, Ethne, Megan, Auriel (SP?) their brother whatshisname, Cameron and Justin and their parents, Ellen Gray and her two brothers, Phil Gray junior, etc. etc. We had good clean snow for the first week, with several light dustings of powder and several nights when it got down to five or ten below. Then it started to rain, and everything was coated with ice. I rolled down the window of our rented car and the ice just stood there, as thick as the glass. I had to go around inside and break all the ice windows out before I could see to drive. So when it got that way, we came home. Altogether a fine ten days. The lodge was comfortable and the meals too good, and we've been taking off pounds, not too successfully, ever since. Grandma stood the trip well. I think she likes snow and cold. We didn't go skiing, but we did go snowshoeing up into the woods back of the Lodge. They pack the trails with weasels, and they run all over— over to Patmos Peak, and up to the top of Barr Hill, and down around by Lumsdens, and through from the reservoir between our house and the

Sugar House, and on down the sidehill through the woods to the Lodge again. Sometime when we're there in summer we ought to try walking them and see where they go.

We have not seen your mother for a week or so, but your dad was up last night and had supper with us. They are both still unhappy and in trouble, as you know. I guess all we can do is stand by, but it's no fun, for them or for any of the rest of us. I hope you don't let it bother you too much at school. Your first job is your classes.

We're sorry the second sweater didn't work out. I guess Grandma has compensated you in coin of the realm, and maybe by now you've bought yourself something that goes better with your face and figger. We had a luncheon for eight people yesterday and served them from your opulent tray of assorted nuts. We thank you—they were very good, and not many remain.

What are we going to do about our united birthdays this year? What would you _like_ to do? Maybe, since you'll be in school, we may have to juggle the dates, but we certainly don't want to let your twenty-first go by without a salute of sixteen guns. Let us hear, by letter or telephone, what you think might please you, and we'll go to work on it. With a month or more to plan, maybe we can come up with an extravaganza, maybe something like Reagan's inauguration—apes, jugglers, sword-swallowers, parades.

Grandma is counting cancelled checks, with compressed lips and furrowed brow. If she weren't so concentrated she'd send her love. As it is, I'll send it for her, with mine. Be good. Be happy. Stay on top of your life.

Love,

Grandpa

« _To: Ansel Adams_ • _July 4, 1985_ »

Dear Ansel,

Dorothy Parker, asked if given the chance she would do it all over again, said yes, she would do it all over again, and do it all over you. This is what Mr. Reagan is about to announce, I suspect.

But that is not the burden of my song. The burden of my song is this: We are coming down to the Carmel Festival on July 27, staying (I guess) at the Mission Ranch and going to some 9 P.M. concert at the Mission the evening of the 27th. We would like to call and say hello, if there's a convenient time and if you'll be at home. I also have, or will have, under my arm a copy of the first edition of *Images* which a librarian lady of my acquaintance hopes I can get you to autograph. If you're going to be at home, I'll bring it; if you're not, I won't expose it to the risks of travel.

Mary recovers, slowly but surely. She has not yet made the decision about which of her several options to choose. Since those options are double radical mastectomy, long and probably debilitating radiation treatments, and watchful waiting, any one of them is sufficiently unattractive. Tomorrow she has a huddle with an oncologist, who may have light to shed on things. Everybody says her cancer is slow-growing and so far non-invasive, so that she can take a while to make up her mind.

Love to Virginia. I hope we can see you for a few minutes on the 27th.

Best,

Wally

« To: Marion Stegner • January 2, 1986 »

Dear Marion,

This in some hurry, so that Rachael can carry it home with her. It's mainly to tell you how touched we are by the two splendid books, which I am sure set you back more than you could comfortably pay. But we love them both, and from here on will know a great deal more about both China and modern primitives. Mary is already kicking herself, as she goes through the China book, that we didn't take the chance and go to China last November—November 1984 that is—with the writing delegation. We do thank you.

Also we want to wish you a happy and prosperous New Year. I wince a little when I write that, but the wish is sincere, even if the chances aren't as foolproof as we'd want them.[46] What we chiefly hope for you is serenity of mind. Prosperity is nice, but can come second. We hope you won't forget where we live, or what our phone number is, and that we'll be seeing and talking to you regularly. The latchstring is always out if you need sanctuary or a rest stop.

---

46. The reference is to Marion's recent divorce from Page Stegner.

Rachael reports a pleasant time and bearable weather in Montana. She is with us now, having come up for dinner yesterday. She stayed over so we could straighten out her financial affairs with Capital Preservation. I guess her car needs some fixing, but otherwise she seems in fine shape, and is going back to school with maximum achievement on her mind.

Be good to yourself, and keep in touch, 1986 or 1996 or 2006.

Affectionately,

Wally

« *To: Marion Stegner* • *March 7, 1986* »

Dear Marion,

This little tape is a sort of token birthday remembrance to serve until the Museum of Modern Art can deliver the two volumes of *Modern Primitives* that Mary ordered for you. Happy birthday, in two installments!

I didn't get a chance to talk with you the other day, and sort of stayed out of the way because I thought you wanted to talk with Mary. But from what I saw of you, and from what she tells me, you have come bouncing back from the low point, and are busy, hopeful, and reasonably content with your altered life.[47] That's good. You have too much going for you to get downhearted. Remember Faulkner's redneck: "They mought of kilt us but they ain't whupped us yit."

Anyway, along with birthday greetings, we both want to tell you that so far as we are concerned, only some legalities are changed. You're still family, we will still want to stay close, we will be more than happy to see you or shelter you or feed you or pour you a drink or listen to you or hear your news or consult with you on problems, any time you feel like seeing or asking us. Legalities needn't interfere with affection; and though we're sad that after 26 years you and Page aren't still together, we hope we can be. Don't write us off or lose track of us or forget us.

Affectionately,

Wally and Mary

---

47. Her divorce.

« *To: John Daniel*[48] • *July 23, 1987* »

Dear John,

In haste, between the cracks of a formidable day of chores, I read with pleasure your editorial on tree-spiking and non-violence. It is an editorial, I think—advocacy of a certain moral and intellectual position—and my guess is that it belongs on the editorial page of some paper, preferably the *New York Times* or the *Washington Post* or the *Los Angeles Times*. Or, perhaps more properly, on the op-ed page. But it's much too long for an editorial, and probably too long for an op-ed piece. If you can see a way of cutting it nearly in half, I'd suggest you try it on one of the papers above.

In almost every way, I agree with your position, though I think you give too much credibility to the tree-spiking advocates such as Foreman: you grant them their premises too freely, I think, though you do later reject them. But when you say, "The violence done to Anderson, in other words, should not obscure the vaster violence being done to the forests," and add, "There is truth in what Foreman says," you seem to me to be a little too complaisant with the tactics of violence. I know you aren't, but you seem so. I guess I would be happier with that paragraph if it started out by saying flatly that "though there is truth in what Foreman says, there is a perversion of logic at work here," or something of the sort, and then go on to your discussion of the faulty parallel between this and King's marches and sit-ins.

Well. No time for debate. I'm getting the yard ready and watering everything, so that you can count on its having been fully watered as of Friday, July 24. I'll clue Marilyn, and you can conduct yourself in accordance with what she has done since that date.

It may be that Lynn will be coming up here for a few days after we leave, and if that happens I will be leaving the two solar systems on. When she goes (if indeed she comes, for all my mind is clouded with a doubt) I'd appreciate it if you'd unplug the kitchen system and throw the switch on the pool system. It's high on the wall, to the left of the control boxes, and it has a label in red ink on it. I'd also appreciate it if you would check

---

48. The poet and essayist John Daniel was a Stegner Fellow who lived for several years with his wife, Marilyn, in a cottage on the Stegner property that had originally been Wallace's study. Daniel worked off rent by helping Stegner in the garden, and in short order the two became fast friends.

periodically to see that the level of water in the tank stays about two or three inches from the top of the tube. My guess is that it will drip some even with the solar heat shut off, and I'd rather not let it go down.

I bought a new fancy extension pruner which is in the corner of the garage with the old one. You get to break it in.

Many thanks. Have a good camp. We'll see you on August 29 or the day after.

> Best,
> Wally

« *To: John Daniel* • *July 11, 1988* »

Dear John,

Thanks for your letter full of news and gloomy prospects. I knew Canada was even worse on timber sales (?) than the U.S. Forest Service, but I expected you to straighten them out. Maybe when they see what you say.

The medicine chest full of stuff has been excavated and assayed. Nobody could fit the imitation eyes, so we threw them away. Rachael and Kerry kept some cosmetics, and the Waste Disposal Program got the rest.

The kids are in and well settled.[49] No particular painting, except the new front window framing, so I was not in danger of painter's colic. Like you, Rachael doesn't see the need of front curtains, especially now that your coon is back. He abandoned the place in despair when you left, but hunger is a great reconciler, and they've been barbecuing, with succulent scraps.

We're pleased that you have found a good house, with garden space and trees. Gradually your California sun-blisters will erode away, and the rain-moss will take their place. Here, in the drought belt, we are flushing only twice a week and restricting our water by 45%. That's not easy, since we seem to have a leak in the swimming pool, or else the dry wind eats water as a chinook eats snow. It goes down an inch a day. Well, we will have to pay the penalty and accept the label of wasters—no time to get the damned thing fixed now, and if we left the kids for the summer without a pool, they'd probably abandon the whole project.

We leave next Saturday. Many telephone calls to make and letters to

---

49. Rachael Sheedy, Stegner's granddaughter and her husband, Kerry. They took over Stegner's old study as living space after John and Marilyn Daniel moved to Oregon.

write and sheets of instruction to post. After that we can in the destructive element immerse, and maybe get something done. Good luck with your forest piece. I'll be watching for that issue. Incidentally, a funny and touching business: The Wilderness Society voted to give me their Bob Marshall Award, and George Frampton called about it, confidentially. But the trouble was, I couldn't—can't—be at Port Angeles, Washington on October 4–5, when the fall meeting takes place, because I'm committed to a talk at the New York Public Library just on those days. So then the Board voted to postpone my award till next year, and give it this year to Tom.[50] He was so touched he almost blubbered over the telephone. But I can't write his citation, as he was going to write mine, because Gaylord Nelson[51] has already stuck his nose in and copped off the prize. Tom should have been the Society's first choice two or three years ago, but all he can think of is how unworthy he is.

Give our best to Marilyn, and enjoy Portland, and keep in touch. It feels like the end of an era around here. Maybe a three-month absence is what is called for, to bridge the gap.

All best,
Wally

« *To: John Daniel* • *September 5, 1988* »

Dear John,
Paper shortage, and all stores closed on Labor Day. Shorthand notes only.

Thank you for your book, and especially for the inscription. I think Hepworth did all right by you, and the poems, as poems are likely to do, look even more sober and sensible and moving and dignified in type than they did in manuscript. Mary and I have been sweetening our mouths with them before sleep, as Increase Mather used to sweeten his mouth with a bit of Calvin. Or maybe it was John Cotton. It's the sweetening that matters.

A note from Tom[52] tells me he has bought another piece of yours, and

---

50. Tom Watkins, the editor of *Wilderness* magazine and author of numerous books about the West.
51. Wisconsin senator and then governor, founder of Earth Day, and counselor for the Wilderness Society.
52. Tom Watkins, editor of *Wilderness* magazine.

that the Old Growth is out. Our copy obviously went to California, and so I haven't seen it, but I will dig it out when we get back.

Which won't be for a while. I've got a date at Dartmouth on the 27th and one at the New York Public on October 4. We're still uncertain whether we'll fly home before I have to go to Boulder on October 19–20, or whether we'll hole up here and fly to Denver direct on October 18. In either event we've got some fall weather ahead. We've already had a couple of nights of frost. As a leaf year, it won't be much—acid rain, drought, and pear blight all hurt the trees. It could be the beginning of something permanent, and anyway our old sugar bush is all as over-age as we are, and it's a question which of us gives out first. This noon a bean supper. That's the way things have been going all summer.

Our best to Marilyn, and our best to you. Reports from Rachael and Kerry indicate that they're surviving and even thriving. Even prevailing.

Let us all take note.

Wally

« To: John Daniel · November 24, 1988 »

Dear John,

It's a long time since October 4, when you wrote us your last letter and sent your poem and the spider essay. It's a time so long and confused that I'm not even sure I didn't already answer you. But on the theory that I probably didn't (when there's doubt there's no doubt), here we go. First, I admire both the poem and the essay, but I want to tell you that if I had known you were going to usurp the poetry-and-essay concession along with the cottage, I'd have had to charge you extra. That essay, as you admit, started in my garden shed, utilizing my spider and my bugs. Never mind that they were going to waste. I might have got around to using them, and if I had, I'd have found them used up, and that's a net loss to me. Nice for Tom Watkins and the world, though, and since you are out of the state, and not extraditable, I'll have to let you get away with it. But I want to tell you that from here on I am keeping a sharp eye on my spiders, and running off intrusive poets and essayists on suspicion.

Catch-up data: I finally got back here a month ago,[53] after my sessions at Colorado, and have been busy writing little essays ever since (using my

---

53. Los Altos Hills, California.

own raw materials, including spiders). Two more little ones to go before Christmas, and I am swearing off little essays for life.

We have had a couple of drizzling rains, about an inch and a half altogether—not enough to help the trees and shrubs, but great for the grass, which is greening up all over. Lots of snow in the mountains, and early skiing for those who love cold hands. Page, Lynn, Pagie, his girl, Rachael, and Bill Wyman, the head of Thatcher School, were here for Thanksgiving yesterday, when I started this letter. Lynn is very pregnant, 8⅔ months, due December 5. The rest of us are about our normal size (extra large), and maybe this morning a mite larger than normal. It's too late now for 1988 resolutions; I'm saving mine for January 1. They involve, as above, no more little essays, and a reduced pot, like maybe ten pounds reduced.

You sound as if you had 1989 wired, though I suspect it would be pleasanter to have Marilyn at home more. But think of the good she does. And you have your mother with you, which is great for both of you. In case another long lapse occurs, let's make this a Christmas letter, with all the best wishes and a lot of prosperity and a whole book of essays for 1989. Our love to Marilyn, and our best to your mother.

Yours,
Wally

« *To: John Daniel* • *November 28, 1988* »

Dear John,
One hour after I wrote you a letter, the mail came with your poem dedicated to me. I'm touched, not only by the poem, which is grave and wise and in your best vein, but by the dedication. I trust I will live long enough to hear your Nobel speech, and tell the awed bystanders that I knew you when you were just a handyman and estate-manager and swimming-pool-vacuumer. It seems to me you are on your way somewhere, and the Poetry Editor's stationery corroborates that impression.

Once again, many thanks, and best wishes to you all for the holidays.

Yours,
Wally

« *To: John Daniel* • *February 2, 1989* »

Dear John and Marilyn,

We're extremely pleased to hear your news. Virtue is rewarded, after all. We can't think of parents who more deserve a baby, or will value it more or treat it better. But you'd better start saving for her/his college! We're alert to the possibilities because, as I may or may not have written you, we became grandparents again on December 2, and Mary Allison is already laying a financial shadow on the future. I am thinking of suggesting that she be apprenticed out at eight to a cobbler, garment-maker, or sanitary engineer, so that her meager wages can be hoarded toward one quarter of Stanford tuition. But she is worth the worry, never fear. Last week she learned a toothless smile, to the idiotic pleasure of parents and grandparents alike.

John, Mary and I read your latest essay with, as usual, pleasure, and we agree that it is a single thing, proceeding from a beginning to an end through an undistributed middle. Nevertheless, something in it, probably the diary form, gives it a greater air of dispersal than it really lives up to. It seems more diffuse than it is, nature either tame or wild being somewhat deliberate in her developments. It is also the sort of ruminative essay, unrelated to any newsworthy problem or crisis, that magazines tend to be wary of. They always look right in books; to the eyes of magazine editors they look like think-pieces, vaguely philosophical and hence of dubious popularity. If I were you I'd try it on some other places before I gave up on it, but I wouldn't be totally surprised if you couldn't place it. In that case, better dismemberment than burial, I should think. Your spider essay, by contrast with this one, is consummated in an hour or two. This one takes a whole revolution of the seasons, and we don't expect that to happen in the space of a short essay. Yvor Winters would not say, but I might, that a little imitative form here, or imitative pace, at least, might help.

Weather dry as a bone, cold at night, warm in the daytime. Precipitation for all of January, .6 inches. Total for the year, 6. inches. Probable result: another serious drought. The reservoirs are at their lowest point ever, according to the radio. So all of us may be knocking on the wooden curtain demanding admission to soggy Oregon.

And so to work. We hope everything goes well for you both, that job and baby cooperate for Marilyn, and that you see some more spiders or grow some more carrots and write some more essays. We miss you in the cottage. Rachael and Kerry are both gone from seven-thirty to about six or after, so that the place seems unnaturally unpopulated until they finally wake up about noon on Saturday. They are getting married in June (about time), and preparations are already beginning to quicken things. True to the modern mix of requirements, they will emerge from that cottage on June 10 in satin and tails. O tempora, o mores.

Best,

Wally

P.S. And O.K., I will not extend any more syntactical rope to poets for them to hang themselves with.

« *To: John Daniel* • *March 8, 1989* »

Dear John and Marilyn,

Ah, what a sad piece of news. We grieve for both of you. We know how you wanted that baby, and we hope that fate will be kind and give it to you yet. Allah kareem, the Arabs say. God is kind. Let's see if he is. Considering the Ayatollah, I'm suspicious of that Koranic statement. Maybe they mean God is kind but Islam is not. Christian or Muslim or Zen, there are a lot of contradictions in religious teachings.

As for your new essay, send it. I have not been so weak as to get myself into any judicial positions.

As for Everett Ruess,[54] the book you are thinking of is *Everett Reuss*, Peregrine Smith Books, Layton, Utah. Ruess's brother, Waldo Ruess, lives, or did a couple of years ago, in Santa Barbara. He is a fervent, even ferocious, advocate of his missing brother. The parents I met maybe ten years ago when I made a speech at Muir College, University of California, San Diego, but I can't give you their home address. (All this may be moot: Waldo Ruess wrote me in April 1985 that he'd be 76 in September.) I have a couple or three letters from him if they'll help you at all.

As for rain: we've been getting it. .3 of an inch in three days of drizzle and fog. Send word to up the ante.

Now your poems. I love "In the Sky Lakes Wilderness." It's descriptively

---

54. At the age of 20 the young artist and wanderer (and endlessly romanticized) Everett Reuss disappeared with his burro into the southern Utah wilderness in 1939. No trace of him has ever been found.

magical, and you work into it your fairly persistent theme of minimal humanity, full of well deserved humility. People will remember this one.

I also love "In the Old Growth Forest." I hope Tom[55] or somebody equally percipient will publish them both. I love death's generous body, I love the way you articulate the death-and-growth cycle of nature. You can be the poet of these times of growing ecological awareness. Take care or you'll become a great man.

Mary and I are going to take a last fling and go to Morocco for a couple of weeks, starting March 21. We shall see if Allah is really kind. If I were a one-eyed kid in a dirt street in some kasba in North Africa, I think I would wonder. Our love to Marilyn, and our sympathy to you both. I hope you can come down on April 30—we'd love to see you.

Best,
Wally

« To: John Daniel · October 9, 1989 »

Dear John,

Sorry to be slow with my response to your letter and manuscript of Sept. 26. We got back here on the night of the 22nd, and have been unpacking and clearing up ever since. An awful lot of things can accumulate in third and fourth class mail in three months, or even two and a half. And since Mary was in need of some medical attention when we got here, we have spent more time than either of us likes at the clinic. Things are settling down now. Diet is the prescribed course of the experiment. She can't eat anything or drink anything—no alcohol, wine, coffee, fruit juice, carbonated drinks, fruit, vegetables (maybe beets). She lives on pretzels and ice cream, or rather frozen yoghurt. Feeling O.K., in general. You ought to try it. My own diet is limited to oat bran.

Your piece seems to me fine and strong and effective, and if editorial requirements were as writers would like them, I would recommend no cuts at all. Everything serves your purposes here. But since even Tom[56] doesn't have indefinite space, I can understand his desire for cutting. So I read through the article for admiration's sake, and then read it again for cutting's sake, and I confess I think you're between a rock and a stone.

---

55. Tom Watkins, editor of *Wilderness* magazine.
56. Tom Watkins.

You're absolutely right about the sections that might be cut if anything has to be—2, 3, and 4 are the only places. 1 and 5 should be inviolate. But 2, 3, and 4 contain an awful lot of the essential information of the piece, and that makes cutting hard. I would think you could condense or leave out the history of the BLM,[57] and concentrate on its functions (thereby weakening the explanation of why BLM knows so little about preservation). Still, you could save maybe 2 or 3 pages in 2 and 3, and another page or two in 4. That probably wouldn't quality for Tom's "more than a little" requirement. And nobody should touch this in that first stage except yourself. My own weak-minded solution would be to go through it with a red pencil, taking out a phrase here, a sentence there, a paragraph or two somewhere else, and then, when you or the computer have compacted it into a solid mass again, turning it over to Tom to finish. He's the editor. He's the guy who wants cuts. When the cuts hurt, and they will, let him take the responsibility, or what's an editor for? Also, at that stage I suspect his eye will be sharper than yours for the extraneous or expandable line. Since Tom is coming by here this Friday to have lunch with us as he junkets hither and yon, I will try to make him assume his proper responsibilities. Because he gave you a job to do, you did it beautifully in the space it demanded. If he needs it in smaller space, he's got to collaborate.

Nothing new here or in Vermont. I seem to have accepted a commission from the *Smithsonian* to do a piece on the history of wilderness acceptance—so far it strikes me as a précis of Rod Nash[58]—but I've got until February 1 to think about it, and I just might do that. Our love to Marilyn, our best to your mother. I'll go to the temple to pray for Common Ground.

Best,
Wally

« *To: John Daniel* • *November 16, 1989* »

Dear John,
Your piece in *North American Review* was splendid, better even than it was when I saw it in manuscript. I think Jim Hepworth has an astute idea, to

---

57. Bureau of Land Management.
58. Roderick Nash, *Wilderness and the American Mind* (New Haven: Yale University Press, 1967).

get together a volume of these essays. They'll reach an audience, whoever publishes them, and I will look smug and say "I knew that fellow when all he could do was rake leaves." (Incidentally, we could use you. We're buried in 'em.)

I haven't had a letter from Tom[59] lately, and so I don't know how he has responded to your cutting in the archeology essay. He is a reasonable man, however, and should be able to compromise between his conscience and his space. And incidentally, he has a fine book coming[60]—the Ickes looks from here like a possibility for a history prize. The whole New Deal, from the inside, is in it.

Honest work? I'm sorry the teaching doesn't seem to open up. And working in a bookstore is one of the better ways to work, though it won't keep you in shape for walking the Burr Trail. Maybe you can get a job as a logger, and help tear down the last old growth forests, saying goodbye to the spotted owls as you go.

My piece for the *Smithsonian* will be purely historical. Don Moser handed me the period from Columbus to Aldo Leopold. Then somebody else will take it from Aldo Leopold to Secretary Lujan, and still a third party will scan the future for signs. I have been re-reading a lot of books I haven't read for years—Rod Nash, William Bartram, Howard Mumford Jones's *O Strange New World*, Castaneda, Audubon's *Delineations of American Scenery and Character*, Cronon's *Changes in the Land*, biographies of Horace Albright and George Perkins Marsh, Marsh's *Man and Nature*. A leaky mind knows no mending, it has to be refilled over and over. As soon as I get all this stuff down into 5,000 words for Moser, I'll have forgotten it again. But I can say, "It's in my notes."

Earthquake. No, the cottage didn't slide down the hill, and so far as we can see sustained no damage except that the vent pipe from the bathroom got flattened out and will have to be made vertical again. Our own house had no structural damage, but lots of breakage, and an avalanche of books from every direction, and a torn-loose water heater. Most of it is now fixed, though I was slow about it because I had the flu when the quake hit, and I stayed in bed for the next week.

Now I have to write a couple of speeches for San Francisco, one to

---

59. Tom Watkins.
60. *Righteous Pilgrim: The Life and Times of Harold L. Ickes, 1874–1952* (New York: Henry Holt & Co., 1990).

introduce the new wilderness film on Pinchot and Muir, one to regale the Friends of the San Francisco Library. Tanya Berry was by the other day, checking out the earthquake damage to her relatives in Marin. Wendell, she says, is retiring from lectures and such, and writing only what he wants to write. God should give us all such options.

Best to Marilyn,
Wally

To: Page Stegner • July 5, 1990 »

Dear Page,

As long as I am housebound, remaking my blood supply and trying to exercise my game hip, I might as well put down in a note how things stand with the car. I have called the Greensboro Garage and asked them to service and inspect it and get it out of storage, but Jackie said there wasn't much chance now, with the Fourth coming in between, that they could have it ready before July 11. If you need the car, better keep on them—they are always overloaded and always slow, but they do yield to pressure if it's applied often enough.

My insides seem to have settled down, and on my new diet of pills that are meant to soothe rather than scoriate,[61] I'm having no problems with them. The hip is a pain in the ass, or near it, but I am now taking exercises and may be able to work it out. If I don't, I'm going to get a good course in indoor living in Greensboro.

One thing occurred to me while I was quarreling with my insides and getting my nourishment in the vein. It has to do with your summer plans. When I got close to the golden door I began to wonder what I would or should have done differently during my life, and one thing I was very sure of was that I should not have accepted every damned assignment that some editor threw at me. I would have written more that I wanted to write, and less of what was only for money. That's right where you sit now, isn't it, with regard to the Sierra Club's proposal? You want to finish the piece you started for Humboldt State, and you can see some excitement in it. On the other hand it's flattering to be asked to do this book on eastern forests. But

---

61. Stegner was on a regime of anti-inflammatory drugs in 1989 to ease the pain of a disintegrating hip. The drugs ate a hole in his stomach and landed him in the Intensive Care unit of the Stanford Hospital. In 1991 he had the hip replaced.

the fact is, you are by no means an expert on eastern forests, either biologically or geographically or historically. You have a choice between spending your whole summer away from Greensboro, Lynn, and Allison, running up and down doing hasty research, and then continuing to do book research after you come home, and finally producing a book that however readable it is can't possibly be very authoritative—between that and staying snug in your log house and writing the thing you want to write, and having your family with you, and some time to look after them and to have some fun. Think it over. If I were in your shoes I am pretty sure I would unload that forest book and do what I was more interested in and more competent to do well. Lynn said the other day, and I just realized the import of the remark, that Wuerthner did not get the assignment to make the photographs. That leaves you even more out there by yourself.

Well, you get my drift. Think it over. Examine your priorities. Can you really do this book right, without paying too heavily? Do you need to do it, either for conviction's sake, or money's sake, or the sake of your dossier? As Cromwell said to somebody, "I beseech you, in the bowels of Christ, bethink you that you may be mistaken."

I hear you don't have air conditioning in your new truck, alas. But maybe you were so baked on the San Juan that the Plains heat felt like a breeze. I hope so.

See you on the 19th. We'll be in touch long before then.

Love,

Pop

« *To: Lynn Stegner* • *September 25, 1991* »

Dear Lynn,

You wrote me a nice warm letter while I was in the hospital, and this morning on the telephone Page said that you had written another. I would have answered the first, honest, except that until this morning I haven't been able to get my leg under the typewriter table, and my handwriting has deteriorated into a shaking scrawl, thanks to the polymyangia rheumatica in the hands. But this morning I feel my powers.

First the operation,[62] which was more of an inconvenience than an ordeal. I've got a wound a foot long on my backside, but it looks worse

---

62. In mid-September Stegner had hip replacement surgery.

than it feels, and it hasn't really hampered me much. I can get around on the walker, and in a week or so will graduate to a cane, a couple of weeks earlier than they prophesied. Sleeping is the worst, because the only safe and comfortable position is flat on my back, so that I'm always waking up with my mouth wide open and as dry as if elephants have been dusting themselves there. But that will change too in a few days, and I will sleep sweetly in my customary fetal position and saunter out each morning with my cane. With luck, I may even be permitted to go down to Stanford next Saturday and do a reading from *Wolf Willow* to welcome Prime Minister Mulroney of Canada. If I'm not able to go in person I will send an audio tape as proxy.

Lots of reading while I'm lying around here unable to write. Amy Tan's latest—not so much, certainly not worth all the Tan-fare. The memoirs of James Reston and George Kennon, both really splendid. A history of the Civil War in the West. R.W.B. Lewis's *The Jameses*, 750 close pages of more than I need to know about Henry, William, and the rest of the family. Nothing there to recommend to you unless you're feeling historico-political, in which case both Kennon and Reston are worth all the time you can give them.

We have seen Page and Shawn,[63] who now are peddling air conditioning and water-purifying units in some pyramid scheme, and will probably lose at least the tails of their shirts. Pagie came down and was helpful for two or three days, and then Shawn drove down and joined him, bringing Sheridan,[64] who looks like a linebacker or tight end and seems to have an equable disposition.

Mary is under some strain, having to look after me, but the nurse's aide who comes for two hours every morning takes some of the burden. She'll come through this week, by which time I may well be on the cane and can help a little. Trouble with a walker is that it takes both hands, and you can't do anything else while you're using it.

The aide is about to leave and will put this in the mailbox for us. We envy you all in the color season, and hope it stays brilliant for you. Give Alison a hug and a big smack from Grandpa, and another one or two from Grandma. See you in a few weeks.

Love,

Wally

---

63. Stegner's grandson and his wife.
64. Stegner's great grandson.

« *To: John Daniel* • *October 7, 1991* »

Dear John,

I'm touched and pleased by your dedication,[65] and I will pretend to myself that it is deserved. I'm particularly pleased and touched because I so admire the book. I read all the essays through, some of them for the second or third time, some for the first, this past weekend, and they hold up beautifully. All of them are serious, thoughtful, provocative; several of them are superb. I was pleased to meet all those owls, spiders, woodrats, and ants again—after all, I have a proprietary interest in them, and they're still around. Night before last one of your screech owls sat on the telephone wires screeching all night, and about four in the morning there was a crash in the eucalyptus clump, and a squealing or twittering, bird or beast I couldn't tell, and then the most profound silence. Owls must eat as silently as they fly. But he sure lit in the bushes with the impact of a guided missile.

Back to the essays. I particularly like "Place of Wild Beasts," "Among Animals," and "The Long Dance of the Trees," probably for the strong sympathy with all life that they demonstrate. But I like your "Desert Walking" for that and other reasons, and there isn't a weak one in the batch. Occasionally I thought I caught you being just a shade more monitory than the traffic will bear, but it's hard to keep from scolding when the children have been so truly bad. And you leave me a little in your wake in the later essays where ecology shades into religion. I share your wariness of sectarian rigidities, and I don't usually mention God for fear of calling attention to myself. But I have to agree that ecology is as close to religious feeling as I'm likely to come, and I have sometimes dreamed of a great convulsive reconversion of the whole bloody race from Christianity, Judaism, and Islam back to good honest paganism, with nobody else around but the friendly little local deities of waterfalls and rain. So I agree with the general curve of your book from immediate back-yard observation to contemplation of the Infinite, and I'm sure a lot of other readers will too. I'll write a more considered letter to Pantheon, and send you a copy when I get time to sit down and think.

I've done a lot of sitting down lately since I had a new hip installed

---

65. To *The Trail Home: Nature, Imagination, and the American West* (New York: Pantheon Books, 1992).

four weeks ago; but now I am around on a cane, not venturing more than a hundred yards, but stretching it little by little. Actually I'm about three weeks ahead of the schedule they gave me, and within a couple of weeks I should be back in game shape. Mary is reasonably well—she's never unreasonably so. Stanford continues to suffer for its bookkeeping slackness, and I'm sorry to see Don Kennedy[66] have to take the rap. But the centennial events went off with considerable éclat. I participated only in the first convocation, parking in my wheelchair while George Schultz conducted the meeting and Prime Minister Mulroney made the keynote speech—a much better and more liberal speech than I would have expected from him. Then I read a little from *Wolf Willow*, in honor of the Canadian presence, and we all tiptoed home hushed and comforted.

And I am green with envy about all that hiking in the Escalante Basin and elsewhere. Maybe with my new hip . . . Love to Marilyn.

Wally

« *To: Rachael Stegner* • *December 20, 1991* »

Dear Rachael,

Grandma and I have been thinking about what we can leave to all of you when we pass on. It won't be a great deal, and the longer we live the less there will be, and we intend to live to be a hundred. But there should be something, and the more we can avoid death taxes the more there will be for each of you. One way to avoid death taxes is to give at least something while we're alive, and so get it out of the estate. This we have decided to do, as we can afford it. There was to be a check enclosed with this, but I ran out of checks and so will have to get yours to you after you come back from skiing.

There is, naturally, some grandfatherly advice that goes with this and with any future checks. This money is not intended to be spending money, unless you get into an absolutely tight bind. It's intended as keeping money. It's part of your inheritance which otherwise wouldn't get to you unless we were both dead. Its best purpose should be as part of your invested capital. Put away in something conservative and safe, it will grow, and maybe have a hand in making your future secure. From here, who can tell

---

66. President of Stanford University.

what the future will look like? The present looks glum enough so that we can imagine it getting worse.[67] In any event, this check comes to you with our love, and our hope that you can use it and any others like it to build a solid and secure life for yourself.

Now Grandma and I can get on with that intention of living through the 20th century.

Lots of Love,

Grandpa

« *To: John Daniel* • *March 29, 1992* »

Dear John,

No, I'm not in full promotional swing, and won't be.[68] All we're going to do is Printers Inc., Books Inc., Black Oak in Berkeley, Clean Well Lighted Place in San Francisco, Thunderbird in Carmel, and, later, when we go east, a couple in New York and maybe one or two in Washington. No big tour. I'm too old. That kind of tour is for young sprouts like you and Ivan Doig.

I'm hopeful we'll still be here on May 28 so we can attend the Pantheon clambake in Berkeley. Even if we don't make Berkeley, I hope we'll be here so you and Marilyn can make us. I will save some mowing and chainsaw chores. Kepler's and Stanford are both accessible to us, so we're pretty sure to get our ear to the crack. I want to hear the applause for your book.

The cruise went O.K., except for some thirty-foot seas and some thirty-foot over-the-rail shots. Hip all fluent, no serious ailments, only the nagging ones. I take 11 pills at breakfast and eight more the rest of the day, but they haven't killed me yet. These modern pills haven't got any oomph.

Everything very green here. Grass grows six inches a week. Lots of poppies and lupine. Besser you should come back and see how it looks in a favorable year.

Our love to Marilyn. Don't miss us.

Yours,

Wally

---

67. Stegner never got over growing up during the Depression. The wolf was always at the door.

68. For *Where the Bluebird Sings to the Lemonade Springs*.

« To: John Daniel • October 22, 1992 »

Dear John,

We're very sorry to hear about your mother's death. We hadn't heard until your letter, but that was hardly your fault. In June we were in Scotland for ten days, in July we were in Vermont, in early August we came back here and tried to straighten out the mess that the post office had made of our mail. At the end of September we went up to Bozeman, where they are establishing a chair in American Studies in my name, and I gummed up the works by collapsing on the stage and getting hauled down to the emergency room. All a tempest in a teapot. What they thought must be a heart attack was only a sudden bout of flu. But it killed the festive occasion. We've been rubber-legged ever since, but perfectly well. So your news comes as a sadness on top of a long frustration, and strikes us not only as a loss but as a memento mori. Your mother was about my age, and I'm going to have to start cleaning up after myself and getting ready.

Your words at her service we're glad to have, for they're affectionate and touching and understanding. Your relationship with your mother, even with all the difficulties of age and growing infirmity, is something I envy. I would have liked the chance to live along with my own mother for a while, to get her out of her imprisonment and share some of the good things of life. It always seemed to us that your understanding with your mother was deep and sure. That has to be a consolation to you, even at the hour of loss.

Great about your Sierra article—and don't knock journalism. It often does some good, and you have a knack of ennobling it. Cecil Andrus I know a little, and you're right about him. It would be terrific to get him back,[69] but I understand his unwillingness. Bruce Babbitt would probably be my choice, if anybody asked me. He's knowledgeable and persistent and tougher than he looks, and he has indicated his general bias by accepting the headship of the League of Conservation Voters. He was here this week, and I could have gone to hear him, but we're still rubber-legged from Bozeman, and in the end we chickened out.

As for your new book project, we will cheer it when it comes. Obviously you're not going to let your agent steer you into a pattern of writing it,

---

69. As Secretary of the Interior.

but a hint is often very useful, and your own sense will tell you as you go whether the direction is right.

And so goodnight. Thanks for the reviews. I like both yours and Slovic's. Why wouldn't I? God bless us every one. And love to Marilyn.

Yours,

Wally

« *To: John Daniel* • *December 18, 1992* »

Dear John,

Jim Hepworth did tell me about the Montana opening, which it seems to me is made for you if you want to move from Portland, but I was waiting until I heard either from you, or from Bill Kittredge, or somebody. Now I have.

There is no need to have my old letter sent to me from the Placement Center. You are an altogether different article from what you were when you asked for that one. Then you were an apprentice poet, now you are a Man of Letters. (Never mind that Louis Untermeyer used to spell that H*A*C*K. He was a spoiled poet.) It seems to me that now, with some years of teaching experience, a book of poems, a book of essays, and various assorted accomplishments that I may not know about, you're ready to step into a university department and carry your share or more, and bring some sanity to the academics in the process.

I guess I won't write any official letter until I hear either from you or from the Montana department. But I'll confide, let us say, in Bill. If this works out, I think you'll like Missoula and the people there. I don't know them all, but Bill Kittredge and Annick Smith are both first-rate people, and Jimmy Welch, though I think he doesn't teach at Missoula, is, or used to be, married to a lady in the English Department; and the head of the department, the last time I heard, was a fellow from the East who had got sold on the West, and wrote a book about the Missoula literary crowd entitled *Ten Tough Trips*.[70] That's the liveliest literary company in the Rocky Mountains, and if you can find a house on Upper Rattlesnake you'll be right in your outdoor element. (Anybody who is anybody lives on Upper Rattlesnake.)

---

70. William W. Bevis, *Ten Tough Trips* (Seattle: University of Washington Press, 1990).

I'm delighted to hear that you've got another book in the works, and sympathetic to hear that you've got galleys coming or come from *Sierra*. Page and I have both had unfortunate experiences with that magazine, which operates somewhat less sanely and humanely than Tom Watkins' *Wilderness*. Good luck.

And a happy Christmas and a prosperous New Year to you and Marilyn. I keep waiting for Clinton to appoint Bruce Babbitt, and if he doesn't I'll be devastated, because it will mean that he has caved in to the Sagebrush Rebels. I don't think he'll cave, though, and I'm therefore hopeful for 1999.

Bless you both. We had a nice dinner with Wendell and Tanya,[71] and a nice lunch down here a couple of days later. I heard him read—well—at Printer's Inc., but like Jesting Pilate, I could not stay for the questions and answers. All our best from here.

Yours,
Wally

« *To: John Daniel* • *March 14, 1993* »

Dear John,
We're happy you're coming down, and we'll be glad to see you out here to help us move spring through the door. I've checked the calendar, and there's nothing in those three days that you'll be here except a couple of meetings that we can go to if we choose but don't have to. Why don't you call us from Di Pietro's after you get in, and we'll work out a time that matches with the rest of your obligations.

About the interview, I'm not so sure. There are few people I'd rather be interviewed by, but there is a profound doubt in my mind that I want to be interviewed by anybody. I get embarrassed, standing up in periodicals piping, "Here I am again." As for the boundaries theme, I'll have to think about that. Boundaries haven't been central to my thinking about the West, or in my thinking at large. In fact, at last year's Founder's Day at Stanford, I found myself a friend of Mulroney[72] because I made a brief speech in which I wished that the boundary between the U.S. and Canada would be as I knew it when I was a boy—an imaginary line dividing like from like.

---

71. Wendell and Tanya Berry.
72. Prime Minister Mulroney of Canada.

But we can resolve that problem when we see you. Meantime, don't give your editor any ideas.

Are you going to be at Babbitt's Timber Summit? If not, why not?

Our best to Marilyn. We wish she was coming along.

Yours,

Wally

The Literary Life

HE LEFT A LEGACY as writer, teacher, and conservationist that once moved Edward Abbey to pronounce him "the only living American worthy of the Nobel." Indeed, Stegner was one of the most important of its novelists. His work, unequaled in the American literature of place, created a new consciousness of the West as America, only more so, a region that embodies the national culture at its most energetic, rootless, complex, reactionary, subdivided, wild, half-baked, comic, tragic, and hopeful. He taught two generations of writers, and after he left teaching he continued to be both model and mentor for what has become an explosion of literary activity in the West. And in matters of conservation he was the most rational and eloquent of the region's statesmen; everyone who values wilderness owes him a debt.

In all of American literature, there is nobody like Wallace Stegner, and nothing quite like his novels. He was a master of his art and though he was a man I would have liked whether or not he had ever written a word, I will take him now wherever I can find him, and I suppose that must mean mainly in his books. I loved him. We all did. He gave us more credit than we deserved and encouraged us to undertake things we would never otherwise have dared to attempt. "All you can do is try," he would say.

FROM "THE QUIET REVOLUTIONARY," BY JAMES R. HEPWORTH

◆ ◆ ◆

« *To: Mark Schorer*[1] • *December 10, 1942* »

Dear Mark,

I don't have any real conviction that this letter will heal the breach which has developed, or even clarify any of the issues. From the tone of your two letters, and from the amount of talking you seem to have done in Cambridge, I judge that you have made up your mind fully, and that any communications between us are likely to come down to "You did!" and "I didn't!" But I have looked over my article as it appeared in *Harper's*, and I have dug up a copy of yours and re-read it, and I have gone over, with somewhat puzzled wonder, the list of crimes you charge me with in your second letter, and at least I can be more specific in my own defense than

---

1. Schorer was a colleague of Stegner's at Harvard and author of *Sinclair Lewis: An American Life*.

I was before, when I was confounded by your attack and uncertain what I had done.

The "misconstructions" you cite, for instance:

a) That I never indicate that the subject of your article is British fiction only. I don't, partly because I was not, whatever you may think, making a running commentary, point for point, on your article. I was using the point of view you represented there, and it is a point of view as common in reference to American as to British fiction. You put it clearly enough: "The earlier Hemingway, Fitzgerald . . . Prokosch, Williams, even Dos Passos—all these enormously gifted writers have, usually against their instincts, viewed with horror the spectacle of modern life; and their fiction has shared the characteristic marks of British fiction." It was precisely because novelists, British and American, viewed their world with horror that I objected, and I can't see that the limitation of your subject makes any difference.

b) That I never indicate that your article is purely descriptive. No, because it isn't, in spite of the protestation in your third paragraph. I think that perhaps you don't realize the implications of your own position, and that you may not have noticed that your first paragraph ends thus: "Yet it is only because the writer has responded immediately to his world and, which is precisely his function, given form to its tone and tempo, that he has been exhorted and upbraided from our quasi-official pulpits. Allow a layman to defend him" (emphasis mine). I don't know exactly what you would have a reader believe. The protestation in paragraph three that you will attempt nothing but description is hardly less disingenuous than your reference to yourself as a "layman." It seems to me apparent throughout your article that you are defending, not describing. You speak of the writer's "honesty," a "scrupulous honesty unknown to an always hopeful citizenry," which leads him to degrade human experience when he would rather celebrate it. I am not sure that one couldn't read "deluded belief" for "honesty," but it is clear from your tone that you do not think so. One of the points I was trying to make, and I had to make it in your teeth because you obviously stood for the opposite, was that intellectual currents can breed a kind of drunkenness, and that writers, being intellectuals generally, have been drunker than the "always hopeful citizenry"—who by implication are dishonest because they don't find the world unbearable.

c) That I suggest all through page 80 that you make a plea for the long-gone Victorian virtues. To that one I can only reply that unless I have lost my ability to read I suggest nothing of the sort. You make a rather strong point of the fact that recent novels repudiate the Victorian virtues, and you imply that therefore they do not exist any more. I agreed that the novels generally repudiated them; I disagreed that the novels were necessarily the best evidence that they had vanished from the earth and left us without a moral reference. I suggested that the moral reference, apparently destroyed, was only altered a little, and that its foundations were as solid as ever. I cannot find anything in the passage which remotely suggests that you are a Victorian old maid, or make a plea for those past virtues. If anybody is making a plea for them, I am. Some of them are gone, and I said good riddance, as you would. But enough of them are left so that we needn't consider ourselves completely adrift. I think you had to dig pretty hard to find this one.

d) That you didn't say what I said you said about experimentation in form and impoverishment of subject matter. You read my "with some truth" as a slur, and you quibble at my restatement of your point. I can't appraise that slur in the phrase, because I am unable to get myself into the frame of mind you seem to have got yourself into. If there's a slur there, I didn't know it when I wrote it. As for my word "sign," at which you boggle, I'll recant on that if you wish, though I should like to take a Gallup poll on how a hundred disinterested readers would read your statement of that truism about technical proficiency and sterility of subject matter. You accuse me of putting in your mouth a much more dogmatic statement than you ever would have made, but read it: it ends, "So true is this generalization that one may very nearly use it as the test of modernity." That leaves little room for exceptions.

Now the more specific charges of paraphrasing and borrowing and utilizing without regard to ethics or friendship:

a) That the suicide note of Virginia Woolf was your documentation, not mine. That one I admit and apologize for, if you wish an apology. It isn't clear that I was summarizing you there. I'm sorry.

b) That the paragraph following refers back to four names in lines 5 and 6 of the same column, etc., which you seem to think should have been put in quotes in the first place. They were not in quotes in the first place because in their original form in your article they simply couldn't be worked into the sentence of quotation I was using. It is perfectly clear that you cited them, and that I am following you. In the second citation of the names I am not necessarily following you. Perhaps I should paraphrase a sentence from your letter here. You remark in that letter that I am not the first to put my money on Hemingway. By the same token, though not in the same tone, I hope, the influence of Newton, Darwin, Marx, and Freud is hardly your discovery. Nobody talking about the apparent collapse of values in our times could have avoided talking about them. Actually there isn't a word of paraphrase in that paragraph: it says essentially what I have said at one time or another to every freshman class I have taught in the last twelve years. The gradual disintegration of man's certainties in the face of scientific and pseudo-scientific discoveries is as indivisible from our mutual subject as yokes are from eggs. And truisms, as far as I can see, need no documentation.

c) That the paragraph beginning "Well, it is hard" is not Stegner but Schorer. That one again I admit. The phrase which was originally in there to reinforce what I think should have been clear anyway got cut out, and I shall not try to make *Harper's* the goat. I apparently cut it out when I was boiling the piece down at Allen's suggestion. Again, I'm sorry.

d) That the "perhaps" introducing the remark about *Finnegans Wake* should be "perhaps this same critic is right in suggesting that *Finnegans Wake*," etc. I'm afraid I can't agree. I'm talking about the possible extinction of the novel as a literary type. You're talking about the changes that come about, particularly the loss of orthodox "plot," as a result of technical innovation and the application of relativist thinking to novel technique. We are not talking about the same thing, and the context is entirely different.

e) That the opening of the next paragraph is more paraphrase. Sure it is, paraphrase of the ideas your generation and mine was weaned on. It refers back, if you like, to your statement (clearly quoted) of those ideas, but if a second reference without quotes when the first has been in quotes is unethical paraphrase I'll eat every word of that passage in letters of cement.

f) Ditto. I was writing for a popular magazine, for God's sake, not the PMLA.[2]

g) That you make some point about the American novel that I use on page 31. If you mean the remark about American novelists being estranged from their world, I must think you both deluded and inconsistent. In another place you insist that you separated American writers, specifically Hemingway and Steinbeck, from your British collection, and that I wronged you by not saying so. Here you think you made my point for me. That point is again one that anyone who has read any modern fiction couldn't miss, and it includes Hemingway and Steinbeck, even *For Whom the Bell Tolls* and *The Grapes of Wrath*. My God, give me credit for a few of my commonplaces, at least.

h) This one I just can't understand. Of course the phrase "no serious writer" had its source in a quotation three pages back. Of course it is now out of quotes. Of course I did it deliberately, for the reasons adduced in (e). And I would guarantee that any reader with a mental age of six or over would know where the phrase came from in the first place, as he was intended to.

What all this controversy comes down to, apparently, is that in two short passages within the section where I was admittedly (and I thought obviously) summarizing your position I have paraphrased without meticulously indicating that I was doing so, and that I omitted a footnote or other reference to your name. The reasons why I left your name out I have already told you; the carelessness about tagging the paraphrase I am sorry for, and I repeat that I hadn't the remotest notion of using or abusing you in an unethical or unfriendly way. But I can't keep from remarking, as the last word I shall voluntarily say in the matter, that if my carelessness seemed unfriendly to you, your instant and overheated reaction seems fully as unfriendly to me, and less pardonable, particularly since in effect you were publicly calling me a thief before you had even made an attempt to see if there was any explanation for what you thought my unpardonable actions. I have canvassed those two articles very thoroughly, and I know

---

2. Publication of the Modern Language Association of America, a scholarly journal.

that if our positions had been reversed I should not have been angry. I can only assume that you wanted an excuse, for some reason, to throw up a barricade.

Yours,

[no signature]

« *To: Katherine Anne Porter* • *May 14, 1948* »

Dear Katherine Anne:

That is a sad story you tell about the Redlands Baptists.[3] If I had known what I was getting you into, we would have tried to send you out of here equipped with a balanced pair of kegs like Noah's Ark, or at least have given you a package of Sen-Sen for the tobacco breath, and I would have given a month's salary to be there when you sneaked into the Mexican pool room.[4] I don't imagine that Pomona is likely to be much better, since the last time I stayed at the Claremont Inn I almost disrupted the smooth functioning of the institution by ordering up some ice about ten in the evening. The bellhop finally tiptoed in with it, saying he had stolen it out of the kitchen icebox. But cheer, if you get really dry, come up here again.

I am glad that you are finding students worth working with and I have no doubt at all that your round of visits will turn out to be not merely the first of a long series, but a high-water mark as well. You left a deep and salty deposit on this campus and we are all very grateful to you.

Our tentative plan for trying to get you here[5] on some kind of part-of-the-year basis appears to be stymied until the regular head of the department recovers from his operation and returns to the position, but I have certainly not given it up, and if you continue to publish with Harcourt Brace I think you may expect a letter from me now and again keeping you posted on how the thing goes forward. I should not want to get you into

---

3. Katherine Ann Porter had written about her three-week sojourn at Redlands, "They are Baptists there, as you know . . . Well, not only did I not hear the word *cocktail*, or even *likker*, pronounced during my stay, I never saw a faculty member smoke, and only once during a last minute little conference at Dr. Nelson's house did I see a student—a boy—light a cigarette." She went on to remark, "I did smoke, of course, guiltily, surreptitiously, hang-doggishly, but not where any student could see. As for alcohol . . ."

4. Porter wrote, "Well, my first act here was to take a taxi and drive to the Spanish section and go into a little Mexican pool room and drink *two* sherries, straight. It occurred to me afterward that I may have created a scandal."

5. Stanford University.

anything that ties you down more than you should be tied, but I think that the administration is sensible enough in those matters that some kind of arrangement agreeable to you, and profitable to us, can be worked out. Sometime during the summer I expect the issue will come clearly up for a decision. In the meantime, thank you again and greetings from many besides your devoted admirer,

Wallace Stegner

« *To: Bernard DeVoto* • *October 21, 1956* »

Dear Benny:

I owe you, as usual, thanks for many things, the latest of which is the collection of Easy Chairs. Those are Fine Furnishings. I know most of them of old, and shall sit in them again for pleasure.

Also I think I owe you for a couple of magazine commissions, one on the Sierra for *Holiday* and another from *Colliers* on the Mormon migration. This last one is embarrassing; you did that migration once and for all in *The Year of Decision*, and my cramping of the thing into six thousand words is a sad comedown, I'm afraid. However, Carl[6] seems to think it'll do, and if it will, I'll settle. The fee, at least, is, as the E Clampus Vitus boys used to say, Satisfactory. The *Sierra* article is in the throes—again the goddam problem of getting an enormous amount of space, time, and material into the space of one article without sounding as if you're concocting General Systems Theories.

Which brings me to the Behavioral Sciences, of which I am temporarily one.[7] I never knew about these things before; I don't know about them now. But I have heard about them. They appear to differ from the social sciences in the way you cut the pie. If you cut it into psychologists, anthropologists, sociologists, political scientists, and all their dichotomies and mitoses, you are thinking in terms of social sciences. But if you cut it with the New Look into Communications Theory, Games Theory, Organizations Theory, and—best of all—General Systems Theory—then you are a Behavioral Scientist, dizzily enthroned.

It's the old business: application of measurement to human behavior,

---

6. Carl Brandt, Stegner's literary agent.
7. In 1956 Stegner was a fellow at the Center for Advanced Study in the Behavioral Sciences in Palo Alto, California.

or the attempt thereunto. In the end, about two-thirds of these boys come down to mathematical formulae, mainly the mathematics of probabilities, and their talk is rich with stochastic processes, Markov processes, Feller processes (not a fast ball), and other mysteries. As for General Systems Theory, that is my dish. That attempts to find a formula which will be mathematically applicable to all behavior of animals, men, and machines, no matter how they are organized—that will be applicable to Social Scientists, Behavioral Scientists, Automats, Historians, and Me. I have a name on that hill: I am the Intelligent Layman, and I will tell you how I come out. From this letter you will judge that this center is all nonsense, but that would be premature. There are a lot of very bright people up there, all talking a language I never heard spoken, and trying to spell the name of a God I never heard of with blocks I can't read. But I'm willing to stick around, because every once in a while I learn something, and that is not so common an event in my life that I can afford to pass it up. On the other hand, I do not expect to become a Behavioral Scientist, as I told a couple of them the other day, to their dismay: I happen to be interested not in Personality but in Character and not in Behavior but in Conduct. They looked at me with fallen jaws. But then.

Thanks again, and love to that admirable woman, your wife.

Wally

« *To Stewart Udall* • *October 20, 1961* »

MEMORANDUM

To Stewart Udall, Secretary of the Interior

Subject: Robert Frost movie

It is very much easier to specify the ways this movie should not be done than to suggest how it should best be done. It should not, for instance, like the recent USIA[8] film, pan over the New England countryside while Robert reads his poems, the camera hunting, sometimes pretty frantically and sometimes sentimentally, for visual equivalents of the poetic images. It should not, as you yourself have said, be poems on a string—not unless the poems are cunningly selected to develop a sequence of themes and unless they are interspersed with talk—become, in fact, almost a part of

_____
8. United States Information Agency.

the talk, as phrases, passages, or whole poems. It should not be simply an interview, the Poet at Home, an Ed Murrow visit to a celebrity.

On the other hand, Frost's most characteristic performance is a monologue, sometimes a walking monologue, sometimes a sitting one, and if the movie is to get at his essence it can hardly avoid being to a large extent Frost Talking. If his age were not too great a handicap, I would say the camera ought simply to accompany Frost on a walk, recording his home place as well as the talk and the poetry he would inevitably generate. That way the countryside could be kept in its place; the figure, face, and voice of Frost would dominate it. At times the voice might go on while the camera made excursions (see "The Quest of the Purple-Fringed," for instance, where the hunt for a flower closes out the season, prepares us for winter, sets up a typical Frost Theme). In any such monologue, poetry and talk are bound to be interwoven; Frost "says" his poems, his talk is poetic and his poetry conversational; and because so much of his poetry is concerned with natural or pastoral subjects, and because his lifelong habit has been to be "out for stars" or hunting the purple-fringed, man and country and ideas and poetry could all be approached through the simple device of a walk and a talk.

Obviously the walking-monologue ought to be steered somewhat, and obviously Frost himself is the person to steer it. But I can conceive of its beginning with the remark Frost makes in the preface to his collected works, that "calculation is usually no part in the first step of any walk." That is actually a statement of a deep-seated disinclination to prefabricate or pre-judge; it expresses not only how he takes a walk but how he makes a poem and how he makes an ethical choice. He wants "freedom to squander"; if he is out for stars he is not hunting any in particular, he "looks up by chance at the constellations." Somewhere or other he remarks that a poet throws ideas out ahead of him like giants throwing boulders to build a causeway, and progresses on what he has just thrown. In still another place he says a poem must "ride on its own melting," like ice on a hot stove. And in still another he compares the starting of a poem to a pushing off from shore in search of some opposite shore that is hidden; one knows when he is there by the fact that his bow quenches in the sand. In all this, and in many poems, he insists on the integrity of the poem as a growing thought: "a poem is the emotion of having a thought while the reader waits a little anxiously for the success of dawn." He is as anti-systematic as Emerson, and he phrases, perhaps more than he himself fully believes, the advantages of loafing and inviting his soul à la Whitman.

Nevertheless what is just as insistently there in his life and his poetry is a perception of the inevitable human limitations and the necessity of choice, sometimes painful choice. From poems which are themselves the records of walks—*Good Hours, The Woodpile, The Road Not Taken, Acquainted with the Night*—(or from the scraps and passages that Frost talking might pick out of them)—the monologue could go on, throwing its road out ahead of it, to the theme SLU [9] mentions, that "men must be together yet apart," and to his statement of the inescapable human condition. Poems such as *The Flood*, or *The Birthplace*, would illustrate it. From those the talk might go deeper, to darker themes and darker poems: *The Wind and the Rain, Desert Places, Bereft*. And from there, on to those very typical stoical and tough assertions of acceptance and resistance (*Acceptance, Come In, A Leaf Treader, Stopping by Woods*) to end on the equally typical faith that the universe is at least a shade in favor of man (*I Could Give All to Time, The Onset, Birches*, and the final couplet of *The Lesson for Today*).

This sounds, and to a degree is, the poems-on-a-string that neither of us wants. There are these differences, however: (1) the poems would seldom be complete poems, and would be embedded in talk, and (2) they would be thematically sequential. Beginning with an apparently random walk, they would move through the acceptance of experience, including its dark side, to the sort of serenity which distinguishes Frost's best poems. I'd like to see him end it with a full reading of *I Could Give All to Time*.

While this talking is going on, what is the camera doing? Somebody who knows cameras better than I do will have to say. But if Frost is there walking while he talks, it can certainly be focusing a good deal of the time on him, as he stops to examine a weed, or sits on a stone wall to rest, or grabs a handful of his hair to encourage a thought. It can, without overdoing it, take in the country side—and I do not mean the sentimentalized prettified countryside, but the sort that is actually there, tart as wintergreen and often rough as granite. It ought to hit some of those abandoned, tarnished-silver farms; if the talk turns to the theme of abandonment and decay, there are plenty of lost cemeteries, towns, schools, churches, farms, being overgrown with skunk spruce, with stone walls disappearing into thick

---

9. Stewart Lee Udall.

woods that were once meadows. There ought to be weather—wind, rain, frost; this whole movie ought to be weathered as Frost is and as Vermont is. When Frost asks for rain he wants it on his head "in all the passion of a banished drouth"; he wants to feel the earth "rough to all his length." This movie ought to catch that in the images the camera chooses. And it ought to catch Frost's face in all its manifold expressiveness. Beyond that I have no suggestions.

    Wallace E. Stegner

« *To: Stewart Udall* • *November 7, 1961* »

MEMORANDUM
To Stewart Udall, Secretary of the Interior
Subject: National Cultural Policy
I have read Mr. Isenberg's statement, and with its general aims (expressed in Part I) I couldn't agree more. It is a time for development of a cultural policy by the Federal Government; and though I do not have too much faith in arts policies which are developed simply as instruments in the cold war, I do think that a sympathetic and helpful attitude toward all the arts on the part of the Government cannot help having useful international results. But I think the Government should support and encourage the arts because they are the arts, the expression of much of the best in this civilization, and not because by supporting them we will win friends abroad.

    We have a long national history of indifference to the arts, or even hostility, to live down. There is no better time to begin than now. And I suppose that, our system being what it is, there is no other way to begin than with some sort of committee such as Mr. Isenberg suggests, though by and large whenever a committee has anything to do with the arts it produces the lowest common denominator of the group taste and imagination: everybody's third-choice suggestion gets selected, instead of someone's first-choice suggestion, which might be creative and hence controversial. But still—a committee, for lack of anything better. Eventually such a committee ought, I think, to be consolidated into a National Arts Foundation, parallel to the National Science Foundation, and it ought to have under its jurisdiction the specific activities which emerge as the proper interest of Government in the arts.

    With a good many of the suggestions implicit in Mr. Isenberg's "Issues Bearing Upon a National Cultural Policy" I don't happen to agree, but since they are proposed here only as a sort of tentative agenda for discussion, there is no point in arguing with them in a memo. (For instance, I would agree with the Federal Government's trying to improve radio and TV programs, but would think the introduction of cultural presentations into the National Park System, other than the interpretive programs now in effect, a mistake. Neither do I think much of motorized cultural caravans or an Arts Corps. Nevertheless Mr. Isenberg has suggested a provocative list of topics for examination. The list suggests what is the truth—that the field is wide open, because largely neglected. I would think the formation of such a committee a step in the right direction and I would hope that it would carry on the sort of thing that you started with your *Night with Robert Frost* and *Night with Carl Sandburg*. I'd like to see those continued, even if only one a year, and a presidential citation, medal, or prize given to the artist selected to be the pièce de résistance.

By and large, as the foundations have discovered, about the greatest encouragement one can give the arts is to buy a talented man's time and let him work, and to honor or reward distinguished performance. There may be something that can be done about stimulating audiences—actually that should be one of the biggest purposes of Federal encouragement of the arts, since the real chorus of any play is in the hearts of its right audience—but that is definitely a long-term goal to be achieved only by massive changes in our national attitudes, educational system, and entertainment patterns. If it could even make a start in this direction, a National Arts Foundation or a committee on a national arts policy would have done more than any agency since the WPA.[10]

I am lunching with Arthur Schlesinger on Monday, and can find out where the project stands.

Wallace E. Stegner

« *To: Stewart Udall* • *December 8, 1961* »

MEMORANDUM
To Stewart Udall, Secretary of the Interior
Subject: Robert Frost film
The consensus of those who have been discussing the possibilities of a film on Robert Frost is that neither he nor the film makers should be confined

---

10. In 1965 the National Endowment for the Arts was created by an act of Congress.

by a formal script. The bulk of the shooting should be done while Mr. Frost himself is steering ideas and poems and speculations through his incomparable monologues. He should not be asked to do anything—tread leaves, swing birches, mend walls, go out to clean the pasture spring, or even read a poem. Though the camera will surely bring in as image and atmosphere a certain amount of "Robert Frost country," there should not be so much of it as to obscure the poet, or to suggest that he is strictly a country poet, a rustic seer. This film should be a sort of poem itself, the portrait of a vigorous and invigorating mind at work, poking around at the edge of the possible, turning over the untouchable, risking getting lost for the sake of making discoveries.

A great amount of footage, then, of Mr. Frost himself, in every mood and in several contexts: in conversation, in student seminars, in his Cambridge home, and on his Vermont farm. The "script" will develop during the editing of this large assemblage of film and sound, which must be selected and edited with care and artistry so that the finished film not only makes a typically Frostian excursion through important and recurring themes, but does it in ways that are sharply and evocatively pictorial without being merely illustrative. The themes such a film should deal with are the themes of Mr. Frost's life and conversation as well as the themes of his poetry: they make a wholeness, a consistent package.

Since we do not intend a script, and hope to catch the man as he is rather than as someone directs him to be, there is no point in guessing how the continuity would go. But I think it certain that there will be a good deal of talk about poetry, about the poem's integrity as a "growing thought," about the way walks, and poems, and lives, should all be conducted without calculation, but only with an openness, a readiness, until the first lines or sets or actions have somehow made a pattern that enforces what follows. I suspect he will be saying something about how to be "together yet apart," and something about the need for minnows to brace up and be sharks, and about the flabbiness of an insured, safe, and protected existence. Also I suspect that a good deal of actual poetry will finally be in this film, because poetry crops up that way in Mr. Frost's talk, like stones pushed up surfaceward by the underground (Trilling's) frost.

Done right, scrupulously, carefully, letting the thought and words of Mr. Frost lead the film, or built out ahead of itself as he describes giants throwing boulders ahead of them to build a causeway, this could be the most intimate, revealing, and enspiriting record ever made of a major poet.

Done right, it will be a must in American schoolrooms for generations to come.

Wallace E. Stegner

« *To: Stewart Udall* • *December 22, 1962* »

Dear Stewart:

If you never write any better than in your article on Robert's[11] visit to Russia, you don't need to worry. It'll do. You do a very delicate and understanding portrait of Marse Robert, the things you select to quote are apt and right on the button, you hold up that old Russian wall and let Robert hop around on it like a sparrow—as I have no doubt he did. It's a fine piece, I'll be looking for it in some magazine. Where, *New York Times Magazine?* Robert, of course, will say he hasn't read it, after it appears. He tells that to all the girls. Maybe he doesn't read things about himself, as a rule, but if he reads yours he can't help being pleased.

Happy New Year. Do you ever write books, or is it always magazine articles?

Sincerely,

Wallace Stegner

« *To: Robert Stone* • *April 19, 1967* »

Dear Bob,

I'm happy to know that the kinks have come out and that your book is firmly scheduled.[12] You'll be competing with Phil Roth, whose third novel is the Guild selection for June. Let's see if you can put him down. He tells me his book hasn't got any Jews in it, so he's given up his strongest ally. I'll be along myself a little later—mine is the Guild selection for September. And God knows who else—Sylvia Wilkinson, Mort Grosser, L.J. Davis, my son Page, all fighting us for that spot in the reader's heart. I'll see you there amid the carnage.

The piece for *Saturday Review* is still, so far as I know, on. I'd greatly appreciate a sort of autobiographical piece—the sort that freshmen are

---

11. Robert Frost.
12. *Hall of Mirrors.*

asked to write their first day in college, plus maybe some quotables on your notion of what you're doing as a novelist. I can't exactly review your book; I'll have to introduce you, so it's bound to get a little personal, and I'd rather have any personal details from you than from rumor or memory.

I was in New York on Monday, and also ten days ago, but in both cases didn't reach you. The first time I didn't have your address with me, and the second time I never got out of the meeting until plane time. But I'll be here now until July 1, and I'll be hoping for an informational letter. Best to Janice.

Yours,
Wallace Stegner

« To: Robert Stone · July 12, 1967 »

Dear Bob,

For reasons that I take to be good and sufficient, I have asked to be stricken from the rolls of Saturday Review—not in anger especially, just in the conviction that I never did belong there, and that the reasons I then thought valid to join up were never good ones. I'll do better as a free lance.

What this does to our notion of doing a brief profile of you to accompany SR's review, I don't know. I shall write Rochelle Girson today and see if she still wants it, presuming that it won't come from an editor at large, but simply from old Teach. I'll let you know the answer. I think it ought to be O.K.

Your vita is a stern one, sir. You've earned whatever you've got. But did you mean that line about living in "a marginal state of near party"? It sounds either political or social, and I doubt it was either. In any case, if I do this little box piece, I shall clean you up and give you a Public School education.

It's the least I can do. Then you can qualify as the first Hippy novelist of top quality. Without a PSE you can't. And a father with a checkbook.

We're here until around November 1, probably, then elsewhere, maybe Africa for a few weeks, then home. I'll be back teaching after New Year. We'll look forward to seeing you in California. And I'll look forward to seeing Hall of Mirrors. And I'll let you know if the SR profile is still on.

Our best to your militant wife,
Yours,
Wally

« *To: Gary Snyder* • *January 27, 1968* »

Dear Mr. Snyder:

Please pardon the lateness of this answer to your letter. I was out of the country and out of touch with my mail, and when I got back I was crucified dead and buried. Now there's a weekend, finally.

I'm happy to have you describe yourself as a preserver, and I'd like to think you are, though in calling you a destroyer I was not entirely guided by the neat antithesis between you and Ronald Reagan. I was going by what you were reported to have said when you talked to the writing group at Stanford last spring. If I misrepresented you, I'm sorry, but I can't think there was any conspiracy to put words in your mouth, because two of the people who reported you as making that remark about leaving nothing of the old order standing thought it was a swell idea and one was appalled. Say they misheard you, or perhaps that you over-stated yourself. In either case I won't accept the word "irresponsible." Neither will I pass it back to you. Though I am sure we disagree on several fundamental matters, we may have more in common than you think—wilderness, redwoods, Indians, poetry (I like some of yours), perhaps even intellectual curiosity. It would take a good many evenings to talk it all out; I'd welcome those evenings, if they ever came about. Meantime, let me reply to one or two things in your letter.

Real values. You say they have nothing to do with social orders, but exist in nature, in human nature. It seems a strange faith for a student of cultural anthropology. I would say that values aren't values at all until some social order, some social agreement or consensus or acknowledgment, makes them so. Until then, they're only human possibilities, alternatives in the genes and the meat and the mind. What gives them any value they have—what makes them conduct instead of merely behavior—is a social agreement on what constitutes legitimate, desirable, or undesirable behavior. How complicated that can be you know as well as I. I cite you Konrad Lorenz on aggression.

You say Western civilization has the great strength of self-appraisal. I agree. It also has the great weakness of eclecticism. I would say your experimental search through the mystical and the Eastern, however admirable as a sign of intellectual unrest and curiosity, is unlikely to turn up anything very substantial for the saving or rejuvenating of Western civilization. I suppose I think we shall (and must) muddle along somewhere between the paralysis of tradition and the chaos of eclecticism, but that the paralysis of tradition is ultimately healthier than chaos. Chaos is a terrible long hard road: Western civilization has taken it and made some sort of settlement, and while I agree that you Daniel Boones who move on when the backhouse needs a door are probably necessary, I think that what gives you value is the society you may ultimately affect $\frac{1}{10}$th of 1 percent. If we were spending any evenings talking, I imagine I would find myself on the other side of mysticism from you, too. I take it you are a mystic, since you embrace both the Buddha and Coyote. I won't take any Christian side against you, because I'm no Christian—though I have to point out that St. Francis had about as much respect for all creatures as even the Buddha. You ask if Jesus saves redwoods? Naturally not. Christians, or pseudo-Christians, cut down all that have been cut. But they also saved all that have been saved. The Old Order that you say is destroying itself has elements, segments, that I respect at least as much as I respect Coyote or even the Buddha. I have spent a lot of days and weeks at the desks and in the meetings that ultimately save redwoods, and I have to say that I never saw there on the firing line any of the mystical drop-outs or meditators. I would have to make a case for the sensitive and responsible segments of even this society, that is—and there we can [illegible]. We would probably agree that kindness, generosity [illegible] against their validity as virtues.

Come by some time, and let me stand up for Greco–Roman stoicism as against, or maybe in addition to, the Buddha. I doubt that I will ever be persuaded that much comes to us from the Indo-European cowboy culture; that seems to me an effaced palimpsest. And anyway, I grew up in a cowboy culture, and have been trying to get it out of my thinking and feeling ever since. I am never going to succeed, fully, because there is no way, so far as I can tell, to remove from the human animal the impressions of the society he is born to. Whatever that society is, it is what makes his values, or most of them, from the time when he is slapped into his first yowl while dangling by the feet from a rubber glove, to the time when he lies on that last bed and looks the farthest he has ever looked in his life.

Anyway I'd like to talk to you. And I shall be regretful if I find that I have misrepresented you.

Wallace Stegner

« *To: Carol Brandt* • *February 20, 1968* »

Dear Carol:

Your exasperation with Viking has its counterpart in me, though it has taken me a good while to make sure it's an exasperation that will last. I think it will—I've thought so ever since they omitted *Live Things* from their Christmas ad, for chrissake. Generally I'm like Lovell Thompson—I can't get mad but I can sure hold a grudge. Or so Lovell says of himself, smiling.

So. Luther Nichols and Ken McCormick of Doubleday have been around here, talking together and then Luther has come down to talk to me. I know what you will probably say to the notion of Doubleday. I would have said it myself. But I am not saying it now; I'm listening to see what they finally say. They are saying it to me and not to you because I asked them to. They suggested going at once to you, I said let's see what you've got before we bother Carol with it at all. What they say they've got is an advance of $35,000 on my next book, or some sort of three-book deal with an advance of $100,000 or so, arranged with adequate tax safeguards, expense accounts, etc. They will put this all down as a package and mail it or bring it, with a copy to you, and then they will hope to discuss. Presumably, since they are frankly interested in a name or two that will enhance their list, they will make some sort of guarantees on advertising, promotion, and sales, and if they should want to use me as a loss leader I would not complain. In fact, I would hardly consider going to them on any other terms. But I will consider going to them, or to someone else, for two reasons: One, I am leaving Viking, no matter what. And two, I am very very interested in some sort of package deal that will let me retire from teaching four or five years early and write books. Some such proposal as Doubleday seems ready to make is what I might eventually want to go for. So if you'll be patient with me, and forgive me for letting them talk before I consulted you, we'll have plenty of time to consider this or other possibilities this spring. I'll be in Washington for a meeting in April, and I will arrange to get to New York for a couple of days at least. Meantime, will you be pondering and staring with glazed eyes into your crystal ball? I have said nothing to Viking since last December, when I called Marshall[13] to see why Viking hadn't at least included me in their Christmas advertising, and got a lot of double talk about how it was

---

13. Marshall Best, editor at Viking.

still moving out of the bookstores but there weren't enough re-orders to warrant further expenditure for advertising, etc. etc.

I can't see that it matters greatly who publishes my next book, if it's somebody who will push it. I am a good enough copy-reader to see that the text is reasonably clean, you and I can reserve the right to pass on design and jacket and blurbs, and I assume that Doubleday has at least as many salesmen in the field as Viking, and that the bookstores deal with them. So I am inclined to listen carefully when Doubleday makes an offer that would make it possible for me to do what I want and rescue my last few productive years. If Nabokov can go to McGraw Hill, why not me to Doubleday?

I sound as if I were all ready to sign. But all I mean is that I am very willing to listen, and that if this one doesn't look right, we should go ahead and investigate other possibilities. Write me what you think of all this.

Yours,
Wally

« *To: Robert Canzoneri* • *October 5, 1968* »

Dear Bob,
It is warm-hearted of you to think of having us stop by, but as they say in Victorian novels, it is not to be. A, we have bought no car, having been loaned one by a friend, along with a large smelly friendly Samoyed dog, who like all large friendly dogs thinks he is a lap dog and is mistaken. Car and dog we will take to Cambridge with us on Monday, where we will put the car in a garage and the dog in a kennel while I dig up some DeVoto data. Then we will drive car and dog to Philadelphia (six hours in a Volkswagen with him is like six hours in the Black Hole of Calcutta), and then we will take the plane directly home. So I'm afraid we won't get anywhere near Columbus. But thanks to you and Dotty anyway.

Page writes in some disgust about the Santa Cruz inability to make up the collective mind[14] (Do I dare to eat a peach?) and speaks of emigrating to Montreal. They are apparently now starting on an entirely new possibility, James Hall (not our James Hall[15]), who used to be at Oregon and is now at Irvine. They will have that college built before they have decided on a man who will decide on how it should be constructed. But maybe

---

14. This is in regard to the search for a provost for the University of California, Santa Cruz's College of the Arts.
15. James Baker Hall, a Stegner fellow at Stanford.

there will eventually come some sort of seismic shock, some bull from the sea, and knock their pillars together and make them act. When they do, I hope they have the wit and grace to give you the opportunity of accepting or rejecting an offer.

I'm sorry about Robin,[16] not surprised about *Per Se*,[17] and delighted about Chip Elliott. Dick Scowcroft writes in general that the Fellows this year, unlike last, are talented, attractive, and eager. I am looking forward to meeting them all, especially Elliott.

Take it easy with all those projects. I admire your energy. Once I too in Arcadia. At least I'm finishing up, this morning, the second section of the novel. And the summer is not lost, since last week we seem to have settled with the Canadian National Film Board to do a movie based on the story "Carrion Spring" plus some other items from *Wolf Willow*. Since Colin Low will be making it, it will probably be a movie I will go to see. People keep calling up with nibbles and feelers about *All the Little Live Things*—the last one was yesterday, some guy who said he was the husband and director of Eva Marie Priest.[18] He spoke of the book as "All the Live Little Things," so that I know if I ever sell it to him I will resolutely look the other way and never look back.

It's gorgeous up here, right at the peak of the color. If we don't get a big rain or a windstorm or something to blow these leaves down, we will leave on Monday most unhappy.

Best to Dotty.
Wally

« *To: Carol Brandt* • *September 20, 1969* »

Dear Carol:

Bless you, that is good news about your back. We have been worried that your back was not coming back into line—there has been a kind of ominous lack of cheery notes from you this summer. This last one reassures us.

Yes, I am working on the novel,[19] of which I have written two short sections and part of a third this summer, sections which I am now revising

---

16. The author, Robin White.
17. A literary magazine published during the 1960s in northern California.
18. Eva Marie Saint.
19. *Angle of Repose*.

and typing up in duplicate so I can put my eggs in two baskets when we leave here. When I have finished this revision and retyping, which I shall do today or tomorrow, I shall have about 375 pages of reasonably finished, though not necessarily final, copy. About 75 pages to go to the end of a draft. Most of that will have to wait until I get home. Then I'll have until when? Sandy guesses March if we want fall publication—to revise the whole thing. I am not sure of it. It's a fairly long, fairly slow novel, mainly historical but with a sort of contemporary subplot. If I decide the subplot doesn't work, I can fall back on the historical one. It's a long way from Portnoy, which I rather like. It isn't Portnoy I like, especially. I like the fact that this one is different. Maybe we should subtitle it "A Victorian Novel." Anyway I see no difficulty in getting it done by March, even though I have to teach one quarter—Jan. to March. I may even have it done by Christmas, and we'll have a few months to brood about it.

I also wrote a treatment of *Carrion Spring*, with additions, for Colin,[20] and I have seen Colin twice this summer. He and his henchmen seem to like the treatment very much, barring two or three small revisions which I shall make before leaving here. Colin has been out to Alberta and determined that the best place to shoot will be the Knight Ranch, on the Milk River Ridge—150 square miles of unfenced range, with 8,000 whitefaces and good logistical facilities and plenty of local cowboys for extras and walk-ons. When he has my revised treatment, Colin and Ian McNeill will go after the Canadian Film Development Fund for their half or three quarters million, or whatever it will take. Don't hold your breath. But however they succeed, I shall be past stage 2 of the contractual arrangement, and entitled to my second payment, as soon as I hand over this script. I would rather not call on them for this until after the end of 1969. By past experience, it might take that long to get it out of them. I will send you a Xerox of the revised treatment. It will not be a screen play, fully developed, but Colin insists he could almost shoot from it now. We shall see. I'll put off any further work on it till I see how their money raising turns out.

DeVoto research has proceeded a little during the summer, also. I will have a good running start on that by the time I'm through with the novel. So I do not feel in bad shape. In fact, I have been working in the woods with a chain saw and I am in pretty damn good shape (knock) and my woodpile

---

20. Colin Low of the Canadian Film Board.

is in even better shape. Which is a good thing. Frost all over the grass the last two mornings. We shall be here at least another week, to get a look at the color, before we start west across Canada. We'll stop and let Colin's father take us around the Knight Ranch, and if there isn't too much snow we'll go up around Banff and Waterton Lakes before heading down home. Did I tell you we'll be driving a camper, with a half-grown Airedale pup? Talk about *Travels with Charley*. Maybe I'll keep a diary.

From my royalty statement I see that Viking has charged off all earnings of all books, including paperbacks against the deficit caused by "excessive returns" of *All the Little Live Things*. I suppose this is legitimate according to the contracts, but Viking is the only publisher I ever had, and I have had a few, who did it. Chintzy. What ever happened to the Old Line Publisher who was reputed to publish authors, not books? When they held out a good round sum of *Wolf Willow* royalties for a year and a half—they said it was a mistake—I suggested facetiously to Anthony Da Fina that we ought to charge them interest. We should have, too. It's what they would have done to us.

Well, it is pleasant to sit in this cold shack blowing on my nails and warming myself by cussing out Viking. Doubleday, I must say, is so far both business-like and on the ball. They let me know what they're doing, and they do what they said they would do, at the time they said they would do it. It would be a hell of a note if this late in life I began to like my publishers.

Take it easy with your back. And don't try to reach me here after about Sept. 28. Don't try to reach me at all, in fact, until maybe Oct. 12. I'll be off traveling with Charley.

Best,
Wally

« *To: Howard Mumford Jones* • *April 2, 1970* »

Dear Howard,

I owe you thanks for two enlargements, the latest your essay on the Genteel Tradition, the earlier one the copy of *Violence and Reason*. I didn't write you about the book because I found it very late. It got mixed up with some fourth-class mail—which is a damned outrage—that came while we were away, and somehow it never got sorted out until recently. I haven't read it all yet, but ever and anon as I read through the first half I rose to my feet cheering. Howard, thou shouldst be living at this hour. So many things need to be said, and being said, go unheard, and being shouted, are shouted down. You've said most of them. Since I haven't heard you being shouted down, I have to assume that you went approximately unheard. It's a pity. But there you will be in your hermit cave, tending the fire and brooding upon the spider, the ant, and other reptiles, when reason comes fearfully back across the devastation the bloody SDS will leave us. Our latest here is that some hooded, gowned, and appropriately masked assailant sloshed red paint over Kenneth Pitzer [21] the other night at dinner—re: the faculty decision, by a close vote, to grant limited ROTC credit on a trial basis. Before the week is out, I believe, they will burn down the ROTC building, currently guarded round the clock by athletes.

My second thanks go for the *Genteel Tradition*, which I have read through, with profit. It happens that I am writing a long, sexless, violence-less novel [22] about a Genteel Female, fl.1847–1938. You have heard of her—Mary Hallock Foote. Her life, genteel or not, is more interesting to me than her fictions or even her drawings, which are pretty good. Rod Paul called the other day to tell me he was publishing her reminiscences at the Huntington. I have been working from those and from her thousands of letters to Richard Watson Gilder and especially Mrs. RWG, the grand-daughter of the Culprit Fay—that's where Rod Paul gets his moniker, too. Anyway, I will send you this genteel novel, in friendship and reciprocity, if I ever get it done. I find I rather like the Genteel Tradition. I can think of a lot of people and some civilizations that a touch of gentility would not harm.

Well. I am Sherwood Anderson-ing you, warming up my fingers before work. And here it is already 8:10. We'll be here through the spring, finish-ing this novel (speriamo), then at the end of June we'll go to Cliveden, Stanford's English campus, for the rest of the summer, returning to Ver-mont for the tail end of the color. We'll be stopping off in Cambridge in October to do some digging into Benny DeVoto, whose biography I have bound myself to write. I'd like to talk with you about him. My impression is that you were never good friends, but that hardly matters. His enemies were as the leaves of the forest, and they probably matter more to me than his friends. I've been trying to get out of Joe Barber exactly what it was

---

21. The sixth president of Stanford University.
22. *Angle of Repose*.

between Benny and Matty,[23] but Joe, he dunno. Do you? Got any anec-
dotes? Spicy incidents? Wise sayings?

Our best to that admirable woman, your wife, and again thanks.

Yours,

Wally

« *To: Robert Canzoneri* • *November 24, 1970* »

Dear Bob:

Don't worry about the delayed publication—that was only a passing notion
of mine. Doubleday tells me not to worry—the new one, they say, will be
a big one, and will need no help from outside. Let us all join hands and
pray they're right. Meantime, for your own sake, I hope you can finish the
Twayne book and get me off your back. I feel like the aged Anchises.

We've been busy—many things to clean up as soon as we got home Nov. 2,
and then on Nov. 18 we had to go back to New York for three days, partly
on the new book business and partly for Doubleday's big clambake on the
short story, celebrating Billy Abrahams' *Fifty Years of O. Henry Collections.*
Quite a show, and some fast horses around—Katharine Anne, Peter Taylor,
Jean Stafford, Cheever, Saroyan, Barth, Kay Boyle, and me in lower case,
squeaking small. We had a couple of symposia, and several large ornate
dinners and lunches, which Mary enjoyed exceedingly but which I enjoyed
somewhat less, having been on the wagon, for weight reducing purposes,
since the first of the month. Lost 8 pounds, too. That demonstrates how
many liquid calories I customarily inhale.

About your proposed essay review of the new book (whose title is *Angle
of Repose* and whose publication date is March 19: Billy Abrahams is going
to do an essay review in the *Atlantic*, he says, and Bill Decker has braced
the *Saturday Review* to do a review, and is scrabbling for galleys so he can
get it in early so SR will publish the review sometime before the book is
remaindered. Those are the only places that I have any line on. How about
propositioning the *Times Book Review* or *Book World*? You can say, with
some semblance of plausibility, that it looks like a big book.[24] Doubleday
is planning a first printing of 50,000, and I must say I'm somewhat exhilarated by the enthusiasm they display. On the other hand, I am all over burn

---

23. Garret Mattingly.

24. It won the Pulitzer Prize, but the *New York Times* never reviewed it.

sores from having indulged in hopes before this, and so I try to maintain a dignified skepticism. I'll believe it if it happens. But you don't have to be skeptical. As my official house critic you can claim special qualifications, and you can cite rumor (please do cite it, and even incite it) to the effect that this will be a book deserving front-page space. But then, I think, what if Canzoneri doesn't like the book? What a position to be in. You'll have to debate that one with your soul.

We saw Fran Utley and his wife at a party yesterday, and I hope your ears burned. They like you in Columbus.

About your opening in creative writing. I'll consult with Dick,[25] who is more informed than I am on the availabilities. One thing I'm sure of—there isn't a black man of any capacity still unhired. We're doing our best to hang onto Al Young, than whom there couldn't be a better, unless Ernie Gaines, who doesn't want to teach. But there may be paler candidates, and I'll see that you get any names we have in our kitty.

Take it easy in the snow. Best to Dotty.

Yours,

Wally

« *To: Howard Mumford Jones* • *December 30, 1970* »

Dear Howard,

I hope you and Bess had a safe and sane holiday season. Ours was the reverse. I celebrated the arrival of God's only begotten son by going off the wagon, after eight weeks of total abstinence. All it did for me was make me question the efficacy of abstinence as a way of life. I have concluded that I am the Addictive Personality.

May I bother you again? I do appreciate your writing to the Philosophical Society, and if it comes through, I shall shortly be able to dictate all my notes to you. But meantime I'm curious about some references in Benny's letters, which I am still laboring through. In a reference to Ted Spencer, Benny remarks that Ted holds the Boylston Chair, a seat that he, BDV, might have been sitting in if God had acceded to the suggestions of some people. Was there any concerted movement, after Bob Hillyer's departure, to put Benny back in the department in that chair, or was that only his delusion? Rumor, notion, serious attempt, departmental vote? And is,

---

25. Richard Scowcroft.

now that I think of it, the Boylston Chair a departmental appointment, or would the settee have to be named by the president or provost? Since Benny was subject to certain self-protective illusions about Harvard, I'd like to know how much evidence he had for the assertion supra, which he made in a letter to Alfred Knopf.

At this moment, only four dread days away, I face the prospect of resuming pedagogy, alas. I can hardly wait for March 21, when it will end.

Our best to you both.

Yours,

Wally

« *To: Robert Canzoneri* • *February 10, 1972* »

Dear Bob,

I'm very sorry to have your letter, not because you're giving up on the book but because your personal life seems to have blown up in your face. That distresses me extremely, for you and Dotty and the children all indiscriminately. I shall offer you no advice. We all tie our own knots, and we're the only people who can untie them, if they're to be untied. But I hope you find a way out of your problem that leaves you without serious or permanent damage to anyone. Which is asking more than we usually get.

As for the book, forget it. Three or four years ago it might have done me some good. Now that I'm retired and tired, weary of the whole bloody literary sweepstakes, I find myself pretty indifferent whether I ever come to anybody's attention or not. Literary fashion is a virus for which there is no vaccine, and if you happen to grow up a smallpox type in a cholera time, you might just as well reconcile yourself to faint praise, faint damns, faint yawns, and the attention of one or two desperate M.A. candidates at Texas A&M or Northern Arizona State. I thought I had a chance with this last one—my last chance, probably. It was a feather in the Grand Canyon,[26] and I'm a little too old to rally up and try 'em again. I'll finish my commitments to Doubleday, since I'm living on their advances, but if the truth were known, and I weren't obligated to write something more, I'd probably spend my time growing strawberries and orchids and sneaking illicit walks in the Palo Alto Foothills Park.

---

26. *Angle of Repose.* This bit of cynicism was somewhat premature and written before the novel received the Pulitzer Prize.

If you want to pass the thing on to your friend Bowman, that's fine with me. But if it's going to be any further drag on you, especially when you don't need any more drags, why not go ahead and scrub it without a qualm.

I didn't see the *Times* review of Page's book. Was it that bad?[27] The SR gave him a pleasant little notice—the only review I've seen. At least he got reviewed in the *Times*; that's better than his old man did. Actually I don't think Page likes this book as well as he did the first one. He's willing to hope for some miracle and be told it's wonderful, but he wasn't too happy about it when he finally let go of it. He tells me he's starting to get some time to write down in Caracas, and he's been making some interesting trips into the back country, including the Andes along the Bolivian border. Maybe next a travel book. Or a revolutionary handbook.

Bob, we do wish you well, and we'll be sympathetic, however your problem works out. Keep in touch.

Yours,
Wally

P.S. Your note about those cigars clears up a mystery. I couldn't read the return address, knew no one in Amsterdam, and couldn't remember any bet that seemed to be spoken of in a scrawl—and it sure was a scrawl—inside. So I didn't know my benefactor, but I enjoyed the cigars. Thanks.

« *To: Merrill Joan Gerber* • *January 30, 1974* »

Dear Merrill,

I had to go off to Santa Fe for a few days, and had no time before I left to write you, but I did slip the bound galleys in a folder and put them in the mail. I hope they arrived.

My reactions to the book itself are going to disappoint you, I'm afraid. It's just not my thing; I was brought up in the wrong time and the wrong place and under the wrong auspices to respond as I am told I should to fiction which is not only overtly and psychologically sexual, but almost exclusively so. I recognize the honesty of your portrait—I don't doubt a word of it—and your writing has all the old precision. You have got better, not worse, during your layoff to raise a family, and you always did have the moves, the instincts, the automatic knowledge of how to do things. But

---

27. Review of *Hawks and Harriers.* It was bad—but it didn't deserve much better.

your subject, which is overwhelmingly Molly's step-by-step discovery of sex, is a subject that my inbred instincts tell me ought to be a little more private and probably less specific. That puts me at odds not only with your treatment of this book, but with nine-tenths of contemporary fiction. My reasons are maybe puritanical, and if they are I will have to accept the term. But they are also somewhat aesthetic. Sex as a direct and openly treated subject tends to become exclusive; it crowds out all other aspects of a character and all other interests that a reader might have. It is, I guess, too easy, even when it is done, as you do it in your book, with the most scrupulous psychological realism and without any leers. I suppose I prefer novels that treat sex somewhat less openly; that let it take its place among two dozen other concerns, some of them (contemporary fiction to the contrary notwithstanding) almost if not quite as absorbing as discovery and manipulation of the genitals. The older I get the more I'd rather be Marcus Aurelius than Petronius, or Casanova, or even Sappho, or Havelock Ellis, or Krafft-Ebing, or Portnoy. Or any poor adolescent devoured by flames. When the aging Sophocles was asked how he felt to be beyond all sexual desire, he said he felt he had escaped from a mad and furious master. That's not the contemporary view, I admit. But as one who hasn't quite escaped, I prefer that to the end described by Buddha, when he remarked on those who strive always for fulfillment, and in fulfillment yearn to feel desire.

These are complicated arid roundabout and somewhat apologetic reasons why I don't feel I can write you a blurb. Much as I admire your gifts and much as I like and admire you, this book isn't my kind of book, and a blurb from me would be not only hollow but a little dishonest. There are plenty of people who will praise it, never fear, because not everybody has my hang-ups and anybody who can read will recognize your perceptiveness and skill. I hope you have a big success with it, and if I am challenged when I enter hell, and made to choose among your book, *Portnoy*, *Rabbit Redux*, and ten dozen more, don't be surprised if I pick yours. But I'd still prefer your writing when it deals with other subjects than the one Molly wants so badly to know.

God bless,
Wally Stegner

« *To: Merrill Joan Gerber* • *February 5, 1974* »

Dear Merrill:

My goodness, my goodness, I didn't mean to dump guilt feelings on you, or to make you ashamed of your book. As a matter of fact, if we're going to have a book almost exclusively about the discovery of sex, this is the way I'd want it—completely honest, without leers or snickers, and taking it seriously as a great mystery. When I said that your book wasn't my kind of thing, I didn't mean at all that it was no kind of thing, or a disgraceful kind of thing. I meant that in this particular, I am not in tune with our times, and it would be dishonest to pretend I was. Those who are in tune with our times are going to like your book for its subject matter more than I do, and anybody with any literary sense is going to recognize its skill. So relax, and let the praise and the shekels roll in, and pray for the emancipation of your

Old Professor

« *To: Howard Mumford Jones* • *July 5, 1974* »

Dear Howard,

How far beyond friendship, duty, and divine love can you go? That is a very pleasant review,[28] and hath an auricular sound like unto bullion. Don't ask me how it could have a non-auricular sound. But you don't indicate where it is appearing. New England Quarterly or so? Or don't you have to do with that journal any more? Wherever it is, I like it, and the general praise you drop on me makes me glad and humble and inclined to kiss the nearest hand, or lady, or even cow.

We have been in Santa Fe for three weeks while Mary tried to get over a spell of breathing problems. It was 110 all the time, and dry as a camel's tonsil, and blowing forty miles an hour, and the whole Rio Grande Valley full of dust. So we came home, where it has been serene and beautiful for a week. How's Bess? Any complications from that fall? I hope not. Please give her our best salaams.

No Vermont for us this year till late September. We rented the cottage, and will come east only to salute the dying year and lock the woodshed

---

28. *The Uneasy Chair: A Biography of Bernard DeVoto* (New York: Doubleday, 1974).

door. Maybe we'll have a day in Cambridge going or coming. If so, we will try to see you, if only for a few minutes.

Started a new novel a while back. Two splendid chapters, and then I realized I couldn't think of any more to say. What do I do now, prof? Invent? That's hard. If I could only invent a little more freely, I would be released into that body of thought that you stirred my depths with a while back. But you can't write a novel without some people, and I ran out at the end of chapter 2. All right, I'll invent. Then I can hang your intellectual linen on their hedges. Trouble is, I am trying to combine a story about Denmark in 1954 with one about old age in California in 1974,[29] and somehow there's a sort of organ-rejection goes on. Persevere. Dr. Shumway has only two or three survivors out of all his heart transplants, and I haven't begun to do as many operations as he has. Also, all I need is one survival, and I'm in. I invoke your prayers.

And take dust in three flowing motions. Blessings on your pinkish pow, Howard Jones my Jo. And on Bess.

Yours,
Wally

« To: Merrill Joan Gerber • June 4, 1979 »

Dear Merrill,

Many thanks for the clipping. It's nice to know that Stegner is finally making it. And that Gerber-Spiro is continuing to make it. That *Redbook* field of yours is the most productive since the first settlement of America, it seems to me. You've sold them more stories than I ever wrote in my long tedious lifetime.

As for the book business, God knows. The Dalton Book kind of merchandizing demeans books and reduces them to merchandise like aluminum siding. But there are occasional bookstores—there are three in this area, thank God—that still like books, hire clerks who read and love books, and make every effort to get a customer the book he wants whether the merchandiser's computer says it's popular or not. So maybe there's hope. Tell me the struggle naught availeth, and I'll ask you what alternative to struggle you can think of. The big hard one to get around is why, in literature as in economics those that have, get, and those that have not get not. I

---

29. *The Spectator Bird.*

could devise a fairer and more equitable system, but nobody has yet called me to the throne and given me the commission.

We're here for the summer, mainly, not necessarily because of gas rationing but because we went to Japan last month, and that used up the budget for travel. Page and his family will inherit Vermont this summer while we try to get the yard cleaned up and the house painted. If you come up this way this summer, you might find us in.

Good luck. In the destructive element immerse. Struggle. Avail.

Best,

Wally

« *To: Marcia Magill* • *September 24, 1980* »

Dear Ms. Magill:

Two and a half months later, as if by magic, I finally get around to reading the galleys of Ivan Doig's *Winter Brothers*. They were worth the wait. Doig's reconstruction of the life of James Gilchrist Swan is informed, sensitive, and lit by a high-powered imagination; and in playing back and forth between 19th and 20th centuries, in putting himself intimately into the mind and territory of Swan, Doig does what I have been wanting western writers to do for a long time: he is finding the western present in the real, not the mythic, western past. Not much in the western present derives from Billy the Kid, Pat Garrett, or Hopalong Cassidy; but a great deal derives from men like Swan, some of them still to be re-discovered. I admired Mr. Doig's *This House of Sky*, a splendid exercise in identity. I admire this one for its broadened horizons and greater historical resonance, and for the way Doig stays stubbornly at the heart of his West, or Wests. He is not only a writer to be watched, he is already important.

If you wouldn't mind sending me Doig's address, I'd like to tell him something like this to his face.

Sincerely,

Wallace Stegner

« *To: Jack Shoemaker* • *September 13, 1982* »

Dear Mr. Shoemaker:

I've now had time to read, with the attention and leisureliness it deserves, the revised and shortened version of Wendell Berry's *A Place on Earth*.

Since I read the novel for the first time many years ago, I can't say whether the new version is better or not. I can say, though, that I admire the novel greatly at any length; and I can't think the loss of 150 pages of Berry anything but a loss.

At any length, it's a splendid, warm, heartfelt novel about countrymen by a countryman. It has no side, there is nothing flashy about it, it can't be read backwards as readily as forward, it has a beginning middle and end, it closes a stretch of life-history and town-history and it leads through feeling to a profound satisfaction. What a pleasure it is to read a book about decent people who love or like or at least tolerate each other, who know, for themselves at least, what the good and the bad are, and who try, and sometimes succeed, to live by "virtue," by obeying their sense of conduct. Wendell is a ruminator, and I love him when he ruminates, because he generally ruminates up some human decency and a lot of human affection and a lot of affection for the earth. It is hard to say whether I like this writer better as a poet, an essayist, or a novelist. He is all three, at a high level. He is, in fact, very special, a sort of national treasure holed up on the Kentucky River. Pilgrimages would not be out of order.

Best,

Wallace Stegner

« *To: Anne McCormick* • *September 13, 1982* »

Dear Anne:

Some weeks ago some Knopf editor sent me bound galleys of Jim Houston's *Californians*, which you are publishing this fall. I have read the book but mislaid the editorial letter, so that I don't know whom to send my comment to. Can I ask you to case the office and see who's handling Houston? He was once a student of mine, one of our so-called Stegner Fellows, and I don't want to miss saying a word for his book. Thus:

It is astonishing how few considered and searching books there are about contemporary California. It appears to be too big and too various; it scares people off, except for eastern visitors who come on a three-day hunt for kooks, and who confine their search to the area between the Los Angeles Civic Center and the Beverly Hills Hotel. But there is a lot more to California than kooks. It is a nation, not a state in the ordinary sense. Nearly one in nine Americans is a Californian; one-twentieth of all

Americans live in three southern California counties. Even able and gifted writers such as Milosz give us only a fragment of the elephant when they make the effort to describe it. James Houston, a Californian born and bred, a steady and acute observer, makes one of the best efforts so far to get the sweep, variety, and vigor of California within the covers of a book. He has a sharp eye and an open mind, he knows the state intimately both north and south, he knows many kinds of people in it, from geologists monitoring the San Andreas Fault to the kooky fringes of Malibu and Marin. He knows, as nearly everybody in California knows, that California is already shaping the future of America. It would pay America to read this lively and perceptive account of what is happening on its western edge.

In haste. Love to you and Ken.

Wally

« *To: James D. Houston* • *June 21, 1984* »

Dear Jim,

You are kind to send on the Art Seidenbaum piece. I had seen it, but when anything is good, there is no such thing as too many copies.

I also appreciate your word on my commentary. Which brings up an embarrassing point. I admired yours very much—a thoroughly informed, thoroughly professional, and deeply felt essay, first rate in every way. And I have a letter on my desk in Los Altos Hills, dated about six weeks ago, saying so. My problem was that I couldn't find your goddam address, didn't have it in any of my lame address books, and couldn't get it from Page and Marion because they were off running the San Juan, in southern Utah. So I never mailed the thing. My admiration was born to blush unseen. At least I can tell you now, and I assure you your address is now in at least one of my lame address books.

We've been here ten gorgeous days, working our silly heads off to get the cottage ready for some Princeton political scientist. Most of our friends are not yet here; some are coming this weekend; we leave Sunday evening. Not the best timing. But great country, and a great time of year. We had forgotten the spring flowers that we used to walk into when we came up from Harvard right after Memorial Day. It's still Lilac time on some shady farms, and the shasta daisies, paintbrush, forget-me-nots, buttercups, asters, columbines, and a lot of unknown flowering bushes, make walking these quiet roads a real blessing. Mary has struck up an acquaintance with a bunch of sheep and some Holstein, Ayreshire, Jersey, and Dutch-Banded cows, and goes around with a drawing pad. Moi, I sand and paint window frames, paint bathroom and bedroom, refinish coffee tables, and cut away young maples, birches, ashes, elms, hemlocks, balsams, spruces, cedars, and other intruders that want to swallow the house.

Our best to Jeannie. It was a pleasure to hear from you. We're back on July 2, probably regretfully.

Yours,
Wally

« To: Barry Lopez • October 17, 1985 »

Dear Barry,

I have delayed my thanks for the copy of Winter Count you so kindly sent, because I was hung up in many things, and didn't have time to read it until the other night. I read it with unsuspended interest, not understanding everything I read but constantly struck by the awareness, the skinless exposure to experience and feeling, the sensitivity to the speech of natural things. Some of these moments I will remember as if they were part of my own experience, for you have managed to report them while leaving most of the mystery in. I am susceptible to mystery even though, by definition, I don't understand it.

Steve[30] seems to have his film on the tracts. I am anxious to see it, because I think he too is susceptible in the ways you are and the ways I would like to be. His film might make an occasional viewer pause and think.

Fall comes on. The coyotes raise their voices these moonlit nights, and the poet who lives in my cottage[31] was visited last night by a family of five coons who sat outside his window and watched him struggle with the Word. The world can't be all bad when that can happen.

Best luck,
Wally

P.S. I'll look into the Seven Visions of Bull Lodge. Thanks for the tip.

---

30. Steven Fisher. *Wallace Stegner: A Writer's Life* was produced and directed by Fisher for PBS, and was narrated by Robert Redford.

31. John Daniel, author of *The Trail Home, The Poet's Funeral,* and *Rogue River Journal: A Winter Alone.*

« *To: Barry Lopez* • *May 4, 1986* »

Dear Barry,

By a happy coincidence, your letter arrived just as I finished *Arctic Dreams*. I had been slow to get to it because of commitments—lectures, articles, the sort of minor irritations one endures in order to live—but once I did get to it I got through it, more or less without interruption, and with consistent pleasure and profit. It is, as I don't have to tell you, a book packed with learning and experience and rich with the sense of history that we both find missing in much of American life. It is also, as again I don't have to tell you, a very personal book—Barry Lopez in confrontation with a difficult and fascinating region, past and present, physically and spiritually and mystically. It's a fine fine book, and I congratulate you. One or two of the people you mention in one context or other—John Teal, for instance, who experimented with domesticating musk oxen, I knew. Teal had a musk ox farm over on Camel's Hump, in Vermont, near our summer place, for a while. But even northern Vermont proved too warm, part of the year. I wish I still had the musk ox sweater that we got from his wife. Softer than cashmere.

You mention that you haven't been in good health. I'm sorry to hear that, and hope it's something that will go away. As we get past seventy-five, we find that a lot of things don't go away. We learn to cohabit with lameness as all our lives we have cohabited with mitochondria and E. coli. That is what Mary is doing. Lame but game. I am lame, but not so game. We plan to assert ourselves against Fate by driving to Vermont and back this year. That will test both the lameness and the gameness.

I too wish we could have a chance to meet again, and talk. We'll be gone all summer and on into the fall, but after mid-November we'll be back. If you get down this way please let me know so that we can get together. I applaud what you're doing and what you intend to do.

Best,

Wally

« *To: Barry Lopez* • *October 19, 1986* »

Dear Barry:

I like your essay very much.[32] I would love to see that horse, but I am getting to an age when I fear to intrude on anything natural or historic or beautiful for fear of calling attention to it. The wonderful thing about your horse is that so much cunning went into its making, apparently—the artist squinted at it in the round, considered the light at different times of day, built it with something like worship. Let us hope some biker won't come tearing toward Jerusalem to be born, and rip it apart.

You say don't bother to reply to your letter and the essay, but I can't ignore the compliment you paid me by associating me with this horse and dropping my name in Bennington. A little earlier, David McCullough dropped my name in Middlebury, during a Commencement Address. Pretty soon I'll be world famous all over New England. I do thank you, and I'm gratified to be thought on your side.

Our stay in Vermont is about over. Three or four hard freezes and our water line has frozen twice in spite of our leaving the water running all night. The geese have been going over for several weeks and the grosbeaks and other late travelers are around us now. Leaves all gone—lasted quick and were never very bright this year. I begin to have Arctic dreams—but mine are all of a warmer climate where my hands don't hurt when I type. Never get old—it's a bummer. We'll be driving across, stopping in Ann Arbor for a week of lectures and then, I suppose, humping it for home the fastest way. After about November 5, we'll be back at our proper address. Keep in touch, and again thanks.

Yours,
Wally

« *To: William Kittredge* • *December 14, 1987* »

Dear Bill:

I am sending you herewith the manuscript I half-promised[33] (I was never sure enough of what I might be doing to promise it for sure). I had the

---

32. "The Stone Horse."
33. An essay on growing up in Great Falls, Montana for an anthology of Montana writers.

feeling I might be fooling around with some reminiscences or autobiographical episodes, and that's what I started to do here. I am not too comfortable with it, and if you look closely you will see that it is a first draft. But your deadline was announced as January 1, and I don't want to foul up the machinery.

On the other hand, if this comes nowhere near filling the bill of what you and the other editors had in mind, don't worry about turning it down. Send it back to me and maybe eventually I will whittle it into something else, and better. For now, it's all I can do.

All the best,
Wallace Stegner

« *To: William Kittredge* • *February 11, 1988* »

Dear Bill Kittredge:
I have a note from somebody with an illegible signature saying I should send you a bio. Here it is. I should also apologize for the piece I sent you—I simply had nothing else that related to Montana. Give me a year and I could do better. And if you think that thing is unusable, don't use it. I will not sue.

The Unreadable One also asks for my favorite Montana books. I am not so much of a regionalist that I keep icons in the niche, but I have enjoyed everything by William Kittredge, everything by James Welch, everything but the whodunits by Bud Guthrie, everything by Dorothy Johnson, whatever I have read of Richard Hugo, everything by Ivan Doig. I have also had a palpitating time with *Tough Trip through Paradise*,[34] and I have learned a lot, though with some revulsion, from the reminiscences of Granville Stuart. When I was younger and more impressionable I was a sucker for the Bar-Twenty tales, and I had a limp like Hopalong Cassidy. Now I have a limp, but not like Hopalong's.

What do you think of your friend Bevis' book on Montana writers?[35] I thought it was a very strong book in need of some revision.

Best,
Wallace Stegner

---

34. Bennett H. Stein, ed., *Tough Trip through Paradise, 1878–1879: By Andrew Garcia* (Boston: Houghton Mifflin, 1967).
35. William W. Bevis, *Ten Tough Trips* (Seattle: University of Washington Press, 1990).

« *To: Barry Lopez* • *February 21, 1988* »

Dear Barry:

I have been slow to thank you for the beautifully inscribed copy of *Crossing Open Ground*. Reasons: flu first, relapses second. The Bay Area has some kind of bug going around that hits you, goes away, comes back and hits you again, and even now and then hits you a third time. Most of the time since Christmas is a blur.

Now that I get up, I find the daffodils and violets and wild plums and acacia out, and your book, still unread, on the bedside table. I will read it promptly and write you again, and I'm sorry I haven't read it before now. I see by this morning's *Chronicle* that I was not needed in the support battalions, because the *Chronicle's* review is lyrical. I know "The Stone Horse" and a version of "Yukon Charley" from having read them with admiration in magazines—in fact you sent me "Stone Horse" last summer in Vermont.

But the rest of the essays are all clean snow, and I will make tracks in them. Just for now, I want to thank you for the book and for your good words.

Yours,
Wally

« *To: Carl Brandt* • *March 6, 1988* »

Dear Carl:

Well, I have pondered, and I conclude that I don't want to undertake the Ansel Adams biography. As I told you on the telephone, I have the feeling that Ansel is being mined, that texts are needed to justify the publication of another profitable book of great photographs. His life has already been very well documented in Nancy Newhall's *The Eloquent Light*, in his own *Autobiography*, and in the forthcoming *Letters*, to which I have written the introduction. I have, in fact, now written four or five essays, long and short, on Ansel, and I haven't a lot more to say—nor is there likely to be much new material available. And finally, having just passed my 79th, I am leery about undertaking a project that, whether it finds anything new to say or not, is likely to take me at least a couple of years, maybe three. That's about all the time they're likely to give me, and I have concluded that I'd rather try to spend it writing something—new novel, essays, memoirs, whatever—closer to my own center. So will you please thank Little, Brown (and Bill Turnage, who I suspect is behind this) and make my regrets?

I'll tell you later what I decide to fill my time with instead. For the next week, Mary and I are going to be over in Death Valley looking at spring flowers.

Best,
Wally

« To: Barry Lopez • April 4, 1988 »

Dear Barry,
If the mills of the gods grind any more slowly than mine, there is little meal being made. You sent me your book at the end of January. At the end of March, after two months of flu, back-braces, domestic crises, burst water mains, termite tentings, and other matters, I got around to reading it.

It's wonderful, as you know but probably won't admit. You not only know a lot, but you know a lot about the right things, and you have developed the appropriately ruminative, deceptively discursive style to convey it. I used to go to bed at night thanking God for Wendell Berry. After *Arctic Dreams* and *Crossing Open Ground*, I have added you to the pantheon, or bitheon. I do thank you for the book and for the inscription and for the general fact of your existence. Stay with it. Don't be diverted.

And let not your heart be troubled, not in this season. It is over a month early, the second year in a row of drought will put a strain on a lot of things, from the white oaks in the pasture to the ring-necked snakes under the dead leaves. But there is a pair of wrens nesting in the wisteria and a pair of mockingbirds nesting in the pyracantha and about forty towhees nesting in the bushes roundabout, and a lot of least bushtits nesting God knows where. This is a season of jubilation, to be followed shortly by drought, grass fires, water rationing, and cats in the birds' nests, to be followed at summer's end by hordes of jaybirds, who survive when all else succumbs. Nevertheless, plant a tree, and celebrate.

All the best,
Wally

« *To: Sam Vaughan* • *December 16, 1988* »

Dear Sam:

Thanks for the encouraging words. I don't know if you can encourage me into writing another book, but I'll see, I'll see. Right now I'm finishing the fifth article I've written in the last five weeks, and when that is done I am going to put my feet up higher than my head and let a little refreshing blood flow down into my brains.

Also, at our advanced age, we have a new grand-daughter,[36] age 12 days, and she is going to take up some time. Our whole effort may be spent teaching her what generation she belongs to, since her youngest sibling is 25 and her next youngest 28.[37] This kid will look upon her brother and sister as her parents, her parents as her grandparents, and us as her forebears, remote in time, legendary as gryphons.

When I get my brain refreshed with new blood, I'll gather together those autobiographical squibs, most of which are duplicative, and send them to you. I doubt that there's a book there, even with vast additions. The drama of a cracked teacup. But really cracked, I'll say that for it.

We hope Christmas is kind to you both, and that 1989 is a bumper year personally and corporately.

All the best,
Wally

« *To: Dan Frank* • *May 26, 1989* »

Dear Dan:

I spoke with Carl on the telephone this morning, and he told me that Doubleday has cancelled its expired contracts with Nebraska, and that you are on the way to taking over several titles. I'm very glad—I hope the arrangement suits you as well as it does me, and that it is satisfying and profitable for both of us.

Carl was unable to tell me what time schedule you contemplate, or what title you will start with. He did say that *A Shooting Star* is entirely free and clear right now, and that if any title can be readied for the fall of 1989, that would probably be it. I am not much of a bridge player, but I do think there

---

36. Mary Allison Stegner.
37. Rachael Mackenzie and Wallace Page Stegner.

are circumstances when you do not want to lead the fourth highest of your longest and strongest suit, but might better lead from aces. In my view, we are going to get more literary notice on any of several other novels—*Spectator Bird*, *All the Little Live Things*, *Big Rock Candy Mountain*, or *Recapitulation*, than on *A Shooting Star*, which did about as well in sales, and better in sales to foreign countries, but is not my favorite novel, nor the favorite of any of the people who follow my stuff. I would like to see a title out for Christmas, but I'd think *All the Little Live Things* or *The Spectator Bird* would be a better bet. *Recapitulation* is actually a trailer to *The Big Rock Candy Mountain*, though I don't suppose that means it has to follow BRCM into print. *Angle of Repose* is I guess still tied up with Fawcett, which has kept that cheap paperback in print for 17 years. *Joe Hill* has been reissued twice.

Of the other stuff, you have the short stories coming up by way of Random House. *Wolf Willow*, which is a book I value, won't be out of Nebraska for a while, I guess, and is also tied up in a complicated way with Macmillan of Canada, as Carl may have explained. *Beyond the Hundredth Meridian* has a small steady sale, and will probably continue to have. *The Uneasy Chair* has just been reissued by Peregrine Smith in Salt Lake, and probably can't stand another edition, at least not yet. And the two volumes of essays, *The Sound of Mountain Water* and *One Way to Spell Man*, might be reissued as a single collected volume, perhaps with some additional essays. That we can talk about later. For now, I just wanted to let you know how I feel in general.

Hurrah.

Wally

« To: Jack Shoemaker • December 7, 1989 »

Dear Jack:

I don't want to delay thanking you (and of course Wendell) for my copy of *Traveling at Home*. It is not only a beautiful little book, comforting to eye and hand, but it is also quintessential, ripe Berry, and the opening essay, "A Walk down Camp Branch," is a little wonder, richer and more evocative even than I remember it from first reading some years ago. As you probably know, I admire Wendell on a good many fronts, but I know no book of his that gives me so much of him in such compact space, and so beautifully laid out. Thanks again, and Merry Christmas.

Best,

Wally

« *To: Ivan Doig* • *September 17, 1990* »

Dear Ivan,

On Saturday came a package with your new novel in it,[38] and I feasted my eyes on it for a few minutes and then had to go on helping my son and his family get ready to go back to California. Yesterday, on a blustery freezing afternoon, I sat down with the book for the first time, and came upon the dedication. What an absolutely cheering thing for you to do! It would be a gross understatement to say you made my day. You made my September, my 1990, and I'm grateful. You can go along a long time without any particular public recognition—none east of the Mississippi—and you can get into a kind of numbed, resistant state where you tell yourself it doesn't matter. But it sure as hell does matter, as I realize now and then, and as I realized yesterday when I read your dedication. It means that I have mattered somewhat, not only to some readers and a few writers, but to some really good writers. I do thank you.

The book is still mainly before me, but I've read enough to be impressed with your ingenious scheme of making the novel open to all of Montana and all of Montana history by means of the Centennial and this Winnebago trip of the Newsprint Twins. It starts active and strong, and I expect it to continue and to finish the same way. But I didn't want to wait the two or three days it will take me to finish it before I wrote my pleasure and thanks about the dedication.

We're hustling a little, first because we're already in the time of frosts and freezes and worries about the exposed water line, but because we have to go to New York and Washington for two or three readings, and I have to make sure I have a couple of clean shirts and a tie. I'll be reading at the 92nd Street Y and maybe at the PEN Center if I feel robust enough, and later at the Politics and Prose bookstore in Washington. It could be a lot more inclusive trip than that, but I'm still recovering from a bout of bleeding ulcers at the end of June that lost me half my blood supply. So I've been living on spinach, raisins, and red meat, but I don't yet feel quite like Popeye; and because of the degenerative hip that brought on the anti-inflammatory drugs that ate my stomach out, I'm still hobbling on a cane. Maybe when I've got a few fall obligations out of the way I'll check

---

38. *Ride With Me.*

in for a new hip. In any case, after a Wilderness Society meeting in the Adirondacks, we'll go home on October 9. If you come through promoting *Ride With Me*, we'll expect you to let us know, and to give us time for a lunch, a dinner, a drink, or something. You've missed us two or three times. I have to go to New York, Portland, and Seattle in November, and to Los Angeles on Dec. 10. Otherwise I'll be at home cheering on the ol' bone marrow.

Thanks again for the confidence-builder. And all the best luck to the book.

Yours,
Wally

« *To: Carl Brandt* • *February 24, 1991* »

Dear Carl:

I don't know if I ever wrote you, or told you on the telephone, that in answer to your note about *Countryside* on February 2, I think I might be able to do a piece, if it's within their orbit. I have done some of this before but I think I have never expressed myself fully about wild berry patches, which in my childhood were both the best of all picnic spots and a real necessity of life, given the fact that we were a frontier village a light year from anywhere, with no local orchards or sources of fruit, and no local enterprise that would import them. We lived all winter on the product of a few days in the berry patches of Chimney Coulee, and with very little mental strain I can revive the feeling, from the smell of the berry patch to the cellar shelves full of mason jars of Saskatoon pin cherries, chokecherries, wild raspberries, wild gooseberries, and varieties of jam made from same.

Let me know if there is any need for this. I seem to be getting closer to that hip replacement, to judge by yesterday's mobility, but this is one I could write on a tape recorder if I had to.

I agree with you, $31,000 seems a big bite to hold back for returns. But maybe Random House knows what to expect, and Mr. Reagan's Recession and Mr. Bush's War obviously shrink the book-buying purse. Well, the Lord giveth and the Lord taketh away. Blessed be the name of the Lord. (In case this paragraph baffles you, it is in response to your latest, the one about the Random House royalty statement.)

Carry on.
Wally

« *To: Bev Chaney, Jr.* • *March 31, 1991* »

Dear Mr. Chaney:

I'm afraid I have little to add to your Stone lore. I have of course known Bob for a long time, and saw him regularly and intimately during his term as a Stegner Fellow at Stanford. But the intimacy had to do with his writing, which the workshop group and I all admired greatly—he was obviously headed for something really good. But Bob's personal life I know little about. The only anecdote that may help you relates to a time when Bob, who had a hypochondriac streak, came in one day with sweat popping out like buckshot on his forehead, and said to me, hoarsely, "I think I'm going blind." It was right at the end of the term, and the end of Bob's fellowship, as I remember. He was afraid he had a brain tumor. The only thing I could do was to lengthen his fellowship by one quarter, so that he would still be eligible for free medical care as a student. He went over to Student Health and, as he reported it later, they shaved his head and cut a hole in his skull and blew him out with a compressed air hose. As it turned out, he did not have a brain tumor, thank the Lord, and did not go blind.

One other item: A CBS or NBC crew was coming to photograph a class, with Hughes Rudd, one of our former students, acting as a sort of narrator. Bob Stone was clearly the best writer in the group, and I asked him to read for the camera, so that we could then film the discussion. He was too shy. He wouldn't do it, and he didn't come to my house that day for the class, and Ed McClanahan took his place. I think Bob regretted the lost opportunity afterward, for he asked pretty interestedly how the thing had gone, and had anybody mentioned him or his book.

That's about it. Ed McClanahan or Wendell Berry could tell you more. Incidentally, I'll be seeing Bob when he reads at Stanford on the 16th of April. Let's see if he's still shy.

Sincerely,
Wallace Stegner

« *To: Carl Brandt* • *April 25, 1991* »

Dear Carl:

Herewith my attempt to do a berrying piece for *Countryside*. Nine hundred words are a pitiful few, alas, and I had to leave out more than I could get in. Also, I regret to say that I have no snapshots whatever of that period of my life. Families like mine had no place to keep albums.[39] I've got an old photograph of the Mounted Police post on Chimney Coulee in 1878–9, and some 1950s and 1970s pictures of the town of Eastend, but none of my family are in any of them. And I have one double-exposed snapshot of a kid I grew up with, Pete Strong, at his father's ranch where the town later grew up. He is a fat boy in chaps and sombrero, seven or eight years old, with a .22 rifle in his hand and the eastern barren edge of the Cypress Hills behind him. I can't see that it would illustrate anything in the berrying piece, but I'll send it and anything else if they want to look.

While I have your ear, what has happened about the trade paperback of *Angle of Repose*? And what, if anything, about the essays? I apparently killed off all activity by getting that letter from the Michigan Press. Out here we live in a Zone of Silence. Have pity.

Best,

Wally

« *To: Barry Lopez* • *May 30, 1991* »

Dear Barry,

It was courteous of you to miss me in Jackson Hole. I regretted not being able to get there, but I have since heard from you, Steve Trimble, and Rick Bass, and so I have a sort of bracket on what went on. You all had a certain bewilderment, which is appropriate in a wilderness, and a question about what are we all doing here? But you all came out somehow inspirited, and I take that as a vindication of Terry Williams and the whole organizational notion.

You're right about the journalists not living up to their responsibilities. For a while the New Journalism was taking over, in the persons of Tom

---

39. To the best of my knowledge only one or two pictures still exist of Stegner's father, George, and two of his mother, Hilda. Of his brother, Cecil, there is only one, age four or five.

Wolfe and others, the functions of novelists; now the novelists have to take over the functions of reporters, especially on environmental matters, which seem like the clammy kiss of death to city editors, apparently.

I keep stalling on the hip, which gives me some problems but has so far not given me so many that I want to go and have it sawed off. I expect that will come in September. We're going to Vermont this summer only for the month of July, and will be back here August 1st ready to start a self-blood-bank, which takes about six weeks. So if you want me this summer you can get me here after August 1, either getting ready for surgery, enduring the damned thing, or getting over it. I could not do it at all except that the limp is bending me into a pretzel.

Hoping you are definitely not the same, and bless you for the good work you do.

Yours,
Wally

« *To: Carl Brandt and Dan Frank* • *July 9, 1991* »

Dear Carl, Dear Dan:

My address book does not contain Pantheon's address, and I have lost Dan's note that came with Terry Williams' new book. But on the assumption that as a division of Random House Pantheon Books has the same address, and that, if it doesn't, and this letter addressed to Pantheon goes astray, Carl will promptly forward, I will send a copy of this note to both places. Because I do want to say a good word for Terry's family history of birds, carcinomas, and refuges.[40] Mary and I have spent enough good hours at the Bear River Bay Bird Refuge to know approximately the attraction it had (has?) for Terry. Also I used to play tennis against Terry's grandfather Sanky, so I feel acquainted with the family. I feel her book from several directions, as I am sure she meant me to.

Terry Tempest Williams' grandmothers and mother taught her to trust her emotions, and she learned the lesson well. *Refuge*, her record of a family whose women have been haunted by cancer contracted from living downwind of the Nevada atomic test site, is an unflinching and wrenching emotional experience. This was a clan of strong women who lived under a curse but loved life to their last breath. Their ordeal is set against the

---

40. Terry Tempest Williams, *Refuge*.

catastrophic rise of the Great Salt Lake that drowned and destroyed the bird sanctuary where Terry Williams spent much of her professional time. The extravagant bird life of the marshes dwindles and all but disappears before the rising tide of salt water, as the women of the Tempest–Romney families—two grandmothers, a mother, six aunts, Terry Williams herself—wilt before the inexorable invasion of disease. There is a lot of death in this book. There is also an exhilarating abundance of life, and it survives flood and disease. But buried in the journal-jottings of this book is an angry indictment of the evasive culpability of the Atomic Energy Commission, and a questioning of the Mormon obedience that led these women to accept so calmly and philosophically the unjust fate they were exposed to. The wonderful thing about this book, though, is that Terry Williams does accept, even while she rages; she is too full of life herself, and too fascinated by all its manifestations, to write a gloomy book, even when the book's subject is disaster and disease. There isn't a page here that doesn't whistle with the sound of wings.

Maybe Dan can find something in that. I hope so.

Best,

Wally

« *To: Susan Houston, National Endowment for the Arts* • *May 17, 1992* »

Dear Ms. Houston:

Your telephone call telling me that President Bush has selected me among those to receive the National Medal for the Arts has put me in a quandary. Until recently I would have received the news with pride and gratification. But I have been distressed by what has been done to the Endowment for the Arts by its congressional and administration enemies, who first forced it to require a humiliating "decency oath" from its grantees, then fired Director John Frohnmayer and subverted his reasonable policies, and finally appointed in his place a censor with veto power over decisions of the staff and council.

I believe strongly in government support for the arts—believe, in fact, that a government that does not support the arts harms both itself and the nation. I also believe that support is meaningless, even harmful, if it restricts the imaginative freedom of those to whom it is given. By definition, creation breaks new ground, and to break new ground must take risks and make mistakes. It was only by taking risks that the human

species, in Lewis Thomas's words, "blundered into brains." The supporting agency must allow for that risk taking, and so must itself take risks.
That was the old, honorable Philosophy of the Endowment, and I trust
is still the faith of many of its officers and employees, though they are
enjoined against it.

So, though I am grateful to people in the Endowment for nominating
me, I am troubled by the political controls placed upon the agency. Though
they do not seem to be applied to me, I feel that I must protest them, for
some artists would feel lobotomized by them and the precedent of censorship is demoralizing. Therefore I must regretfully decline the honor that
is offered me. I shall not be there on July 21 and 22.

    Sincerely,

    Wallace Stegner

« *To: Carl Brandt* • *July 8, 1992* »

Dear Carl:

You ask about Scotland. Scotland, especially if you choose to see the highlands from the Royal Scotsman train, is about as plush as this world of woe
gets. A throng of happy servitors who act like friends greet you as you arrive
on the platform, and offer you trays of champagne. Pipers pipe you aboard.
A handsome girl in kilts escorts you to your stateroom and shows you the
bathroom, the closets, the cunning storage drawers, the windows that
open, the beds that accept the weary human frame with comforting firmy-
softness. When you unpack and adjourn to the observation car you are
greeted by a butler whose whole joy is [to] serve your needs, or even anticipate them. Will you have Glen Grant? Glen Fiddich? Glen Finnian? There
are something over 300 single-malt whiskies made in Scotland. He has them
all. Or if you want to stoop, there is always Chivas Regal. Dinner is a gourmet
delight. Your kilted faerie unfolds into your lap a napkin as stiff as tin. You
start with a parmesan and truffle panache with elder-flower and chive dress-
ing, proceed to monkfish on a bed of buttered leeks with chili pepper and
coriander vinaigrette, go on to roast fillet of lamb with a peppercorn coriander crust, red currant and port sauce. This is served with courgette batons and
Chateau potatoes and washed down with bottle after bottle of St. Véran,
Les Grandes Bruyères, Roger Luquet, 1989. You finish off with fruit creams
with pithiviers, whatever they are, and with the brandy or cordial of your
choice.

It goes on like that, breakfast, lunch, dinner. You roll through the valleys and up the glens, you park at night on quiet sidings in stone-quiet little stone towns. When all else palls they stop the train and the accompanying bus appears and takes you to Cawdor Castle, or Glamis Castle, or some other castle. The Brits aboard are bored. ABC, they say. Another bloody castle. Not us Americans. Among us was a crippled and very obese businessman who couldn't utilize the bus, or didn't want to. He sat in the observation car, attended by the butler and a footman, and tried to reduce the national stocks of single malt whiskies. We also had a retired general who did petit point in the observation car.

Altogether it was a hell of a trip, and exhausting, and for those who had to pay, très expensive. But worth the time of any work-worn literary agent looking for a psychic break. And the service, up and down and across, all the way, was absolutely impeccable. When I grow up I want to marry one of those girls in kilts.

You also ask about the hip operation. That has been a resounding success. I'm sorry to hear that Clare is looking forward to one, but if she has to look forward to any operation, that's the one. They cut an alarming hole in you, and I hesitate to recite what they do, but it's evidently as foolproof as any simple engineering job. I was in the hospital 8 days, at home in bed but mobile (with a walker and a part-time nurse) for another two weeks, and then back on my feet. I had to use a walker the first couple of weeks and a cane for the next month. After that I was home free, though not the lithe and lissome athlete that in my youth broke Olympic records. Three months, though, should cover all the worst of it, and only the first three weeks are really troublesome. As of now, ten months after the operation, I have totally forgotten it. My only trouble is that while enjoying all the luxury of Scotland—or rather, after being evicted and thrown out on my own—I muscled some luggage in the wrong way, and now I am in a corset and a snit. I will recover from both.

Hoping you are the same,

Wally

FYI: Sometime soon, perhaps already, *People* magazine is running a story on the NBA[41] squabble, which will apparently include some statements and a photograph chez moi. We are above *People* magazine in these parts, but if in your A&P browsing you happen across that issue, whichever one it is, I would be curious to see it. I have also just concluded a three-day

---

41. National Book Award.

marathon interview with a girl from Edmonton, Alberta, who is doing a one-hour radio program about me on the CBC. Again, I have no firm date. I will try to inform you and Sam. On the 21st of this month *Vermont Magazine* is sending an interviewer over to do a piece. And on August 6, heartily sick of all this repetitive yammering, but submissive because I am told is it Useful, we will escape back to California, which I never thought was safe but which is evidently safer than Vermont.

« *To: Carl Brandt* • *October 9, 1992* »

Dear Carl:

It's just as well we missed connections in Bozeman—you might have been holding my hand in the emergency ward. It was a floperoo. I had some sort of bug, and was burping on the roadside on the way to the museum where I was supposed to read. Missed the ceremonial dinner because I was a little too nauseated to risk it. Got fifteen minutes into the reading and collapsed, barely missed doing a George Bush on the podium, staggered outside, but was pursued and hauled off to the hospital. They thought I was having a heart attack. I wasn't, but for a while there I wished I was. So all the careful preparations for wooing a bunch of contributors to the endowed chair went by the board. Missed the next day's luncheon, fled off to Fishtail with the Heynemans and spent four days in their guest cabin recovering. As I recovered, Mary came down. So we limped home disheveled and disgraced, and have been rubber-legged ever since.

Now that I'm a little more compos mentis, I have pondered your September 24 letter about the Penguin audio people. I'm not sure what pages they're counting—whether the hardback edition, which has only 276 for the whole book (hence a cut to 225 wouldn't be so bad), or the paperback, which has something like 541. I guess that in either event I'm inclined to risk it, partly because people in Bozeman who take long trips and use a lot of tapes kept asking me if *Crossing* or *Angle* or any of the novels was on tape. None is. Maybe even a castrated version would be better than nothing. So if Penguin is willing, I'm inclined to go ahead, always with the provision that I can approve the cut, and maybe have a chance to mend it if I think it needs mending. But I don't want to do the reading myself; this last episode has persuaded me that I am a frail old fart and had better not put myself under a lot of strain.

Hoping you are the same,
Wally

« *To: Ivan Doig* • *November 10, 1992* »

Dear Ivan;

Thank you for the word on Carsty. Curiously, I was thinking about him as I drove home today, before picking up the mail with your letter in it. I was thinking that we were approximately the same age, and that he and I were the only survivors that I could think of of the group of graduate students that used to hang out together in Iowa City in the thirties. So I just thought of him in time. He was a very amiable, very sensible, very likable man. He made Maquoqueta, Iowa look good by being from there. But I don't much like being the last leaf on the tree. Too many years.

Thanks, also, for the books from Shadbolt.[42] He is a writer I have read about, but never read, and he or you did send a couple of his novels, with a very pleasant inscription. I will now repair the leaks in my education. If you have his New Zealand address, I'd appreciate your putting it on a postcard and sending it down—I'd like to thank him, and send him some book in exchange.

Also, the mystery of the third book, *Who is Sylvia?* is now solved. It wasn't by Shadbolt, and I never heard of Lynley Hood, so I had a hard time figuring out why it came to me. Now the answer. It wasn't supposed to. Here it is, as fresh as when it came from Down Under.

Pray up a little rain for all of us, if you know the chants. We're starting our seventh dry year, and God knows what Egyptian plagues will come down on us if we don't get some rain this winter. God knows how many Californians will flee off to the better-watered Northwest, too. It's in your own best interest. Pray, man. Our best to Carol.

Yours,
Wally

« *To: William Kittredge* • *December 28, 1992* »

Dear Bill:

Word has come in by grapevine that there is a position at Montana that John Daniel is being considered for. I have just updated my 1986 letter

---

42. Maurice Shadbolt, author of eleven novels, the most famous of which was *Season of the Jew* in 1987.

of reference for the Stanford Career Planning and Placement Center, but I want to add a personal note.

John was a Stegner Fellow in poetry, a category that when Yvor Winters was alive we saw little of, because he sheltered them from pollution. John Daniel was another kind. He is a poet with a strong environmental conscience, somewhat in the vein of Wendell Berry but with a wilderness bias. His last-year book of essays, called *Coming Home* or *Going Home* (I loaned my last copy and find myself as foolish about titles as some people who write me about *"Angel" of Repose*) is a very solid, thoughtful, and eloquent performance. He has a volume of poems, published a couple of years ago by Jim Hepworth at Confluence Press, and he has a new book in preparation. He has been poetry editor of *Wilderness* magazine for the last couple of years. And he is a superb, dedicated teacher, and a man who will fit into the Missoula group like a hand into a glove. I guarantee that you will like him. I hope you can find the place for him. He has written so far only essays and poems, but he could teach fiction too, if necessary. And his wife is an environmental engineer skilled at disposing of municipal and industrial wastes. You could assign her to the pulp mill.

Finally, he is about six feet four, a former logger, a mountain climber and wilderness hiker, and a great companion. If you ever take any recommendation of mine seriously, take this one.

You up there in Missoula are making yourselves a reputation in the world. Wonderful. I had hoped to see you and Tom McGuane and Scott Momaday, all ex-Stegner Fellows, at that Academy of Distinction clambake in Glacier late in June, but at the moment there is doubt that I can make it. I will hope. Meantime, have a good productive satisfying New Year. It already looks better than the old one.

Best,
Wally

Stanford:
1945–1971

To Malcolm Cowley, June 1, 1957
To David Packard, May 1959
To Richard Scowcroft, July 25, 1959
To Richard Scowcroft, July 26, 1959
To Richard Scowcroft, March 1, 1960
To Richard Scowcroft, March 13, 1960
To Richard Scowcroft, October 30, 1960
To Richard Scowcroft, August 2, 1962
To Wendell Berry, January 18, 1968
To Wendell Berry, December 17, 1968
To Wendell Berry, April 9, 1969
To Richard Scowcroft, November 27, 1973
To John L'Heureux, July 24, 1982
To John Crowe Ransom, May 14, 1989

STEGNER ESTABLISHES the Stanford University Creative Writing Program, 1945:

I arrived at Stanford just as the GI students were flooding back—the best students, and the most motivated, that any professor ever had. Many of them were gifted writers; the first story I read in a Stanford class was one by Eugene Burdick which was later published in Harper's and won an O. Henry prize. I scurried around to find some means of encouraging all this talent, found some prize money from John Dodds and the Division of Humanities, and the next year, by a concatenation of circumstances too complicated to go through here, found permanent funding, through Dr. E. H. Jones of San Angelo, Texas, for both fellowships and prizes. That was 1946. Through the years the program developed and changed, dropped its prizes (too many hassles, too much bitter competition, since our prizes were a thousand dollars), and gradually leveled out as a program of fellowships for advanced students and a ladder of courses, of increasing difficulty and expectation, for undergraduates. The models were . . . Iowa, Harvard, Bread Loaf. Fellows were asked only to help pick their successors, for with several hundred applications and a small faculty the reading burden was enormous. Otherwise, they wrote. They didn't, and still don't, have to be candidates for degrees. They didn't, and still don't, have to be qualified to matriculate at Stanford. They had to be good writers, and a lot of them were.

Bud Burdick, of Ugly American notoriety, was the first, but there have been many since. An article on western writers in the *New York Times* recently (in which, characteristically, they managed to call me the "Dean of Western Writers" and get my name wrong, all in the same instant) featured Tom McGuane, Ed Abbey, and Scott Momaday, all former writing fellows. Tillie Olson was a fellow, Robert Stone, Jim Houston, Larry McMurtry, Ernest Games, Wendell Berry, Max Apple, Nancy Packer, Philip Levine. Ken Kesey and my son Page, though never fellows, were students in the program. There have been many good ones since I retired a dozen years ago—Bill Kittredge, many others. It's a long list, and a long shelf of books—many of them first-rate. There is also a long list of people who went through the program and wound up not writers but editors, teachers, foreign correspondents, and so on. Bill Decker, long an editor at McGraw-Hill, Dial, and Viking, and now a novelist as well, was in the program; so was Don Moser, the present editor of *Smithsonian*. Many others. They have been a talented and productive group. I sometimes had the feeling that I was reading American literature just a few months ahead of its breaking on the world. And there have been some prize-winners: Robin White won the *Harper's* Novel Prize, Scott Momaday the Pulitzer, Bob Stone the National Book Award. I try not to take credit for any of that. The people who won fellowships in that program were so talented that there would have been no holding them down. A year or two at Stanford helped them get their act together.[1]

But by 1971, enough is enough.

I . . . was pretty fed up with the disruptions of the sixties. It was no fun teaching. That didn't apply to the writing students, actually, because writing students were still a pleasure to teach; I enjoyed them and learned from them. But the undergraduate teaching that had to go on was so disrupted, and the kids were so hassled in so many directions. The intolerable ones came with answers and not questions, and the others came with just confusions. Between them there was no way you could feel you were not wasting your time in the classroom. So I decided I had other things to do, and it was getting on toward the time when I had only a few years to do them in. I retired at sixty-two, knowing that I had some books I wanted to write, and I didn't know how many years I might have. I have, after all, a history of a senile grandmother and I might not have my buttons. So I retired, and I've managed to get three or four books into the years since.[2]

◆ ◆ ◆

1. Both passages above excerpted from *Conversations with Wallace Stegner on Western History and Literature*, Richard Etulain and Wallace Stegner (Salt Lake City: University of Utah Press, 1983).
2. Seven, actually, including a Pulitzer Prize and a National Book Award.

« *To: Malcolm Cowley* • *June 1, 1957* »

Dear Malcolm;
Many thanks for your interesting Hopwood Lecture. With all its proposals to make a writing program professional instead of either arty or
critical I could not be more loudly in accord. And I am about ready to agree
that a new look has to be taken at the course offering and the method of
approach. My feeling about our own ship is that it falls between the two
stools of the arty and the critical; that perhaps in (I hope amiably) resisting Winters' general push toward the critical and traditional and even
dogmatic approach, we have encouraged the free expression of opinion
and the free experimentation in method until we risk the loosest kind of
expressionism and everybody's way becomes as good as any other. This, it
seems to me, is the most consistent danger of the workshop method; the
encouragement of critical comment from the students not only encourages the alternatively harsh and too-tender criticism you speak of, but
it also subtly encourages the student to think his opinion is as good as
teacher's. The teacher may ultimately abdicate his right to tell 'em—and
sometimes they do need to be told. My own experience this past year was
a little unsatisfactory in that way; with a somewhat apathetic, no matter
how talented, group, there is a sort of inert resistance to actual teaching,
even the teaching of what makes a sentence a good sentence. I have been
half of the opinion that it might be better to turn the whole thing into
a kind of tutorial system, and cut down on the class meetings, for that
reason.

But about your concrete proposals: The project proposal I'm all for; one
thing a group like ours needs is a sense of solidarity and a sense of common effort. If literature is the loneliest trade, it doesn't necessarily want
to be lonely, and the kids would generate enthusiasm on a group project.
The book does it somewhat for us, but I'm going to take your suggestion
and turn over the whole editing chore to the class, I think—selection,
preparation for the press, proof-reading, jacket-matter, everything. I
think we can't run a magazine in competition with *Sequoia*,[3] but we can
do something in that line, and I think likewise, that participation of the
group in the programming of visitors would have salutary effects. We tried
it with Aldous Huxley this spring—threw him to the student lions, so to

_____
3. Stanford's literary magazine.

speak—and though he worked like a dog, I think he enjoyed it, and so did they.

The professional courses you mention are harder to visualize in our set-up here. For one thing, we are, by the terms of our endowment, indissolubly linked to the English Department. And I can't see the department holding still for courses which are definitely not content courses in literature, or even method courses in writing, but something that could be sniped at as Journalism School practicalities. I totally agree with you that they—and the professional attitude they assume—are essential, but they do have that trade-school smell that the traditionalists in the department would deplore. So I think that the best we can do here is to import a good deal more of that sort of thing into the courses as we have them set up; perhaps to use one meeting a week for these practical matters, and one for the usual workshop on manuscripts, or perhaps to have occasional evening meetings, with or without visitors but probably with some practical assignments. The Jones Room is a good place for such meetings, and I think they might be very profitable.

Now I've got to get busy packing to start driving east. We'll be in Vermont all summer and part of the fall; if we pass anywhere close to Sherman we'll give you an advance call and at least try to stop long enough for hello.

And one further, rather wistfully hopeful question. Dick is to be off next winter quarter—January to around March 20—and I think we'll need someone to fill his place. Is there a chance that you and Muriel could be lured out here again? If there is, when you have recovered from your latest stint of teaching, write me at Greensboro, Vermont, where we'll be after June 25. Nothing would delight us more, though I am painfully conscious of the shortness of the term and the shortness of the salary we can offer. At least we could try to elevate it somewhat above last time. Will you ponder, and drop me a note?

Mary sends her best, with mine, to you both. I picture you in your exurban quiet among the butterflies. When we get to Vermont I will send you a symbolic porcupine quill (erithyzon dorsatus) as a token of solidarity.

Best,
Wally

« *To: David Packard* • *May 1959* »

Dear Mr. Packard:[4]

I listened to your talk before the local chapter of the AAUP[5] last Thursday evening with great interest, and many things that you said I was very
pleased to hear. I share your optimism about Stanford's future and at least
some of your satisfaction with Stanford's present. I do believe that this
university is just getting the vision of greatness, thanks in considerable
part to the present board and the present administration, and that it faces
an incomparable opportunity for service to the community, to the nation,
and to human learning. In particular, I was pleased to hear you say that the
plans for development of the Sand Hill Road area of Stanford land have
been suspended for further study: quite seriously, many of us would give
up other benefits, if necessary, to see Stanford preserve that land open
and unmutilated in the midst of the ringworm suburbs. It is perhaps un-
American to think that a four-lane highway is not necessarily better than
a two-lane one, or that a population of four thousand per square mile is
not necessarily better than half that. So be it. If it can preserve some of
the character of the local landscape and the openness and expansiveness
of what has hitherto been the Stanford community, I should say Stanford
has the opportunity to be un-American in the very best sense of the term.
Beauty does not ordinarily win out in a competition with the chance for
dollars; it takes an institution of both integrity and vision to resist the short-
term good for the long-term, and I am sure you will have the enthusiastic
support of a very large portion of the faculty in your effort to save that hill
land from what they call Progress.

Some other aspects of your talk on Thursday left me somewhat uneasy.
To bring them up then would have extended the discussion long past its
proper time, and so I venture to write you of them now. In discussing the
purposes and opportunities of the university you were emphatic on its
obligation to turn out scientists and engineers who would be useful in the
weapons race; and linguists and diplomats capable of holding their own in
the cold war, and capable of taking a persuasive part in cultural exchanges

---

4. Packard was cofounder of Hewlett Packard, and was Deputy Secretary of Defense in the
first Nixon Administration. Stegner and Packard were well acquainted, though possibly not
by 1959. Nevertheless, the formal tone of this letter suggests that it may have been written
for an audience greater than one.

5. American Association of University Professors.

aimed at solidifying international friendships, and humanists who could, as you said, collaborate with psychologists and others as communications experts; and so on. Perhaps I misinterpreted you, and perhaps you were taking for granted much of what is now on my mind, but I did understand you to look upon the university's purposes with a highly practical eye, and judge its performance by purely practical criteria. We seemed, from your words, to be an institution dedicated to the production of technicians, scientists, experts, leaders—a sort of "human accelerator" as Arthur Wright put it, shooting out its business end experts and specialists with half their electrons missing and with their nuclei knocked whobberjawed. We seemed, as you described us, to be something like the Stanford Research Institute, subsisting on government research contracts and bending all our efforts toward the production of limited experts and the application of science and other knowledge to practical ends. Perhaps you did not mean to give this impression, but I think you did, especially in your commentary on the debate between generalists and specialists, where you clearly chose the side of specialization. Now I don't quarrel with specialists, but I do think the other side needs stating more than you stated it. I suspect that what we most need is neither generalists nor specialists, but specialists who can generalize and generalists with a specialty. And I further suspect that we do not attract, develop, or hold this kind of faculty and train this kind of student unless we concentrate on being something that you did not mention at all: a community of minds, a fellowship of people who know something, are willing to communicate it, and are always wanting to know more. What makes a university, for me, is the climate of absolutely free intellectual inquiry, the pursuit of knowledge wherever it leads us, the almost anarchic emancipation from all applied or practical ends, from government preoccupations, from cold war needs, even from such common pedagogical intentions as the training of "leaders" or "'citizens." Obviously Stanford and all other universities must depend to some considerable extent on government research contracts and to some lesser extent on private or industrial research contracts. But these activities are not the university. If, as I think you did, you intimated that the professional and research facilities were the most important part of the university, I must disagree, for it seems to me that the core of this university and any other university is the college or school of humanities and sciences, in which knowledge is not applied but "pure," to be studied for its own sake. Keep that part of the university in health, and the production of experts and leaders (and specialists who can generalize and generalists with specialties) will follow automatically. Try self-consciously to produce specialists and leaders in that pre-professional college, and you will, I am convinced, produce half-men, limited men, men with imperfect vision and low horizons. And I would call to your attention, in connection with your general satisfaction with the undergraduate program at Stanford, that the School of Humanities and Sciences which does two thirds of all the teaching done by the university gets a whole lot less than 66% of the budget. I would have been better assured that Stanford is going to realize its potential as a university if in your talk before the AAUP you had given more stress to that indispensable core of humanities and sciences: the best that has been thought and said in the world on the one hand, and the purest and most adventurous pursuit of new knowledge on the other.

This letter has gone on so long that you can see why I did not raise these questions and this apparent difference of opinion the other evening. I do agree with you that Stanford, which has always been a good university, is trembling on the brink of becoming one of the small number of great ones.

At such a time, especially, the question of direction and goals is vital. I respectfully submit that our goal ought to be the goal of becoming the finest center of learning, the finest community of scholars, scientists, teachers, and students, that we can become; and that the short-term goal of producing practical troubleshooters and specialists will, if it is pursued too far, end by forcing us to abdicate our strongest position as a university.

Sincerely yours,
Wallace Stegner

« *To: Richard Scowcroft* • *July 25, 1959* »

Dear Dick,
I've been putting off writing you because I had some business about Frank O'Connor to discuss, and was pondering how best to approach it and what sort of proposal to make. Maybe there'll be room in this letter for it, maybe I'll write you another in a day or two. This will have to concern itself with the problem you raise about fellows teaching, and specifically about Evan Jones' proposed appointment as an acting instructor half or third time.

I can sympathize with Evan's need for more funds, and he's in a special position as a foreign student. Nevertheless I do not think that he or any other writing fellow should, as a matter of policy, be allowed to teach, or should be encouraged to do more than casual outside work. This, as you know, is in line with departmental and university policy with regard to fellowship holders; and I think we would actually be in a strong argument with the administration if we held otherwise with regard to our writing fellows. Our own avowed purpose in establishing the fellowships was to assist in the support of young writers, within the university community, while giving them as much time as possible for writing. I don't think we further our purposes, or theirs, by encouraging them to work outside or by granting them graduate assistantships in addition to their fellowships. Every Humanities fellow and other fellow in the university would have a right to demand the same treatment. I am strengthened in my convictions in this by several recent talks I had with Neilma here in London. (And incidentally, Jones does not get 2,500, he gets 3,000. Neilma raised the ante for the specific reason that she thought 2,500 too little to let a man devote his full time, comfortably, to his writing. That relieved us of the offer of 500 that I had made to him in an earlier letter.)

It is just as well this came up when it did, for I am sure we should have established a policy before this. Browning,[6] for at least part of last year, was in direct violation of the terms of his appointment as a fellow, since he took an outside full-time (I think) job, did not register in the university, but still drew his fellowship check and attended the poetry group. If I am wrong in this I would like to be corrected, but I believe it is true, and I had intended to speak to Yvor[7] and to Browning before I left, but got swamped. Surely there is no objection to young poets and young novelists staying alive; and surely it would be pleasant for them to live as well as they can; but until we can raise the fellowship amount, or devise some sort of sinking fund for people going down for the third time, I am afraid that the people who accept the fellowships will have to accept them in full knowledge that they can't take jobs or assistantships. If they can't accept on those terms, they shouldn't accept. If you will recall, I refused Abbey[8] the same sort of special arrangement that Yvor evidently gave Browning. And I would do so again.

---

6. A Stegner Fellow in Poetry.
7. Poet and Stanford professor Yvor Winters.
8. Edward Abbey.

Perhaps the best thing to do now is to discuss this with John Loftis and with Phil Rhinelander,[9] and if they agree, to pass it on to Yvor and Jones. I shall write Jones and explain my reasons and express my regrets. Neilma had a letter from him which she read us here in London; it said he was perhaps going to become, with his wife, the sponsor of the International House, and it asked permission to leave one quarter early, since his work for the degree would be completed then. Neilma thought this a sensible notion, and I think has already mentally applied that thousand-dollar rebate toward the next Fellow from Australia.

Ultimately, I feel sure, we'll have to adjust the terms of these fellowships. If the estate is ever settled and we get the full endowment, we can raise the ante and still have six fellows. If we don't get any more, I suspect we'll have to reduce the number and raise the stipend; or else we'll have to develop an emergency fund from which people in difficulty can be loaned or given a few hundred dollars. Think what that would have done for Strucinski!

London is pleasant, hot, jammed with sociability. Snow[10] gave a party for us the other night, full of lords and ladies gay and all of London's reviewers and editors. We've dined a couple of times with Storm Jameson, who is a great lady in all the best ways. Tonight, for causes which I cannot understand myself, we're having dinner with Martha Gellhorn. The Joneses are fat and sassy, and today we had a note from Larry Ryan asking us up to Cambridge. Shrubbs, Jacobsons, and Gutwilligs all gutty and willig. V.S. Pritchett, I discovered the other night, has never been to Florence or Rome. He made me feel like a cultivated American.

A chapter on the novel got done yesterday, a piece for the *Atlantic* last week. Argument against teaching-fellowships. Love to all of you, more tomorrow.

Yours,
Wally

« *To: Richard Scowcroft* • *July 26, 1959* »

Dear Dick,
This is the second installment of the letter I sent you yesterday. And I can't emphasize strongly enough that I agree with you and Loftis entirely, and

---

9. Acting Chair of the Stanford English Department and Dean of Humanities, respectively.
10. C.P. Snow.

if Yvor[11] wants to play Khrushchev he will find, I trust, an adamantine foreign policy looking him in the eye. My own notion is that people ought to sacrifice a little something, if necessary, to get a year for doing nothing but writing.

The O'Connor business is this: When we got to Dublin we found Frank[12] healthy, or nearly, but grumpy after a winter in Dublin and wanting to go where he could talk to somebody. O'Faolain won't enter his house, on account of Frank's adultery, and the Dublin winter doesn't toss many talkers of Frank's kind onto the beach. So he raised the question of coming to Stanford; Harriet, he said, had opposed it because she doesn't want him to teach, it interferes with his own work and disturbs him. Frank, over a pint in Davey Byrne's pub, confided that he wanted to teach again, and that since his doctor had forbidden him Irish whiskey, and put him on a wine diet, he wanted to go where wine was plentiful and good, which it is not in Dublin or even Maryland or Brooklyn. So, since Malcolm[13] is committed only for one quarter, though we urged him for two; and since there may be at least one quarter and perhaps two untenanted, I said I would see whether or not we couldn't arrange a year's visiting professorship which Frank and Malcolm could divide. It is my own notion that if Malcolm (or Muriel) could get off the hook for the second quarter, he or she would; and Frank specifically said that he would like six months better than three. This is of course all exploratory still, though we have committed ourselves to Malcolm for one quarter, and two if he'll take them. It seems to me that Frank is as good a man as can be found to take your novel seminar and perhaps a course in the 18th or 19th century English novel. He would also like a writing course each term, which could be 203 one term and either 135 or 133 the other. Malcolm could be used either for one writing course and an American Literature course, or for two American Lit courses. The salary necessary to acquire the two of them for the full year, splitting however they might want to split it, would be $12,000. That is the basis on which we hired Malcolm, and it is agreeable to Frank.

Now the question: Will you, at your convenience, broach this double appointment to John Loftis[14] and also to Phil Rhinelander?[15] And will you

---

11. Yvor Winters.
12. Frank O'Connor.
13. Malcolm Cowley.
14. Acting Chair of the English Department.
15. Dean of Humanities.

either ask John to write Virgil[16] about it, or speak to Virgil about it yourself when he returns? I know for sure that the department will have to replace you, and I feel fairly certain that for American Literature courses Phil may be able to find a little helping money from the Coe Fund, if it proves necessary. However the money is found, these are two good men, as good as we can find, proved and demonstrated and available. I think we should close wit 'em. Unfortunately you may have to do the closing, since we'll be a long way off. The biggest problem would be working out the division of time between them.

I don't think the need for action in this is too pressing, but I think it might be settled, if possible, in the early fall. Can I pass that on to you? You know, too, that the university is bringing Jim Farrell[17] for four lectures (November, I believe) and that he is an indefatigable talker who might be of interest to the writing people and American Lit people. Mrs. Clark will probably be in touch with you; if possible, bleed some other entertainment fund; if necessary, use ours.

No Russia. I thought only two days on that one. I would have liked well enough to go, but it would have taken a full 50 days there (all under Soviet steering and planning), plus briefing sessions beforehand and undoubtedly a clutter of correspondence and interviews afterward—especially since Nixon and K. started it off with such a bang. It would have cost me nearly two months on the book. I decided to wait for the Stalin Prize before taking in Moscow. For a while, though, it was sort of lively, with the State Department calling from one side and Ted Weeks from the other, urging us to go. Alas, I have no patriotism. I hate Soviets bad enough already without going to Moscow. Breathes there a man with soul so dead.

London, on first examination, looks pretty expensive—much more so than when we were last here in 1950. A moderate meal at Rules last night cost about 6 bucks. The Shrubbs, for a pretty decent house (not nearly as pleasant as you live in) far out in the country, pay ten guineas a week. We pay 14 guineas for a very shabby little flat. The Gutwilligs pay eight for a flat without a real sink. Cosi fan tutte. At the moment we are three hundred bucks over our estimate for the time. Kismet.

Wally

---

16. Virgil Whitaker, Chair of the English Department.
17. James D. Farrell.

« *To: Richard Scowcroft* • *March 1, 1960* »

Dear Dick:

I hope you haven't picked anybody to fill Berry's shoes as Jones Lecturer in writing, because I have just been talking with Philip Roth, and we can get him. He would want to come for two years, which would suit our purposes fine; he is, as you know, the author of *Goodbye Columbus*, a very-much-talked-about volume of stories; he got second prize from Mary in this last O. Henry; he is now on a Guggenheim and his volume of stories was a Houghton Mifflin Fellowship volume; and he won the *Paris Review*'s Aga Khan prize last year. Besides this he is one of the decentest, pleasantest, most intelligent, and altogether nice people Mary and I have met for a long time. He has an M.A. and taught for two years at the University of Chicago. I have told him that unless you and the department head have arranged the writing program completely he is assured of the Jones Lectureship; this does not, naturally, commit the department, since it can easily say it has made other plans: it only commits me, and I must say I like being committed; I think we would gain a great deal by having Roth around, and he comes very cheap at $3,000 for half-time. I have told him that if the appointment can be made, he might get an English 5, English 133, or English 135, depending on how things were already allocated. He would prefer 133 or 135 to the beginners, but would not boggle too much at the 5.

Inasmuch as you were having a certain difficulty in your last letter finding staff for the writing courses, I hope this will work: I very much hope it will work, in fact, because I think Roth is one of the best young writers in America and we ought to get him while we can. He will write his way out of the job in a couple of years, but meantime he will have enriched the mixture, I think.

Last night we were at his house, where were gathered Bob and Hatch Williams (Viking has just taken Bob's novel); and Don Hall (he's in Rome to interview Pound for the *Paris Review*), besides some of us local scrittori and poeti. All this a little tiring because we'd got off a boat from Sardinia at five that morning, and in Rome people do not go home at ten. Tonight we're having dinner with Watson, he of the hallucinatory mushrooms, and after that going to a Beaux Arts ball at the Academy, attended by representatives of all the other academies in Rome. Anticipate a pale note of recovery two weeks hence.

The novel is done, or at least I think so. I shall send it off about Wednesday.

Ora pro nobis. And please let me know as swiftly as possible about Roth. As you know, this appointment comes out of the department to the extent of a graduate assistant's wages, and out of us for the balance.

A thought occurs to me: R.E. Fowle met Roth at our place ten days ago. Mum's the word.

     Yours,

     Wally

    « *To: Richard Scowcroft* • *March 13, 1960* »

Dear Dick,

Many thanks for the prompt action on Roth,[18] whom I spoke with a half hour ago and who is now set to come. For our records and the Department's, he will be paid $2,000 for teaching one course per quarter, as Berry[19] was this year; and like Berry's, his salary will come out of Department funds to the extent of a half-time acting instructor's wages, the rest to be supplied out of Creative Writing. I think he should be assigned to teach one section of 133 and the two sections of 135. His title will be E. H. Jones Lecturer in Creative Writing. All of which you know.

About the *Esquire* clambake I am of two or more minds. My spies report that the Iowa session was (in addition to being widely publicized and a sort of celebrated airing of far-out opinions) somewhat outrageous. Mailer was brought in primarily as a gunslinger, to provoke angry retorts by his outrageous remarks, and I guess he succeeded. And I guess it all suited *Esquire* down to the ground. But I wonder if it did Iowa any good, and I wonder if it would have been done at Harvard, and I somewhat wonder if it should be done at Stanford. Stanford students like Kesey[20] (ex-Stanford students) would have found such a session delightful, probably. The working ones might have been diverted by it in more ways than one. We ourselves, or whichever of us was on, would undoubtedly have lost weight and sleep and repose of outlook. This latter consideration is given extra weight by the fact that next fall I'll have to be running off for a day or two here and there for delivering Phi Beta Kappa lectures, and that sounds like quite enough shenanigans. Add to all that the fact that you're probably much too busy

18. Philip Roth.
19. Wendell Berry.
20. Ken Kesey.

to want to be occupied setting this up, and that I'm too far away and not especially eager anyway, and that there might be a real hassle with *Esquire* when we came to picking the symposium-eers. Likewise a joint session with SF State and Cal would be difficult because of the quarter-semester problem, difficult because of differences of taste and point of view, and dubious because it would inevitably leave Stanford looking like a third wheel, a country cousin. Unless it was held at Stanford, which as a three-ply thing it undoubtedly would not be.

In view of all this, I'm inclined to stall, if you are. You might when you get a chance discuss it with Phil Rhinelander, who might have a university attitude to express. Since Stanford would be entering into a partnership with *Esquire*, the university would have to give its consent. But even if Phil thinks it might be a good idea, what do you think of stalling until this summer, when we have both had time to think, and when I'll at least be back where I can conveniently communicate with both *Esquire* and Stanford? My real fear is that *Esquire*, for publicity purposes and (supposedly) for coverage in the argument, would insist on some far-out character like Mailer. And I doubt that truth is ever arrived at by the process of saying something preposterous, getting an angry and quite as preposterous reply, and ultimately forcing even the most level-headed into saying things they don't mean. If we could really pick good people—Thornton Wilder, say, or Arthur Miller, or O'Connor or Malcolm, or even a young one like Bill Styron—people who have done something good and who look as if they might go on—then it is possible Stanford might gain something, and I might be willing to sweat it out. But on the Iowa basis, it is *Esquire* that stands to gain.

None of this, naturally, has to be communicated to Rust Hills.[21] Maybe you can write him that it seems best, since I will be on duty next year, to wait till I get back before committing ourselves to anything. Ask him to write me after July 1. And meantime, I wish you'd write me what you honestly think. Maybe we need something like this now and then to keep from looking or being middle aged and suburban. But my confidential and scowling adviser thinks we ought to go slow, and I think she's right.

Addio,
Wally

---

21. Fiction editor at *Esquire* magazine.

« To: Richard Scowcroft • October 30, 1960 »

Dear Dick and Anne,

We are reassured, now that you're staying in Madrid and reconciling yourself to the Spanish language. We think you should stay in that 2 cent martini country. In Italia noa si trova, believe me. It is somehow a sign of spiritual health in you that whenever you start off on sabbatical you land in a country where the drinking is cheap. Be! Consume one for us.

You'll be happy to know that we have survived the Benny DeVoto memorial meeting (which was superb, really—Schlesinger[22] and Kitty Bowen both very good and Edith[23] wonderful), a party for C. P. Snow, the *Esquire* symposium (which was about what I expected, somewhat silly but apparently stimulating to the undergraduate mind, and productive of some running arguments among the faculty, who found it hard to be as alienated as the *Esquire* speakers). So we have survived, and now all we have to get past is a visit from Robert Frost on Nov. 8–9–10, another visit from Snow on Nov. 2, a visit from Jack London's old light-of-love Anna Strunsky next Tuesday, midterms, term papers, finals, Phi Beta Kappa trips to Reed and Utah, and the usual problems of classes. I strew sacred cornmeal in the direction of your Iberian peace. I have read six M.A. novels so far, including Simckes' (passed), Broder's (bad), Reid's stories (back for more work), Segre's stories (bad), Jo DeEds (more work), and Gwen Davis (terrible). La Davis came in the day after I'd finished her book with the word that Doubleday had bought it; I then turned it down as an M.A. thesis. Now I am reading her other one, the one she was doing in your class, to see if there is a thesis there. Sound familiar? Nancy is very good, steady, intelligent, responsible. Malcolm[24] and Muriel are fine, but somewhat quieter than previously because he is still getting over a prostate operation and is not drinking much. No word from the O'Connors.[25] No action on an American Literature man. I plugged Claude[26] hard, but it doesn't look too hopeful. Yvor,[27] Virgil,[28] and Dave Levin (that grateful boy) not convinced. But

---

22. Arthur Schlesinger.
23. Edith Mirrielees.
24. Malcolm and Muriel Cowley.
25. Frank and Harriet O'Connor.
26. Claude Simpson.
27. Yvor Winters.
28. Virgil Whittaker.

maybe there's still a chance, and since Phil Rhinelander just added me to the Coe committee, I'm sure as hell going to make it difficult for anybody else's boy to make it, unless and until they give Claude a tumble.

Carvel[29] is married, as perhaps you know. Nobody I ever heard of. I am writing a belated congratulation tonight.

Yvor has been in the throes of firing his poetry fellow Mezey, a sort of dirty-ankled Beat who didn't respond to the Master's voice ex cathedra. I cheerfully offered to be Yvor's executioner, since it was clear that having blown his top to this boy, mainly because the kid writes sexual poetry and doesn't wash and doesn't attend class regularly and doesn't admire (but he just won the Lamont Poetry Prize), Yvor was getting cold feet. So I passed on the word from Yvor that the boy was probably out—after less than five weeks. Kid pretty sore and glum. Wife an art student in North Beach, no money except fellowship. Then old Yvor telephoned in the dark of night to say, "Think we're being too harsh?" Which was exactly what I knew the bastard would be doing, so then I passed on the word to the kid that he could stay if he wanted to attend class and kiss ass. I guess he's kissing. At least I have now met a Poetry Fellow.

Election grows close and hot. All of us finally converted to Kennedy, even Franny. He's all right, I think, though not the most charming personality in the world. Prospects look pretty even, right down to the wire. I shall vote in absentia, since I'll be up in Portland talking literature on election day.

Before I forget, let me congratulate you on the Stanford Short Stories. Your introduction is shrewd and pointed and well turned. The book itself may be the best one we've had. I think the two-year lag permits a stricter standard and a better book. Also, R.F.[30] has stirred up the family (both Nancy Riley and Mrs. Langston came out this fall to look us over) to provide the usual deficiency appropriation, and it appears that both Deirdre and Mrs. Langston may want to contribute something—the rumor on Mrs. Langston is $20,000 to $30,000 to the endowment in January, so maybe we'll sometime be at the point of living off our income.

---

29. Carvel Collins.

30. Richard Jones, former Chairman of the Department of English at Stanford, whose brother endowed the Creative Writing Program that Stegner founded and directed until his retirement in 1972.

Most of this letter is only to reassure you and let you know what you're missing. Continue to miss it. [Word illegible] life's worth missing.

Best,

Wally

« *To: Richard Scowcroft* • *August 2, 1962* »

Dear Dick:

It will delight you to hear, if you haven't already, that Gwen Davis is suing Viking for libel in connection with Kesey's[31] book—she thinks she is the silly Red Cross female named Gwendoline who visits the hospital. Viking's lawyer I talked with on the telephone today. Gwen has affidavits from a Math instructor and an English TA (who?) saying that the portrait matches her (fat, blonde, and with a funny way of talking). Kesey himself is not being sued, for reasons I don't comprehend; maybe the pickings were thought better at Viking. The suit is a New York suit, and Viking is afraid it may have to pay, though it would naturally rather not. Apparently Helen Taylor, one of Viking's editors, plans to come to Palo Alto in September and ask around to see if Gwen had any reputation that could have been soiled, and any character that could have been maligned. My own feeling, and I think this lawyer's too, is that the farther we keep out of this the better. But just for my own satisfaction and information, could you check your gradebook, or Janet's, and see who was in that writing class with La Davis. I'd like to know whom Helen Taylor is likely to find still around. Page, who is now in New York attending a wedding, has told me that Davis made passes at both Art Edelstein and Jon Baumbach, and used to pester both households. I know nothing, happily, and at the moment I'm torn between a half impulse to spike Davis' guns if possible, and a one-and-a-half impulse to stay out of the flying mud and keep all of Stanford out with me. I should think it's up to Kesey to find character-assassins to match Davis' character-testifiers, but I'd like to know who's potentially close to all this.

Letter from Virgil yesterday says he sees no reason Blair[32] can't feel sure of a third year, and that the prospects for permanence are not entirely dim if Blair produces strongly and shows continued good teaching. So I'd

31. Ken Kesey.
32. Blair Fuller.

appreciate it if you'd ponder (over a period of months and years) whether Blair is the man we want and can push for semi- or actual permanence as a writing teacher.

For two days in a row, the first two such days since we arrived, the sun has shone. We have had about two winters' worth of rain, Palo Alto style, in three weeks. Nevertheless we thrive. Ted[33] and Kay Morrison came over for the day, in a deluge, Tuesday, and we walked five miles through the soaking bracken and under the dripping trees. We have seen no one else. Next week we're going down to Hanover to draw some books from the Dartmouth library, and maybe in mid-August we'll go over to Breadloaf and see Avis[34] and others. That'll be our literary summer. Mormonism proceeds apace;[35] at the moment I am strongly tempted to muckrake the Pioneers, sainted though they be. They kept their souls in tight little coin purses, with moths and silverfish eating at them.

I have read Katherine Anne;[36] only moderately impressed. Am reading Roth:[37] he's very bright and perceptive but he doesn't know when to turn it off. Have fun, be happy, stay out of libel suits.

Love to Anne.

Wally

« To: Wendell Berry • January 18, 1968 »

Dear Wendell,

A quick and perhaps impertinent question in the five minutes before I drag a batch of papers home.

We have now got all our fellowship applications in, and are starting to read. The poetry folders, thirty-odd of them, will go to Kenneth Fields, a young assistant professor and one of Yvor's ex-poetry Fellows, in a day or two. But as you perhaps know, I have been quietly resisting the narrowly Wintersian view of poetry for a long time, and I don't know Fields well enough to know whether his judgment is his own, or borrowed. And you will be dealing with whatever poetry fellows we select, dealing with them for six months. It occurs to me that you might want a hand in selecting them. If we can weed them

---

33. Director of the Breadloaf Writer's Conference.
34. Avis DeVoto.
35. Stegner was working on *The Gathering of Zion*.
36. Katherine Anne Porter's *Ship of Fools*.
37. Philip Roth.

down to a manageable number, would you have time to read them and give us your judgment? Then I suppose I shall have to make some final adjudication between your selections, Fields', and my own. Hopefully, we may coincide.

If this strikes you as either unnecessary or pesky, tell me so. But if you'd like an advance look at your fellows, here is your chance. We select two Fellows in poetry, four in fiction. But with the fiction you won't have to be concerned, since we've got a battery of talent headed by Ed and Nancy[38] to help select those.

We're home, I guess, but it hardly seems so. Bales of paper to work through, millions of minutiae at school. Farmers on the Kentucky, pray for us. Your novel is on my bed table, but not yet read. And we did have a fine warm time stopping over with you. Our thanks to you both.

Yours,
Wally

« *To: Wendell Berry* • *December 17, 1968* »

Dear Wendell:
As Ed[39] has probably told you, I had to let him know yesterday that there is virtually no chance of his making it through the Department to a regular appointment as Assistant Professor, and the time has long since run out on the Jones lectureship that he holds. In a way, this seems to cut off an able and loyal man because of an inflexible departmental system. As I explained to Ed, it isn't quite that. The system is one I devised myself, to give young writers a backlog, half-time job for three years while they wrote their way out of it. In practice, the system hasn't always worked that way. Often the fault has been ours, because as in Ed's case we wanted to hang onto an able teacher. But I think our extension of the lectureship may have slowed Ed's novel down and cost him his momentum; and the lectureships were designed, and still are, to help writers write rather than encourage them to drift into teaching. So I have to agree with the system, and am not being coerced by anyone. The only chance to continue Ed's teaching here—and believe me we would all love to do it—would be to get him through the department as an Assistant Professor. There he does run into the usual

---

38. Ed McClanahan, former Stegner Fellow and Jones Lecturer in Creative Writing, and Nancy Packer.
39. Ed McClanahan.

conditions and requirements and even cliques, and with his somewhat slim and spotty publication record I know he'd get cut down. The best I could do for him was to assure him of another full year beyond this.

So this note is a regretful one. I appreciated your letter about Ed, and agree with your estimate of him. He has nothing but friends in the Creative Writing faculty, and his students love him. It was not easy to tell him what I thought the realities of the situation.

Best,

Wally

« *To: Wendell Berry* • *April 9, 1969* »

Dear Wendell:

That's a pleasant sort of note. I'm glad you enjoyed it; I'm sure they enjoyed you. Your good wife and I never settled that fisticuff argument we were going to have, her trim welter against my over-middleweight verging on light heavy. She'd have killed me. But tell her not to settle too fast for the Black Panthers against the cops, and the BSU–SDS[40] against Hayakawa. The Panthers in Oakland are breaking up, with assassinations yet, and charges that Seale is turning them into a black KKK, and the SDS, having won its point—and a good point—against SRI,[41] will have to invent a new excuse to raise hell. I will then report on whether she should rejoin them, or quietly regret. Gurney, as you probably know, is going to have an anti-pollution happening at the Little League ballpark on April 19. We'll be on our way to Italy, and can't attend, but I sit here in my closed room smoking cigars and risking emphysema and applaud him. Ed[42] says, Come on over and sign a petition against them sonsofbitches, and I told him I would if he'd rephrase it to a petition against us sonsofbitches. We'll all drive there in cars.

I just bought a camper and a ¾ Dodge truck with pickle, onion, relish, mustard, and everything. Page and Marion will drive it to Vermont, we'll drive it back. Pray for us.

It was fine to have you both out here. Since I have resigned as director, I can't exactly say come again any time, but I expect I have enough influence

---

40. Black Students Union and Students for a Democratic Society.
41. Stanford Research Institute.
42. Gurney Norman and Ed McClanahan, former Stegner Fellows.

to swing it, and Dick has enough mother wit to be swung, in case you ever want to.

I'll send you a copy of my feeble little western essays one of these weeks. Thanks for your new poems. How do you do all this, teaching at our shop. Didn't we work you? Best to Tanya.

Wally

« *To: Richard Scowcroft* • *November 27, 1973* »

Dear Dick:

No doubt I should have written you immediately after the faculty vote on my promotion, to thank you for having created it and to assure you that I'm satisfied with the ⅗ time (for the present). I think I can live on it (the salary plus other money) and it will give me time to do some writing which I am discovering that I miss a bit.

Of course I don't know who voted how or even exactly how the argument and counter-argument went, and I devoutly hope that you will find out all these things and tell me, just to satisfy my old woman's curiosity. What I do know is that the avant-garde, whoever that really is, seemed to think that full-time would take up too much space in the program with traditionalists. My sneaking feeling is that there was a tad of blackmail lurking somewhere in all that but I don't know. The hilarious thing was that the meeting took place at the height of Albert's[43] big conference on something called "creativity" or something like that, and I can't at all understand how he could find the time, energy, and absence of hangover to wage any kind of battle. I believe that I also hurt my chances and got everybody's hack up by submitting as part of my papers the soon-to-be-published essay on Fiction's New Form, which of course is a manifesto for realism and manages to take a poke at avant-gardists in universities. The only thing anyone has discussed with me (which means Polhemus, Carnochan, and Bender) is that little piece. Actually even Ruotolo who said he agreed with it thought it a bit "unfair." Unfair? Who said anything about fairness anyway? I gathered from what Bliss said that he was fearful of picking up opposition from the scholarly types who couldn't accept a non-Ph.D. teaching lit. courses if he mentioned that I had already said I didn't want to teach more than 2 creative writing courses. So, to allay

---

43. Albert Guerard.

one fear—that the realists would be too dominant in CW (why not?)—he would have had to arouse another—that the non-scholars would take up too much room in lit. courses. The scholars didn't mind my being full-time in CW, the avant-garde didn't mind my being in lit., and the compromise is ⅗ which really is fine with me, especially since now I don't have to break my brains trying to dream up a seminar in Chekhov and Joyce, which I would have done.

All goes reasonably well in the CW area. I have spent the past week reading informal applications and find that everything is melting into one puddle. I am going to search my notes, and Dolly's files (immature writers would put a parenthetical Haha here) for info as to how many you encouraged to apply last year and how many of those you actually accepted in the program.

Ellen Nold called me at the beginning of autumn and asked if it was all right for her program to give creative writing credit. After a moment of being a nice guy, I said No. Apparently she misunderstood and later in the fall wrote me and said her understanding was that in unusual circumstances she would provide creative writing. I then wrote her a three-page letter saying No and explaining, and I must say I convinced myself so much that I've about decided Freshman English ought not teach CW either, unless they do it with our people and under our supervision. However, I shall not wage that war without you. Nold called up and said my memo was "beautiful" and she concurred. I don't quite get that, but I accept it.

I read Chuck Kinder's novel and I think he really is awfully fine. In fact, it seems as good as anything to come out of our program. I will say I'm glad I don't have his nightmares.

One small but satisfying bit of gossip: the 390 class[44] is an exercise in praise from the master and the only constructive teaching going on is Kittredge[45] who feels some compulsion to tell the kids what he thinks. He told me that he was embarrassed to do it because he didn't want to undercut Albert. In a moment of pique in talking to Bender (who said he too thought it would be good for the CW program to have someone avant-garde—which really shows how basically naive and impressionable people can be) I said to get poor teaching the thing to do was to load the

---

44. Albert Guerard's Voice Project in creativity.
45. William Kittredge.

program with avant garde types who by the very nature of their values can't have anything to teach.

My friends the Cappallettis will be returning to Florence at the end of December and I hope you will get together with them. A real treat is to go to Santa Croce with Minima so that she can discourse on the artist she did her doctorate on, one Giovanni di Milano who has a chapel at SC. You perhaps do not remember the Cappas very well, but let me say she is the least malicious person I ever met and one of the most generous and serving, even though that sounds yukky. She is also very smart. Mauro, too, is very kind and warm once you know him, but he is a bit of a Great Man and very serious. When in Italy, he works all the time except after 9:30 at night and Sunday afternoon. I think you will enjoy them and they you. I hope that you and Anne are over-eating, getting drunk nightly, and in all ways having a marvelous time. As you know, I consider myself re: Stanford as your Eliza Doolittle. That out of a guttersnipe you could create something acceptable to a bunch of English professors strikes me as nothing short of miraculous, Mr. Higgins. (Since I can positively hear your exclamation over that sentence, let me hasten to say that you had first-rate raw material!)

Have fun. Best to Anne.

Wally

« To: John L'Heureux • July 24, 1982 »

Dear John:
Your letter revives some of the distress I felt when the English Department made its decision last spring, but it doesn't change my mind.

I believe the department made an egregious mistake, or several of them. Having a distinguished appointment to make, and with the whole English-speaking world to hunt in, it came up with a coterie writer of minimum distinction. If it had made a trial appointment of a year's term, the mistake could have been corrected. Instead, they rushed to appoint Sorrentino[46] to tenure, and whatever he stands for will be built into the writing program for fifteen or twenty years. On the evidence of his dossier, Sorrentino is a fairly inexperienced teacher; on the evidence of the advanced writing class

---

46. Gilbert Sorrentino, precisely the kind of avant-garde, postmodern, metafictionalist Stegner could not abide.

he is not a good one. But there he is, locked in. I don't know Sorrentino and have nothing against him personally. He is apparently a pleasant man. But I am convinced he is the wrong one for the job.

Whether the department made its mistake out of ignorance of what a writing teacher ought to be, or out of some notion of "balancing" or "mixing" the offering (as if it hadn't always been mixed and always perfectly open to every sort of tendency) doesn't matter. It doesn't even matter if the department was conned into its vote by a person or persons bent upon muscling in and taking over. The reasons may be many, but they still resulted in what I feel is a danger to the future of the writing program and a complete repudiation of everything I tried to do when I was building it.

One inescapable conclusion that I draw from the whole matter is that Creative Writing has now been taken over and is being directed by the English Department. Up to now, it has been semi-autonomous, especially in the matter of initiating its own appointments. It has now achieved full second-class status, and in danger of being dominated by English professors ambitious to control it, or unaware of its needs, or indifferent to them, or actively hostile to the whole notion of writing as a university discipline. The most revealing—and alarming—aspect of the Sorrentino appointment is that the English Department voted it over the expressed opposition of Nancy Packer, Ken Fields, and the united Jones Lecturers—everybody on duty in the writing program. What your recommendations were I don't know. My understanding is that you recommended a year's trial, but that rumor may have been wrong. Dick Scowcroft, who as retired head of both the English Department and Creative Writing should have been consulted, opposed the Sorrentino appointment and was not heeded. If anybody had consulted me, I would also have opposed it, and would also not have been heeded, I imagine. There seemed to be an overwhelming desire to ram the appointment through and get it out of the way.

So, seeing Creative Writing being led in directions I can't approve, and coming under the domination of an English Department that I think is not competent to make sensible decisions regarding it, I have to ask myself what my part is in all this. Being long retired, I can't legitimately interfere in appointments, and wouldn't want to. But since my name is still associated with the Writing Program as its founder, and since my name is still on the fellowships and is sometimes used in advertising or promotion or money-raising, I can ask myself if I want it there. I conclude that I don't.

You urge that the name Stegner should not be removed from the program, but in all the important ways it already has been. If the program can keep its equilibrium under the new rules (and you and Nancy are the best guarantee that it can), it doesn't need my name on it anywhere. From here on it's yours, or I hope it is.

Please, therefore, do see that my name is taken off the fellowships and out of the catalogue and all Writing Program leaflets and announcements. If it takes a letter to Development to change the terms of the endowment, I'll write it. There is nothing in the terms of the endowment that obliges me to leave my name on something I no longer want it on; and since the program itself is left intact, I am sure the university will agree.

Just erase the name and the association, that's all it takes to make us all easier in our minds. In some circumstances, Unthink is the soundest thought.

Yours,
Wallace Stegner

« *To: John Crowe Ransom* • *May 14, 1989* »

Dear John,
It's wonderful to have a letter from you. Hark from the Tomb. The spike deer you hid in our bushes fifty years ago is still gloomily surveying the driveway from the front of our carport, and some of the people you knew here have been around helping out with the celebrations of the writing program. But the closest we came to you was Don Allan, who was living in Paris when you were at 44 Avenue Kleber, and who was here (I think) when you were. He's now in Basra or Baghdad, running down Middle Eastern atrocities for news organizations. On my birthday in February some old students came back and held a dinner—Allan Wendt, Boris Ilyin, Carol Burdick, Connie Crawford, Bud and Rich Arnold, and others—and Don wrote us a hilarious letter from Baghdad (hark from the tomb indeed) and made himself a member of the wedding. I wish you had been there—it would have been fine to see you after so many years.

We remember so well those days in Paris when we slept on your floor at 44 Avenue Kleber, and went to the Folies Bergère, and waltzed on the one o'clock pavements of the Left Bank. I also remember a night (on a later trip, I think) when you lived in a fourth-floor walk-up with one of those

French lighting systems that let you get up half a flight before going out. That was the night, I think, when you had come into an inheritance, and were feeling like a Henry James character.

I'm not looking forward to seeing the 21st century but I must say I did enjoy parts of the 20th. Not the last month or two. We made the mistake of going to Morocco in March, and Mary got a bug that has kept her in bed since, until just a couple of days ago. Now that we're out of bed, we're getting ready for the marriage of our granddaughter, which will take place on June 10. So it goes, from century to century.

Good luck and much pleasure in your retirement. And keep in touch.

Best,

Wally

On History
and Historians

◆

To Dale Morgan, November 24, 1941

To Dale Morgan, March 4, 1942

To George Stewart, February 16, 1945

To George Stewart, April 18, 1945

To George Stewart, May 7, 1945

To George Stewart, September 11, 1945

To Bernard DeVoto, October 20, 1947

To William Culp Darrah, December 29, 1947

To George Stewart, November 4, 1958

To George Stewart, May 1, 1960

To Fawn Brodie, February 7, 1969

To Fawn Brodie, March 6, 1969

To Fawn Brodie, November 5, 1970

To Fawn Brodie, January 2, 1971

To Fawn Brodie, May 9, 1971

To Fawn Brodie, January 27, 1972

To Fawn Brodie, February 8, 1972

To Fawn Brodie, June 19, 1972

To Fawn Brodie, March 13, 1973

To Fawn Brodie, January 26, 1974

To Fawn Brodie, March 15, 1974

To Fawn Brodie, April 24, 1978

I SUPPOSE EVERY history I ever read has had some affect on me because it taught me something, and I had to get my education in public and by myself. I never was trained as an historian, and I don't know anything about the trade. So I've learned it from reading other historians, insofar as I've learned it at all. There are people scattered all up and down the historical spectrum who have taught me something. William Byrd's *History of the Dividing Line* taught me something. Castañeda taught me quite a lot. There are people who have dealt with Mormon history or western history, people like Dale Morgan and Juanita Brooks, who have taught me plenty. Ross Toole, in Montana, his histories of Montana. Paul Horgan. Chittenden on the fur trade and Yellowstone park.

And Webb—I should certainly not have forgotten Webb. Certainly Sam Morison can't be left out of any major list.

My involvement in history is personal, not scholarly. I wouldn't have got into Mormon history if I'd never lived in Salt Lake and lived at the wardhouse on Tuesday nights. I wouldn't have written Powell if I hadn't known the Southern Utah plateaus, and I wouldn't have written Benny DeVoto's biography unless I had known him. All the history and biography that I've done has been an offshoot of personal experience and personal acquaintances.

BOTH EXCERPTS FROM *Conversations with*
Wallace Stegner on Western History and Literature,
RICHARD W. ETULAIN, 1983.

♦ ♦ ♦

« *To: Dale Morgan* • *November 24, 1941* »

Dear Dale,
I have a couple more questions to try your patience with.[1] They arise out of your really fine job on the State of Deseret in the *Utah Historical Quarterly*,

---

1. Stegner was at work on his book, *Mormon Country*, and consulted the historian Dale Morgan, of the Utah Writers Project and author of *The Great Salt Lake*, on a number of occasions. This letter has been abridged to include only its interesting parts. The full text is available at the Bancroft Library in Berkeley, California.

and both have to do with the statutes. Thus: The law provides shooting, hanging, or beheading as alternative punishments for murder. Is there any instance in the history of the state of someone's being actually beheaded? And I wonder also if the practice of courts was to allow the prisoner to choose his method, as at present. The second question has to do with the vagrancy ordinance of Feb. 10, 1851. You remark that Brigham was later to gather up a lot of these "loafers" and send them out to found colonies. Is there specific backing for that statement? Did he send them out in gangs, or salt them into more reliable groups of draftees? Is there any record of an entire settlement enterprise being accomplished by "vagrants" gathered off the streets? And how did the vags like it? That's a pretty mess of questions. I ask them because I come more and more to a condition of astonishment at the parallelism in methods between Utah in the early days and any totalitarian state today. The whole thing is there—private army, secret police, encirclement myth, territorial dynamism, self-sufficiency, chosen people, absolute dictatorship operating through party rule, group psychology, esoteric symbols, sacred or distinguishing uniforms (garments), New Order and all. Now if I find a parallel in Utah to Hitler's methods of solving unemployment by work gangs and public construction, it's that much better. I have heard gossip (told to me as gossip, not really believed by the person who told me) that Hitler informed Reese, former head of the German missions, that he had been baptized into the Mormon Church in Austria as a child, and had studied the Book of Mormon and Mormon history. Immediately after that conversation, says my gossip, Hitler instituted the monthly fast day, the proceeds to go to the poor. One thing is sure—there is some kind of affinity, because Hitler did lay off the Mormon missionaries, and Reese did write a glowing article on Hitler Youth and the Church for *Germany and You* in 1938. I do not, actually, expect to make anything out of this, because even if it were true it would mean nothing but that every dictator could have learned things from the Mormon leaders. But I am rather curious for facts on the colonization by vagrants.

 Yours,
 Wally Stegner

« *To: Dale Morgan* • *March 4, 1942* »

Dear Dale,

This, I hope, is the last request I shall have to make of you. It concerns Joseph Musser and his little group of serious polygamists, and particularly their paper, *Truth*. If I could lay my hands on a copy or two of that paper I should be about ready to do a chapter on survivals of old-line Mormonism among the lunatic fringe. Do you have, or have information where I could borrow or buy that paper? Its editor is Joseph P. Musser, but I have no notion of where he is to be reached, and whether I would get a reply if I sent in for information. If I were in his shoes I wouldn't give me any.

I keep hearing your praises sung by Benny DeVoto, who considers you (and why should he not?) the last authority on Utah history. You can take considerable pride in what you've done for Benny's book. It will be a good one. What you've done for mine you can quietly forget, because you won't be proud of that association. But I hope you'll help me once more anyway.

Sincerely,
Wally

« *To: George Stewart* • *February 16, 1945* »

Dear George,

Don't worry about the cancelled public appearance of this brother in the Princeton quad. Neither your students nor I will miss much, probably, though since I have never been in Princeton and since we would have liked to see you again we are sorry the bets are off.[2] The army job, if it turns out to be army, sounds interesting. Or even if it turns out to be civilian. I don't mean to imply that only the army is interesting. I mean to say it sounds like a nice active sort of job.

Our own job here is about as vague as it could well be. Apparently we get a quarter system superimposed on a trimester system in a month or so, and that too will be active, if guesses mean anything. Personally I am rather dubious at the prospect of teaching (me a civilian) a roomful of

---

2. Though at Princeton at this time, George Stewart (novelist, historian, toponymist) would eventually move to the University of California, Berkeley where he and Stegner would continue their long friendship.

uniforms, but I am girding my loins to be a Christian soldier and see that our armed forces split not the infinitive and splice not the comma. At present I am two-thirds at Radcliffe and one-third at Harvard, which is a blessing, inasmuch as the Harvard boys are generally demoralized and the Radcliffe girls are determined to take over all the intellectual pursuits their brothers are shut out of. Result, they work like beavers.

After two weeks in Cambridge, or after one day for that matter, we pine for the clean snow and the neighborly neighbors and the low thermometer and the peace and quiet of Greensboro.[3] Democracy stops at the New Hampshire line, apparently.

I hope your duties will bring you toward Boston, and even slightly beyond it, across the Charles. Don't fail to notify us if you're coming this way, so we can make a preparation. Mary adds her best to mine, to all the family.

> Yours,
> Wally

« *To: George Stewart* • *April 18, 1945* »

Dear George,

This is not a voice from the grave, it's simply a grave voice, breaking now and then into cackling insane laughter. Partly *Look* magazine is responsible for what has happened to my once bright wits; partly the housing situation in Palo Alto; and partly the *Literary History of the United States*, which I got front-footed into over two years ago and haven't been able to look at till now, and now all of a sudden what I thought was a month's work expands into a year's—or more's—and I sit cowering with volumes of Bret Harte under my arms to protect them from the rain of tears and wonder how in hell I get through what I said I'd get through. I gather that you are also a Literary Historian of the United States, and since I have been hornswoggled into doing a section that you should have done, and you're doing something related but different I thought I might learn something if I hung around you and let my ears hang out. To be coherent for a minute, have you done that job of Western Literature as viewed from the East yet? And if so, could I borrow a copy or an outline or something, partly to help me fence my own bailiwick but more for pure brute information? I don't think we're

---

3. Village in northern Vermont.

likely to cross boundaries except that in a general discussion of local color and Bret Harte the eastern popularity can't simply be ignored, and at that point and perhaps others we might cross-reference. I'm still a very long way from done. In fact, I'm just beginning. But about June 1, when we move up to Palo Alto (did you know we were going to be neighbors of yours at Stanford?) I'll be about in condition to stagger into the Bancroft for a few days each week, and Mary and I shall be hoping that the Stewarts have not gone for the summer. The only time I got up to the Bay Area on the *Look* job [4] was last October. I called, but Jack said you were in Washington and Ted was away visiting.

I notice that your place-names book is out, [5] but I haven't had a chance to get one yet. For the sake of your academic reputation, I hope you didn't spell out some of the Arizona names of anatomical memory. But I shall see shortly.

As if we couldn't bear a mild sort of leisure, Mary and I have taken on a job as Houghton Mifflin's West Coast editors, to fill out the vacant hours at Stanford. While I am not out soliciting manuscripts, and should mutter a little if many came in, as long as I'm turning Early-Californian, yet a good book or even a promising book is always extremely welcome, and if you know of anything around Berkeley that's in seeable shape I'd appreciate your steering it in our direction.

Best to Ted and Jack and Jill,
Wally Stegner

« *To: George Stewart* • *May 7, 1945* »

Dear George,
It was very thoughtful of the Germans to surrender today, on Mary's birthday, so I had legitimate reasons to cease reading Ambrose Bierce at 4 o'clock. Only good thing about this confounded *Literary History* business is that I am catching up on the works of Stewart. Latest one the Squibob.

Thanks very much indeed for the copy of your chapter. I note with some interest the extreme eagerness with which the editors embrace fresh points of view and fresh judgments. My God, who is this snotty little STW guy? Oh, I know he is Stanley T. Williams, but who does he think he is? One

---

4. *One Nation.*
5. *Names on the Land.*

of the greatest lessons I have drawn from the loan of your manuscript is the lesson of how to react when I finally get some copy to and back from the editors.

I'm sorry you haven't had happy experiences with Houghton Mifflin. My own experiences have been nothing but pleasant. Actually, I think Houghton Mifflin has altered considerably since you published the Bret Harte. Both Paul Brooks and Lovell Thompson, who direct the place now, are comparatively young and vigorous, and I really do think that Lovell is probably the best advertising manager in any publishing house, old or new line. This isn't to feed you a sales line and try to attach your next book—much as I'd like to, it's merely to justify my own connection with the firm. If they were stinkers I wouldn't work for them, I hope.

I hear rumors of a *Life* option on *Names on the Land*. That's a curious and interesting notion, but then your notions are often curious and interesting, and beget their kind. I hope it works. By practically bursting a bellyband, I have reached page 20 of a new novel. Maybe by the time we move to Stanford on June 16 I'll be through chapter four, and steaming along famously toward a conclusion sometime in 1955. This is my Nobel Prize novel, so I'm in no hurry. See you in Stockholm.

Thanks again for the letter, news, and article. I'll be up to work in the Bancroft this summer, and shall be seeing you. And once we get grooved in our furnished flat in Stanford, and start casting eyes out on the permanent housing situation, we'll hope to see you down in Palo Alto both frequently and lastingly.

Best,
Wally

« *To: George Stewart* • *September 11, 1945* »

Dear George,
So now, maybe you have quit chasing forest fires, us we have quit chasing bears out of the grub box, and are back at the home stand. This note is about three things. One, I finished *Names on the Land* during the camping trip, and it's a beautiful job, full of humor and sense and understanding and a lot of hard work. I shall read it again, piecemeal, a good many times probably, but I'm glad I read it through first. American history is a fresher matter than it used to be.

Two, we're expecting you, now that rationing is off, to drive down this way and have dinner and spend the night sometime. Let us know a date, and whom you'd like to break bread with, and we'll see what we can do.

Three, I'd like in the interest of a friend of mine, to ask you a question. He's dug up a piece called "Incidents on the River of Grace," by one "Midas, Jr.," and published in the heretofore unknown Porter's *Spirit of the Times*, 10th volume (1861). Collins, my Harvard friend, is going to edit and publish the account, which apparently describes life in 1851–52 on the Merced River. But he's baffled by who is Midas, Junior, and asked me to dig him up a capable researcher in the Bay Area to see if the identity could be established. Just on the chance that you might recognize this bird offhand, I'm sending along Collins' letter. And in the case that you don't recognize him, could you put me in touch with someone who knew the Bancroft and the California Historical Society libraries, and would be willing to undertake this search for not too exorbitant a sum? This is a good deal to ask: I wouldn't ask it if there were the library facilities or the researchers around here to fall back on. And I wouldn't ask it, either, if I didn't think this piece might interest you for itself. I am seeing what I can do about getting it for the Stanford Press. Donald Bean, whom I just talked to, seems enthusiastic about the idea. Maybe I ought to collar it for Houghton Mifflin.

Sorry to have missed you last time we were up. Our best to all of you. If you see Paul Taylor you might tell him that I have had proofs on the picture book, and that I did use two of his wife's photos.

Sincerely,
Wally

« *To: Bernard DeVoto* • *October 20, 1947* »

Dear Benny:
It appears that I have been sitting on my can a little too long and that some other gent is finishing a biography on Powell.[6] I wondered if by any chance you might know him and if you could tell me enough about him so that I would know whether to charge up the work I have already done to experience, or whether to go on gathering this stuff in the expectation that I could do a better book on it than the competition.

This gent's name is William Culp Darrah and he lives at 122 Lincoln Road, Medford 55, Massachusetts. I had heard about him vaguely from

---

6. John Wesley Powell.

Henry Nash Smith a couple of years ago, but Henry had him living in New Bedford, and I was never able to hunt him down. He is apparently doing a full-length biography, in which the exploratory section of Powell's life is only an incident. This would have to mean a pretty heavy concentration on Powell as a bureaucrat and planner—which is the part I'm just getting around to.

There is a bird at Columbia doing a Ph.D. thesis under Commager[7] on Powell's governmental career, but this does not bother me nearly as much as Mr. Darrah. Since he's almost done, there's nothing I can do except to hope he does a bad job and then to come along behind him several years hence, sweeping up his remains.

I am a hundred pages along in *Across the Wide Missouri*, and it's wonderful stuff. Sometimes you make me mad; you know too much. It's a swell book and a very beautiful one I think.

Our best to Avis and to you. Dick[8] seems to thrive as a transplanted plant, and the air is already beginning to be thick with visiting Scowcrofts.

> Yours,
> Wally

« To: William Culp Darrah • December 29, 1947 »

Dear Mr. Darrah:

Some time ago, after I heard from Miss Sinclair of the Utah State Historical Society that you were well along with a book on Powell[9], I asked friends in Cambridge if they would find out how far you were along and whether there was any point in my trying to finish my own book on Powell, which is by no means near completion. Carvel Collins, who dropped out to see you, undoubtedly told you what my situation was. He was full of admiration for the thoroughness of your research and indicated that I could not hope to add much if anything in the way of new information, since your own collection of materials was pretty exhaustive.

This note is simply to say that I cannot possibly hope to beat you out

---

7. American historian Henry Steele Commager.
8. Richard Scowcroft, Stegner's co-director of the Stanford Writing Program.
9. John Wesley Powell. Darrah's book, *Powell of the Colorado*, was published in 1951 and reissued in paperback by Princeton University Press in 1969.

with the Powell book and that at the same time Powell intrigues me so much that I probably won't let the subject go but will hope to finish my own book some time within the next two or three years and hope also that yours hasn't completely satisfied the thirst for Powell in the reading public.

I imagine that you have everything that I have in the way of documents, but if I have anything that you can use, you are very welcome to it.[10] I know you have all the diaries and journals, and I know you have combed the New York Public and the Archives. Whether you have all the relatively unimportant materials from Illinois Wesleyan and Illinois State Normal and the reports of the Board of Education of Illinois during Powell's teaching period, I don't know. There is also an M.A. thesis by a man named Morris, of which I have a copy, besides various letters, newspaper stories, and pictures, and other small miscellaneous items from the period of the explorations. If there are any gaps in your own stuff that any of these things will fill, please let me know.

Sincerely yours,
Wallace Stegner

« *To: George Stewart* • *November 4, 1958* »

Dear George,
I refuse to send you one of these Steig cards, these Get-Well things that suggest being sick is just the funniest damn thing on earth. I expect you don't think it's funny at all, and you should be permitted to enjoy your distaste for it. So I will venture to say, without fear of successful contradiction, that I don't envy you at all, but that we're both very pleased to know that things go well, and that the surgery wasn't quite as drastic as anticipated.

Jack was over to dinner the other night, along with Page and one of his roommates. He looks in health and spirits in spite of living at the Village, which is only a cut above jail, and which may be a cut or two below any modern jail. But he tells us he is moving into Crothers Memorial at the end of the quarter, and there he should have some moderate plush. Mary contemplated introducing him to Marg Coolidge, of the Greensboro-Cambridge

---

10. This seems a remarkably generous offer to a competing author. Stegner's own book, *Beyond the Hundredth Meridian*, would not appear until 1954, but when it did it eclipsed everything written before and since about Powell and aridity in the American West.

Coolidges, but then she got cold feet. Marg is getting a divorce and has four children. That looked like a slight overload.

A million things to do before dinner time. I just wanted you to know that we thought of you and wished you jet-propelled health. Best to Ted.

Wally

« *To: George Stewart* • *May 1, 1960* »

Dear George,

I remember Backus well, and I'll be glad to see what I can do when I get back to Stanford in July. At the moment I haven't the slightest idea of what is going on in the department except as it concerns writing classes and not too much about those. Dick Scowcroft writes that he has picked out Stanford fellows and that the Jackson selection has been made—not to a Stanford man. What the hell goes on? I thought we had that wired, as they say in Joisey City.

I'm interested that you may do the California Trail. You're a lot farther along with it, actually, than I am with the Mormon Trail. I had Page doing some work for me for a while, but he got too busy with graduate classes to be any use,[11] and so I guess I'll have to do the dern thing myself. Since we're just across the Platte from each other, so to speak, maybe we should take the opportunity for frequent consultations. As for wagons, I know nought. I can tell you about the construction of 1856 handcarts, but not wagons. If you do decide to do the California Trail, when are you promising delivery? I've not promised anything earlier than 1962, though I hope to beat that some.

Hey, would you like me to put you on the list of potential Writers in Residence at the American Academy? Dick Kimball, the director, asked me the other day for a list of such. Maybe I just won't ask—I'll just put you on. But if you'd like to include Rome in your itinerary when you come to Florence next summer, it's possible the Academy could at least offer you an apartment or rooms for a week or two or three or four weeks. I do not say they would; I say only that they sometimes do if the rooms are not already occupied by some blighter like me. Summer is a somewhat different

---

11. A scurrilous slight. Page read and summarized about 200 Mormon diaries of the hand-cart crossing to Zion. Of course all of them said essentially the same thing: "Made 11 miles today. Hot. Mother died and so did the pig."

matter, though; they've got a bunch of high school classics teachers, and no fellows to speak of. So maybe there's nothing in it. Anyway I'll put your name down as a possibility. There is no fee. There is a free apartment with maid service, telephone, and light; facilities of the Academy including 75-cent meals; company; no duties, aside from social ones.

We'll be back on July 1, and we'll want to see you soon and talk about—among other things—Greece. The coldest, rainiest, windiest, bleakest of earthly habitations. And I had sinusitis so bad I was asthmatic the whole time. But that's what we get for going in March. Only those who went in April got the same thing. Maybe May is the time.

Mary is now in bed with bronchitis, but we are learning that this is the way life is lived in Rome. I've finished the novel twice and am now on the final (I hope) revision. After a USIS[12] talk on the 12th, I ought to be in the clear.

Hoping you and Ted and all the younger generations are the same.

Yours,

Wally

« *To: Fawn Brodie* • *February 7, 1969* »

Dear Fawn:

Remember that book on the Indian pictographs that Dean[13] was once going to do, and that you asked me to do an introduction to? What ever happened to it? Has Dean written it, or prepared prints or transparencies of the cliff paintings? If not, is he going to? About a year ago in Salt Lake I spoke to him about sending some pictures and a brief text to *The American West*, which is set up to do a spectacular job on just that sort of illustrated piece. Nothing ever came. Now I am writing you to see if you can't nudge him. We'd be very interested indeed to have a look either at the book or at an article, or very probably both. We think we're as appropriate a place as any he could find to publicize those cliff paintings, and we think we can give him better illustration, in better color, than anybody else. And in the event that he is too busy or too tired (I can't imagine that) to do something

---

12. United States Information Service.

13. Dean Brimhall, Fawn Brodie's uncle, and a great explorer of the canyonlands of southern Utah. Fawn Brodie was a Utah Mormon girl who drifted away from the faith and went on to become a biographer (Joseph Smith, Thomas Jefferson, Richard Nixon) and professor of history at UCLA. She died of cancer in 1981.

with these pictographs, how about your doing something with them? We don't need a lot of words. With a thing like this, which would be lavishly illustrated, 2,500, or even 2,000, would be enough for an article. The book, of course, could take its own shape and size.

I'm going to write to Dean in five minutes, putting a burr under him and suggesting that if he for any reason can't do it he should get after you to do it. Do not try to escape the editorial net.

Our local radicals are hot after RAND[14] now. Barricade the doors. Here comes idealism with all its wolf teeth bared.

All the best,

Wally

P.S. It goes without saying that if you have any short article of your own that you think might fit us, we'll be overjoyed to get it. We pay $150 to $200, depending on length, and we specialize in finding good pictures.

« *To: Fawn Brodie* • *March 6, 1969* »

Dear Fawn,

How do you like a university history department by now? You join the pedagogues just about the time the rest of us are ready to jump from the mast or slide down the anchor chains.

I haven't replied to your letter of Feb. 9 because I hoped I might hear from Dean. I haven't—maybe he's out on his tote goat exploring some new canyon. To tell you the truth, I doubt that he's ever going to write those pictures up. I proposed a book to him last May, and he said then that he would send down an outline and some pictures: never did.

I imagine he'd a lot rather find pictographs than write about them. On the other hand, your proposal that you take the introduction you have already done, put Dean into it as the hero-explorer, and make us an article for *American West*, is something that we are all very interested in. Are you in fairly frequent communication with him? Could you propose this, and see if he'll supply photographs? If he will, then I hope you will send us something soon, the sooner the better. If this is four-color stuff, we have to work several issues ahead. And please don't forget, or let Dean forget, that we're also interested in talking to him/you about the book, whenever and if ever he gets to that point.

One further note, quite a long way from the main subject of this letter:

---

14. A nonprofit think tank first formed to offer research and analysis to the U.S. military.

I have signed up to do a biography of Benny DeVoto—did I tell you this already? I am naturally interested in talking to anyone who knew him, worked with him, corresponded with him, or was in any way associated. Knowing how much he admired *No Man Knows My History*,[15] I can't think you didn't have some contact with him. Did you know him well? How? When? Where? And would you be willing sometime either to talk to me about specific things—his own work in Mormon history, for example—or failing an opportunity for us to get together handily, could I send you a cassette for a tape recorder and get you to talk me a tape-full? I'm in no big hurry—it'll be two years until I even begin to write. But I am making like a squirrel so that things will be assembled when the time comes.

All the best,
Wally

« *To: Fawn Brodie* • *November 5, 1970* »

Dear Fawn:
Many thanks for your piece on Dean. He's getting too secretive in his old age—it's long past time you smoked him out of his hole, and I very much hope that *American West* can make use of your article, or some version of it. As you may or may not know, I haven't been associated with the magazine for nearly two years now, not because I've lost interest but because I've been concentrating on getting some books written before I go senile.

So I can't answer for the editorial response. My guess is that the editors will find the piece too long for the magazine, as you feared; and I have the sense also that they may want the emphasis shifted somewhat. As it stands, it's a sort of profile of Dean Brimhall, with the Barrier Canyon and other murals an incident in his life. I suspect that for *American West* readers the Barrier Canyon murals may be central to the text as well as to the illustrations; and this suggests to me that it would be easy enough to shorten the article substantially by concentrating on the pictographs and giving Dean's background, personality, and foreground incidentally or as thumbnail sketch. But that the magazine will want some form of the piece I am confident. I'll leave it to the editors to communicate with you about that. As for me, I'll take the article and pictures down to the office this afternoon.

I'm sorry I couldn't make the Salt Lake City meeting, and hear you on

---

15. Fawn Brodie's study of Joseph Smith.

the subject of the manipulating of history. Since I have been manipulating history for the purposes of fiction for three years, I'm interested. Is it O.K. if I twist events and personalities for fictional purposes? Or have I sinned? (I'm fairly sure I have—I've got that feeling.) At least I am now open to correction, and that stimulates the writing of history.

I'll be in touch with the *American West* office about what happens with the article.

All the best,
Wally
cc: George Pfeiffer[16]

« *To: Fawn Brodie* • *January 2, 1971* »

Dear Fawn:

I had lunch with the *American West* people last week, and they told me that they were planning to run your piece in two parts, so as not to lose either the biographical part or the pictograph part. That's a splendid resolution of what looked like a problem of length. I hope it pleases you. I'll be looking forward to seeing Dean looming up in full Technicolor on the pages of *American West.*

Our best for 1971. What are you working on? Got another good book in the mill? Me, I'm now sinking slowly and inexorably into the morass of Benny DeVoto's endless correspondence. Years from now I will surface, having lost my terrestrial limbs and acquired flippers and a layer of insulating fat like a sea mammal, and waddle toward publication.

Let us hope.

Yours,
Wally

« *To: Fawn Brodie* • *May 9, 1971* »

Dear Fawn:

I had heard of Dale's[17] death, but no details. It's a great loss, he was so fine a scholar that almost one's first thought is of the unwritten book—and not

---

16. Editor of *American West.*
17. Dale Morgan, 1914–71. Western historian, author of *Jedediah Smith and the Opening of the West* and *The West of William H. Ashley.* Morgan was at work on a definitive history of Mormonism at the time of his death.

only the Mormon one but the fur trade one. And that's heartless, really, because he was also so fine and decent and generous and long-suffering a man that one should think first of the person we've lost, and not the books.

It seems to me the University of Utah might be a very sound place to give his letters. That library deserves to have some sound sense filed in it.

I've heard some echoes of your iconoclasm about our great democratic heroes. It's O.K. to talk about Richard Burton,[18] but who gave you leave to smear the memory of one of our founders and authors?[19] Shyme.

The novel goes along about as I expected, reviewers are about their old proportion of stupids to wise men, illiterates to those who can and do read. Though it doesn't for some odd reason show up strongly in the lists, the sales have been very satisfying, better than anything of mine. So I assume an angle of repose and see what the next hour will bring forth.

Many thanks for your note, and best luck.

Wally

« *To: Fawn Brodie* • *January 27, 1972* »

Dear Fawn:

Help!

In Benny DeVoto's correspondence there are several long letters to "Madeline," whom I have determined to be Madeline McQuown, maiden name unknown to me. In them Benny justifies his novels against her criticisms, and argues with her at length about history, and applauds the work she herself is doing, which seems to be a biography of Brigham Young. I know no biography of Brigham by any McQuown, and the Stanford Library doesn't contain one. But just as I was about to go down and get varicose veins standing before the Union Catalogue I saw a mention in one of the letters to "your uncle," who had just expressed his displeasure at Fawn Brodie's *No Man Knows My History* by excommunicating her. If David O. McKay was her uncle, Madeline McQuown has to be some sort of cousin of yours. Last autumn, on a quick trip through Ogden, I checked the telephone book: no McQuowns. Can you tell me (a) who exactly she is, or was, and how associated with Benny, and (b) what ever happened to her book on

---

18. *The Devil Drives: A Life of Richard Burton.*
19. Thomas Jefferson.

Brigham, which seemed to be near completion when this correspondence was going on in 1947. I'd be, as ever, very grateful.

I'm also curious to know what you think, now that you're deep in Jefferson, of Benny's thesis that Jefferson had in mind from the beginning, when he bought Louisiana, the notion of playing for the entire continent—that he was not just steering the fur trade into American channels when he sent out Lewis and Clark, but was continuing a game he had started before the Louisiana Purchase, and that he had in mind all along the consolidating a continental nation. Fred Merk disagreed with that notion violently, maybe others did too. And I'm damned if I've got time to read the whole history of continental imperialism to find out how sound the theory is and what historians have thought of it. I rely abjectly on you.

I hope you'll have a few minutes for this. And I hope sometime I'll know something that you might need, but my hope is not excessive. Scholarship is foreign to my nature.

How does the Brimhall project go? I hope well. By now, maybe, Emil Haury and Ned Danson, of the University of Arizona and the Museum of Northern Arizona respectively, have talked to him about the future of his collections. If they haven't, and need stirring up, let me know.

All the best, and many thanks,
Wally

« To: Fawn Brodie • February 8, 1972 »

Dear Fawn:

Many thanks for the resonant word on Madeline McQuown. That's an amazing story, in more than one respect, poor Dale's part in it not least. And I wonder why Benny took Madeline's criticisms of his novels and histories so seriously, and why he wrote to Knopf or somebody (I haven't looked this up through the mass of notes) that Madeline's Brigham Young would be the definitive biography when it appeared? He must have been duped, as Dale was, and that must have taken a certain skill in the duper. I think I shall check out the San Jose telephone book to see if she still exists, but I doubt that I want to get into the basket of snakes she might turn out to be. She isn't really important to my book anyway, except as an earnest of his continued interest in Ogden, Ogdenites, and Mormon history.

A visit the other day from a gent named Leland Fetzler, from San Diego

State, who is writing a piece for *Dialogue* on DeVoto's changing attitudes toward the Mormon Church. Seems an intelligent fellow—he might rejuvenate Benny in a few unforgiving Utah breasts.

There is a connection between these two paragraphs, even if there doesn't seem to be. For Jarvis Thurston was accused by Madeline of having absconded with Benny's letters to her—absconded and refused to restore them to her hands. Maybe he took the Brigham MS too, as she told you. He must have cleaned out the desk. Maybe I'll write and ask him. Is he still at Washington University in St. Louis? I have just looked back through the letters and find that on March 31, 1946 Benny wrote Madeline two separate notes, one full of discussion of your book, Dale's objections to Benny's review, Widtsoe's response to the recanting letter Benny allowed to be published in the *Rocky Mountain Review* and later in the *Improvement Era*; the other advising her to request DeVoto's letters to Madeline back from Thurston, who had no right to them, and if he refused, to see a lawyer. Explicit pars una.

Next step, the San Jose phone book. And if you do catch Jefferson plotting continental hegemony, leave me in on it.

All best,
Wally

« *To: Fawn Brodie* • *June 19, 1972* »

Dear Fawn:
Your two letters reached me at Logan. I had heard about Dean's death, and felt it for the loss it was. In Salt Lake we had the chance to see Lila[20] twice. She is, as you would imagine, magnificent. Also, at Logan we saw Juanita Brooks,[21] and Lila gave us a copy of the memorial service talks, so that we have had a good picture. It sounded like something Dean himself would have approved.

In Logan I also talked to Everett Cooley about the pictures. He and Lila clearly hope that some way may be found to keep them in Utah, but both agree that Jennings has shown no interest, and we all know that Dean swore Jennings shouldn't have a chance to acquire and ignore them.

---

20. Lila Brimhall.
21. Utah historian and author of highly acclaimed books on the Mountain Meadows massacre and on John D. Lee.

Alternatives seem to be Cooley's Western Americana archives, where I suspect they would be well displayed and used, or the University of Utah Art Museum. Both, if the details can be worked out, would seem more appropriate than the University of Arizona or the Museum of Northern Arizona, which Dean asked me to make inquiries of last fall. There seems to be enough money in the Brimhall Fund for Research in Indian Art to pay for the assembling and clarifying of the pictures—getting notes and pictures matched, and all that. There also seems to be in Everett Cooley's mind—and in mine—the hope that you will write the book, and Knopf will publish it. I told Cooley that if you would do it, and Knopf would publish it, and if all parties involved wanted me to, I would write the introduction. But I'd already promised you that.

Now all that remains to do is for you to sit down and write. How goes Mr. Jefferson?

Best,

Wally

P.S. Re: Benny's interest in psychoanalysis: I've talked with Greg Rochlin as well as three others of Benny's analysts (he had six, at one time or another). Benny knew about as much in that line as his analysts did, which made him a hard nut to crack.

P.P.S. I just talked on the telephone with George Pfeiffer of *American West*. I told him about the proposals for a book on Dean's pictographs, and ran into one of his headlong enthusiasms. He is eager to enlarge his anthropological offerings (latest will be a long piece on anthropological studies along the Alaska pipeline), and he has been having greater and greater success with his books. For instance, *Living Water* has sold 40,000. *The Great Southwest*, not out yet, has sold nearly 20,000 by subscription, before publication. It is clear that George has the lists and the know-how for subscription publishing, and he is being pestered by Knopf, Doubleday, and others to merchandise their books for them. He won't. But he can merchandise his own, probably better than an eastern publisher can (Doubleday's book on the Sierras sold 4,700 copies; George sold 20,000). And he is enthusiastic about the notion of a book by you on Dean's pictures. It could be a better business deal for you than Knopf. So in case Knopf is lukewarm or indifferent, you might bear George in mind. I'll help as I can, naturally.

« *To: Fawn Brodie* • *March 13, 1973* »

Dear Fawn;

Many thanks, however belated, for your absolutely persuasive quotation from Jefferson. It will go into a footnote as if I found it myself, and you shall be thanked among the acknowledgments page without having it known that you provided the substantive scholarship and not the helping hand.[22]

I'm glad the Dean Brimhall book will get made, and that you'll have the biggest hand in the making. If you still want the foreword, I'm still willing.

Recently I've been reading Leonard Arrington's life of David Eccles, written for the Eccles Family, or some of them. Am I cockeyed in thinking that Eccles was one of the biggest land pirates, timber pirates, coal pirates, railroad pirates, in the West? You'd never know it from Arrington's biography, and I am (being pressured by Joe and Jess Quinney and by Nora Eccles and her husband to comment on Arrington's book) about to suggest that he wipe off the whitewash and do the old buzzard as what he was: a hell of an acute buccaneer whose conscience stopped at the edge of the family, or at the farthest, of the Church, and did not extend into business enterprises where the public lands, the laws of the United States, or other irritating irrelevancies were involved.

Arrington, from what I know of him, is a perfectly nice guy; but if anybody ever wrote a Faith-promoting, Saint's-Life, exemplum of a biography, he did. Can he be reasoned with, you think, especially now that he's Church Historian?

And I agree with you about teaching. Three years ago I swore I'd never again try to teach anybody young.

Best,

Wally

« *To Fawn Brodie* • *January 26, 1974* »

Dear Fawn,

Many thanks for sending me the clip of your review,[23] and even more thanks for writing it. It's a very just review as well as a friendly one.

---

22. As per Brodie's request.
23. Review of *The Uneasy Chair*, Stegner's biography of Bernard DeVoto.

On the issue of "censorship," I suppose I have to plead guilty. I had a choice to make, and made it for what I hoped was better but what may have been worse. The fact is, I wasn't, and am not now, particularly interested in Benny's private life insofar as that private life was sexual or conjugal. That's his business, so far as I am concerned. And, as you remark, Avis is still alive. So are the two boys. If I had elected to get into the tense emotional relationship between Benny and his older son, I would have had to skimp something else, and even with my limitations upon it the biography was already getting too long. So somewhere in midstream I decided that his private life, his life as husband, lover, and father, was none of my business, and that I would write of his private life only as it plainly affected his career and his solution of his problems by work. So I concentrated on his depressions and his panics and his triumphs over them. Revealing the emotional life of a man like Benny can make him look like an awful fool, perhaps an irretrievable fool. And that was not what my biography wanted to say. What it wanted to say was that he survived his own worst enemy, himself.

Well. That isn't a defense. Maybe it's a confession. But I suppose if I were doing it over, I would do it the same way, and my reasons would be both protectiveness for Avis and the boys, and a conviction that full revelation would be a distorting mirror, not a clear one.

You had quite another situation in Jefferson, and rose to it like a 25-pound German Brown to a black gnat. Result: splendid. But would you write, say, Dean Brimhall's life in the same way? Some day you must instruct me in the proprieties of history and biography, of which I have only an amateur's understanding. And incidentally, how does the Brimhall project proceed?

All the best,
Wally

« *To: Fawn Brodie* • *March 15, 1974* »

Dear Fawn,
This is a pleasant business, trading compliments. I appreciate your comments on *The Uneasy Chair*, including those you sent to Doubleday, and I can return them redoubled. *Jefferson* is a splendid book,[24] the intimate history you promise, and a touching and troubling one. I confess I first had a little shock at not finding anything about the Louisiana Purchase

---

24. *Thomas Jefferson: An Intimate History.*

and the Lewis and Clark Expedition—those two things included all I ever knew about Jefferson—but I could see why you deliberately omitted all but the running outline of his political career. He sounds like a good deal more reluctant president than our present disaster, and an infinitely more human one. The other night, quite by the way, I dreamed that Nixon had published his Meditations, more or less on the model of Marcus Aurelius, and the very thought woke me up sweating. Jefferson, by contrast, could have published his Meditations and enriched the world. In a very real sense, you publish them for him, and you too have enriched the world by taking a figurehead off his pedestal, to coin a splendid phrase, and humanizing him. What you may have done to the democratic politicians is another matter. Let the wind out, probably. Isn't it wonderful how laggard and unwilling the truth is, when a myth is more politically useful.

You can't help making a stir with this. I will be rooting and promoting.

Auguri.

Wally

« *To: Fawn Brodie* • *April 24, 1978* »

Dear Fawn:

You tempt me to say that anybody who would set out to write a book about Nixon deserves what she gets. But I am kinder hearted than that. I wish you well with your grisly task. Incidentally, do you know Jessamyn West, and have you talked to her? She's Nixon's cousin, and grew up with him. She lives, as you probably know, in Napa.

The piece on the Mormons that you speak of probably was written in the Church Library. After all, you can't ask the boys to knock their own show. The mistake was made by the Harvard Encyclopedia. If they want to substitute my piece I'll charge them double as a penance.

And you're being rehabilitated in Utah. That is the benign influence of Spencer Kimball. Wait till Ezra takes over—out you'll go on a rail.

And thanks for your kind words about the *Atlantic* piece.[25] It was hard enough to do so that it ought to have been important. I don't know if it is. But it was fun collaborating with Page. Gives you feelings of immortality.

Why don't we ever see each other?

Yours,

Wally

---

25. "Rocky Mountain Country" (with Page Stegner), *Atlantic Monthly*, April 1977.

Conservation

To David Brower, September 2, 1953

To David Pesonen, December 3, 1960

To Stewart Udall, September 22, 1961

To Stewart Udall, October 23, 1961

To Mrs. Kenneth Brown, October 26, 1961

To Stewart Udall, No Date, 1961

To George Stewart, November 1, 1961

To Stewart Udall, December 30, 1961

To Stewart Udall, December 9, 1962

To Stewart Udall, December 7, 1963

To Stewart Udall, February 14, 1967

To Randy Morgenson, January 26, 1972

To Tom Graff, Environmental Defense
    Fund, November 10, 1984

To Margaret Owings, April 14, 1985

To Charles Wilkinson, February 26, 1986

To Charles Wilkinson, November 19, 1986

To Charles Wilkinson, April 21, 1987

To Charles Wilkinson, October 17, 1987

To Charles Wilkinson, March 24, 1990

To Dave Brower, May 16, 1990

To Dave Livermore, March 9, 1991

To Dave Livermore, May 17, 1991

To Margaret Owings, August 24, 1991

To Charles Wilkinson, October 28, 1991

To Dave Livermore, October 30, 1992

To Harold Gilliam, No Date, 1992

To Dave Livermore, March 5, 1993

S TEGNER'S INTEREST in conservation began in the 1930s when he was still teaching at the University of Utah and began reading western explorers like John Wesley Powell and Clarence Dutton, but he didn't begin writing about wilderness and the need for its preservation until the mid-forties when he did a piece for *The Reporter* called "Public Lands and Itchy Fingers." Several articles followed over the next ten years, and then in 1955 David Brower, executive director of the Sierra Club, persuaded him to edit a book called *This Is Dinosaur* that led to the defeat of two proposed dams in Dinosaur National Monument, dams that would have flooded and destroyed forever a spectacular region of northeastern Utah and northwestern Colorado canyon country. It was the first major environmental battle since John Muir fought the City of San Francisco for the preservation of Yosemite's Hetch Hetchy valley, and Stegner was at the center of it. Muir lost; Stegner and company prevailed.

Over the next three decades, and particularly in the aftermath of his famous "Wilderness Letter" (included here), Stegner would find himself, often reluctantly, involved in conservation activism of one form or another. In 1959, in an attempt to restrict development in the California Coast Range above the San Francisco Bay Area, he cofounded the Committee for Green Foothills, an organization that thrives to this day. He served on the governing boards of both the Sierra Club and the Wilderness Society, on the councils of the Trust for Public Land and the Greenbelt Alliance, on the National Parks Advisory Board, and for a brief tenure as special assistant to the Secretary of the Interior, Stewart Udall, during the Kennedy Administration.

Asked by Richard Etulain in *Conversations with Wallace Stegner on Western History and Literature* if he enjoyed all this conservation activity, Stegner replied, "Not really, no. But I feel obligated, since I think I know something about it, to say how I think it is . . . No, I don't enjoy it, and I don't suppose I'm going to do it very long, but I did have a certain obligation, I thought, and people told me I did." A typically modest disclaimer from the man T. H. Watkins referred to as "one of the most important figures in the modern conservation movement . . . one of the most eloquent and intelligent voices in defense of the voiceless that our literature has ever produced." Or as Stegner himself put it, ". . . a paper tiger, Watkins, typewritten on both sides."

• • •

« *To: David Brower* • *September 2, 1953* »

Dear Mr. Brower:

Thanks very much for the film script, which I have had time only to read through hurriedly, but which strikes me offhand as admirable. I did question that the national parks began in Lincoln's day—wasn't Yellowstone the first, in 1873?—but that sort of historical detail is obviously going to be corrected in the editing. One omission that seemed to me unfortunate was the part Earl Douglass played in the establishment of Dinosaur: it was he who dug at the quarry for many years after 1909, and he who eventually promoted the establishment of the national monument to discourage mineral claims within the fossil area. I have a chapter on him in *Mormon Country*. It is called, I believe, "Notes on a Life Spent Pecking at a Sandstone Cliff." Mrs. Douglass, whom I knew, once wanted me to write her husband's biography. He got a dirty deal from the University of Utah and died poor, but that monument is really his baby, and he would have been 1000 percent in sympathy with the spirit of your movie. Can he be given a paragraph of narrative when the camera runs over the quarry site?

I suppose you knew, incidentally, that Al Millotte (who shot *Beaver Valley*, *Seal Island*, and other animal films for Disney) shot the whole length of the Green and Colorado canyons in 16mm color four or five years ago. We went down the San Juan and Glen Canyon with him and saw a lot of his stuff later. It's marvelous photography, even if I do say so as I shouldn't, having shaken the aspens on the Kaibab to simulate storm and done other personal services to Art. Probably none of that stuff is available since it was intended for a massive full-length life-and-animation movie on the Colorado Basin, and may yet be so used. But there may be services that Al or the Disney office might be willing to provide, shots or sequences that they might be induced to loan or donate, to fill in possible holes in your own.

As for the Four Corners, I am afraid I can't help much, since I have never been through there but once, and then I was pulling a one-wheel trailer. I imagine that I am the only living man who has taken a trailer across that Dinnehotso road, but I spent so much time under it repairing the hitch that I didn't see as much of the country as I intended. From the road, it is extremely barren, and for most people's taste forbidding. Its canyons and gulches are probably every bit as worth saving as a lot of other southwest canyons. Since it is within the Navajo reservation, much of it is already preserved after a fashion—though I had a letter a few years ago from a Texas gentleman who had a big idea for a hotel right on the Four Corners, with a dining room in four states, and an opening night in which the governors of four states sat down at one table—but each in his own state—and then played a round of golf back and forth among their respective domains. The Texas gentleman was sure he could fix it up with the Navajo. I guess I wouldn't worry about such gentlemen as he, and such projects as his, but the prospectors for vanadium and uranium are all over that country now, and mineral claims might easily be spotted all across it. What can or should be done about that I don't know; the region is still so inaccessible that not fifty people a year are likely to go through it. But all it would take is a road, and a dam on the San Juan, and it would be moved in on.

My own feeling, off the cuff, is that the Wayne Wonderland in southern Utah is a good deal more spectacular and more worthy of preservation as a monument and recreation area, but it isn't at the moment or in any conceivable future time likely to be threatened by major dams. Again, the big threat is mineral claims, especially uranium, and the airports and installations that accompany strikes. More immediately threatened than either of these regions is the Glen Canyon, which ought properly to be added to the Rainbow Bridge National Monument, but which is, I guess, already doomed by dam-makers.[1] You probably know Glen Canyon; for my money it's better than the Yampa–Green section, and it has the Navajo Mountain Rainbow Bridge as well as the Natural Bridges monument on its fringes.[2] Really sound planning would reserve the natural bridges, Glen Canyon, and the Rainbow Bridge as a single national park—and you could throw in the Four Corners without straining probability too much.

Obviously we ought to talk sometime. Obviously I would be glad to write something sometime for the SCB[3]—maybe a section could be lifted out of my forthcoming biography of Major John Wesley Powell, who first ran the canyons and who fathered all the reclamation activities which now

---

1. This is certainly one piece of evidence that Brower was forewarned about the great importance of Glen Canyon, but having never seen it himself, he traded it away for Dinosaur, promising not to oppose a hydro-power plug in Glen Canyon if the Bureau of Reclamation would abandon its plans for a dam at Echo Park.

2. In 1962, after spending twenty-one days in Glen Canyon, Brower wrote to Stegner, "There could be no more unconscionable crime against a scenic wonder of the world than Glen Canyon Dam. You said it long ago, and now I know it—Dinosaur doesn't compare."

3. Sierra Club Bulletin.

threaten other interests. We return to Los Altos on September 12. Why don't you give me a call sometime so we can arrange for lunch and a talk and a drink? I'd be very pleased to know more specifically what the Sierra Club is doing and plans to do, and happy to do what I can to help.

Sincerely,

Wallace Stegner

« *To: David Pesonen* • *December 3, 1960* »

Dear Mr. Pesonen:[4]

I believe that you are working on the wilderness portion of the Outdoor Recreation Resources Review Commission's report. If I may, I should like to urge some arguments for wilderness preservation that involve recreation, as it is ordinarily conceived, hardly at all. Hunting, fishing, hiking, mountain-climbing, camping, photography, and the enjoyment of natural scenery will all, surely, figure in your report. So will the wilderness as a genetic reserve, a scientific yardstick by which we may measure the world in its natural balance against the world in its man-made imbalance. What I want to speak for is not so much the wilderness uses, valuable as those are, but the wilderness idea, which is a resource in itself. Being an intangible and spiritual resource, it will seem mystical to the practical-minded—but then anything that cannot be moved by a bulldozer is likely to seem mystical to them.

I want to speak for the wilderness idea as something that has helped form our character and that has certainly shaped our history as a people. It has no more to do with recreation than churches have to do with recreation, or than the strenuousness and optimism and expansiveness of what historians call the "American Dream" have to do with recreation. Nevertheless, since it is only in this recreation survey that the values of wilderness are being compiled, I hope you will permit me to insert this idea between the leaves, as it were, of the recreation report.

---

4. David Pesonen was consultant to the Outdoor Recreation Resources Review Commission, which was reviewing the need for wilderness legislation to present to Congress. Even before this famous "Wilderness Letter" was published as part of the commission's report, Secretary of the Interior Stewart Udall obtained a copy of it and was so moved by its eloquence that he substituted it for his prepared speech at a wilderness convention in San Francisco. In no small measure the letter contributed to the passage of The Wilderness Act in 1964.

Something will have gone out of us as a people if we ever let the remaining wilderness be destroyed; if we permit the last virgin forests to be turned into comic books and plastic cigarette cases; if we drive the few remaining members of the wild species into zoos or to extinction; if we pollute the last clear air and dirty the last clean streams and push our paved roads through the last of the silence, so that never again will Americans be free in their own country from the noise, the exhausts, the stinks of human and automotive waste. And so that never again can we have the chance to see ourselves single, separate, vertical and individual in the world, part of the environment of trees and rocks and soil, brother to the other animals, part of the natural world and competent to belong in it. Without any remaining wilderness we are committed wholly, without chance for even momentary reflection and rest, to a headlong drive into our technological termite-life, the Brave New World of a completely man-controlled environment. We need wilderness preserved—as much of it as is still left, and as many kinds—because it was the challenge against which our character as a people was formed. The remainder and the reassurance that it is still there is good for our spiritual health even if we never once in ten years set foot in it. It is good for us when we are young, because of the incomparable sanity it can bring briefly, as vacation and rest, into our insane lives. It is important to us when we are old simply because it is there—important, that is, simply as idea.

We are a wild species, as Darwin pointed out. Nobody ever tamed or domesticated or scientifically bred us. But for at least three millennia we have been engaged in a cumulative and ambitious race to modify and gain control of our environment, and in the process we have come close to domesticating ourselves. Not many people are likely, any more, to look upon what we call "progress" as an unmixed blessing. Just as surely as it has brought us increased comfort and more material goods, it has brought us spiritual losses, and it threatens now to become the Frankenstein that will destroy us. One means of sanity is to retain a hold on the natural world, to remain, insofar as we can, good animals. Americans still have that chance more than many peoples; for while we were demonstrating ourselves the most efficient and ruthless environment busters in history, and slashing and burning and cutting our way through a wilderness continent, the wilderness was working on us. It remains in us as surely as Indian names remain on the land. If the abstract dream of human liberty and human dignity became, in America, something more than an abstract dream, mark it down at least partially to the fact that we were in subtle ways subdued by what we conquered.

The Connecticut Yankee, sending likely candidates from King Arthur's unjust kingdom to his Man Factory for rehabilitation, was over-optimistic, as he later admitted. These things cannot be forced, they have to grow. To make such a man, such a democrat, such a believer in human individual dignity as Mark Twain himself, the frontier was necessary, Hannibal and the Mississippi and Virginia City, and reaching out from those the wilderness; the wilderness as opportunity and as idea, the thing that has helped to make an American different from and, until we forget it in the roar of our industrial cities, more fortunate than other men. For an American, insofar as he is new and different at all, is a civilized man who has renewed himself in the wild. The American experience has been the confrontation by old peoples and cultures of a world as new as if it had just risen from the sea. That gave us our hope and our excitement, and the hope and excitement can be passed on to newer Americans, Americans who never saw any phase of the frontier. But only so long as we keep the remainder of our wild as a reserve and a promise—a sort of wilderness bank.

As a novelist, I may perhaps be forgiven for taking literature as a reflection, indirect but profoundly true, of our national consciousness. And our literature, as perhaps you are aware, is sick, embittered, losing its mind, losing its faith. Our novelists are the declared enemies of their society. There has hardly been a serious or important novel in this century that did not repudiate in part or in whole American technological culture for its commercialism, its vulgarity, and the way in which it has dirtied a clean continent and a clean dream. I do not expect that the preservation of our remaining wilderness is going to cure this condition. But the mere example that we can as a nation apply some other criteria than commercial and exploitative considerations would be heartening to many Americans, novelists or otherwise. We need to demonstrate our acceptance of the natural world, including ourselves; we need the spiritual refreshment that being natural can produce. And one of the best places for us to get that is in the wilderness where the fun houses, the bulldozers, and the pavements of our civilization are shut out.

Sherwood Anderson, in a letter to Waldo Frank in the 1920s, said it better than I can. "Is it not likely that when the country was new and men were often alone in the fields and the forest they got a sense of bigness outside themselves that has now in some way been lost . . . Mystery whispered in the grass, played in the branches of trees overhead, was caught up and blown across the American line in clouds of dust at evening on the prairies . . . I am old enough to remember tales that strengthen my belief in a deep semi-religious influence that was formerly at work among our people. The flavor of it hangs over the best work of Mark Twain . . . I can remember old fellows in my home town speaking feelingly of an evening spent on the big empty plains. It had taken the shrillness out of them. They had learned the trick of quiet . . ."

We could learn it too, even yet; even our children and grandchildren could learn it. But only if we save, for just such absolutely non-recreational, impractical, and mystical uses as this, all the wild that still remains to us.

It seems to me significant that the distinct downturn in our literature from hope to bitterness took place almost at the precise time when the frontier officially came to an end, in 1890, and when the American way of life had begun to turn strongly urban and industrial. The more urban it has become, and the more frantic with technological change, the sicker and more embittered our literature, and I believe our people, have become. For myself, I grew up on the empty plains of Saskatchewan and Montana and in the mountains of Utah, and I put a very high valuation on what those places gave me. And if I had not been able periodically to renew myself in the mountains and deserts of western America I would be very nearly bughouse. Even when I can't get to the back country, the thought of the colored deserts of southern Utah, or the reassurance that there are still stretches of prairie where the world can be instantaneously perceived as disk and bowl, and where the little but intensely important human being is exposed to the five directions and the thirty-six winds, is a positive consolation. The idea alone can sustain me. But as the wilderness areas are progressively exploited or "improved," as the jeeps and bulldozers of uranium prospectors scar up the deserts and the roads are cut into the alpine timberlands, and as the remnants of the unspoiled and natural world are progressively eroded, every such loss is a little death in me. In us.

I am not moved by the argument that those wilderness areas which have already been exposed to grazing or mining are already deflowered, and so might as well be "harvested." For mining I cannot say much good except that its operations are generally short-lived. The extractable wealth is taken and the shafts, the tailings, and the ruins left, and in a dry country such as the American West the wounds men make in the earth do not quickly heal. Still, they are only wounds; they aren't absolutely mortal. Better a wounded wilderness than none at all. And as for grazing, if it is strictly controlled so that it does not destroy the ground cover, damage the ecology, or compete with the wildlife it is in itself nothing that need conflict with the wilderness feeling or the validity of the wilderness experience. I have known enough range cattle to recognize them as wild animals; and the people who herd them have, in the wilderness context, the dignity of rareness; they belong on the frontier, moreover, and have a look of rightness. The invasion they make on the virgin country is a sort of invasion that is as old as Neolithic man, and they can, in moderation, even emphasize a man's feeling of belonging to the natural world. Under surveillance, they can belong; under control, they need not deface or mar. I do not believe that in wilderness areas where grazing has never been permitted, it should be permitted; but I do not believe either that an otherwise untouched wilderness should be eliminated from the preservation plan because of limited existing uses such as grazing which are in consonance with the frontier condition and image.

Let me say something on the subject of the kinds of wilderness worth preserving. Most of those areas contemplated are in the national forests and in high mountain country. For all the usual recreational purposes, the alpine and forest wildernesses are obviously the most important, both as genetic banks and as beauty spots. But for the spiritual renewal, the recognition of identity, the birth of awe, other kinds will serve every bit as well. Perhaps, because they are less friendly to life, more abstractly non-human, they will serve even better. On our Saskatchewan prairie, the nearest neighbor was four miles away, and at night we saw only two lights on all the dark rounding earth. The earth was full of animals—field mice, ground squirrels, weasels, ferrets, badgers, coyotes, burrowing owls, snakes. I knew them as my little brothers, as fellow creatures, and I have never been able to look upon animals in any other way since. The sky in that country came clear down to the ground on every side, and it was full of great weathers, and clouds, and winds, and hawks. I hope I learned something from knowing intimately the creatures of the earth; I hope I learned something from looking a long way, from looking up, from being much alone. A prairie like that, one big enough to carry the eye clear to the sinking, rounding horizon, can be as lonely and grand and simple in its forms as the sea. It is as good a place as any for the wilderness experience to happen; the vanishing prairie is as worth preserving for the wilderness idea as the alpine forests.

So are great reaches of our western deserts, scarred somewhat by prospectors but otherwise open, beautiful, waiting, close to whatever God you want to see in them. Just as a sample, let me suggest the Robbers' Roost country in Wayne County, Utah, near the Capitol Reef National Monument. In that desert climate the dozer and jeep tracks will not soon melt back into the earth, but the country has a way of making the scars insignificant. It is a lovely and terrible wilderness, such a wilderness as Christ and the prophets went out into; harshly and beautifully colored, broken and worn until its bones are exposed, its great sky without a smudge or taint from Technocracy, and in hidden corners and pockets under its cliffs the sudden poetry of springs. Save a piece of country like that intact, and it does not matter in the slightest that only a few people every year will go into it. That is precisely its value. Roads would be a desecration, crowds would ruin it. But those who haven't the strength or youth to go into it and live can simply sit and look. They can look two hundred miles, clear into Colorado; and looking down over the cliffs and canyons of the San Rafael Swell and the Robbers' Roost they can also look as deeply into themselves as anywhere I know. And if they can't even get to the places on the Aquarius Plateau where the present roads will carry them, they can simply contemplate the idea, take pleasure in the fact that such a timeless and uncontrolled part of earth is still there.

These are some of the things wilderness can do for us. That is the reason we need to put into effect, for its preservation, some other principle than the principles of exploitation or "usefulness" or even recreation. We simply need that wild country available to us, even if we never do more than drive to its edge and look in. For it can be a means of reassuring ourselves of our sanity as creatures, a part of the geography of hope.

Very sincerely yours,
Wallace Stegner

« *To: Stewart Udall* • *September 22, 1961* »

MEMORANDUM:
To Stewart Udall, Secretary of the Interior
At the 45th meeting of the National Parks Advisory Board in Olympic National Park, September 15–19, 1961, Larry Cook reported on the experimental mothering by the Park Service of a group of African students during the past summer. Later the Advisory Board unanimously passed a

resolution urging continuation of this hands-across-the-sea program by the National Park Service, as one means of counteracting in the African and Asian mind the idea that America is a country built of, by, and for materialistic gain. Our system of national parks, the resolution points out, is visible and inspiring proof that aesthetic and spiritual values are built into America and that the nation has made persistent efforts to maintain them.

The resolution and the action it proposes are admirable, but I wonder if there is not a much greater opportunity open to us. If one summer under the wing of the National Park Service will give a handful of African or Asian students a broader, warmer, friendlier, and more humane view of America, then the national parks and the philosophy behind them—a philosophy completely American and in its civilized implications in advance of the whole world—are worth being exported to the millions of Africans and Asians who will never see America. I do not mean travel posters, nor film shorts of inspiring scenery, nor even excellent scenery-and-wildlife movies such as Disney's *Roosevelt Elk*. I mean a serious, full-length movie on the National Park System, as carefully written and professionally made as the Williamsburg film, and put together in such a way that, while holding an audience's attention with the sheer beauty of the scenes in which it is filmed, it is also the stirring presentation of an idea and an ideal.

One of the surest signs of maturity in an individual or a nation is the strength to stay one's hand, to forego or renounce, when one has the power to do otherwise. Our National Park System is a willed renunciation by the present in favor of the future, a foregoing of material and short-range profit in favor of long-range public good. There is no aspect of its national life where America shows to better advantage than in its system of national parks. Though the idea has been copied around the globe, I do not believe that we have ever adequately told the national parks story in our program of overseas information. It is customary to fill USIA[5] library windows with blow-ups of Old Faithful in eruption and of tourists hanging their heels over the rim of the Grand Canyon, but there our propaganda exploitation of the national parks is likely to end. The films that are shown in USIA libraries and sent around to provincial centers in Europe, Africa, and Asia are commonly films on TVA,[6] industrial production, reclamation, and

---

5. United States Information Agency.
6. Tennessee Valley Authority.

other subjects which fit in with the "nation-building" preoccupations of emerging nations. That is, in the very selection we make from our own civilization, we strengthen the image of America as a nation obsessed with practical and materialistic matters, and at the same time we subtly corroborate the bulldozer bias of nations eager to industrialize as rapidly as possible. By showing these nations another and more humane side of our country, we might not only persuade them that our democracy has flowered in non-material ways, but teach them, for the world's good and their own, to make reservations of their own scenery and wildlife for the future.

A National Parks movie, in other words, might serve the purposes both of American overseas information and of the broad conservation movement. It would also, beyond question, be a most effective instrument for furthering the conservation movement among our own citizens. The idea which you have been so effectively hammering home, that our opportunity to save something more for the future will come within the next ten years or never, can get substantial help from such a movie as this. An intelligent, dramatic, and effective presentation of what we have done is one of the ways of suggesting what we might do. For years to come it could be a major element in the interpretation programs of all our parks.

Now is no time to prepare a shooting script of a movie that has neither a producer nor funds, but it is clear to me that there are a thousand opportunities for beautiful photography as well as some dramatic episodes. There is a good deal of voltage in the story of the birth of the idea, when a group sitting around the campfire with Hayden's Survey in Yellowstone got a kind of simultaneous inspiration and vowed to get that beautiful country made into a park; and later, when, with the aid of W. H. Jackson's photographs and Thomas Moran's watercolors, they absolutely swept the Congress off its feet. There is much that could be done with Muir in Yosemite, and with Powell in the Grand Canyon, and much more that could be done with the great periods during the administrations of Theodore Roosevelt, Wilson, and F.D.R., when the National Park reservations were so largely increased. I do not imagine we want any inter-bureau wrangles dramatized, but if we do, I can write you a stirring sequence on Dinosaur. But mostly, I suspect, what this movie should have in it is a pictorial record of how the idea born around the Yellowstone campfire has flowered in terms of human use, human responsibility, and human enjoyment. That story is almost the only evidence we have that God was right in entrusting a virgin continent to us.

We should learn, as Robert Frost says, to take our own side in an argument, and make use of it. I spoke briefly about all this to Connie Wirth and Dan Beard at Olympic. They tell me that there is no such movie in existence. The closest thing to it is a recent National Geographic Society film which does not seem to fill all the bill. I have not seen it, and so cannot say how close it comes. It appears too that though the National Park Service is expanding into these public relations fields, it does not have the funds now, and will not have them in the foreseeable future, to do a movie of the length and elaborateness which I have suggested. There are, however, two possibilities, not mutually exclusive, which occur to me. One is that Ed Murrow be approached to see if his expanded budget does not include funds that might be diverted to the purpose of a National Parks film made primarily for overseas consumption but authorized for domestic showing as well. The other is that Laurance Rockefeller might be asked to underwrite a National Parks film to be made available to all interpretation programs in our national parks and monuments and also to Mr. Murrow's program of overseas information. The spectacular success of the Williamsburg film offers both a model and a precedent, and Mr. Rockefeller's lasting interest in conservation suggests that he would not be hostile to the idea.

If you see anything in this notion, which for all I know may have been proposed many times before and which may have impassable difficulties in its road, I suggest that we might try to organize a meeting including yourself, Mr. Murrow, Mr. Wirth and Mr. Beard in the projection room of the National Park Service offices, where Connie Wirth could arrange showings of all the available park films. From personal viewings and from other information I am convinced that none of these will do the job, though it is possible that Mr. Murrow could find some stop-gap use for some of them. If they do prove to be inadequate, and if Mr. Rockefeller or Mr. Murrow or both are interested in exploring the idea further, I would be happy to dig into Park Service history and try to prepare some sort of treatment for future consideration. There is probably no chance of its being half so dramatic as the Williamsburg film, but still there are dramatic episodes and I should think that what we may lack in dramatic intensity can be made up by beautiful photography and by the driving force of an idea now nearly a hundred years old and fresher than it ever was.

Wallace Stegner

« *To: Stewart Udall* • *October 23, 1961* »

MEMORANDUM:

To Stewart Udall, Secretary of the Interior

Subject: Building a conservation backfire in Utah

During the Escalante Basin trip we discussed at length, and on several occasions, the possibilities of organizing the conservation sentiment that undoubtedly does exist in Utah, but seldom makes itself heard. Dean Brimhall, Bates Wilson, and Bill Krueger all felt that local opinion in proposed park areas is pretty largely ignorant and indifferent. Where it is formed at all, it is likely to be formed by resource interests such as uranium, oil, and grazing, and by the politicians subservient to these. They might be very much more effectively opposed if the hierarchy of the Church were not generally in the same camp, drawn there by its considerable wealth and by its general conservatism. This frame of mind, the Resource-Republican variety of States Rightsism, is common enough throughout the West. It is probably least diluted in Wyoming, where the stockmen dominate the State, and in Utah, where the existence of the Mormon Church creates a special condition and a special difficulty.

When the Church chooses a side, it is difficult for the garden-variety Mormon to resist it publicly, though he may do so in the secrecy of the polls. Moreover, the influence of the Church on all state affairs does not wane, but increases. When I was a student in Salt Lake City, the Mormon–Gentile proportion in the city was about 40–60; now, according to Dean Brimhall, it is more like 70–30. In back-country towns like Escalante, it is about 95–05. The starvation of opportunity about which Utahns complain is a reality: the State has exported much of its best and highest-trained manpower for decades. But if opportunity within the State is meager for a Mormon boy, it is even meagerer for a Gentile, and this, plus a continued campaign for home missionary work, has made Salt Lake increasingly Mormon in its population and its attitudes. The Church has always owned the *Deseret News*; now it also owns a controlling interest in the *Tribune-Telegram*, and has in effect joined forces with the Gentile mining and refining and industrial interests that founded the *Tribune* in the first place as an opposition paper. There is no opposition paper now. I don't believe there is an opposition radio station or television channel either, though I have not had time to look into this.

Since the hierarchy is generally on the Clyde-Bennett side, and since it controls the media of communication, and since it absolutely controls Brigham Young University, largely controls Utah State, and considerably dominates the University of Utah, the organization of any opposition opinion will be difficult and slow. It will have to proceed without actively offending the Church—will have to pretend the Church doesn't figure in this, as technically it doesn't. It will have to mobilize opinion that is largely democratic and often Gentile or jack-Mormon, and do it in such a way that it does not drive away those good Mormons of good will and good sense who probably hold the balance of power in the State.

The first step must be the organization of the scattered supporters of the park-and-wilderness philosophy into some body which can, with both the force and the anonymity of a group, create a conservation movement in Utah and make it clear that Clyde and Bennett speak not for the people of Utah but for special interests, and not for the welfare of the State but for the fast buck benefiting the few. Such a Utah Conservation Council could operate in several ways. (1) It could—and should, early—hold a well-publicized meeting, with a speaker of impressive stature, which would get the program stated and make it plain that this sort of opinion exists. (2) It should enlist the aid of all the conservation societies, whether they have branches in Utah or not. (3) It should promote the showing of Utah park-lands movies, if there are any available, or slides, if that is all we have, to groups of all sizes and political complexions. (4) It should answer the pseudo-economic arguments of the Clyde-Bennett axis with economic arguments on the other side, pointing out with all the figures available, that a park is an eternally renewable resource and that its economic value over any extended time will surely be greater than that of all the uranium mines or oil wells in the area. In this connection, the Council should have made available to it as early as possible the study of the potential benefits of the Canyonlands Park which is currently being made for the NPS by the University of Utah.

None of this can be done in a month, or even a year. To begin, I shall communicate discreetly with a certain few people in Utah of whose opinions and energy we are sure, to see if I can get them to the point of organizing, and to assure them of the very great amounts of help that will come to them as soon as they do. I can cite them the example and the experience of similar associations in other states (e.g., the Great Basin group in Nevada) and suggest at least a preliminary program aiming at passage of the Wilderness and Canyonlands bills. In this first group I would surely write to Dean Brimhall of Fruita, Clyde van Hemert of Escalante, Angus Woodbury of Salt Lake City, Ernie Linford of the *Salt Lake Tribune*, the Points and Pebbles Club of Moab, the Wasatch Mountain Club, perhaps the Utah Wildlife Federation, perhaps (I don't know him) Carl Bauer, Utah vice president of the Federation of Western Outdoor Clubs, as well as to Grant Prisbrey and other of your personal correspondents. Once there is an active existing core, I know many Salt Lake people who would be attracted to it; they would be too inert to start it, but sympathetic enough to be eventually galvanized.

In all of this I stand in a rather odd position. I am known to be a liberal and a democrat, and I was active in the Dinosaur fight, and for these I am looked on with suspicion. On the other hand, I am in many eyes a Local Boy Who Made Good, and besides that I have written a good many things about Utah, and Utah is fantastically sensitive to praise and publicity "outside." I think that anything on Utah's park possibilities that I wrote would be more persuasive to university people, especially, than someone else's writings on the same subject. I am supposed to Know, in a hometown way, and to be sympathetic with Utah at large. For that matter, I am. So I shall immediately write Art Deck of the *Salt Lake Tribune* to see if I can write him a feature on the Utah parks situation. Somewhat later I would like to write at least one travel article (probably on the Escalante Canyons) for some national magazine and in the midst of a lot of praise of Utah scenery, get in a plug to make a lot of it Parks for America. Another possibility is a piece on the High Plateaus of Utah, with a conclusion that would ask for the inclusion of part or all of Thousand Lake Mountain with Capitol Reef to make a great national park.

These proposals are in line with our conversation this morning (Oct. 23). I shall go ahead on them at once. If there are fees involved in any of the articles that may result, I assume that while I am with the Department there is some rule specifying where they should be sent. But even while I am with the Department, I think it might be strategic for me to work as an individual in placing the articles, at least those on any aspect of the Utah situation.

Wallace E. Stegner

« *To: Mrs. Kenneth Brown* • *October 26, 1961* »

Dear Mrs. Brown:

What I am doing in the Department of the Interior is more or less what I have been doing, in my off hours, for years: trying to promote conservation thinking and conservation acting in as many ways as I can, from neighborhood green belts to national parks. I am not specifically doing any writing; mainly I am assisting to frame policy, but if it takes some writing to do that, I am willing.

You speak of the writer's involvement in his society. I think too many writers are far too little involved. They sit in the middle of their own skulls, or their own endocrines, and snipe at the saints, politicians, working people, house-wives, and bureaucrats who have to keep their world running. This doesn't mean I am anti-literary. The highest thing I can think of doing is literary. But literature does not exist in a vacuum, or even in a partial vacuum. We are neither detached nor semi-detached, but are linked to our world by a million interdependencies. To deny the interdependencies, while living on the comforts and services that they make possible, is adolescent when it isn't downright dishonest. And I would as soon say it to Henry Miller as to the book reviewer on the *Des Moines Register*.

As for writing workshops, they are just that, but they are also places where a human being can grow a centimeter or so if he tries. I am not so much interested in teaching "techniques," which are after all only the art of packaging. I'm interested in what's in the package, thought in the way of idea and belief—and I hope I don't have to agree with it before I respect it.

Sincerely,

Wallace Stegner

« *To: Stewart Udall* • *No Date, 1961* »

MEMORANDUM

To Stewart Udall, Secretary of the Interior

Subject: A Film on the American Land

The intention is to create a film which will present, in poetic and evocative images, the natural environment which we as Americans have inherited and in which we live as fish live in a pond. Implicit in this film will have to be attitudes of respect toward the natural and, in Schweitzer's phrase, reverence for life. It would not be the intention of this film to celebrate nature over the machine, but to celebrate nature beyond the machine, in addition to the machine. For if the machine provides much of the material goods we depend on, nature provides much of the quality of our living, and this too many people living a termite life in glass and asphalt and air-conditioning are likely to miss.

The base from which we take off will probably be the Ansel Adams–Nancy Newhall book, *This is the American Earth*. How much can actually be done to transfer those magnificent photographs to the motion picture medium is something that the actual making of the film will have to test. Perhaps the correspondence can be close, perhaps the film will have to diverge fairly sharply. Certainly the book's theme of the development of a "land ethic," what Aldo Leopold defined as "a harmony between men and land," should transfer intact. But there are some things that can be done in motion pictures that cannot be done in stills, however magnificent; and there is an audience that will attend and profit from movies that will rarely read books; and these are the justifications and the opportunity for the film we propose.

For example, it is possible in a film to give a far more graphic picture of the damage and destruction we have done during our occupancy of this continent. Instead of a static gully, the motion picture can present, in a few seconds, the whole process of gully erosion. Instead of a hillside of blackened stumps, the movie can show great trees coming down, the cats crushing through the understory, fire gulping the slash and crowning off across a virgin stand of timber. The movie can present in more telling terms not only the unhealthy bedlam of overcrowded slums, freeways, amusement parks, rush-hours, and assembly lines, and the sterility of a life of glass and stone, but also the very sound and shine of mountain water, the living dart of bird or animal, the identity and dignity that a human being achieves the moment he is alone and quiet in the open.

More than this, with modern techniques we can go below the surfaces of the life around us, show a chick forming as red lines and the throb of a heart within the egg, show plants germinating, roots probing the soil, aphids working the tender shoots and ants herding the aphids. We can go underwater and watch raindrops pebble a pond, or a beaver or muskrat building a stick lodge. We can treat the community of life of which we are a part, treat it at any level, and treat also the violences we do to it, the exterminations we threaten to commit, the steps we take to protect this life community against its worst enemy, ourselves. However we do this, the theme should be respect for the land, reverence for life. It is a miracle we live on, and we are part of it, and all parts of it depend on all other parts.

We live, literally, by courtesy of the earthworm. Somehow, in striking visual ways but without any didactic statement, without preaching, this film ought to illustrate Francis Thompson's "Thou canst not stir a flower / Without troubling a Star," and Donne's meditation, "No man is an island, entire of itself but every man is a part of the continent, a piece of the Main."

Obviously the unity of such a film will depend on the script, and I am not prepared to write a script yet. Nancy Newhall's text, though somewhat tiptoe and lush, gives many clues, and contains some striking images. I think the true continuity must be that of the interdependence of life—all life, even the apparent pests—and the losses men suffer when they forget this and act not as part of nature, but as its irresponsible masters. What is at stake is the quality of our living. We could make the film test that by examining the life around us in all its variety and mystery.

And none of this, done right, need be the slightest bit corny or sentimental. It can be, and should be, a kind of hymn.

Wallace E. Stegner

« *To: George Stewart* • *November 1, 1961* »

Dear George,

We're sorry we missed you when you got back. I guess we might have overlapped just a few days, since we went up to the Olympic Peninsula to attend a meeting on Sept. 1? or so, and you may have been back by then. We were too swamped to do much but get our gear aboard, or we would have called before we left.

We're still swamped. Pleasantly so for me, somewhat drearily so for Mary, at least during the week. I find this boondoggling a most demanding job, and leave here before 8 AM and get home about 6. The house we took sight unseen is a gloomy three-story barn, sparsely and whimsically furnished, and poor Mary with her lust for light has to get outside to get any. Also we know only a few people, and she's had some days to spend all by herself. On the other hand, we've got around some evenings and weekends, and have met some interesting people in and out of government. Last weekend, passing through Gettysburg, we murmured your name reverently.

My chores are concerned mainly with policy and planning in several areas of conservation, and by whatever means offers itself. It's a little like a three-headed boy trying to scratch his head with both hands full of pencils. But it's exciting, and there's an opportunity to do something, right now, that if it isn't done now can never be done again. So on occasion we even get urgent. Much of what we're urgent about won't show until after January, but I hope it shows then with some logic and persuasiveness.

We return to Los Altos either just before or just after Christmas, depending on whether Page and Marion have agreed to visit her parents in Ohio, or not. In either case we'll be in residence, and hot for conversation with the Stewarts, after Dec. 28.

My trails book lies cold and dead right where I aborted it.[7] Saskatchewan isn't quite finished, even[8]—I've got to rewrite the last 100 pages, and was going to evenings and weekends. Hah. Under no circumstances am I likely to have the Mormons under control before next summer, alas.

Best to you both,
Wally

« *To: Stewart Udall* • *December 30, 1961* »

Dear Stewart:
Herewith the annotated outline,[9] with my apologies for the fact that it comes a few days late, and without an adequate bibliography for several chapters. The misbegotten university library closed down totally for the holidays just when I wanted to use it. I have, however, kept a carbon of the outline, and I'll send on some supplementary bibliographical suggestions after the first of the year. Maybe there is enough here to keep you busy.

As one who has written too many books, and got trapped in too many of the customary pitfalls, let me urge you not to think of this outline as anything holy. It is a suggestion, a sort of hypothesis, a way of getting started, and your reading and thinking as well as the reading and thinking of the people working with you may well alter the direction or the organization of any part. Similarly, the four chapters that I drafted are only rough drafts. If I were carrying on with them myself, I would certainly insert and delete and revise several times before letting go of them. There is actually no real

---

7. *The Gathering of Zion.*
8. *Wolf Willow.*
9. An outline Stegner made for Udall's book, *The Quiet Crisis.*

way of telling what they may ultimately need, until the whole book has been finished in rough draft. Then the inter-relation of the parts, and the way ideas have to be cross-referenced between chapters, will begin to come clear. And always, always, there is the possibility of more learning, more knowledge. No book is ever finished, in the sense that its author knows the whole subject and has said it just as he wants to. Every book is eventually relinquished, with bugs still in it, and weak spots, and places where the author would like to do some more reading and thinking. In a quick book like this one, the discomforts of early relinquishment may be greater than usual. Fortunately there is no doubt at all about the theme, and the final chapter, containing the Program, is a matter of your personal conviction and personal politics, so that it's bound to end strong. I even think it will begin strong and continue strong, but I wish I had been able to leave you something a little more finished to work from.

Al Josephy writes that he couldn't make it after all. I'm sorry, he would have been a help. As a matter of fact, he asks how he might be able to help you from New York, and I am going to write him that he could help a great deal with illustrations, and perhaps with checking continuities and organization as the draft emerges. I'll be sending you sometime in the next couple of weeks some rudimentary suggestions for pictures. Meantime, I think you'd be well advised to put Al to work from the outline, and also to ask Al Edwards to get his friends at the Museum of Natural History working on the problem. Don Moser, if he manages to get down to you, has had some experience in that line, too, and should be helpful. I am writing him to give him the goose.

The news about the Frost film is fine. Let us now praise famous men and pray these movie makers do something worthy of their subject. I'll keep in touch with Foote and Kay, and I have promised Foote to go over his rushes and comment on them.

I think I have not yet said, for record, what an exhilarating experience Washington was. As my grandmother used to say, I enyoyed it. I also got a good inside glimpse of your vision of the next few years in conservation, and I'm sold. I'll help any way I can.

Yours,

Wally

« *To: Stewart Udall* • *December 9, 1962* »

Dear Stewart:

Many thanks for the kind words about *Wolf Willow*. The most remarkable thing I can think of, practically, is that you should find time and energy to read it. That you should like it is an extra dividend. It may even be, though, that your prediction that it won't sell is premature. After a slow start, it seems to be beginning to move—not big, but pretty steady. And if it doesn't fulfill your prediction about being around a while, I'll haunt somebody. I felt this one the way old Robert feels some of his poems. I wanted to put it out there where they couldn't overlook it even if they wanted to. So if they overlook it in spite of me I'll begin introducing cobras into the drains of critics and booksellers.

I never did write you of the Hawaii meeting[10] because I did not suppose you had time for gossipy letters, and there was nothing outside of the official resolutions to say—except that we all had a hell of a good time, saw Hawaii going to the devil even faster than California, ate indigenous and drank exotic, and came home with the flu. I got to know the Board members somewhat better, and I remain firm in my conviction that Stan Cain is the best man among us. But I gather that you feel the same way, since you've put him on your Wildlife board too.

I hear that as a member of the Sierra Club and the Wilderness Society I am engaged in suing you. Well, anything to make you do your duty.

I'm glad that you have Harold Gilliam working on the book.[11] He's a good one, if I do say it myself, as taught him. And I hope you can keep him around until a complete draft of the book is finished. I imagine that you're well aware, without my telling you, that a book suffers from a series of short-term workers. If Harold could take it clear through to the end, and you take it over from there and put your fingerprints on it, it would come out looking and feeling more like a single continuous thing than if it's put together by a committee first, and then you try to make unity of it. What I saw last summer looked very promising, and what I heard from Harold in Volcano House sounded good. I'll be looking forward to the whole thing. I do not envy you, though. I've been doing nothing but reading Mormon history for five months, and I haven't yet started to write. Saturation, they

---

10. National Park Advisory Board.

11. *The Quiet Crisis.* Udall credits "my friend Wallace Stegner, who joined my staff for a few weeks in the fall of 1961" for the original outline of the book.

tell me, is the historian's ideal. But it's hard to manage when you have another job or two in hand.

Mary joins me in greetings to you and Lee. We remember Washington with a slow country wonder. Have a Merry Christmas and a New Year full of New Parks.

Yours,

Wally

« *To: Stewart Udall* • *December 7, 1963* »

Dear Stewart:

The first thing I did when we got home was to read through *The Quiet Crisis*. It was a great experience—seeing the ideas we had often talked over put down finally and persuasively. It's a fine and moving book. I am pleased and astonished at how you have been able to take the rough drafts or rough ideas of many different people and make them all your own. You have made a shorter book than I would have—and that is a compliment: one of the marks of your personal style is that things are boiled down to their essence. I might have wasted time on rhetoric, if I had been doing it, and would have made every chapter longer. But your way is better. You lay it out clearly and without frills or waste. The modifications you have made in my original, hasty suggestion for an outline are all sound—the Olmsted[12] chapter, the chapters on the Roosevelts and on the philanthropists, are splendid; and I'm pleased at the way the philosophy-action relationship is worked out, section by section. Altogether, a splendid job. I imagine you must feel very good about it. Because we've been out of touch, I have seen only one review, that in the *New Yorker*, but that, even in that snide and snitzy magazine, was very respectful, so that I imagine you must have got a good press. The pictures are as good as I would have imagined them, from my quick look at some photostats in Al Josephy's[13] office last September. It could be a rallying cry; let's hope it will be. I'm proud to have been even briefly associated with it, proud of your acknowledgment of my simple-minded efforts to suggest a way of beginning, and touched by your dedication and inscription.

---

12. Frederick Law Olmstead.

13. Alvin M. Josephy, Jr., author of many books on the American Indian. He served as a consultant to Secretary Udall, and was appointed a Commissioner of the Indian Arts and Crafts Board of the Department of the Interior in 1966.

Since I last saw you to talk to you, several important and even disastrous things have happened, and because I've been away in a far country I have a lot of catching-up to do. I wish I could see you and talk to you. The disaster of the President's death must obviously have shaken you clear down to the ground. It did us—we were in Athens, and for ten days were constantly being approached, often in tears, by Greeks anxious to express their fellow-feeling and sympathy, as if we had all suffered a personal loss, which indeed we had. I realized after I had got home that I was half expecting to get back here and find it not true—like one returning from a nightmare. But it miserably is true, and what it does to your program, what it does to you personally, what it does to the whole liberal cause, what it does to the sort of honor and probity and high-mindedness Mr. Kennedy stood for—these are rough questions. I hope that Mr. Johnson is sympathetic to conservation as an idea, and I hope that sheer shame may help Congress get a few things through. But mainly we watch in uncertainty to see what events will bring forth.

There is much that I must catch up on with regard to the Advisory Board,[14] Connie's[15] departure, etc., etc. I never, in fact, felt so frustrated, lost, and at sea. But I shall try to discover the answers to a few things from other sources, and not to bother you for answers. My principal reason for writing this letter is to tell you how well I think the book comes off, and to thank you for the warm inscription. I do not expect or intend to miss any more meetings of the Advisory Board while I am a Member of it, and so I expect to see you in the spring in Washington. If you come out here any time, whether in connection with the 1964 campaign or on any other business, will you give us the chance to put you up? I promise not to stall you at the valet parking at the airport a second time. And if there's a chance you might be induced to speak at Stanford, please give me warning, as far in advance as possible, so that I can set it up.

Our very best to Lee. I tried to call her when we were in Washington briefly in September (you were off climbing Kilimanjaro), but didn't catch her in.

Again, congratulations on the book.

Yours,

Wally

---

14. National Park Advisory Board.
15. Conrad Wirth, Director of the National Parks.

« *To: Stewart Udall* • *February 14, 1967* »

Dear Stewart:

I read your essay with real enthusiasm, cheering and waving my hat. As you know, and as we have all known for much too long, considering how little we have done about it, the crux of the Great Society, the Good Life, Quality in Living, Conservation, and much else is over-population or its threat. A bunch of businessmen that Bill Patterson of the *Saturday Review* spoke to recently listed the population problem sixth or seventh on their list of things that had most shaken and endangered and affected the world in the last quarter century. They should have put it first. Ten years from now they will.

Meantime, your essay: I have put a few, a very few, marginal comments on it. It has your customary punch and directness; it doesn't let a reader roll with anything, but hits him again while he's rolling. Whether in fact you dare say these things only you can decide. You aren't as vulnerable as Bobbie Kennedy, but with six children you will sure as hell come in for some journalistic ribbing. (I am not recommending that you drown any of them.) You can also appraise the response of Cardinal Cushing and Cardinal Spellman as well as I can. The Pope carefully missed a beautiful chance to put the Church on the side of sense when he visited this country a year or so ago, and in spite of some straws and dirt in the wind, I don't see the Church accepting calmly the ideas you propose. In fact, my Mormon friends (I have a couple) assure me that in the eyes of the LDS Church an infant is a soul before the sperm ever finds the egg, and what does that do to birth control?

Apart from how much you dare say from a Cabinet and Family Room position, I have little to suggest on how you say it. Only in a half dozen places you slip from a level of diction that is clear, dignified, sober, and persuasive into a sort of political-speech argot, and I think that each time you do it you weaken your case. Sweeping things under the rug, using phrases like population-wise and time-wise, speaking of the be-all and end-all, and warnings that are writ large, you lower the level of the discourse along with the level of the diction.

With regard to your query on page 35, about what else you might add in a scarehead way to characterize an America of a billion people. Put it in terms of cities 5 times everything—5 New Yorks, 5 Greater Bostons, 5 Los

Angeleses, 5 Philadelphias, 5 Dallas–Fort Worths, and on and on. Or cite what I heard the other day—right now, at less than 200,000,000, schools in Oakland are making a practice of sending busloads of school children to the Duveneck Ranch, just over the hill from us, to let the kids see cattle, horses, and barnyard fowls. Multiply that by five. Or spread the Megalopolis that now stretches from Portland, Maine to Jacksonville out by a factor of five— it can't go anywhere but inland. Multiply by five the pollution of Lake Erie and the other Great Lakes—which Thoreau a little over a century said would remain unpeopled wilderness for many generations. Multiply deaths from emphysema by five or more. Thicken the air on 20th Street in Washington five times—you'd need an airplow to get you to work. Thicken the Potomac five times and you could plow it, and plant greenery to re-start the carbon cycle.

This could go on. It's a science fiction job, essentially. And for every condition that you multiply by five, don't forget to multiply by five the engines and installations and committees and protest groups and public agencies designed to cope with it. Jesus, it makes my head ache even to consult on this.

Please let me know if I can do anything more. You needn't worry about the writing—it is clean and crisp, with only the few slips that I have mentioned. Coming from you, with your authority behind it, it will be front page. I hope you will feel that you can speak this candidly, because unless you shock and jolt people they won't pay attention. As Flannery O'Connor said when asked why she wrote such grotesque stories, "you can only make a deaf man hear you if you shout."

Our best to you and Lee. I've got a piece on the Everglades coming soon in *Saturday Review*. Let us hope it makes some ammunition for the poor old NPS.[16]

Yours,
Wallace Stegner

---

16. National Park Service.

« *To: Randy Morgenson* • *January 26, 1972* »

Dear Randy:

Forgive the delay in answering you, and commenting on your two essays.[17] We've been remodeling the house, and I haven't been able to find anything, much less deal with it.

I've been interested to read your two pieces. They're literate, sensitive, and earnest, and they probably made you feel good when you wrote them, because it is always a satisfaction to try to nail down precisely what it is one feels, and how. But I doubt that they'll do for publication, and I'll try to tell you why, always with the risk of being blunt and seeming unfriendly. I can't help saying what I think, because it's the only way I ever found of being helpful to a young writer, and it hasn't always worked even then. But being soft wouldn't work at all.

So: first the Yosemite piece. It's all about your feelings and sensations, and those don't communicate well to a reader. He half feels you indulging a sort of yeasty nature mysticism, and he has no way to join you in it because you give him nothing concrete enough to see or smell or touch or hear. Your pictures are all generalized pictures. There is no foreground, middle ground, background; there are not even details, but only generalizations of details. "As warm sunlight reached into the canyon, chipmunks and chickarees chase over Sierra slickrock and across dried grassy places"—not any special chipmunk, not any special grassy place. The sunlight doesn't come into the canyon through the slot of any particular upper canyon, it touches no special surface or plane or color of rock, it casts no shadows. It is a generalized sunlight hitting not a place, Yosemite Canyon, but a generalized Nature crossed by anonymous and generalized little beasties. I would feel the emotions this morning arouses in you if I could put myself in your shoes, look in a given direction, see a particular cliff in a particular state of sun and shadow, watch a particular chickadee doing something special in a particular piece of grassy meadow.

And so through the whole essay. You come at us emotion-first. You try to evoke the emotions without ever giving us the particular place, picture, actions, sense impressions, that might let us feel as you do. Does this mean

---

17. Randy Morgenson was a seasonal backcountry ranger in Yosemite National Park who vanished in July of 1996 and was never seen again. A book about his life and disappearance has been written by Eric Bhelm entitled *The Last Season*.

anything to you? It may be you're feeling the influence of Muir, who did get away with a lot of generalizing of that kind. But he got away with it partly because he had a sort of exclamatory genius, he was a whirling dervish of Nature, and not all of us can be anything like that. Also he gave us a lot of very particular pictures, and he derived his emotions primarily from such particular actions as climbing up a particular pine in a high wind, or inching out beside the lip of Yosemite Falls and listening to the bombs of water thunder by his ear. If I were you, I'd follow Thoreau or somebody like that rather than Muir. Read Thoreau on the ant battle, and see how very particular that is. As for the emotions themselves, those you try to evoke in us seem a little standard, perhaps because they don't arise out of a particular dramatized situation or scene. You may take it as my version of an almost-infallible rule of thumb that nature description by itself is very hard to get away with—it's necessarily pretty inert and undramatic; that Nature description with added emotional responses is almost as hard—especially if you give even a hint of swooning with ineffable feelings; and that the best Nature description is that which is particular, special, and dramatized, so that it communicates its own emotional responses, and the author doesn't have to pump at them. You know a lot about the mountains that doesn't *show* here. If you tried to tell us what you know, your feelings about the mountains would probably come across more strongly than they do when you work on the feelings exclusively.

The Indian-village sketch has some of the same misplaced emphasis and generalized pictures. I never see these Indian farmers or feel them as people, I never see their fields or houses or village streets. Where is this? Somewhere on the Deccan plateau? Hyderabad? Wherever it is, we ought to see it. If it's Hyderabad we ought to see those rocky outcrops, we ought to see the horizon broken by the dome of a Mogul tomb, we ought to see gypsies going by with mirrors sewn into the bright cloth of their dresses, we ought to smell the smell of earth and wood or dung-smoke, we ought to know whether these farmers are black or brown, skinny or fat, smiling or dour. We ought to know whether they wear the dhoti, whether they're half bare—all sorts of things that we don't know. We ought to know, for that matter, exactly what province we're in, what language they speak, whether they're Hindu or Moslem or Jain. We ought to have some particular picture, some particular dramatization, of a native ceremonial day, so that when we get around to Christmas (is it Christmas? You don't tell us) we have something solid for a cross-cultural transfer to walk on. Just as a sample: Once in Hyderabad I watched a tribe of the local gypsies, a tribe whose name I can't now remember—Dravidians, I suppose they were—conducting a child's funeral. They came along the road singing and dancing and laughing, carrying that little three-foot coffin on their shoulders with the sun glinting off the pieces of mirror they had sewn, along with shiny rocks and bits of porcelain and God knows what else, into their clothing. They glittered and glanced like a trout in the rainbow at the bottom of a clear creek, and they seemed to be having the happiest time in the world. Well, if I had been wanting to make an essay on cross-culture sympathy, I could have set up a contrast between their sort of funeral and one of our own—somber, black-draped, tearful, absolutely at odds with our supposed Christian hope of immortality. And I could have posed it in dramatic terms by having that Dravidian child's funeral the funeral of a child of a friend of mine, and the Christian funeral a funeral in my own family—brother or sister or mother or father, somebody close. Then I think I could have made my point about the brotherhood of man that shines through all cultural differences, and I think a reader might have got what I meant without my having to tell him.

Does this mean anything to you? I hope so. I do think that you have to steer away from the general, quit looking at the heavens and thinking large vague thoughts and feeling large vague feelings, and start watching the pebbles and ants and sunshine and shadow right under your feet. If you can learn that, and discipline yourself to keep remembering it, you can do with words what you obviously want to do with then.

Good luck. My best to your family, who were one of the pleasantest things about Yosemite. And just a last word: A French friend who yesterday blew in from Paris tells me that France has totally banned snowmobiles, anywhere. Who are we that we should trail behind the French? What's the status on snowmobiles in the park, now? Any decisions? I haven't heard.

Best,
Wallace Stegner

« *To: Tom Graff, Environmental Defense Fund* • *November 10, 1984* »

Dear Tom Graff, Environmental Defense Fund
(and members and guests):
First my regret that unavoidable business will keep me in New York and force me to miss this celebration, to which I had looked forward.

Next my thanks to Margaret Owings, who has kindly promised to carry my greeting.

Finally my congratulations to this organization and all associated organizations and individuals who have done so much in the past year to insure us a future worth inheriting.

Because of the late triumph on the Tuolumne, it is of rivers that we think when we summarize the past year. Rivers have always appealed to the human imagination as symbols of life itself—its purity, its depth and mystery, its evanescence. A river is always passing but always there; it will take you with it or let you off. Once, writing about the first mountain river I ever knew, Henry's Fork of the Snake, I said that by such a stream it was impossible to believe that one would ever be tired or old. Now that I am demonstrably both, I can still value wild rivers both for the memories they provide—and Margaret can fill you in on the Colorado, which we went down together—and for the illusion they can revive of youth and life and freshness. No American should go through life without knowing a river, some river, and the wilder the better. I would not for any money relinquish my memories of swimming down Split Mountain Canyon on the Green, well before the sport of river running was invented. I treasure my memory of the little quiet river I was a boy on in Saskatchewan, where I snared suckers with a loop of copper wire from the footbridge, and learned the ways of ducks, muskrats, beavers, frogs, bank swallows, and a lot of other fellow creatures.

I am making myself homesick. What I intended to do was greet you at this dinner and applaud your support of the natural environment and the organizations such as this that defend it.

Sincerely,
Wallace Stegner

« *To: Margaret Owings* • *April 14, 1985* »

Dear Margaret:

The composite picture we might draw of you (like one of those drawings of suspects wanted by the police) might not strike you as very attractive, but believe me, you are hard to draw. You are as elegant and elusive as one of the mountain lions who owe you their personal and species life; as sleekly domestic as one of your sea otters floating comfortably on the swell and cracking shellfish on your stomach; as immovable, resistant, and ascendant as the Santa Lucia Mountains under whose loom you live; as restlessly active as the Pacific that beats at their feet; and visible from as far out to sea as Pico Peak.

Never mind how the elements of that picture fall together. We mean it in love and respect. For more than mountain lions, sea otters, coast redwoods, and the coastal mountains are in your debt. We are all in your debt for bringing such grace and conviction to the rescue of threatened life forms, and for the lesson that hope arises from dedication, effort, and a feeling for the relatedness of all life and the dependence of all life, including our own, on a healthy environment.

God bless. We salute you though we are unable to be present at the Environmental Defense Fund dinner which celebrates your leadership and inspiration.

Affectionately,
Wally

« *To: Charles Wilkinson* • *February 26, 1986* »

Dear Mr. Wilkinson:

I'm deeply indebted to you for sending on the copies of your two articles ("Western Water Law in Transition" and "The Greatest Good for the Greatest Number"), as well as your op-ed piece from the *Denver Post*. It is probably just as well that you left Colorado for Michigan about the time that was published; your life might have been in danger. I confess that I read both it and the Western Water Law piece with yells of delight and a sense of having come finally to the source of contemporary, up-to-date information that I have been looking for. It happens that I am to give the Cook Lectures at Michigan in the week of October 27 this year. I profoundly wish that you were still going to be there; and I warn you that I will be using a lot of your knowledge of recent water law. The subject of my lectures is supposed to be, broadly, the development of western institutions; and water is at the heart of those. I have the feeling, and it is correct, that I am barely beginning on the job of preparing these three talks—I'll have to spend the entire summer on them, and even then they will be far from the definitiveness I would like. Most of my ideas were formed on Powell and Webb, and both obviously need updating. Donald Worster, whose book *Rivers of Empire* is just about to come out, has been of great usefulness to me. So, in a less reliable, more journalistic way, has Marc Reisner, in a book called *Cadillac Desert*. But these books are only the popular summaries of certain problems I have to deal with; and in your articles, as well as the footnotes and citations therein, I get a lot of solid help.

How can we get together? I'll be here, with minor excursions of a few days to a week, until about mid-June. Then I'm going to Vermont again, with a carload of books and Xeroxed authorities, to brood from a distance about the West. Will you be coming through this way on your way back to Oregon before June 15? Or will you be in the East at all this summer? Our summer address is simply Greensboro, Vermont (Justice Rehnquist's too, if you're interested). If you're anywhere close it would be a great privilege to talk to you. Our own cottage is more like a shack, but we can find you a primitive bed and plenty to eat; or we can get you a room at the local inn. In case you're coming through the Bay Area before we leave, it's easier and somewhat less spartan.

I hope we can make contact in person. If we can't, maybe we can rely (reluctantly) on the U.S. Postal Service.

Sincerely,

Wallace Stegner

« *To: Charles Wilkinson* • *November 19, 1986* »

Dear Charles:

I cost myself two weeks of self-satisfaction and smugness by not getting around to your letter and lecture earlier. We got home two weeks ago, and I have been digging out ever since, and some things took precedence. But this morning I finally opened your envelope, and was (quite apart from the purring that your last page aroused) charmed, persuaded, and exhilarated by your lecture. It couldn't have been better said. It couldn't have been better-tempered, or more conciliatory to all parties of the nagging western dispute, or more likely to bring the warring parties into some sort of consensus that will not only work but will grow. I congratulate you. I will shamelessly steal from you. And if you don't mind, I will Xerox your speech and send it to some rancher friends of mine in Montana, even though they may have been in Billings to hear you, as well as to some environmentalists who have (like me) got a little rigid and self-righteous in their antagonism to both ranchers with grazing privileges on the public domain and to the bureaus who manage that domain. I hope (you have to) that you will publish it. I assume that it will be incorporated in some form in "The Lords of Yesterday,"[18] which I will look forward to with increased excitement.

Do you know Robert Redford? Have you participated in any of his peacemaking, consensus-building conferences at Sundance? You should have, and I will see that he gets a copy of this. If he already has it, then he will have two, which is all to the good.

Obviously you give me a hell of a lot more credit than I deserve, but I will take it, happily. Nothing would please me better than to have been even 2% responsible for starting you on your career of making the West work.

Cheers,

Wally

« To: Charles Wilkinson · April 21, 1987 »

Dear Charles,

Many thanks for the Indians volume. Pretty soon you will have every aspect of western land and water law tidied up and made intelligible, if not credible. I have had no time to read the book yet, being buried under proofs, deadlines, obligations, and requests. I don't know what I did to get hit with more work after retirement than I ever had before it. Knowing no other way, I am putting one foot after another, but it may be two or three weeks before I can find even bedside time for reading, and I want you to know how much I appreciate your thoughtfulness in sending it.

One of the smaller of my chores is the proofs of the Cook Lectures at Michigan, which the Michigan Press is publishing.[19] They are no more than a wide general summary, and will teach you nothing you don't already know by heart, but I will see that you get a copy anyway when the little book appears. One of the lectures, I think the one you were present at, will be published earlier in the *Michigan Quarterly*. Part of the third will appear in *American Heritage*. Apart from that I have done nothing but write angry letters in the environmental wars (and quarrel with the town council of Los Altos Hills about its subdivision ordinances). And some days I can't even get around to the angry letters. Maybe summer will be quieter.

---

18. Reprinted in Wilkinson's *Crossing the Next Meridian* (Washington, D.C.: Island Press, 1992).

19. *The American West as Living Space* (Ann Arbor: University of Michigan Press, 1987).

I have not seen Joe Sax since he moved to the Bay Area, but hope to soon. And I hope we see you if you get down this way. Don't overlook us.

Yours,

Wally

« *To: Charles Wilkinson* • *October 17, 1987* »

Dear Charles:

Last night I sweetened my mouth before sleeping with a hundred pages of Wilkinson, and came to the end of Chapter 5. It's going to be a splendid book.[20] You have a gift for clear, unconfusing, sequential exposition, and you've got any quantity of important facts to expose. The focus on the effect that laws have in freezing practice, often corrupt or misguided practice, is very effective. Most of us who don't know any law just work our mouths; you show how the cowboys and miners did it. I learned a lot from just three chapters. I will learn from every additional one.

Being an old freshman theme reader, I couldn't resist putting a few pencil marks in the margins—almost never anything but a question of idiom, or choice of word, or a minor solecism. You can ignore these if you want, for they are all trivial, and you have the invitation to kick me for impertinence next time you see me. But now and again I find that even fine writers don't know when they're dangling a participle.

The question of publication is not a question of if, but one of where. It's a more-than-publishable book, on the strength of three chapters. Whether a trade publisher who has to sell ten thousand copies or more to break even will think there are enough readers to warrant his risking it is another question. Almost any university or regional press would jump at it, and that at least gets it into libraries and into the hands of a select audience. I still think that Island Press, whose catalog I enclose, is a strong possibility for you. It's a sort of cross between a trade publisher and a specialty press, and its natural customers are precisely the people you hope to reach. Maybe you met Charles Savitt at the Wilderness Society meeting last month. In any case, he is one whose nostrils would begin to quiver at the possibility of getting this book, so keep him in mind. If I can help any with Random House or Doubleday or Viking, let me know what you'd like—letter to an

20. Eventually published as *Crossing the Next Meridian: Land, Water, and the Future of the West* (Washington, D.C.: Island Press, 1992).

editor or whatever. You won't need any helping letters to Island Press, I'm positive.

I'm still warm from that flattery you poured on me in Montana. Now how do I scramble up to the level you put me on? Alas.

All the best. Carry on.

Wally

« *To: Charles Wilkinson* • *March 24, 1990* »

Dear Charles,

Many thanks for the tape of the award proceedings. I like my curmudgeonly stance so well that I will probably adopt it permanently, and assault all reporters, interviewers, reviewers, and club women in that vein. I thought you rallied gamely from the assault, though. And I am really touched by the naming of the awards for me, in spite of my curmudgeon behavior. The awards went to two first-rate people. Let's hope they will inspire others to exercise themselves on behalf of the environment. And not merely pollution-cleanups, important as those are. As Aldo Leopold said, the science of land doctoring is well advanced; the art of land health is in its infancy. (Something like that he said.)

Now later. I began this letter this morning while sitting here waiting for a camera crew to get set up to show me At Work. So I thought I might as well do something useful, and started this letter. Then I got involved in a lot of nonsense, and only now, in the cool of the day, get back to finish.

We are reasonably—never unreasonably—well, and hope to stay that way. Some bookstore appearances for the *Collected Stories* will occupy the next month or six weeks. Maybe in June this film will be finished, and I may have to go wherever it premieres—Salt Lake or Los Angeles. In July we'll go to Vermont and I'll tear up the telephone by the roots and try to get in two months of quiet work. In September I hope to see you in the Adirondacks. Further than this, deponent sayeth not, because deponent doesn't know further than this.

Take it easy in the stretch, and save some of your energy for the fall meeting. This time, I really hope to make it. My best to Patty Limerick when you see her.

Best,

Wally

« *To: David Brower* • *May 16, 1990* »

Dear Dave,

Your autobiography[21] is in our hands, and though this new book of mine has kept me from having much reading time, I have read enough in it to recognize a lot of people and situations and battles, and to get an overview of the tremendous sweep and scope of your life. I knew it already, of course, but to see it put together in one continuous narrative is to be deeply impressed. Though we have not always agreed on tactics, particularly in that one bruising instance,[22] I never doubted that you were and are the most effective fighter for the environment in the whole round world. That impression is strengthened by the browsing that I have been able to do in the Life and Times. America, the world, all of us, are in your debt for your constancy, persistence, imaginativeness, and vision. I hope your book does more than well. I hope you live forever, and in a sense you will.

Our best to Anne.

Yours,

Wally

« *To: Dave Livermore* • *March 9, 1991* »

Dear Dave Livermore:

Thanks for your letter of March 5. I am saddened by it, for I hadn't known of Scott Matheson's death. That's a serious loss to Utah and to the cause of environmental sanity. It is absolutely appropriate that the wetland preserve at Moab should be re-named from Moab Slough to something commemorative of Scott Matheson, who was a good governor of Utah and a good friend of the earth.[23]

I don't know what to say about your invitation to speak on June 1. I would like very much to be there; I don't see any reason at the moment why

---

21. *For Earth's Sake: The Life and Times of David Brower* (Layton, UT: Peregrine Smith, 1990).

22. When Brower began to assume absolute power over Sierra Club policy in 1969, many among its leadership, including Stegner, opposed him. After a long and divisive battle, he was removed as director.

23. The Moab Slough is a large wetland on a bend of the Colorado River at Moab, Utah. It was renamed the Scott M. Matheson Wetlands Preserve at a dedication ceremony in June of 1991, which Stegner did attend.

I couldn't. But I am not young anymore, and I have learned to be cautious. Let me say that if I can't be there—and the condition of my aging skeleton will dictate the answer to that—I will definitely write a letter or message to be read on that occasion.

I would appreciate a reminding letter sometime in May, so that I don't foul things up by forgetting. But if indeed I can be there in person, I will let you know as early as I know myself.

Sincerely,
Wallace Stegner

« *To: Dave Livermore* • *May 17, 1991* »

Dear Dave:

Many thanks for your communiqué and the brochure on the Castle Valley Inn.[24] You have our itinerary exactly right, and we'll be happy to see you or your henchman at 11:58 AM on the 31st. Thank you for the meticulous arrangements, which we will take advantage of, be sure.

The Castle Valley Inn looks very special, and if it suits your arrangements, we'd like to stay there both Friday and Saturday nights. Our aged quirks are so many that we think it's best to drive, as we planned, even though it would be a privilege to go down in the Lear jet with Babbitt and Andrus.[25] The Monday night space at the Marriott is fine, and we thank you. And there's no need to reimburse us for anything, mainly because you've taken care of most of it in advance, but also because I can easily send you a summary after we return.

One question: My son Page and his wife will be putting the boats out at Green River about Saturday noon, after a run through Gray and Desolation Canyons. They will probably have to start immediately back to California, but if they don't, I wonder if I could ask them down to the barbecue at Ken Sleight's ranch on Saturday night.[26] Page writes a good deal of environmental stuff, knows Sleight and others in the Moab area, and runs the San Juan or the Green or Cataract Canyon at least once every year. It would

---

24. Castle Valley is fifteen miles east of Moab, Utah along the Colorado River canyon. The Stegners attended the dedication of the Scott M. Matheson Wetlands Preserve in Moab on June 1st, 1991.
25. Bruce Babbitt and Cecil Andrus, the Secretary and former Secretary of Interior.
26. Ken Sleight, legendary river runner and Utah environmentalist, owner of the Pack Creek Ranch south of Moab.

be a great moment for him and Lynn if they could end this year's river run with a party at Pack Creek. No need to do anything about accommodations. They can unroll a sleeping bag anywhere, or find a bed in Moab. But the barbecue, if they have time, would be a pleasure to all of us.

As I get closer to clearing the desk, I get more and more excited about this. We'll greet you with cheers at the end of the month. We're grateful for the invitation and the assistance.

Best,
Wally

« *To: Margaret Owings* • *August 24, 1991* »

Dear Margaret,
Mary and I have just spent three or four of the pleasantest and most inspiring evenings of our lives fighting over your Oral History and reading it far into the night. What a life you have had, and what the world owes you! You and Nat, for you always did things as a couple. Along with the exhilaration that comes from reading how much good a sensitive sensible wise stubborn woman can do comes a lot of nostalgia for those days, as they say, of yesteryear, when we were all a good deal younger and fresher and we enjoyed your hospitality in Jacona and Big Sur and occasionally got together on some environmental issue. You make me ashamed of having always been a benchwarmer, but then not everybody has the energy that you have, or the plain savvy.

Enough. We loved the book and are grateful that you sent it. It has been a real joy to know you and watch you work. And we hope that's not all over, though Nat is no longer here to add his impetuous enthusiasm to any project, and the rest of us are depleted somewhat. Maybe more than somewhat. Sometimes I ponder myself as a habitat—for all sorts of creatures from mitochondria and E. coli to dandruff germs, mites, ticks, and fleas live in or upon me—and if I am a habitat, then anything that endangers me also endangers all those dependent creatures. I am thinking of applying for protection under the Endangered Species Act; and if worst comes to worst, I might even ask you to form a Friends of the Stegner Habitat foundation.

We have done little since we last saw you. I went over to Moab and helped dedicate a Nature Conservancy wetland in June, and then later in June we were in New York for a week. July we spent in Vermont, and on the first of August came back here. We have become great-grandparents, which insures a certain biological continuity, and by applications of 1080, DDT, rotenone, and 2-4-D we keep the habitat sterile. Mary has just about had to give up the piano because of her arthritic hands; a great distress to her. But no fatal flaws yet. We will survive a while.

We hope your health is blooming, that you have not fallen over any Pekingese and broken anything, and that your energy and grace are as always. Bless you, you are very special.

Love,
Wally

« *To: Charles Wilkinson* • *October 28, 1991* »

Dear Charles,

Dan Frank sent me bound galleys of *The Eagle Bird*, and I sweetened my mouth with it last night and lost a couple of hours of sleep. It's a splendid book, clear all the way, orderly all the way, and impassioned whenever the script calls for passion. And informed, oh my. This is the best one-shot summary of the western past and present, and the best forecast of the western future, that I know. I will be quoting you, and maybe stealing from you, if I ever again get around to writing anything. I will write Dan a more coherent note for publicity purposes, but I want you to know how good I find your new book. Somehow you have managed to make a lot of disparate lectures and articles take a systematic and satisfying holistic look at the region.

I missed the Wilderness Society meeting, as you will have noticed. Six weeks ago I got a new hip, and it doesn't respond to much casual sitting yet, either in airplane seats or in seminar-table chairs. By another couple of weeks I should be able to drive a car again, and then I'm a little looser in every way. Also, by then I may be able to get my leg under a typewriter table and get it back out again without worrying that the hip joint (pure titanium, guaranteed not to ring the buzzer in airport security systems) won't come with it. Altogether, I look forward to years of jogging and gentle walks among wilderness wildflowers.

Tell me something, while we're on the line. Do you know why Tim Wirth voted against the moratorium on mining claims (the Bumpers Amendment) a couple of months ago? And Baucus of Montana too. Is there something I don't know about that amendment? And what are the chances that your old friend the Lord of the Past will finally get revised?

My best to Patty Limerick, whose name I see in the papers every hour and a half. And to you too. It's a real pleasure to know people who not only have all the right instincts and responses, but who know something.

Cheers,

Wally

« *To: Dave Livermore* • *October 30, 1992* »

Dear Dave:

I'm sorry I wasn't in when you called the other day, and sorry to have been slow in responding to your October 9 letter. Mostly I've been cooling my heels (which are not that hot to begin with) in doctors' offices, and donating my blood to the vampires in medical labs.

In response to your questions about my possible helpfulness in various projects, I guess Mary told you about where we stand. I have pretty much had to swear off doing forewords and introductions to books, coffee table or otherwise. Not only was that sort of thing beginning to take all my writing time; it was also beginning to wear out its own usefulness. I am not an expert on everything in the West, or a spokesman for every organization. I might like to be, but I can't. Now, of course, I find myself getting old and falling apart. I made the mistake of feeling pretty good and going up to Bozeman for the kickoff of a Chair in Western Studies three weeks ago, and wound up in the emergency room, where I've more or less been since.[27] So I think the answer to Sydney Macy and the national office of the Conservancy has to be no, much as I would like to help out both projects. To you and Dave Freed and the Bright Edge campaign it can be a cautious yes. I'm already involved in that campaign to some degree, and if I have steam for only one, that should be the one.

Now the Steve Fisher film.[28] God knows what keeps delaying Steve. He called me about six weeks ago and said he had done the final cutting and

---

27. The Chair in the History Department at Montana State University was to be named in his honor. Fifteen minutes into an inaugural speech, Stegner collapsed from the effects of a vicious intestinal flu and was rushed to the hospital in Bozeman.

28. Steve Fisher, a Berkeley filmmaker, produced a documentary on Stegner's life, a project that dragged on for nearly four years.

was now completing the narrative text that Bob Redford is to speak. Silence promptly ensued. If he ever gets it done, and it's ever aired, it may turn out to be a memorial.[29] But if I'm still kicking, there is the chance that we can appear somewhere. Nothing sure—I wouldn't dare say for sure.

To go back to the Last Great Places project: I can't write anything new for it. If John[30] and the national office want something of mine, the best I can suggest is that they pick something out of one of the three books of essays that are already in print.

Thanks for the video. And of course we'd love to see you anytime you get down this way.

> Yours,
> Wally

« *To: Harold Gilliam* • *No Date, 1992* »

Dear Hal,

I'm sorry I can't be present to see you receive the first "Defender of the Trust" award from the Mono Lake Committee. I can't think of any individual who deserves it more. And not merely from the Mono Lake Committee. Every environmental group in the Bay Area owes you one, for you have not limited your efforts to one cause or organization, but have seen the environmental crisis as a web of entangled and interrelated crises, all brought on by the pressures of human greed, on a finite and fragile earth.

A thing that strikes me forcibly is how long you've been at it. Since you appeared in my Stanford class—when was it? 1946?—you have spent decades in the same This World pulpit playing the same multiple role as teacher, reporter, preacher, gadfly. We have always known where to find you, and you have always been there when any part of the environmental movement needed you. Even when you took a break from the *Chronicle*, you never went far from your field of endeavor, for you were doing much the same thing in Secretary of the Interior Steward Udall's office that you have done since leaving school.

---

29. It did, in fact, turn out to be a memorial. The film was not completed and shown until after Stegner's death in Santa Fe, New Mexico in April of 1993 from complications resulting from a car wreck.
30. John Sawhill, president of the Nature Conservancy.

Like any good teacher, you can take satisfaction in having helped educate two generations of *Chronicle* readers.[31] Like any good preacher, you can take credit for saving some souls. Like any good environmentalist, you have helped preserve what without you and others like you would surely have been lost.

If you can think of any feasible way to clone yourself, I'll be happy to help you promote it. Meantime please accept my personal thanks along with the thanks of the Mono Lake Committee and other groups, for all you have done.

Yours ever,
Wally

« *To: Dave Livermore* • *March 5, 1993* »

Dear Dave:
A thousand things, including income taxes, have descended on my helpless head all at once, and to cap it, I have to go to Santa Fe for four or five days, staring Friday. But I have the draft of the brochure, and I think I know what the Bright Edge program is about, and if God is kind I'll have a brief foreword off to you within a week or so[32]—probably just after we get back from Santa Fe. Will that serve? I'm afraid it will have to, or else I'll have to clone myself and put us all to work like typing-pool slaves.

In haste,
Wally

---

31. For many years Gilliam was a columnist and environmental writer for the *San Francisco Chronicle*. He is also the author of a number of books on the natural environment: *An Island in Time, Above Yosemite, Above Carmel, Monterey, and Big Sur*, and *The San Francisco Experience*.

32. God was not kind, and the foreword was never written. Stegner was badly injured in an automobile accident in Santa Fe sometime after midnight on the 28th of March. He died at St. Vincent's Hospital on the 13th of April from respiratory problems contracted in the Intensive Care ward.

Acknowledgments

In selecting from the hefty accumulation of Stegner's correspondence preserved in the Marriott Library at the University of Utah, and from libraries around the country whose holdings contain the archives of many of the public figures with whom he corresponded, the only criterion for inclusion has been this editor's sense of a letter's particular importance to the oeuvre, to thoughts and opinions, or to the general course of a literary life. They have been reproduced in their entirety, including paragraphs of occasional chitchat that may seem verbose or irrelevant (there are not so many), though in deference to the company accountant in the immaculate white suit I have repaired typos and spelling errors. Punctuation has been left as it was inserted because Stegner did not use marks and signs to conform to style guides but rather to indicate the cadence of a sentence. I have tried to limit the annoyance of endless footnotes, except for identification of people not likely to be recognized, and where some sort of reference is helpful to an understanding of the content.

I am indebted to a great many libraries and librarians for assistance in searching archives and providing leads to material that I would otherwise have overlooked—in particular, but by no means limited to, Greg Thompson and the able staff of the Marriott Library at the University of Utah, where the bulk of Stegner's papers have been deposited; Maggie Kimball, head of Special Collections at Stanford University; Amy Cooper, Special Collections Librarian at the University of Iowa; Erika Castano, Special Collections at the University of Arizona; Leslie Calmes at the Center for Creative Photography, University of Arizona; Diana Sudyka at the Newberry Library in Chicago; William Marshall and Claire McCann at the University of Kentucky; Robert Blesse at the University of Nevada, Reno; Alan Ritch at the Bancroft Library in Berkeley; and Margaret Gordon at the University of California, Santa Cruz, the institution where I was once incarcerated for thirty years before escaping into early retirement. She was ever patient with the stupid questions of a man who never got over, or past, the demise of the card catalogue.

I am also eternally grateful to those many individuals who provided me with copies of letters from their personal files, particularly Carl Brandt Jr., Jackson Benson, and the family of Philip and Margaret Gray. The others are all included in the text, and need no further introduction, but I would particularly like to thank Jim Hepworth for relinquishing his own interest in editing this collection and encouraging me (perhaps I should say hammering me) into doing it myself; and Philip Fradkin, currently completing a new biography of Wallace Stegner, who generously shared with me materials unearthed during his own research.

Chronology

1909	Born on February 18th in Lake Mills, Iowa, to George H. and Hilda (Paulson) Stegner.
1910–14	Family moves from the Paulson farm in Iowa to North Dakota, then to Redmond, Washington, and eventually to Eastend, Saskatchewan.
1914–20	George Stegner homesteads a farm on the Canadian side of the Montana line, and settles his family in Eastend.
1920	Family moves to Great Falls, Montana, after going bust trying to grow wheat. George makes a living bootlegging whiskey into the United States from Canada.
1921	Family moves again, this time to Salt Lake City, where they remain for the next ten years and where Wallace attends high school and college.
1927	At age sixteen, he graduates from high school and begins college at the University of Iowa.
1930	Graduates with a B.A. from the University of Utah, and begins graduate work in English at the University of Iowa. His brother, Cecil, dies of pneumonia.
1932	Receives an M.A. in English.
1933	Because his mother is ill and he does not want to be as far away from her as Iowa City, he enrolls in the Ph.D. program at the University of California, Berkeley, with his friend Milton "Red" Cowan. On November 1st his mother dies of cancer.
1934	In February he and Red Cowan drive to Iowa City in Stegner's Model A Ford, named "Laura," and enroll in doctoral programs at the University of Iowa. To make ends meet he takes a temporary teaching job at a Lutheran college, Augustana, in Rock Island, Illinois. He meets Mary Page, of Dubuque, Iowa, whom he marries on September 1st.
1935	Returns to Salt Lake and accepts a teaching position at the University of Utah. Completes his Ph.D. dissertation on the geologist and writer Clarence Dutton.
1936	A shortened version of the dissertation is published, *Edward Dutton: An Appraisal* (University of Utah Press).
1937	Stuart Page Stegner is born on January 31st. The day before, the novelette *Remembering Laughter* wins the $2,500 first prize in Little, Brown's best short novel contest, a sum considerably exceeding Stegner's yearly salary at that time. The offer of an instructorship at the University of Wisconsin moves the family to Madison in the fall. *Remembering Laughter* is published (Little, Brown and Company).

1938   Publishes *The Potter's House* (The Prairie Press). He is invited to teach at the Breadloaf Writer's Conference during the summer, where he first meets Bernard DeVoto, Archibald MacLeish, Robert Frost, and Theodore Morrison.

1939   Accepts, at Morrison's behest, a prestigious Briggs-Copeland Fellowship to teach at Harvard, and the family moves from Madison to Cambridge.

1940   Publishes *On a Darkling Plain* (Harcourt, Brace and Company). His father commits suicide in a fleabag motel room in Salt Lake City.

1941   Publishes *Fire and Ice* (Duel, Sloan and Pearce).

1942   Publishes *Mormon Country* (Duel, Sloan and Pearce), a volume in an American Folkways series edited by Erskine Caldwell. He takes a year off from Harvard, which he spends working on *The Big Rock Candy Mountain* at the seasonal home of the Stegners' friends, Peg and Phil Gray, in the small Vermont village of Greensboro.

1943   Publishes *The Big Rock Candy Mountain* (Duel, Sloan and Pearce).

1944   Leaves Harvard and moves to Santa Barbara, California, where he goes to work on a series of articles for *Look* magazine that takes him all over the country during that year. The articles were to be published serially in the magazine and then as a book called *One Nation*, but the subject, prejudice and the treatment of minorities in America, eventually scared the editors of *Look* off and they only published a fragment of what Stegner wrote.

1945   Publishes *One Nation* (Houghton Mifflin Company). He wins both the Houghton Mifflin Life-in-America Award and the *Saturday Review*'s Anisfield-Wolf Award for the year's best book on race relations. He is offered a teaching job at Stanford University and the family moves from Santa Barbara in June.

1946   Begins teaching at Stanford. Many of the students in his writing class are soldiers returning to college on the G.I. bill. The excitement of teaching them inspires him to draw up what he later refers to as a "rather grandiose" plan for a major creative writing program.

1947   Publishes *Second Growth* (Houghton Mifflin Company).

1948   The Stegners buy ten acres of land in the Los Altos Hills, a few miles from the Stanford campus, and begin plans to build a house.

1949   The hilltop house, with its view of the Coast Range mountains and the foothills north toward San Francisco, is completed and the family moves in at the end of the summer. Except for numerous excursions abroad and summers in Vermont, where they maintain a summer cottage in Greensboro, he will live here for the remainder of his life.

1950   Publishes *The Preacher and the Slave* and a collection of short stories, *The Women on the Wall* (both with Houghton Mifflin Company). Wins first prize in the O. Henry Memorial Short Story Award for "The Blue-Winged Teal."

1951 Stegner, with his family in tow, spends a good part of this year traveling around the globe on a Rockefeller Foundation fellowship to meet and exchange literary and cultural ideas with many of the world's most important writers.

1952 Publishes *The Writer in America* (The Hokuseido Press, Kanda, Japan).

1953 Most of this year is spent teaching at Stanford and working on the biography of John Wesley Powell that will become *Beyond the Hundredth Meridian*. During the summer he revisits (incognito) his childhood home in Eastend, Saskatchewan, as part of the research for the book that will become *Wolf Willow*.

1954 Publishes *Beyond the Hundredth Meridian* (Houghton Mifflin Company). He begins a year's fellowship at the Center for Advanced Studies, located near the Stanford campus. From April to August the Stegners live in Copenhagen, Denmark, where he does research for a book comparing three small, rural villages: one in Denmark, one in New England, one in Saskatchewan. Only Saskatchewan survives and becomes *Wolf Willow*.

1955 Edits the book *This Is Dinosaur* (Knopf), copies of which are distributed to all members of Congress, and results, ultimately, in the defeat of the Bureau of Reclamation's plan to install dams at the confluence of the Yampa and Green rivers in Utah and flood Dinosaur National Monument. This is the first serious environmental battle since John Muir's attempt to save Hetch Hetchy in Yosemite National Park, and establishes Stegner as a major player in the conservation movement. In November Stegner and his wife travel to Saudi Arabia where he is hired by the Arabian American Oil Company to write a history of Arabian oil development.

1956 Publishes a new collection of short stories, *The City of the Living* (Houghton Mifflin Company).

1957 Edits *Great American Short Stories* (Dell Books).

1958 Edits *Selected American Prose* (Rinehart & Company).

1959 Spends the summer in London, and the fall at the American Academy in Rome.

1960 The Stegners spend winter and spring at the American Academy in Rome, returning to the United States in early summer. In December he writes the famous "Wilderness Letter" to Dave Pesonen.

1961 Publishes *A Shooting Star* (The Viking Press). He accepts a temporary position as Special Assistant to Secretary of the Interior Stewart Udall, and lives for part of the year in Washington, DC, returning to Stanford in late December.

1962   Publishes *Wolf Willow* (The Viking Press). He helps found the Committee for Green Foothills, a group dedicated to the preservation of the Coast Range above the San Francisco Bay Area, and is named its first president. He is appointed by Interior Secretary Udall to the National Parks Advisory Board, a service he performs for the next five years.

1963   Accepts a Fulbright appointment to Greece, where he and Mary spend a good part of the year living in Athens. Shortly after Kennedy's assassination they return, sick at heart, to Stanford.

1964   Publishes *The Gathering of Zion* (McGraw-Hill Book Company).

1965   Edits *The American Novel from James Fenimore Cooper to William Faulkner* (Basic Books, Inc.).

1966   With Richard Scowcroft and Nancy Packer edits *Twenty Years of Stanford Short Stories* (Stanford University Press) and writes an introduction to the collection.

1967   Publishes *All The Little Live Things* (The Viking Press). During the spring he teaches at the Stanford campus abroad in Semmering, Austria.

1968   Receives the Commonwealth Gold Medal for *All the Little Live Things*.

1969   Publishes a collection of his essays, *The Sound of Mountain Water* (Doubleday & Company, Inc.).

1970   "Beyond the Glass Mountain" is republished in *Fifty Years of the American Short Story, From the O. Henry Awards* (Doubleday & Company, Inc.).

1971   *Discovery: The Search for Arabian Oil* is published (Middle East Export Press, Beirut). Publishes *Angle of Repose* (Doubleday & Company, Inc.). Disenchanted by the campus disruptions over the Vietnam war (he supported the sentiments, but disavowed the tactics), and wanting to devote his remaining years to his own work, Stegner retires from Stanford.

1972   *Angle of Repose* receives the Pulitzer Prize for fiction.

1973   Spends the fall lecturing at the University of Toronto. Writes a lengthy introduction to his good friend Ansel Adams' book *Images* (New York Graphic Society).

1974   Publishes a biography of Bernard DeVoto, *The Uneasy Chair* (Doubleday & Company, Inc.).

1975   Publishes *The Letters of Bernard DeVoto* (Doubleday & Company, Inc.). In the spring he is a fellow at the Rockefeller Study Center in Bellagio.

1976   Publishes *The Spectator Bird* (Doubleday & Company, Inc.). In November the San Francisco Opera premiers *Angle of Repose*, music by Andrew Imbrie, libretto by Oakley Hall.

1977   *The Spectator Bird* receives the National Book Award for fiction.

1979   Publishes *Recapitulation* (Doubleday & Company, Inc.).

1980   Receives the first Robert Kirsch Award for Life Achievement from the *Los Angeles Times*.

1981   Publishes, with Page Stegner, *American Places*, photography by Eliot Porter (E. P. Dutton).

1982   Publishes a second volume of essays, *One Way to Spell Man* (Doubleday & Company). The Sierra Club presents him with the John Muir Award for service to the environment.

1983   *Conversations with Wallace Stegner on Western History and Literature*, with Richard Etulain, is published (University of Utah Press).

1984   Writes an afterword to a fine letter press edition of John Steinbeck's "Flight" (Yolla Bolly Press). Writes the foreword to *Montana and the West* (Pruett Publishing Company). Writes the foreword to David Rains Wallace's *The Wilder Shore*, photographs by Morley Baer (Yolla Bolly/Sierra Club Books).

1985   Writes a new foreword to a reissue of *This Is Dinosaur* (Roberts Rinehart, Inc.).

1986   Delivers the Cook Lectures at the University of Michigan in October. *The Sense of Place* is published by the Wisconsin Humanities Committee, Silver Buckle Press at the University of Wisconsin, Madison. He and his wife take a trip during the summer to Bora Bora and Moorea.

1987   Publishes *Crossing to Safety* (Random House). Cook Lectures are published in book form in *The American West as Living Space* (University of Michigan Press). Receives an honorary doctorate from the University of Montana.

1988   Writes the foreword to the Ansel Adams collection *Letters and Images* (New York Graphic Society/Little, Brown and Company).

1989   At the end of March, the Stegners travel to Morocco for a vacation.

1990   Publishes *Collected Stories of Wallace Stegner* (Random House). Receives the PEN USA West Lifetime Achievement Award. Receives the Western History Association Prize.

1991   Receives the Governor's Award for the Arts from the California Arts Council.

1992   Publishes a new collection of essays, *Where the Bluebird Sings to the Lemonade Springs* (Random House). He declines George H. W. Bush's nomination for a National Medal for the Arts Award in protest over controls imposed by the administration on the National Endowment for the Arts. PEN USA West gives him the Freedom-to-Write Award. Montana State University establishes a chair in his honor.

1993   Receives the Cyril Magnin Award for Outstanding Achievement in the Arts. Receives the Bay Area Booksellers Award. In March, in Santa Fe, New Mexico, where he had just received an award from the Western Booksellers Association, Stegner and his wife are involved in a car accident. Two weeks later, on April 13th, he dies of respiratory complications contracted in the intensive care ward at St. Vincent's Hospital. In July, during a private family service in Greensboro, Vermont, his ashes are scattered in the ferns beside the cottage where he spent so many summers of his life.

Index